CW00662041

STUDYING ORGANIZATI
CRITICAL REAL

Studying Organizations Using Critical Realism

A Practical Guide

EDITED BY PAUL K. EDWARDS,
JOE O'MAHONEY, AND
STEVE VINCENT

OXFORD
UNIVERSITY PRESS

UNIVERSITY PRESS

Great Clarendon Street, Oxford, OX2 6DP,
United Kingdom

Oxford University Press is a department of the University of Oxford.
It furthers the University's objective of excellence in research, scholarship,
and education by publishing worldwide. Oxford is a registered trade mark of
Oxford University Press in the UK and in certain other countries

© Oxford University Press 2014

The moral rights of the authors have been asserted

First Edition published in 2014

Impression: 1

Published in the United States of America by Oxford University Press
198 Madison Avenue, New York, NY 10016, United States of America

British Library Cataloguing in Publication Data
Data available

Library of Congress Control Number: 2013955763

ISBN 978–0–19–966552–5 (hbk.)
ISBN 978–0–19–966553–2 (pbk.)

Printed and bound in Great Britain by
CPI Group (UK) Ltd, Croydon, CR0 4YY

Foreword

ROY BHASKAR

This book is a very welcome and important addition to the existing critical realist literature. Stemming from the work of the Critical Realism in Action Group (see Preface), it is an exercise in practical or applied critical realism (henceforth ACR). In this Foreword, I want to say something about the primacy of ACR (first section) and its transcendental or overarching features in the social world (second section). Then in the third section, I want to identify what I see as a big danger to research in the social field and at the same time to post what I feel promises to be a corrective to it. Then in the fourth section, I consider ways in which the work in this book may be complemented, perhaps in a second or follow-up volume, by exploiting the ontological and conceptual innovations of subsequent developments in theoretical or philosophical critical realism (specifically, in dialectical critical realism and the philosophy of metaReality). Finally, in the fifth section, I conclude with some reflections on complementary perspectives which may help to consolidate the achievements and develop the project of this book.

THE PRIMACY OF APPLIED CRITICAL REALISM

It is a pleasure to be asked to write a foreword to a book on applied critical realism. Of course, if CR is to be 'serious', it must be applicable (on this criterion see Bhaskar 2013: 11–12). Furthermore it is in its applications that, on its own self-understanding, the whole point and value of CR as an *under-labourer*, and occasional midwife, lies. So much so, that one could say that applied or practical critical realism or indeed 'critical realism in action' is, or should be, the soul or heartbeat of CR.

Despite this, there is a dearth of such texts. For even when one has begun to grasp some principles of basic critical realism, it will not be obvious how exactly one is to 'do it'. How, for instance, as the editors in the concluding chapter of this book ask, does one identify a mechanism when it is not observable and so can only be known through its effects? Indeed it is something of a scandal that the CR community has not produced such a book before now.

The book is itself the outcome of a practical project: an ESRC-funded series of seminars and workshops. The papers represent a rich seam of work recently completed or in progress, drawn mainly from the fields of management, business, and organization studies. The reader may expect some homogeneity of content, but will surely be delighted by the diversity of topics and approaches in the collection. These are prefigured in the gentle introductory chapter, nicely classified in terms of their research design in chapter 2, and revisited in the sagacious conclusion.

TRANSCENDENTAL PROPERTIES OF ACR IN THE SOCIAL FIELD

Transcendental Features of ACR

1. There is a *double specificity of method* in the research process in applied CR: first with respect to subject matter (in the intransitive or ontological dimension of the scientific process), and second with respect to where in the total research process the investigation of the particular subject concerned is (in the transitive or epistemological/social dimension).

For just as critical realism purports to be ontologically maximally inclusive, in allowing not just knowledge (and epistemology), but even false beliefs and illusions, when causally efficacious, to be real and so part of ontology, it lays claim to provide a more general and comprehensive epistemology than its irrealist rivals. These typically remain fixated on a particular moment of the research process. Thus if one defines a round of scientific inquiry as the movement of the research process from knowledge of one stratum of reality to knowledge of the next, then one can note how classical empiricism or Kantianism or Popper's falsificationism (for example) all derive their plausibility from a particular phase of scientific enquiry. By contrast CR attempts to provide an account of the whole research cycle (e.g. in the DREIC model of natural scientific discovery, to be discussed in a moment), so providing a fuller, more comprehensive account of epistemology.

2. CR research is characterized, as Stephen Ackroyd and Jan Karlsson note in chapter 2 by the *primacy of ontology* in the research process, whereas for its irrealist rivals, such as positivism and social constructivism, epistemology is primary. Accordingly, as they say, 'the interest of realists in empirical research is typically *exploratory*'. Indeed it is typically to identify, discover, uncover (and in more engaged, participatory research, test

the limits of) structures, blocks, and (generically) *causes*, and the particular sequences, combinations, and articulations of them at work in specific times and places; whereas for positivists and constructivists it is typically to prove/disprove and justify *propositions*, theories, and so forth.

Moreover CR is of course primarily interested in *explanation,* and only secondarily in prediction (Bhaskar 2008 Appendix to ch. 2; but see also Naess 2004).

3. In CR our focus is on *structures and mechanisms*, not regularities or patterns of events; that is on the domain of the *real*, rather than the *actual* or *empirical* (Bhaskar 2008: ch. 1.6). Moreover there is a mismatch between the domains of the real and the actual caused by the fact that almost all we study, at any rate in a field like this, occurs in open systems. We find causality without correlation, and correlation without causality.

4. It follows from this that for CR scientifically significant generality is not on the face of the world, but at a remove, a depth from it: that it is *transfactual*, not empirical or actual. CR is interested in *theoretical* (transfactual), rather than empirical, *generalizations* (see Ackroyd and Karlsson, ch. 2).

5. As Ackroyd and Karlsson point out, CR thus involves specific *research designs,* with distinct logics of scientific discovery, involving centrally neither induction nor deduction (though both continue to have a place, namely in what I have called the Humean and Liebnizian moments in the process of scientific discovery: Bhaskar 2008: ch. 3.3). Rather *abduction* and *retroduction* come to the fore. *Abduction* involves redescription or recontextualization, most usually (in CR research) in terms of a characteristic causal mechanism or process which serves to explain it. *Retroduction* involves imagining a model of a mechanism, which, if it were real, would account for the phenomenon in *question.* (These two can often shade into each other: there is only a relative difference between them.)

6. Retroduction features centrally in the *DREIC* model of theoretical (natural scientific) inquiry, which I have differentiated from the *RRREIC* model (involving both abductive redescription and retrodiction) of applied scientific research. In the DREIC schema, D stands for the *description* of some pattern of events or phenomena, R for the *retroduction* of possible explanatory mechanisms or structures, involving a disjunctive plurality of alternatives, E for the *elimination* of these competing alternatives, I for the *identification* of the causally efficacious generative mechanism or structure, and C for the iterative *correction* of earlier findings in the light of this identification. In the RRREIC schema, the first R stands for

the *resolution* of the complex event or phenomenon into its components, the second R for the abductive *redescription* or recontextualization of these components in an explanatorily significant way, the third R for the *retrodiction* of these component causes to antecedently existing events or states of affaires, E for the *elimination* of alternative competing explanatory antecedents, I for the *identification* of the causally efficacious antecedent, and C for the iterative *correction* of earlier findings in the light of this (albeit provisionally) completed explanation or analysis (Bhaskar 2011: ch. 1).

Features of ACR in the Social Field

Elsewhere I have discussed the differences between the experimental natural and the social sciences (Bhaskar 1998a: ch. 2). These fall into three main types:

(i) epistemological

(ii) ontological

(iii) relational

I have space here only to discuss the most important differences of each type.

(i) A hugely important epistemological difference is that social phenomena only ever occur in *open systems*, where events are determined by a multiplicity of mechanisms, perhaps of radically different kinds; that is to say such open systems are characterized by both *complexity* and *emergence*.

7. It follows from this that it will not in general be possible to specify how a mechanism operates independently of its context. Hence we must not only relate mechanisms back to explanatory or grounding structures (as in natural science), but also to context or field of operation. This means that in the social field in principle we need always to think of a *context mechanism couple, C+M,* and thus of the triple, mechanism, context, outcome, CMO, or more fully the quartet composed of context, structure, mechanism and outcome, CSMO.

This is also part of the reason why we do not have a body of independently validated theoretical knowledge of structures and mechanisms, which we can apply straightforwardly to retrodict antecedently existing states of affairs (as in the RRREIC model). For in the social world, even if we know what the mechanism is, we do not know (or cannot be certain in advance of our investigation) how it will operate in the specific context concerned.

8. It follows from this that discovery and application must often proceed
   in tandem, and may be only analytically distinguishable, and so we have
   the theorem of the contingent *duality (and simultaneity) of discovery and
   application,* together with that of the (again contingent) co-incidence
   of retroductive and retrodictive moments in research. This means that
   every application of CR in the open-systemic world is potentially (or at
   least readily begets) a creative process of discovery.

More formally, it is possible to develop a unified general model applying
properties of both the DREIC and RRREIC schemas, combining retroduction
with, on the one hand, retrodiction or, on the other, abductive redescription
(Steinmetz 1998; Danermark et al. 2002: 109–11).

(ii) The most important ontological differences are the activity- and concept-
     dependence of social, in contrast to natural, structures; which we can
     take together with (iii) the important relational difference that the social
     sciences are internal to their subject matter, that is, part of their own field
     of inquiry.

9. Ontologically, the social world is an emergent, concept- and activity-
   dependent, value-drenched, and politically contested part of the natural
   world. In it, social structures pre-exist and enable or constrain human
   activities, which are in turn (through the intentional causality of reasons) causally efficacious in the material world (Bhaskar 1998: chs. 3.1
   and 3.2). The fact that we are *material,* as well as *conceptual,* beings
   means that social life, *though concept-dependent, is never exhausted by its
   conceptuality,* and that our conceptualizations of it are *always potentially
   subject to critique,* including *explanatory critique* in the context of practical and hermeneutical struggles over (inter alia) discursively moralized
   relations of oppression (as in master-slave-type relations).

10. It is the necessity for, and contingently critical character of, hermeneu-
    tics in social science, which taken together with its internality to its
    subject matter, generates the model of explanatory critique; just as the
    value-drenched and politically contested nature of a relationally defined
    social world means that the exploratory conception of social research
    easily veers over, in action-orientated research mode, to a transform-
    ative model in which *learning about* and *changing* the world are two
    moments of what I have called the *'depth struggle'* in emancipatory axi-
    ology (Bhaskar 2009: ch. 2.7; 1993: ch. 3.10).

11. As noted, we are equally and irreducibly material, embodied and part
    of nature, and emergently, conceptualizing, reflexive, and self-conscious
    beings. It is the fact that social life has an interior, at least partially

conceptualized and reflexively accessible, that makes possible the rich, thick descriptions of *qualitative* research, stressed by Joe O'Mahoney and Steve Vincent in their introduction to this volume, and which feature so prominently in so many of these chapters, as discourse and document, identity and subjectivity, ethnography and case study, agency and critique. Many of these hermeneutic features can be seen time and again to be complexly interwoven with extensive materially embodied features of social life, susceptible to *quantitative* research. Social research involves a constant toing and froing, a jobbing back and forth between the inner and outer, the internal and extensional, the intensive and extensive.

Anti-reductionism and Laminated Systems

The condition of possibility of actualism and monocausality is closed systems. But outside the natural scientific laboratory and a very few naturally occurring contexts, we are almost always confronted by open systems, where the determination of phenomena by a multiplicity of mechanisms, perhaps of radically different kinds, is the rule. In order to guard against the constant tendency of mainstream-influenced thought to actualizing reductionism, that is to flatten or one-dimensionalize, to de-stratify or de-differentiate reality, Berth Danermark and I (Bhaskar and Danermark 2006) purloined our colleague Andrew Collier's (1989) notion of a 'laminated system' to mark the irreducibility of the mechanisms at the levels specified. Since our article, various concepts of laminated system have come into currency.

Our first original kind of laminated system was one constituted by a number (in the original case seven—namely physical, biological, psychological, psycho-social, socio-economic, socio-cultural, and normative) of ontological levels, earmarked for the understanding of a specific disability. This model is similar to WHO's notion of a human being as, for health purposes, a bio-psycho-social mix. Gordon Brown (2009) employed a similar kind of laminated system for education (posting physical, biological, psychological, [we should perhaps add here, socio-economic], socio-cultural, and curricular [normative] levels) and others developed kindred laminated systems for ecology, social work, and elsewhere.

This type of *laminated system, LS1,* is composed, *in a case-specific way,* of *irreducible ontological levels* (for the case at hand).

However, in our article, we had already mentioned two other types of laminated system.

LS2—four planar social being. This model, first introduced in *Scientific Realism and Human Emancipation,* as an elaboration of the 'transformational model of social activity', sees social life, and in principle every social event, as occurring simultaneously on each of four planes of social being (Bhaskar 2009: 130). These are constituted by: (a) material transactions with nature; (b) social interactions between people; (c) social structure *sui generis*; and (d) the stratification of the embodied personality.

This model, like the first type of laminated system, highlights the irreducibilty of planes or levels of being that the researcher or analyst might otherwise be inclined to overlook. One obvious immediate virtue of the four planar social being model is that it pinpoints the ecological dimension of social being that social theorists have been prone to ignore.

LS3—seven scalar social being. In articulating a laminated system based on levels of scale, ranging from (i) the sub-individual level of motives and depth psychology, through (ii) the individual level of the biography of the embodied personality, (iii) the micro-level of small-scale interaction, (iv) the meso-level of functional roles and structural positions, defined in relation to ongoing practices and institutions, (v) the macro concerned with the properties of large wholes, such as the UK economy or contemporary Norway, (vi) the mega occupied with geo-historical stretches over swathes of space-time, such as medieval Christianity or feudalism, to (vii) the global, that is, the planetary whole, or even (vii)* the planetary whole of world geo-history (of course itself embedded in cosmic geo-history), it was not my intention to suggest an exhaustive taxonomy. Clearly the pie can be carved in other ways, and, for example, various regionally specific classifications inserted. However, one virtue of the seven-scalar model articulated is that with it we are less likely to illicitly abstract from levels of social causation, which are practically indispensable for, but different from that of, the analytical focus of the study.[1]

However, following the publication of our 2006 article, another kind of laminated system quickly moved into view. In looking at emergent spatio-temporalities in my book on dialectic, I had mentioned the possibilities of intersecting or overlapping spaces and times or more generally rhythmics (Bhaskar 1993: ch. 2.2). This raised the possibility of a fourth type of laminated system constituted by co-present spaces, times, space-times or rhythmics (or spatio-temporalizing causal processes), forming so many condensed geo-historical layers, as in the *pentimento* or layered levels of drawing or painting found on the canvas of an old work of art[2].

So we have:

LS4—co-existent emergent space-times (or rhythmics) or pentimented social being. However, it now became clear that in principle the idea of a laminated system could be used in *any* case where it was important not to

---

[1] For use of this third type of laminated system in relation to the explanation of gender-based violence in South Africa see Price (forthcoming).

[2] For a development of this idea in relation to mental health practice, see Moth (forthcoming).

leave out an irreducible and necessary but causally variable element in the non-reductionistic explanation of a phenomena. Thus one could extend the idea to include the members of a set, where each member is irreducible and necessary for the set as a whole; that is, to specify any multiplicity of different components, where each component is irreducible and necessary, for example, the elements of a diet, the components of a curriculum, the aspects of a good education or hospital or government. This then leads to *LS5: irreducible and necessary components in a complex whole.*

While I have hitherto mainly presented laminated systems as a heuristic which is especially apt for interdisciplinary work (e.g. Bhaskar 2011), a laminated system may be useful even where the distinct mechanisms at work are known under the descriptions of a single discipline; that is quite generally, wherever one is dealing with cases of both complexity and emergence or qualitative novelty.

UTILIZING FURTHER DEVELOPMENTS IN CR: DIALECTICAL CRITICAL REALISM AND THE PHILOSOPHY OF METAREALITY

Ultimately, I hope it will be possible to regard CR as a box of tools for applied critical realist research without differentiating the toolkit into compartments marked 'basic critical realism', 'dialectical critical realism', and 'philosophy of metaReality'. However, at present the slow, and sometimes jaundiced, reception of non-basic critical realism means this is how we must proceed.

Dialectical Critical Realism: I want to illustrate some of the rich potential here by reference to just a sprinkling of figures:

> *2E: absence.* Absence is a hugely valuable diagnostic category. Looking at what is missing in a social context/situation or entity/institution/organization will often give a clue as to how that situation and so on is going to, or needs to change. The absence of rain presages shortages, inflation and food riots; lack of free speech the demand for civil society, a public sphere, constitutionality, and democracy.

> > *epistemological dialectic.* On this schema, we start with some relevant absence or incompleteness. This generates anomalies or problems which become increasingly troubling; as inconsistencies and contradictions in the cognitive or practical situation proliferate. These contradictions act as a signalling device to the relevant community, telling them that something is radically wrong, and in particular that they have left something out of the theoretical or practical mix. This entropic degeneration can

only be halted (and consistency restored to the situation) by repairing the omission, namely by incorporating what had been excluded in a more comprehensive or inclusive totality. (Such a totality in turn may leave something relevant out, triggering a further round of this dialectic.) It is largely this schema which (I have argued) Marx hailed as the 'rational kernel' of Hegelian dialectic (Bhaskar 1993: chs. 1 and 2).

rhythmic. We have already encountered this in LS4. This connotes some tensed spatializing process which consists in the exercise—in space and time—of the causal powers of a structure or thing. Thus for many purposes we may want to take the causal, spatial, and temporal properties of a process together. The seasons, agriculture, industry, the university term, Kant's daily stroll around Köningsberg, the office Christmas party each have their own rhythmics. Rhythmics may clash, coalesce, reinforce, or undermine one another or other processes in a variety of different ways.

3L: *concrete universal (or singular).* Universals in the real open-systemic world are not abstract universals, specifying that a is always b, but rather that this particular a, while sharing the universal tendency of a to b (whether it is actualized or not in this case), is characterized by distinctive mediations, Xi...Xn, a specific geo-historical trajectory, GxHy and an irreducible (concrete) singularity. It is the concrete universal that allows someone to say, 'Yes I am a woman, but I am not a feminist' or 'though I was born in Chelsea, I support Arsenal'. Every universal in the world is of this type, and every particular thing has these four aspects (universality, mediations, geo-historic trajectory, and singularity) (Bhaskar 1993: 130). In critical realism, we must move both from empirical to transfactual (theoretical) and from abstract to concrete universality.

holistic causality. Holistic causality presupposes internal relations between the members of a complex, such that what happens to one element affects the other, so that for explanatory and research purposes they cannot be treated individualistically, but must be taken together. This is clearly a widespread condition in the social world. This sentence is internally related to the last; your well-being is affected by that of your family and community. Generally in holistic causality, the form of the combination of elements causally co-determines the elements; and the elements causally co-determine each other, and so causally co-determine the form of the whole.

constellationality. This is a figure which describes the relationship between two terms which are distinct and initially defined in relation to each other, but where one term overreaches and contains the other. Thus being may be said to constellationally contain thought or knowledge, while at the same time the distinction between knowledge and its object is maintained. (So epistemology is both part of ontology and distinct from it.)

4D: *four planar social being*. We have already discussed this notion; but it is interesting to note that it, like holistic causality, was already introduced in basic critical realism (Bhaskar 2009: 130).

From, *1M: Tina Compromise Form*. This is the theory/practice compromise which results from the combination of a theoretical falsity and a practice which, in accordance with axiological necessity, nevertheless upholds or respects the categorial truth theoretically denied. Understanding Tina compromise formation enables us to see how ideologies can render themselves plausible.

Concrete utopianism. This is an exercise which invites us to think how a constraint or a necessity could be better satisfied with the same set of resources. It is grounded in dispositional realism, the idea that possibilities as well as their actualizations are real. From this perspective the actual is only one (contingent) instance or manifestation of the real, and other different and better manifestations of it are possible.

The philosophy of metaReality. I will be briefer with this. However it is worth noting that it can be used to sensitize us to levels or aspects of social reality of which we may not normally be aware. Thus the *axioms of universal solidarity* and *axial rationality* can be used to show the limiting conditions under which participants in a conflict situation would no longer be disposed to give radically incommensurable descriptions; while the *identification of a metaReal level in some particular instance of 'demi-reality'* can indicate a level of human goodness (or neutrality) on which some social horror or evil depends, a level which once recognized and mobilized can begin the process of transforming it (Bhaskar 2002).

Concluding Reflections

Including some studies which utilize Dialectical Critical Realism and the Philosophy of MetaReality in a second or follow-up volume would be a good way of developing the project of this book. At the same time this book will surely stimulate similar enterprises from fields other than business studies; and it is to be hoped that in a follow-up to this book or some parallel one, attention will be given to the very important topic of interdisciplinary applied critical realism touched on in the third section, 'Anti-reductionism and Laminated Systems'.

Meanwhile, the reader of this volume may like to reflect that, although the philosophy and systematized meta-theory of critical realism is new, it has nevertheless always been the driving logic of all good science (at least if my arguments are correct). This opens up another huge field for study and comparison: that of CR as *implicit* method in action. From this implicit CR, there will of course remain much to learn, even if CR today need no longer disguise itself in or masquerade behind some Tina compromise.

In the meantime, this volume will go a long way to satisfying the demand, with which I am often besieged, for examples of self-conscious critical realism in action. Sometimes I suspect this demand is really the mistaken residue of the longing for a formula or recipe or algorithm, which (while supplying a guarantee of methodological rectitude) could be mechanically applied to a pre-given subject matter. But no such subject matter or formula is possible. The reader should remember the *duality of discovery and application* and, recalling the irreducible singularity of concrete subject matters, rejoice in the fact that even the seemingly most humdrum empirical research shares the *double specificity* of all ACR here. However, even though the demand for an algorithm is a chimera, we can certainly learn by example, and this book has much to teach us about the variety of research perspectives, strategies, and techniques in ACR.

This book will also go a long way to satisfying another common demand, namely for a demonstration of how CR 'makes a difference'. However, there is also, I suspect, a problem with this demand. For lurking in or behind it may be the idea that CR should be a better way of doing what standard or mainstream meta-theories do. But this is not so: CR can certainly show how (in its immanent critique of them) other meta-theories fail. However, it is not a better way of doing what they do (or would do, if they could). Rather it is a way of doing something rather different. For CR is oriented to discovery, understanding, and transformative change, rather than prediction (manipulation and control), justification, and apology. It is a striking virtue of this book that it shows this. CR is indeed a new game, continuous for sure with current and past science, but not with the way the textbooks have presented it.

Preface

This book derives from the work of the Critical Realism in Action Group (CRAG) which was set up in 2007, and specifically a seminar series funded by the Economic and Social Research Council (Grant RES-451-26-0775) which we ran during 2009 and 2010. Some of the early work of CRAG was also supported while Edwards was a Senior Fellow in the Advanced Institute of Management Research, also funded by the ESRC. The objectives of the group, the series and the book are simple: to show how scholars interested in critical realism can deploy its ideas empirically, and to explain to other scholars some of the attractiveness and promise of CR. Although some of CR's concepts and arguments are abstract, it has some very practical implications that we aim to draw out.

We are very grateful to participants in the seminar series for their eager engagement for the project. We would particularly like to thank Chris Smith, who as well as contributing to this volume facilitated the first CRAG meeting in London, and Lee Martin of Nottingham University Business School for organizing several CRAG-related events there. We are also grateful to Val Jephcott at the Industrial Relations Research Unit, University of Warwick for acting as coordinator of the CRAG network and to Trixie Gadd for preparing the consolidated bibliography.

We are especially grateful to Roy Bhaskar. Apart from the obvious fact of being the inspiration behind CR, Roy kindly facilitated a workshop at the Institute of Education, where draft chapters of this book were discussed, and graciously agreed to write the Foreword. His enthusiasm for scholarly debate and his good-hearted encouragement of other scholars stand as an example to us all.

Paul K. Edwards
Joe O'Mahoney
Steve Vincent

Contents

List of Tables   xxi
List of Figures   xxiii
Contributors   xxv

1. Critical Realism as an Empirical Project: A Beginner's Guide   1
   Joe O'Mahoney and Steve Vincent

2. Critical Realism, Research Techniques, and Research Designs   21
   Stephen Ackroyd and Jan Ch. Karlsson

3. Employing a Form of Critical Realist Discourse Analysis for
   Identity Research: An Example from Women's Talk of
   Motherhood, Childcare, and Employment   46
   Wendy Sims-Schouten and Sarah Riley

4. Researching Identity: A Critical Realist Approach   66
   Abigail Marks and Joe O'Mahoney

5. Critical Realism and Grounded Theory   86
   Steve Kempster and Ken Parry

6. Critical Realism and Interviewing Subjects   109
   Chris Smith and Tony Elger

7. Critical Realism and Ethnography   132
   Chris Rees and Mark Gatenby

8. Critical Realism and the Organizational Case Study: A Guide to
   Discovering Institutional Mechanisms   148
   Steve Vincent and Robert Wapshott

9. Comparing Cases   168
   Ian Kessler and Stephen Bach

10. Critical Realism and International Comparative Case Research   185
    Ayse Saka-Helmhout

11. Pulling the Levers of Agency: Implementing Critical Realist
    Action Research   205
    *Monder Ram, Paul K. Edwards, Trevor Jones, Alex Kiselinchev,
    and Lovemore Muchenje*

12. History and Documents in Critical Realism   223
    Alistair Mutch

13. Critical Realism and Mixed Methods Research: Combining
    the Extensive and Intensive at Multiple Levels   241
    Scott A. Hurrell

14. Realist Synthesis   264
    Joanne Greenhalgh

15. Probability and Models   282
    Malcolm Williams

16. An Appraisal of the Contribution of Critical Realism to
    Qualitative and Quantitative Research Methodology:
    Is Dialectics the Way Forward?   300
    Andrew Brown and John Michael Roberts

17. Concluding Comments   318
    Paul K. Edwards, Steve Vincent, and Joe O'Mahoney

Bibliography   327
Index   357

List of Tables

1.1 Examples of Abduction 17

2.1 Eight Designs Relevant to Realist-informed Research and Some of their Characteristics 27

4.1 Ten Realist Principles and their Consequences for Identity Research 78

5.1 Structure of the Chapter 88

7.1 Categories of Ethnographic Data 141

9.1 Distribution of HCA Roles by Trust 181

9.2 Distribution of HCA Roles by Type of Ward 182

10.1 Key Subsidiary Characteristics and the Nature of Transferred Practice 190

10.2 Key Institutional and Organizational Characteristics Related to Type of Agency 193

10.3 Illustrative List of Codes 198

10.4 Truth Table Indicating Necessary and Sufficient Conditions 201

13.1 Sectoral Distribution of Soft Skills Deficits in Scotland 2002 248

13.2 Generative Mechanisms and Methods Used to Investigate Them within Case Studies 253

13.3 Breakdown of Case-study Response Rates and Respondents 256

14.1 Different Types of Realist Synthesis 276

15.1 Logistic Regression Main Effects Model of Variables Associated with Migration from Cornwall 1981–91 (1981 variables) 296

15.2 Odds Ratios of Variables Associated with Migration from Cornwall 1981–1991 (1981 variables) 296

List of Figures

1.1 Levels of Realist Theorizing   15

3.1 Model for the Interactions between Discourse,
     Embodiment, Materiality, and Social Structures   53

3.2 Critical Realism in Discourse Analysis in Three Phases   59

3.3 CRDA in Action   63

4.1 The Transformative Capacity of Agency   73

5.1 Causal Configurations of Two Contexts   90

5.2 Hycner's 'Phenomenological' Analysis   99

5.3 Building a Grounded Theory   101

5.4 A Retroductive Grounded Theory of Leadership Development   102

5.5 Example of Contrastive Causal Configurations   106

7.1 Causal Mechanisms   142

8.1 Significant Types of Causal Mechanism   151

12.1 Mentions of Retailing in Brewery Company Annual Reports,
      1970–1990   231

13.1 Overview of MMR Research Design   246

14.1 Template for Realist Synthesis   270

14.2 Web-based Description of a Programme as an Example of a
      Source of Programme Theories   272

Contributors

Stephen Ackroyd is Emeritus Professor at Lancaster University Business School.

Stephen Bach is Professor of Employment Relations at King's College, University of London.

Professor **Roy Bhaskar** is World Scholar at the Institute of Education, University of London.

Dr **Andrew Brown** is Senior Lecturer in Economics at Leeds University Business School, University of Leeds.

Paul K. Edwards is Professor of Employment Relations at Birmingham Business School, University of Birmingham.

Tony Elger is Emeritus Professor in the Department of Sociology, University of Warwick.

Dr **Mark Gatenby** is Lecturer in Organization Studies, Southampton Management School, University of Southampton.

Dr **Joanne Greenhalgh** is Principal Research Fellow in the School of Sociology and Social Policy, University of Leeds.

Dr **Scott A. Hurrell** is Lecturer in Work and Employment Studies at Stirling Management School, University of Stirling.

Trevor Jones is Visiting Professor, Birmingham Business School, University of Birmingham.

Jan Ch. Karlsson is Professor in the Arbetsvetenskap Group, Karlstad University.

Dr **Steve Kempster** is Director of Leadership Development at Lancaster University Business School.

Ian Kessler is Professor of International Human Resource Management at King's College, University of London.

Alex Kiselinchev is Research Fellow, Leicester Business School, de Montfort University.

Abigail Marks is Professor of Work and Wellbeing at the School of Management and Languages, Heriot-Watt University.

Lovemore Muchenje is PhD student, Birmingham Business School. Formerly: Research Fellow, Leicester Business School, de Montfort University.

Alistair Mutch is Professor of Information and Learning at Nottingham Business School, Nottingham Trent University.

Dr **Joe O'Mahoney** is Lecturer in Organizational Studies, Cardiff Business School, Cardiff University.

Ken Parry is Professor of Leadership at Bond University, Australia.

Monder Ram is Professor of Small Business and Director of the Centre for Research in Ethnic Minority Entrepreneurship (CREME) at Leicester Business School, de Montfort University. His co-authors are associates of CREME.

Dr **Chris Rees** is Senior Lecturer in Employment Relations in the School of Management, Royal Holloway, University of London.

Dr **Sarah Riley** is Senior Lecturer in the School of Psychology, Aberystwyth University.

Dr **John Michael Roberts** is Senior Lecturer in Sociology and Communications in the School of Social Sciences, Brunel University.

Dr **Ayse Saka-Helmhout** is Reader in International Management at Surrey Business School, University of Surrey.

Dr **Wendy Sims-Schouten** is Senior Lecturer in the School of Education and Continuing Studies, University of Portsmouth.

Chris Smith is Professor of Organization Studies in the School of Management, Royal Holloway, University of London.

Steve Vincent is Professor of Work and Organisation at Newcastle University Business School.

Dr **Robert Wapshott** is Lecturer in Entrepreneurship in the School of Management, University of Sheffield.

Professor **Malcolm Williams** is Director of the School of Social Sciences, Cardiff University.

1

Critical Realism as an Empirical Project
A Beginner's Guide

Joe O'Mahoney and Steve Vincent

INTRODUCING THE BOOK

This book offers a practical handbook for critical realist (CR) researchers. More specifically, it explores the methodological consequences of committing to a CR *ontology*—by which we mean the assumptions that researchers from this tradition make about the nature of reality. These assumptions are important because ontological commitments, which relate to what we believe exists, often affect our *epistemological* concerns, which relate to our beliefs about how whatever exists can be studied and known. Thus, for a researcher, ontology and epistemology are important because they have consequences for the possibilities and limits of the research methods, techniques, and analyses that they employ.

The contents of this book are aimed at both experienced social science researchers and students, in a variety of social science disciplines, who want to reflect on ontological issues and their consequences for research practice. The book has been developed in order to fill what we saw as a significant gap in the literature. Whilst there are numerous contributions outlining CR theory in sociological and organizational research (for example, Fleetwood and Ackroyd 2004), as well as many more general texts about realist ontology (Collier 1994; Cruickshank 2003), work delineating the consequences of these views for research *practice* is an emerging area of interest (for a more recent general collection see Olsen 2010). Consequentially, when our co-editor (Paul Edwards) suggested we set up a series of seminars titled 'Critical Realism in Action' to explore the practical consequences of a commitment to critical realism, we jumped at the chance.

This book represents the outcome of the seminar series, and, in terms of its constitution, reflects the nascent nature of critical realism as an empirical project. Indeed, as the reader may have noted, whilst all the contributors are 'realists' of one persuasion or another, some would deny that they are *critical* realists. However, as critical realism is itself an emergent and developing project, progress is better achieved through inclusive debate rather than exclusion. Within their respective chapters, contributors have been free to make qualifications that allude to their own ontological preferences—although we have reserved the right for a final comment in the last chapter. Finally, we are also indebted to those contributors who come from academic worlds outside of business schools, as their chapters will broaden debates and spread know-how across disciplinary boundaries.

The development of critical realism, as a philosophy of science, is generally attributed to a series of books by Roy Bhaskar (see Bhaskar 1989). It has proven to be influential, not least because it has an affinity with many people's views about the way the world fits together, both within and outside of academia. As a result, experts have spent a good deal of time and effort refining and exploring the philosophical details of critical realism and debating its key concepts. In our view these ideas are important, but their prose contains a good deal of specialist jargon, which can be off-putting to newcomers. As an attempt to cut through the thickets of jargon, our introduction first and foremost offers a 'beginner's guide': an opportunity for those new to the area to dip their toes into the water before deciding whether to read any further. It also outlines some of the opportunities and challenges the CR philosophy presents to scholars seeking to undertake empirical research. As a result, and unlike the following chapter which provides a more extended consideration of the research practice of critical realist scholars, this chapter is relatively rudimentary. Therefore, if the reader is already conversant with critical realism and the methodological challenges that this presents, they may wish to skip forward to consider the rest of this volume. For readers interested in exploring the theoretical debates further, books by Collier (1994), Danermark et al. (2002) and Elder-Vass (2010) offer accessible and thorough accounts of CR ideas.

The sections immediately below offer a basic outline of some, but by no means all of the concepts that are used to generate CR accounts of the world. Initially, an effort is made to outline how CR is different from other ontological positions, before exploring CR ideas in more detail and considering some of the challenges these present for research practice.

BEYOND SUBJECTIVISM VS. OBJECTIVISM

Critical Realism holds that an (objective) world exists independently of people's perceptions, language, or imagination. It also recognizes that part of that world consists of subjective interpretations which influence the ways in which it is perceived and experienced. This double recognition is important and relatively novel in social science research. Many research textbooks, for example, employ a simple dichotomy, between objectivist (positivist, deductive, and empiricist) approaches, which are typically aligned with quantitative methods, and subjectivist (social constructionist, inductive, and interpretive) approaches, which are typically aligned with qualitative methods. From a CR perspective, employing this dichotomy creates a false illusion of two distinct worlds: objectivists deal with numbers and facts, social constructionists explore meaning systems of social selves. The former, who claim to be the guardians of 'proper' science, chastise the latter for failing to provide robust findings that can be confidently generalized across the broader social formation. The latter, who claim that discourses generate 'realities' that are local and fragmented, chastise the former for assuming their measures correspond to some objective world 'out there', when ultimately all knowledge is discursively relative and interpreted subjectively. Below, we explore these two positions in more detail and outline their weaknesses.

More than just Events

Ontologically considered (that is, in terms of the assumptions made about what exists) empiricists and positivists share a realist commitment to an objective world that exists independently of researchers. However, empiricists and positivists differ from critical realists in that they limit this world to empirical 'facts' (i.e. things that are observable) which they often quantify and correlate to in an attempt to generate universal statements or 'laws' about the world. This commitment to an empirical ontology, following the early natural sciences, means that positivists are hostile to 'metaphysical notions about which it is not possible to make any observations' (Blaikie 1993: 14). In simple terms, this means that things cannot be real if we cannot observe them.

The theories empiricists and positivists develop tend to be based upon statements about event regularities and the manner in which such regularities are correlated. As regularities are best demonstrated through the empirical observation of events, it follows that more observations means better science. As a consequence, positivists tend to favour large and quantitative data sets, often the product of the answers to questionnaires, which can be mined for statistical regularities and correlations. The objectives of such research are to (a) induce strongly supported propositions from empirical observations and (b) to test and improve these in the effort to assert invariable laws through experimentation. Typically, some percentage of variance in a *dependent variable*, such as how many hours a social grouping typically works in an average week, is 'explained' by *independent variables*, such as their profession, age, ethnic origin, gender, the number of dependent children, their location, and so on. Once statistically significant relationships are 'confirmed' any laws generated to describe the regularities observed are deemed to be universally applicable. This assumption emerges from methods that perceive numerical relationships about the social world in a 'closed' way, as in laboratory experiments, with numerical data about specific phenomena isolated and studied independently.

From a CR position, this reification of correlations rather disregards the independent role(s) of broader context(s), which social phenomena cannot be arbitrarily separated from. As a result, positivists and empiricists produce 'thin' accounts of research phenomena, which can only describe, but not explain, empirical events. For example, positivists might assert that performance related pay (PRP) is correlated to better overall organization performance, but they would often be less interested in or fail to recognize the existence of mechanisms which may, or may not, explain how these two phenomena relate (Hesketh and Fleetwood 2006). Critical realists would argue that there may be a number of 'knowable' reasons why PRP might be correlated with higher performing companies which have little to do with performance being *caused* by such schemes. These might include wealthier companies being able to afford such schemes or that PRP and higher performance are both triggered by a third factor (such as proactive managing directors), whilst they actually have no direct relationship at all.

Critical realists would argue that an explanation of *how* PRP and performance are related (if at all) cannot be elicited through a deductive, positivist approach, because the social world is not closed like a laboratory but open to a complex array of influences which change both temporally and geographically, often in unexpected ways. Thus, even if we use an alternative methodology to find compelling evidence that PRP *can* generate higher performance, we also need to specify under what conditions this might be the case, as a number of contextual factors, such as the labour market, cultural norms, employment regulation, and institutional arrangement might influence this relationship (see also Greenhalgh, this volume).

Such complex, open systems mean that, for CR researchers, useful research is necessarily rich, 'thick', and explanatory as opposed to the 'thin' descriptive approaches that positivism necessitates. Thus, whilst numbers count, they are meaningless without a broader explanatory framework (see Williams, this volume). At best, the conjunctions positivists construct suggest connections that might warrant further explanation or investigation— they are not explanations in themselves but associations of facts. As such, numbers should be viewed as a potential justification for further research that might explain the associations which have been observed (see Hurrell, in this volume).

More than just a Text

On the other side of the subjective-objective dichotomy, subjectivist or *constructionist* approaches (sometimes also identified as idealism or relativism) suggest that 'true' knowledge of an external 'reality' is impossible either because it is claimed there is no external reality outside of texts or discourses (strong social constructionism) or because if there is an objective reality, we can know nothing about it (weak social constructionism). Instead (although what follows is, in itself, a truth claim) many social constructionists argue that knowledge is entirely discursive and, as a result, is inherently 'unstable, fragmented and susceptible to frequent rewriting' (Webb 2004: 724). Epistemologically, social science becomes an effort to explore and reinterpret subjective meaning systems, primarily through the identification of discourses and their construction of meaning. And, when being critical, constructionists frame truth (a term they often place in quotation marks) as an Orwellian hegemony generated through dominance (see Willmott, 1993). However, ironically, in doing so, they also frequently imply generalizing claims to truth concerning the properties and relations of discourses, identities, and reflexivity (O'Mahoney 2011).

CR researchers agree with constructionists about the political nature of science and are equally sceptical of its truth claims, many of which simply represent the current orthodoxy within scientific communities. Take 'objective knowledge' outside of this community and it quickly comes to have a substantively different meaning. In this regard, *claims* to objectivity often serve to obscure the ways in which knowledge is subject to reinterpretation across broader social domains. For example, managerial access to, and claims for, superior knowledge has often been used as a basis for justifying political decision-making in which the interests of managers and business owners are prioritized over other groups (see Braverman 1974). CR researchers and social constructionists would, then, agree that claims to objectivity and truthfulness can have negative consequences, depending on the circumstances and vested interests of those 'in the know'.

Yet, the constructionists' rejection of the possibilities of (knowing) a non-subjective, non-discursive reality means that constructionist researchers must not only take narratives, stories, and discourses at face value, they must also reject any claims of (natural or social) science to provide 'better' understanding of the world which we inhabit: all theories are equal and 'reality' is what people say it is. Yet, such a position runs aground on hard facts. In the natural sciences, more accurate scientific representations of reality have enabled moon-landings and mobile phones that work simply because scientists now have a better, though not flawless, understanding of the natural world. Whilst the researcher is right to be both sceptical about the benefits of new knowledge and sensitive to the social meanings ascribed to it, the achievements of applied science are testament to the greater accuracy of modern knowledge compared to beliefs, for example, that lunar eclipses were caused by the moon being swallowed by a black boar. To use a sociological framing, we would hope discourses that girls are naturally bad at science, that Western cultures are superior to others, or even that tribal societies are necessarily more sustainable than capitalist ones, would not be accepted solely on the basis that some groups believe these statements to be true.

In the social sciences, critical realists hold that, whilst an 'open' social system does not allow the precision afforded by the laboratories of natural science, explanatory theories, such as patriarchy, or concepts, such as exploitation, can be generated to offer better explanations of social phenomena. These can be contrasted with the common-sense theories of the 'layperson' precisely because lay-knowledge tends to be susceptible to the self-interested narratives of powerful groups and neither critically evaluated nor tested. In short, the layperson's predilection to accept the truthfulness of widely accepted socially constructed versions of reality is often part of the problem in the first place, so unless our ontology is able to separate people's beliefs from the reality they represent we will end up with another form of thin explanation. Ultimately, social constructionists' denial of better truths—that is, more accurate descriptions of reality—inhibits the potential of research to emancipate us from debilitating social relations. If patriarchy is seen to exist only in locations or periods where there are discourses that describe it, we circumscribe our ability to critique such systems.

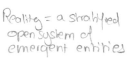

THE CRITICAL REALIST ALTERNATIVE

Stratification and Emergence

For CR researchers, reality is a *stratified, open system of emergent entities*. We will return to the idea of stratification or *depth ontology* in the next section, as this is a big idea in itself. Here we break the rest of this mouthful down into simple parts, starting with the idea of an *open system*. In basic terms, this means that the parts of the universe (or entities), which ultimately interact to cause the events we observe, cannot be studied or understood in isolation from their environment. Unlike 'closed' laboratories, open systems, such as societies or organizations, contain complex and unpredictable feedback loops that prevent history being conceived as determined or predictable (Thompson 1968: 4).

Entities are things which 'make a difference' in their own right, rather than as mere sums of their parts (Fleetwood 2005: 199) such as molecules, individuals, or organizations. Entities may be material (e.g. water) or immaterial (e.g. employment law). So, as Fleetwood argues (2005), they may be real in different ways. For example, the tooth fairy is not materially, but ideationally real: the discourse about it has real effects, for example, on the bedtime activities of children, even though it does not exist. Entities are organized hierarchically in that they exist at different levels. For example, the entity 'organization' is made up from (among other things) people; people are made up of tissue and organs; tissue and organs are made up from cells, and so on. It is important to note that greater explanatory power is to be found in understanding how different entities relate as part of a greater whole—to really understand what a heart or a coin is, it is necessary to place it in the context of the body, or the monetary system. The concept of the 'laminated system' is useful here (Bhaskar 1993; Elder-Vass 2010)—that different distinct layers make up both physical and social systems, all of which the research needs to consider when attempting an explanation.

However, this does not mean that the 'top' entity or system is always determined by the lower entities, or the parts. Why not? This is where *emergence* comes in. Emergence happens when an entity has causal properties that are greater than the sum of its 'lower level' parts (Elder-Vass 2010). In the natural world, H_2O (water) has properties that an equivalent quantity of separate hydrogen and oxygen atoms do not. In the social world, teams can do things that the team members cannot accomplish independently and, at a different hierarchical level of social reality, the capitalist economic system is constituted of a complex array of related entities (money, commodities, the stock exchange, and the characteristic relationships in the economy, and so on) which result in enduring patterns of institutions and events across history. In each case, properties of the collective are not reducible to the properties of the parts that constitute it—that is, the sum is different to the parts—although knowing the parts and how they tend to associate helps develop a better understanding of emergence at the hierarchical level that takes our interest.

So, water, teams, and capitalist societies can be considered as *entities in themselves* not simply assemblages of the things that constitute them. Indeed, it is the distinctive properties of each that renders the concepts 'water', 'team', and 'capitalism' analytically useful in the first place. As such, entities have *emergent properties* which are dependent upon, but irreducible to, their 'lower level' components. For example, 'wetness' is a property that water has that would not exist if either oxygen or hydrogen were removed, even though neither oxygen nor hydrogen feels wet themselves. For the social world: exchange, commodification, and exploitation appear to be ubiquitous properties of capitalism, yet these outcomes could not happen if money, surplus value (in the sense that we create more goods than we need to survive), and property laws did not also exist, even though money, surplus value, and property laws do not, in isolation, create the conditions necessary for exchange, commodification, and exploitation.

The properties of entities can be usefully conceived of as *essences* and *causal powers*. An essence is 'what makes something that thing and not something else' (O'Mahoney 2011: 726). Water is H_2O and has the power to soak; organizations have directors and the power to employ; money has legal status and has the power to purchase.[1] The notion of causal powers is also useful for understanding change, because change often occurs when the powers of one entity interact with another: water can be heated by fire, teams may elect a leader, and organizations might get bought by other organizations. Such mechanisms often transform entities: water might turn into steam, a new leader might develop a new strategy, and a purchased organization might be asset-stripped. So, changed and/or emergent entities, created from the interactions of entities and causal powers, will often have new properties and powers.

Furthermore, powers may be possessed, exercised, or actualized. An entity may possess a power simply due to its properties (the state has the power to spy on your internet activity); this power may be exercised by the power being triggered (the state may attempt to spy on your internet activity); yet this power may or may not be actualized (i.e. be effected) because there may be countervailing powers, (e.g. your use of anti-spying software or the government agent spying on the wrong IP address). The social world is full of powers, the actualization of which is often retarded by other powers within the open systems in which they are located. The potential of entities to possess, exercise, and actualize powers provide critical realists with a more sophisticated and nuanced representation of social reality which is in stark contrast to flatter empiricist or constructionist approaches where things either are, or are not.

Any power necessitates at least one mechanism for the potential exercise of that power: the possessed power of heat to transform water into steam implies a mechanism (the increased vibration of molecules) by which this occurs. In the social world, powers depend on mechanisms that relate one (or more entity) to another (or more). The power of a state to spy on your private life implies the existence of mechanisms for this to occur. It is not only access to the appropriate technology that is needed. More crucial is the existence and compliance with instructions of specific agencies. The mechanisms of interest are, therefore, mainly relational, they connect and (potentially) transform distinct groups and institutions; often, though not always, creating empirical tendencies in certain contexts when there are no, or weak, countervailing mechanisms. Thus: sufficient heat will tend to turn water into steam at 100 degrees Celsius at sea level, providing there are no countervailing mechanisms (such as a low pressure weather system); and the state will tend to represent the interests of powerful economic groups under conditions of neo-liberal

---

[1] Although we need to be careful when using terms like 'essence' and 'power', it is important to note that without some idea that an entity has one or more essences or powers it is indistinguishable from anything else.

capitalism providing there are few countervailing mechanisms such as strong democratic institutions.

We might note that entities are necessarily related and because of this they generate physical or social structures (Sayer 2000). This is an important general proposition because it leads us to consider the ways in which different social entities are related to each other and how, in the case of social science, the social world is actually constituted. Employers (entities which have certain properties) form a social structure in their relationship to employees (entities which have other properties). Employers have (limited) powers to sack employees through the mechanisms of law—more specifically the mechanisms of redundancy or disciplinary legislation. However, in the course of many employment relations these mechanisms are used infrequently, due to countervailing forces such as labour markets, trades unions, and the fact that employees tend to 'do a good job' (or add value in a way that means their employer continues to make a profit). It is ultimately, then, the manifestation of these interacting mechanisms in actual day-to-day events, and patterns of events, that allow critical realist researchers to examine their existence without assuming that their manifestation is either predictable or determined. The task of the researcher, then, is to work out a better and causally accurate, correct, or reliable explanation for these patterns of events via the development of more adequate accounts of the powers, entities, and mechanisms which created them.

Depth Ontology

We now turn to the notion of stratification and the view of causal powers this implies. In contrast to the positivist ontology, which equates reality with recordable events, and the constructionist position, which collapses ontology to discourse, critical realists adhere to a *stratified* or 'depth ontology'. In particular, a distinction is made between the 'empirical' (what we perceive to be the case: human sensory experiences and perceptions), the 'actual' (the events that occur in space and time, which may be different to what we perceive to be the case), and the 'real' (the mechanisms and structures which generate the actual world, together with the empirical). This perspective is important because it facilitates a better understanding of how powers which operate in different locations and/or, often, at different hierarchical levels relate.

In the natural sciences, such distinctions are straightforward. We might, *empirically*, witness an apple falling. Further investigation, examining other apples or additional objects might indicate that objects *actually* tend to fall, which might lead us to imagine an invisible *real* mechanism that explains these occurrences (i.e. gravity). Further investigation of the actual properties of gravity in different contexts might allow us to refine our assumptions by examining other potential (and context dependent) mechanisms (such as the surface area of the object or air resistance) that interact with gravity to change its effects in the actual world.

In the social world we can apply a similar framework. In a chemicals factory, for example, we may *empirically* observe a team of operatives follows testing schedules and standard operating procedures detailed within a Code of Practice. We may also observe that they do this independent of supervision, even when they have done the same test at the same time in the equipment's operating cycle hundreds of times previously and never once had an 'unsatisfactory' test result. For critical realists, in order to explain such dutiful following of the rules we may need to look beyond the events observed. The existence of the team and the reasons the workers espouse for following the rules is unlikely, in itself, to provide a very complete explanation of the causal mechanism that produced the pattern of events. At best, we are likely to achieve what Elder-Vass calls a '*level-abstracted* view of it—a view that considers the effect of the whole entity [in this case, a team] in isolation' (2010: 49).

At a 'deeper' level, or the *actual domain*, the causes of the empirical regularity may be accessed beyond the immediate context of the observed regularity. So, whilst we may assert that the existence of intra-team relationships is an important determinant of the behaviour observed, other events, such as the activities of engineers in constructing the Code of Conduct, requirements for pre-entry professional training and random surveillance from supervisors, may all play a role in determining the observations made. This suggests other influences, such as research and development procedures, national training systems and the routines of supervisors, of which participants may be unaware, are important precursors of observed behaviour. In short, reality is more complex and multiply sequenced than may be apparent in 'raw' observations and the *actual* causes of events may no longer be observable. Ultimately, CR researchers see reality as 'multiply determined', with no single mechanism determining the whole result (Bhaskar 1978): multiple causes must be teased out from detailed explorations of the setting.

It follows that a key commitment of critical realist research is that there are deeper levels awaiting discovery. Beyond direct observation it is also possible to posit various other *potential mechanisms* that may be (in part or whole) neither manifest nor readily observable, but still have an effect. For example: *potential* harm caused by minor chemical deviations, such as may be the case with some medicines, may affect the creation of Codes of Practice; *potential* for local communities to lobby politicians for more costly legislative regulation in the event of a tardy health and safety record may inform operating practices. Yet none of these causal influences may be actualized within the observed entity [team]: the chemicals do not deviate, the community does not lobby, and the regulators do not act precisely because the team follows the rules.

Claiming this stratified ontology enables critical realists to recognize that 'powers may exist unexercised, and hence what has happened or been known to have happened, does not exhaust what could happen or has happened' (Sayer 2000: 12). The assumption is that causal potentials, such as those outlined above, can affect events in *transfactual* ways. This means that they affect what happens (actually and empirically) because the specific powers of the entities observed owe their continued existence to their ability to preclude the specific powers of other entities (see Ackroyd and Fleetwood 2000a). Put another way, the stability (or *morphostasis*) of the observed pattern of events (in our case, the team following the rules) is predicated on the ongoing obviation of the causal powers of other entities. As such, if it were not for the existence of these deeper levels, there would be no logical reason for the pattern of events observed to be as they are. This is not to suggest that deeper levels are inevitably required in a causal explanation, but the possibilities of causal mechanisms at deeper levels must be considered.

From Explanation to Emancipation

CR social scientists, who maintain there is the possibility of improving the human condition by explaining social relations and structures more adequately, are in a double bind: they are seeking to articulate the relations of entities and powers, which may not be empirically manifest, in language that is both the means to a solution and part of the problem to be addressed. In the effort to make headway, the analyses CR researchers tend to deploy involve two intertwined activities: firstly a description of empirical things and events (often in research itself) and, secondly, an analysis that theorizes the mechanisms that generate these. Thus realist research and scholarship tends to be iterative and to involve a movement from consideration of the intransitive world of actual events, mechanisms, and structures to the transitive world of measures, descriptions, and theories.

Critical realists hold that such a movement is possible because the two domains are dynamically engaged: language, though not necessarily reflecting the 'true' nature of reality, is not arbitrary. Discourses both 'run up against' and transcend the intransitive referents to which they relate. In this sense, language is simultaneously transitive and intransitive. In order to communicate effectively it has structures (grammar, meanings), powers (to signify, convince), and historical trajectories (a context) which can be subjected to realist analysis (Fairclough 2002). CR researchers must, then, be sensitive to the political potentials and implications of the research they do. Labelling and identifying the disempowered can be debilitating where those at a disadvantage are also incapable of altering the structures that dominate them (see Bhaskar 1986). Semiotic devices can have negative effects on human relations and conditions.

As a result, and in order to *really* emancipate, we must do more than identify the disempowered. As Collier explains:

> When it is *just* a set of false beliefs that enslaves, their replacement by true beliefs *is* liberation. But the vast bulk of human bondage, misery and repression is not like that. The extension of emancipatory critique from cognitive error to unsatisfied needs makes it clear that false belief is not the only chain that binds us...unemployed workers, homeless families, bullied wives, tortured prisoners, may all know exactly what would make them free, but lack the power to get it...Hence cognitive enlightenment is a necessary, though not a sufficient, condition of their emancipation. (Collier 1998: 461)

[handwritten margin note: Action Research? → P. Freire]

Furthermore, the ability of the social scientist to make value judgements is not, according to many critical realists, beyond their rightful scope. Sayer (2011), for example, argues that an accurate, scientific description of humans is one that acknowledges their fundamental needs to avoid suffering and to flourish. Thus the acknowledgement of these needs necessarily implies an ethical, normative stance for the researcher. Sayer (2011) and other realists have also sought to move beyond this position to detail a number of properties that they believe all humans possess which imply ethical practices for how they should be treated (see Smith 2010; Nussbaum 2006). The point is that emancipation and the achievement of human rights often depends on the transformation of structures, in the sense that to be 'free' from previous bondage requires both self-awareness and the ability to choose wanted and needed sources of determination. Such 'in-gear' freedoms require 'hard work, transforming recalcitrant structures, with the technical and social means at our disposal, into other, more congenial structures' (Collier 1998: 464)—CR researchers should therefore be challenged to consider the means required to act on and change the world (see Ram et al., this volume).

CRITICAL REALIST RESEARCH

Whilst questions of research strategy and design are dealt with in more detail in the next chapter and thereafter in this book, the following sections of this chapter provide an introductory overview of some of the distinctive features of the CR approach to research.

Starting with Theory

As a philosophy of science, CR, as opposed to applied CR, is a meta-theory and is not a testable body of ideas. Thus CR acts as a general orientation to research practice, providing concepts which help create more accurate explanations of (social) phenomena than those which currently exist. It does not provide the concepts (or prescribe the methods) that are necessary for *successful* empirical research. Thus, CR-influenced researchers do not have detailed preconceptions about which particular causal mechanisms may be at work, which kinds of data may be important to showing their operation, and how their existence can be demonstrated. CR-influenced researchers are, however, interested in looking for and establishing as correct particular causal relationships and for understanding the necessary connections between these. Thus, the CR-informed researcher is inclined to seek out and to clarify the generative social mechanisms at work in any given situation.

As a consequence CR studies of social organization are necessarily deeply conceptual. It is difficult to imagine how the world that is perceived can be understood without the help of ideas to clarify and simplify what is observed. Such ideas are likely to structure the perceptions of people, but not to the extent that their conceptions cannot be changed. Thus, ways of seeing are not only corrigible by being tested against experience, but by being systematically tested and improved in the process of research. Thus in a basic way, for the CR scholar research is iterative—it moves between conception and application, so that ideas are tested against what can be found and observed in empirical research. The good researcher must be to some extent a theoretician.

Reviewing the Literature

Thus, the CR researcher basically seeks to provide a theoretical explanation for the social world and accepts that some views of the world are more accurate than others. There are some obvious reasons for thinking, for example, that modern explanations for thunder represent reality better than those of eleventh-century Germanic pagans. Similarly, there are ways in which the CR-informed explanations for the (occasional) effectiveness of HR policies are better than those proposed by HR professionals and business leaders. In seeking to develop theoretical explanations the researcher may have to start with recognizing that there is only limited knowledge of the domain she is researching, because for example the area is new, novel, or for other reasons under-researched. In such circumstances there are a number of options, such as to take a grounded theory approach (see Kempster and Parry, this volume). However, researchers can often get a head start by reviewing literature by discovering the ideas and theories that already exist and then critique, or attempt to improve them. Indeed, some approaches see this as a valuable end in itself (see Greenhalgh, this volume). Literature review typically takes one of two forms:

- Standard literature review

A standard review of the literature for a CR researcher will attempt three things. It will first aim to distinguish more realistic from less realistic theorizing, often drawing on a historical analysis of the phenomena under study. Second, having identified the more realistic theories, it will seek to identify the mechanisms that a researcher might expect to be at play in the research area and the contexts in which these might be best studied. Third, the literature review might seek to identify gaps concerning the interplay of mechanisms and contexts which warrant further study. The development of research questions and thus the choice of suitable research methods will, to some extent, depend upon the mechanisms which the research expects to be underlying the field of research in which they will be immersed.

- Immanent critique

A complementary approach for the CR researcher is to undertake an 'immanent critique', which provides a critique from within a theoretical position and identifies contradictions, ambiguities, or inconsistencies (Antonio 1981). It seeks the 'Achilles heel' (Bhaskar and Hartwig 2010: 79) of an existing theoretical position in order to identify theoretical weaknesses that require further investigation. For example, Archer undertakes an immanent critique of conceptions of the social agent within economics and social-constructionist sociology to demonstrate the need for a new theory about the ways in which humans are conditioned by, but irreducible to, social norms and structures. This then spurs Archer's (2000) investigation and development of a theory of humans which incorporates the notion of morphogenetic cycle and the subjects' 'inner dialogue'.

As we discuss shortly, this process may, depending on one's methodology, be iterative: the identification of 'best-fit' theories may emerge as more and more data are collected, and theories that are developed become those to be critiqued. What might be developed during this process might approach what Cruickshank (2003) calls a 'domain-specific' theory (Figure 1.1)—when the general realist theory is drawn upon to develop a framework for studying a specific empirical domain.

Describing the Social World

Once a literature review or an immanent critique has been undertaken, the CR researcher will begin the process of data collection with at least some idea of the *potential* mechanisms active in the empirical domain. However, knowledge of extant theories will not *determine* what the focus of the researcher should be because (a) theories are expected to be fallible and thus may not be applicable, may be wrong or in need of correction, (b) the mechanisms

Metaphysical realism
A metaphysical ontological argument (with no specific
claims about being) about reality existing independently of
our own perspectives and ideas

General Realist Meta-Theory
Meta-theoretical ontology: emergent properties in open
systems

Domain-Specific Meta-Theory
Applying realist precepts to a research debate

Domain-Specific Theory
Developing specific theories based on empirical research

Figure 1.1 Levels of Realist Theorizing
(amended from Cruickshank 2003)

specified by theory may not be actualized and thus difficult to explore, and (c) the context or research environment may not permit the study of the events which are associated with the actualization mechanisms. For example, whilst theories suggest that innovation is enabled by cross-industry collaboration, a researcher studying innovation might be sensitive to the fact that (a) this may not be true in all instances, (b) in a period of recession other mechanisms might prevent such collaboration from having an effect, or (c) even if the mechanism is actualized, they may not have access to data which reflects this. However, although the critical realist approach to the specifics of data collection may not differ considerably from any other approach, the researcher is likely to be guided by a (potentially implicit or unfinished) 'domain-specific' theoretical framework which indicates where attention might be focused.

In seeking methods for data collection, a CR approach is necessarily inclusive. Whilst a (strong) constructionist approach necessitates a search for discourse (and therefore a focus upon methods such as interviews or textual analysis), and a positivist approach would necessarily involve the quantification of empirical data, CR research can and should usually incorporate data of different sorts, quantitative and qualitative, historical and current—anything that the researcher (or their research subjects) have good reason to think 'makes a difference'. Furthermore, the CR commitment to emergence means that social phenomena both should not be reduced to their discursive descriptions, nor to their component parts, but can be treated as entities in their own right. Thus, it is expected that a multilevel description will often emerge from realist research, for example. A study of team working, for example, will consider not only the dynamics of the team itself but also the vertical, horizontal, and temporal relations of that team. In terms of the vertical relations within an organization, this might also include the phenomena from which the team emerges (e.g. team members, formal and informal rules, practices) and the properties which are emergent from the team (for example, group norms). As critical realists hold that context can often trigger or retard the actualization of causal mechanisms, methods should also be sensitive to the empirical context at a variety of levels.

At this stage, all the usual caveats apply to the methods that are used to ensure that the data are both accurate and collected ethically. For example, when collecting data about the world, the researcher must be reflexive, not only about the extant models, concepts, and terms which they might draw upon to better understand phenomena, but also the inherent biases and assumptions that any researcher might possess which influence both their own data collection and the future theories and models that they might develop to explain that phenomenon.

Analysis

Positivist and constructionist research tends to prioritize epistemology over ontology by generating (in our view often impoverished) theory through descriptions of empirical data. As neither position allows the existence of causal mechanisms, their explanations can only refer to what is evidenced empirically. Thus, positivists seek to create generalizations from inducing relationships between atomized variables without seeking to ask 'why?'—a question that would demand a richer explanation than can be provided in an equation. For example, if statistical analyses show a correlation between firms that implement teamwork and organizational performance, then an HR manager wanting to improve her employer's profit margins might consider implementing teamworking. But remembering that correlation is not causation, this 'thin' explanation would be critiqued by realists who would ask what mechanisms, and in which contexts, enabled the two phenomena to be related, if indeed they were at all. Conversely, many constructivist, ethnographic and anthropological accounts, whilst providing very 'thick' accounts of the phenomena under investigation, are ontologically bound to keep such descriptions local rather than seek to create theoretical explanations of the mechanisms at play in their field. However, it should also be noted that many constructivist approaches do indeed seek to develop theoretical explanations which often posit mechanisms and entities despite such activities being inconsistent with their professed ontologies.

In their own research practice, critical realists recognizably use two distinct explanatory logics, moving from the empirical to the real through the use of *abduction* and *retroduction*. Put simply, abduction re-describes the observable everyday objects of social science (usually provided by interviewees or observational data) in an abstracted and more general sense in order to describe the sequence of causation that gives rise to observed regularities in the pattern of events. It involves combining observations, often in tandem with theory identified in the literature review, to produce the most plausible explanation of the mechanisms that caused the events. For example, a researcher looking at HR practices might interview a group of workers about their appraisal and seek to explain these data in terms of theory about disciplinary power of managerial discourses (what is said in the appraisal situation) in the employment relationship, wherein it is theoretically assumed that the bargaining position of the appraisee (worker) is weaker than their appraiser (manager). Here, and if the explanation of the mechanisms is successful, theory and data will be consistently and effectively 'fitted together' in such a way as to render the nature of the mechanism clearer. A few examples are provided in Table 1.1 which extends three of Danermark's et al. (2002) examples.

Retroduction, on the other hand, seeks to ascertain what the world (i.e. the broader context) must be like in order for the mechanisms we observe to be as they are and not otherwise. This often involves first identifying patterns over periods of time and in different contexts to creatively asking 'what if?' to identify often hidden causal mechanisms. For example, extending the example

Table 1.1 Examples of Abduction

Empirical observation	Potential generalized explanation	Potential: (1) entities (2) mechanisms (3) structures
Men and women communicating	Communication as mutually constituting identities of gender	(1) Men and women's bodies, male and female identities, text and conversation (2) Socialization, construction through discourse (3) Gendered relations
Pupils and teachers interacting	State ideological power being exercised	(1) Pupils, teachers, schools, lessons, books, rules, physical architecture (2) Socialization, learning, construction through discourse, power relations, rule creation and enforcement, communication (3) State ideological power, school organization
A funeral	Social ritual to normalize death	(1) Funeral, mourners, deceased, religious texts, songs, burial, clothing (2) Social norms, ritualized displays, public grieving (3) Religious, family, or community institutions

used above, we might observe (1) that some managerial discourses are more persuasive than others, and (2) that in certain organizational contexts (opportunity structures, labour markets, etc.) workers are more inclined to accept the managerial version of 'the truth', however this might be constructed. This, in turn, suggests a number of other causal processes are also at play to affect the mechanism observed, suggesting the opportunity to understand more about the relationship between the mechanisms we observed and the contexts in which it operates.

In order to build better explanations of the interconnections between strata which might explain such variance within a known mechanism, we must either bring in or develop other theoretical resources. For example, we might use comparative analysis to demonstrate that it is those appraisers who are able to transpose the dominant cultural tropes of their appraisees into the appraisal meetings who prove to be the most persuasive. As a result, we might develop a new theory that connects the organizational outcomes with broader cultural contexts. Alternatively, and drawing on existing theory, we might consider the nature of opportunity structures within the broader labour market in order to explain why it is that, say, managerial trainees and those with opportunities for further technical training have a greater interest in being complicit with managerial discourses than, say, those with little opportunity for career advancement. In either case, new lines can be drawn between the operation of a mechanism, at one level, with the context(s) within which the mechanism resides.

In addition, and as different theories which emphasize different aspects of mechanisms that are simultaneously implicated in an observer pattern of events, retroduction implies a commitment to *theoretical pluralism*, at least at the outset of an investigation. Multiple theoretical lenses can be considered for what they tell us about the various and stratified influences that are affecting the things we observe (for an example of an empirical paper that uses this approach, see Vincent 2005). As a result, abduction and retroduction can *potentially* say much more about the world than deduction or induction, because they *add theory* to data, unlike induction and deduction which do not. It is important to note that the generalizations from realist theorizing concern the properties and exercise of transfactual, hidden, and often universal mechanisms, which are in contrast to positivist generalizations which are concerned with an empirical population (Danermark et al. 2002: 77). In other words, the critical realist researchers seek to 'generalize, not about populations, but about theoretical propositions' (Montano and Szmigin 2005: 367). This distinction is important because theoretical generalizations are more enduring and can be applied through time and space: a theoretical generalization that capitalism tends to commodify should not only be applicable in all forms of capitalism (including future ones), but when one finds empirical evidence to the contrary, it prompts the researcher to retroduce further mechanisms that might be at play to prevent the mechanism being actualized. In contrast, a generalization that notes only the empirical instances of capitalist commodificaton is a much thinner proposition that has limited explanatory value because it simply identifies the empirical event and says little about why, to what extent, and in which circumstances. Moreover, evidence to the contrary simply modifies the generalization and does not prompt a pursuit of counter-mechanisms.

Thus, when abduction and retroduction succeed, they offer a new and often unanticipated view of things: what was hitherto unobserved becomes the basis of new understanding. By postulating a new view of an organization, the properties and character of existing organizations are recast in the light of a new or existing theorization. A successful realist study, therefore, involves a reconceptualization of the subject and the processes in which it is connected. Finally, it should be noted that many researchers, for simplicity, treat abduction and retroduction as one movement, often from qualitative data to the best theory that explains the data (Mingers 2006; Ketokivi and Mantere 2010). As we believe that abduction necessitates some form of retroduction, and vice versa, we do not disagree with this combination.

CONCLUSION

For those readers new to critical realism, we hope that this chapter has provided an accessible introduction. Yet, we do recognize that even the terms used here may seem unfamiliar and awkward, especially for those more used to positivist or constructionist approaches. However, the key point for us is that this terminology enables a much more sophisticated representation of the natural and social worlds than that offered by other positions. For this reason alone, the (reflexive and critical) journey into critical realism is one that we believe will enrich all researchers—even if they end up disagreeing with the ontology, they will be more able to justify their own beliefs and practices.

We would also stress that the terminology of critical realism makes a lot more sense when put into practice. The explanatory power and clarity of distinguishing between entities and mechanisms, or between real, actual, and empirical levels of reality, or between possessed, exercised, or actualized powers, was, for the authors at least, a powerful reason for choosing critical realism over the more dominant positions of positivism and constructivism. Moreover, the commitment of critical realism to both truth (in contrast to constructivism) and 'thick' explanation (in contrast to positivism) means that it offers researchers a more powerful *critical* approach which not only accepts that beliefs can be false, but also that the identification and retardation of those mechanisms that create false beliefs can contribute to emancipation.

Finally, we would also reiterate that critical realism is still a relatively new movement, with significant opportunities for researchers to critique and amend the vocabularies and assumptions which the original theorists developed. Thus, as you examine the chapters that follow, bear in mind that many of them are tentative and exploratory movements into what has recently been unchartered territory. Fortunately for us, the commitment of critical realism to a progressive and truthful social science means that critique and debate are fundamental to the survival of not only critical realism, but credible social science.

2

Critical Realism, Research Techniques, and Research Designs

Stephen Ackroyd and Jan Ch. Karlsson

INTRODUCTION

Realists think that, although organized social life is undoubtedly complicated, it is not impossible to develop reliable accounts of it from research activities. In particular, it is possible to account for key social processes that are at work beneath surface appearances and explain otherwise puzzling outcomes. As has been argued in the introductory chapter of this book, in order to do this, critical realists put ontological questions (in this area, questions such as: what are organizations and what does management do?) before epistemological ones (how can organizations and management be studied?). The issue for CR-guided researchers is always: what concepts are required to understand the data available and to bring into focus the processes or mechanisms that are really at work?

Conceptual issues are always important in research, whether they are acknowledged or not. Ideas and concepts of some kind are necessary to identify and collect the information that is potentially relevant to any research endeavour. It is ideas again, this time at a higher level of generality, that are necessary to make particular interpretations of any evidence produced. Researchers guided by CR make a virtue of this realization by repeatedly asking the question: what concepts do I need to understand and explore more fully the social mechanisms under investigation? In answering such questions both concepts and data are necessary. In general, in CR-guided research the goal is to synthesize from the available ideas and relevant data an account of what is happening to key social mechanisms and processes (see also Greenhalgh, this volume).

For CR-guided researchers, the role of a research method is essentially to connect the inner world of ideas to the outer world of observable events as seamlessly as possible. How this is to be accomplished, however, is not obvious and there are few reliable rules about how to proceed. In the end, there is only the suggestion that the researcher should think through the implications of her developing understanding of the area under consideration and to think about what further information might provide more insight. Indeed the approach of the CR researcher to research methods is usually highly flexible and adaptive by comparison with other researchers. Others are almost invariably wedded to the use of particular methods in standard ways. Positivists submit questionnaires to large samples of respondents to generate statistically analysable data sets, for example, whilst constructionists utilize ethnographic research to understand the meaning attributed to events by their research subjects. CR researchers by contrast may well use different techniques—depth interviews, questionnaires, or direct observation—at different times or even at different points in the same research project, where possible combining information from different sources. In this approach, research techniques are mainly used to gain access to information that is seen to be particularly important in further developing the researcher's understanding. They are not, as they are for others, ends in themselves. If one technique does not work or is not available to find out what is wanted, then something else will be used to make do. In this view, successful research depends on intellectual creativity not on following methodological rules.

ECLECTICISM AND CREATIVITY IN CR RESEARCH

The CR researcher is potentially interested in many kinds of data, especially at the outset of research. Later, when some headway has been made, there will typically be more focus and comparatively greater interest in specific types of information. This is because it is not clear in the early stages of research what causal mechanisms there are, let alone how they work. This eclecticism and adaptability is difficult for some to understand. So fixated are some observers on the proposition that particular approaches to research should each have their own preferred kind of method, that they do not accept or take on board the eclecticism of CR research practice. Accordingly CR researchers are sometimes seen as failing to do quantitative and qualitative research properly. The fact is, however, they do not conceive of research in orthodox ways. Realists may be fairly described as having a 'beg, borrow, and steal' approach to research techniques. Thinking about possible mechanisms is matched by ingenious research practice which explores possible uses of new data and information that could indicate their existence and character.

However, it is not true that there are no recurrent general designs in CR research, and it is these that we wish to identify and to discuss in this chapter.

Whereas almost any research *technique* (i.e. detailed procedures for data collection) may be turned to account, there are some recurrent approaches at the level of research *design* (the overall strategy of research) which tend to be habitually used and to recur as choices by CR researchers. We suggest that research designs for CR-research projects have the abductive and retroductive logics of discovery—discussed in the introductory chapter—embedded in them. For this reason realist research is distinguished by the use of particular designs and not others. We suggest below that there are actually eight distinctive research designs which are set out schematically in Table 2.1. However, clearly, only some of these designs are in practice designs of choice for CR researchers, and habitually resorted to. Chief among these are the ordinary case study and the comparative case study, and for that reason it is necessary to consider the merits of the case-study design carefully—which we do in the next section of this chapter.

The other research designs outlined in the second half of this chapter are possible designs for CR-informed research, but which are only sometimes approximated in practice. We include consideration of these not because they exemplify current practice—as the chapters which follow this one clearly do—but because they offer research designs which can be used in CR research, and which have interest because they point the way forward, and suggest directions in which CR research may develop.

THE CASE FOR CASE STUDIES

The claim that the case study is *the* basic design for realist research might be thought surprising by some readers. In many discussions of case-study research, especially those influenced by positivism, the procedure is not regarded as an important activity at all, never mind being a key research design (cf. Yin 2008). In such discussions it is suggested that few cases will be representative of the generality; and, since which cases are in fact representative is not known, no case can be trusted as a basis for generalization. It follows that case studies can only be marginally useful—say in exploratory studies or the initial stages of research—to throw up possible hypotheses for more rigorous investigation. But this is to assess the case study by reference to the logic of inductive [Positivism] inference. Amongst other things, one problem with this position is that some of the most celebrated and widely accepted research projects—one thinks of work by Gouldner (1954), Beynon (1973), Burawoy (1979), Pollert (1981), and Delbridge (1998)—are case studies. In addition, there are numerous valued research projects that are either extended comparative case studies themselves, or make their arguments by comparing the findings of a number of similar cases undertaken by different people. In order to understand the contribution

CASES

Broadly Conceived

of these works, we have to revise our understanding of case-study research and why it can be so effective. Cases do not have to be narrowly drawn (as in a case study of a particular work group or single organization); they can be more broadly conceived (investigating a generic type of organization or management system, such as bureaucracy, the Taylorized factory, or even an example of a particular type of economy).

Causation or Causal mechanisms

??? How is Causation established?

For CR researchers, one goal of research is to identify the sequences of causation or causal mechanisms at work. Case studies are a suitable vehicle for examining such sequences, with successful designs identifying a context in which a specific causal mechanism is identified and explored. The aim of research is to bring to light formative processes which cause particular outcomes, when they operate, and which are best conceived in their totality or as near to it as possible. The logic applied in reaching for this complete process is abduction (as opposed to induction or deduction). When such processes are found there is every reason to suppose that the same mechanism is operative in many places, working itself out in similar ways and indeed everywhere that similar outcomes are noted. For the realist, then, a case study represents an opportunity to identify the operation of a mechanism or a process in whole or in part. Actually of course, mechanisms cannot be directly observed. In fact, idealized characterizations of them are created using intuition to interpret the available evidence. It is only the *operation* of mechanisms that can be identified from our empirical observations.

Another research question follows on from the identification of a mechanism. We can also consider the question of how it is the mechanisms we have identified have come to exist, to ask the classic question: what must the world have been like for the mechanism we have now identified to come into existence in the first place? This use of retroductive logic broadens the scope of case-study research.

The idea that realist research is less valuable because it relies on case studies and comparative case studies must be firmly set aside. Contrary to the view of many positivists, it is the well-chosen and well-made case study, rather than the statistical inference, that is often crucial in the development of scientific knowledge, especially in applied subjects such as biology, medicine, and social science. These often depend on the accurate description of key mechanisms to advance. Studies of the life cycles of plants or animals or the aetiology of diseases can only get so far by observing that there are statistical associations between measured variables. How a disease process actually works is not clear until there is a perception of the key mechanisms involved. In such cases, very strong statistical associations which have no theoretical warrant can be misleading.

Thus, for example, for decades the presence of water in areas where malaria was rife misled doctors into supposing a parallel between the causes of malaria and of cholera. Because of this association it was guessed that the infective agent was in the water (which in a sense it was) and it got into people by being ingested (which it did not). Actually another and in the long run much more helpful correlation noted the high incidence of flying insects in areas that are malaria prone; but this was not a decisive breakthrough either. In this example the key observation was neither of these strongly attested associations: this came from finding the infective agent for malaria (already identified in the blood of patients with the sickness), in the gut of two mosquitoes. The necessary steps towards understanding were two: the largely empirical one of focusing research on the insects rather than the water and the theoretical one of thinking that the mechanism of transmission of malaria involved the insects as well as the people.

Ronald Ross's research, which is taken to have definitively solved the problem of the cause of malaria, was published in the *Lancet* on the basis of the identification of the malarial infective agent in the two mosquitoes. As far as is known, nobody suggested that the research was invalid or that the real cause of malaria had not been found on the grounds that the two mosquito cases were unrepresentative. Actually, they were very *un*representative: not all types of mosquitoes (and not both sexes of the right type) pass the infective agent with their bite. But this does not invalidate the essentially correct depiction of the life cycle of the malaria parasite, which Ross's cases made all at once suddenly conceivable. The mechanism of interest here is broader than the part embodied by the cases of infected patients and of the carrier insects, but it is difficult to imagine how this disease might have been understood without the notion of a complex mechanism being central, and efforts made to piece together an understanding of the overall process.

A CLASSIFICATION OF REALIST RESEARCH DESIGNS

Case studies are important because they provide a situation in which mechanisms may be to some extent isolated and then studied, allowing abductive logic to be brought fully to bear. But the well-chosen case study is not the only research design utilized by realists, important though it clearly is. We suggest that it is insightful to see realist research designs as varying along two dimensions. Other descriptions of the range of possibilities for realist research have consistently suggested that the distinction between intensive and extensive studies is important. The suggestion is that case studies tend to be intensive, but realists may also study social phenomena more extensively by other means. In this account we develop this idea by suggesting that intensive research is [Intensive methods] distinctive because it is focused on the discovery of generative mechanisms, while extensive research looks at the context in which mechanisms operate. [Extensive methods]

Abduction
vs
Retroduction

Detach
vs
Engage

The difference is also between utilizing abduction or retroduction as the principal logic of discovery. In Table 2.1 we limit possibilities along this dimension to four.

The second dimension concerns the extent to which researchers take a stance of relative detachment from their subject matter. We treat this dimension as a dichotomy between involvement and detachment of the researcher in the situation under investigation. On the one hand there are studies which attempt diagnosis only. On the other, there is research which tries also to influence the phenomena under investigation. This dimension may also be thought of as a continuum.

The result is a typology of eight possible designs. This typology does not aim simply to reflect the current state of realist research in organization and management studies. Neither does it simply find a place for and discuss the research designs that CR researchers use most frequently. The idea is to do this, but also to move beyond this and to consider a range of research designs that are logically possible given critical realist philosophy and meta-theory. This allows us to discuss some infrequently used but important research designs which might well become more popular in the future.

Dimension I: Intensive and Extensive Research

This dimension relates to the scope and purpose of research, and has been used several times before in the presentation of realist research (Sayer 1992; Danermark et al. 2002). Hitherto this has been thought of as a matter of degree with a range of possibilities. At one end of the scale—the intensive end—research is held to be focused and the situation under study is considered in depth. At the other end of the scale, it is the broad characteristics of groups—often whole populations—that are of interest.

In our account we have broken down this continuous scale and consider four distinctive research designs, which are separately labelled in Table 2.1. What distinguishes these designs is the extent to which they rely on abductive or retroductive logic. Until a mechanism, existing in but distinct from its context, has been abducted no very satisfactory explanation has been achieved: without being able to set out a clear and causally effective process like this it is difficult to see the outcome of CR research as constituting science. On the other hand, any such mechanism is difficult to imagine existing outside a particular context. Hence the context contributes, if only in a minimalistic way, to the production or reproduction of the mechanism. In this regard, it is possible to see that the context shapes the mechanism to some degree, and that the two intersect without serious interactive effects. This may be compared with a situation in which mechanism and context do interact, and the context decisively shapes the outcome of the mechanism. With the simple case

Table 2.1 Eight Designs Relevant to Realist-informed Research and Some of their Characteristics

	Distinctive Research Strategies			
	Intensive ←→ Extensive			
Research Procedures:	What is the mechanism? (Context as given)	How do context and mechanism: typically interact?	historically intersect?	What is the context? (Mechanisms inferred)
Detached Study	Case studies (1)	Comparative case analysis (2)	Generative institutional analysis (3)	Research surveys and census data (4)
Engaged Study	Action research (5)	Intensive realist evaluation (6)	Barefoot historical research (7)	Extensive realist evaluation (8)
Dominant Logic of Discovery:	Abduction	Abduction	Abduction/ Retroduction	Abduction/ Retroduction

study, which reveals the operation of a mechanism, it is possible to assume that the context is simply the inert container of the process. However, we can distinguish explanations of outcomes in terms of the extent to which they are the outcome of a generative process per se or the outcome of mechanism plus contingent features of the context. Finally, then, realists can ask the retroductive research question: what must the context have been like to have allowed the emergence of a given generative mechanism? This is a distinct explanatory task and considering it takes us in the direction of extensive studies.

Dimension II: Detachment and Involvement

Critical realists usually assume that complete detachment from their research subjects is impossible. Further, it has been common since the work of Bhaskar (1978, 1986) and the emergence of an explicitly *critical* realism (Danermark et al. 2002; Sayer 2000), to abjure even the attempt at detachment and to acknowledge that a committed position is appropriate for realists. Bhaskar (1986) suggests it is necessary to acknowledge and to seek to develop the potential contribution of social science to human emancipation. In realist social theory the social world is produced and reconstructed by the actions of participants (Archer 1995; Elder-Vass 2010): all social groups, from small work teams to multinational corporations, are held to be produced and reproduced by the people within them as they go about their daily activities. In principle then it ought to be possible to effect at least some change by intervention. Research clearly has some potential to influence events and to induce change because it is, precisely, an intervention in social relationships.

However, although social reproduction is occurring everywhere, change away from existing patterns is difficult to bring about because of the generative mechanisms already at work. The outcome of the interactions producing and reproducing groups and organizations is not equally in the control of the different groups involved; some groups have much more influence over outcomes than others. Most social roles have limited capacity for doing more than to reproduce their mode of participation in the institutions they are part of. Existing generative mechanisms, which reproduce social relations in their existing patterns, are largely beyond the apprehension as well as the control of many participants. Thus, it is in practice difficult for research to have a significant or enduring effect on changing social relationships and institutions, especially with larger groups, or in effecting change in directions contrary to existing processes.

However, there are growing exceptions to a detached stance. The second four designs we discuss involve more active involvement of participants in the process and outcome of research (see Ram et al., this volume). A research project that merely interprets data will not effectively test the nature and strength of existing generative mechanisms; it will merely recognize and acquiesce in their being there. Such research will not discover what is possible in redirecting and changing existing mechanisms. Researchers may, in some circumstances, intervene indirectly in social processes by giving advice to policymakers (Pawson and Tilley 1997; Byrne 2004) and attempt to change relationships and institutions to discover the limits of the powers of groups and the possibilities of inducing change through action. Despite the difficulties of this type of work, the emergence of more varied applied and engaged CR research has developed and can be expected to develop further.

We now discuss examples of each design. In each case we outline its character, give an example, and comment on the logic of discovery.

REALIST RESEARCH DESIGNS INVOLVING DETACHED STUDY

Case-Study Design

We have already noted some seminal research monographs based on single cases that are clearly realist: Gouldner (1954), Beynon (1973), Burawoy (1979), and Pollert (1981), for example. However, many early case studies cannot be considered examples of realist research. The studies undertaken by Selznick (1949) and

Blau (1955), for example, though well known and regarded by some as foundational for organization studies as an academic field (Reed 1985), supposedly produced a comprehensive account of an organization's functioning. By contrast with this, however, the realist type of case study, although clearly alive to the possibility of emergent properties, makes no claim to holism. It concentrates instead on identifying particular but nonetheless highly formative causal processes (Gouldner 1954). Intensive studies like this bring to light particular generative mechanisms, and make expedient use of the organizational context to do this.

A valuable example of realist case research is that of Burawoy (1979), which is based on a sustained observational study of a Chicago machine shop. Among other things, Burawoy wishes to explain why his industrial workers did not develop high levels of solidarity and militancy. He notices that workers engaged with their work as if it were a game. Employees approached their work by responding to the challenge to 'make out' in their negotiations with supervisors and, more especially, work-study engineers. 'Making out' meant achieving marginal increases in pay for each machining job and gaining higher wages than co-workers. The game-like qualities of the daily interactions with engineers and rate-setters created rivalry between fellow workers as opposed to solidarity. Individuals competed to achieve high earnings and, when successful, they also gained higher status in the group. As a result of these relationships, vertical antagonisms between workers and managers are displaced by horizontal rivalries between worker and worker. By noting the existence of these rivalries and the extent they preoccupy workers, Burawoy shifts debate about how workplace behaviour should be interpreted. He shows that relationships in the workplace can change from relationships constituted by resistance of workers to managerial control, to the 'manufacture of consent' through the workers' willing participation in bargaining games.

This example explains regularities in the outcome of social processes. It identifies regularly reproduced social patterns, but not in previously expected forms. We have a factory with an administrative system that produces neither the disciplined conformity expected by management, nor the class-conscious resistance expected by Marxian theorists. Although realist research often features organizations, and shows that they tend to work with predictable regularity, explanations are not reducible to the suggestion that human interactions simply adopt expected forms and patterns. The explanation offered by Burawoy features: (a) recurrent patterns of interaction involving different groups with different motivations and (b) in which there is a central role for discretionary behaviour in (c) constituting, reproducing, and changing those patterns. The ability of people to make informed choices is a key part of the reason the mechanisms identified by the researcher take the precise form it does, giving rise to continuity and change. Finally, though these explanatory accounts were found in specific contexts, they are not unique to them. The account can be taken as realist, though Burawoy himself does not use this language, in at least two respects. Firstly, sets of causal factors influencing workers' acceptance of making out are identified, such as the structure of collective bargaining and the grievance system—a structure that gives workers apparent rights as equals with managers. Secondly, these factors are ordered, with some, like this structure, operating at the level of the actual and others lying more deeply in the organization of capitalism—what Burawoy calls the simultaneous securing and obscuring of surplus value. A single case, albeit benefiting from the fact that the factory had been studied many years previously by Donald Roy and hence that comparison was possible over time, offers explanatory generalizations.

In terms of research techniques, as suggested already, CR researchers tend to be empirically wide-ranging. Clues about the character of generative mechanisms are found in many places—in the attitudes of group members, the actions to which these give rise, and the interaction between groups. Only following the sustained observation of behaviour and through noting particularly deviations from sanctioned beliefs and expected patterns of action, does recognition of the precise nature of the generative mechanisms begin to emerge, understanding of their nature begin to be developed, and extent of their effects confirmed. For this reason, realists suggest ethnography is a suitable basic method for their work (Miles and Huberman 1994; Porter 2000; Reed 2008; Rees and Gatenby, this volume). However, as the research proceeds, interest in particular kinds of data may also develop. As his study progressed, Burawoy became more interested in the rivalries between workers, for example, and collected data about them. As we have also discussed earlier in the chapter, changing attention to different kinds of data as knowledge advances is a feature of realist research.

Although there were only twenty or so machinists in Burawoy's vicinity during fieldwork, there is no doubting the general relevance of his findings. The key point is that accounts of generative processes discovered in case studies involve the conceptual interpretation of causal sequences. Such work offers a new and unanticipated view of organizational processes: what was hitherto largely unobserved is the basis of new understanding. Once having seen a familiar organization construed in a new way, it is difficult to revert to the old way of seeing. A well-executed realist study, therefore, involves a reconceptualization of the subject and how it works. To the extent that an account of generative processes establishes a new and different account of the subject, it is an abduction as defined by Danermark et al. (2002). (See also Dubois and Gadde 2002 and Easton 2010.)

Comparative Case-study Research

Case-study research is not confined to single cases. Looking at several similar or related cases to compare the similarities and differences allows processes

and outcomes, generative mechanisms, and conclusions about causes and outcomes to be drawn more effectively.

The limitation on justifiable generalization from case studies is theoretical rather than empirical. On the other hand, there will be variations in the
way a generative mechanism works itself out in given situations. Comparative
research helps to clarify both the nature of a mechanism and the range of
variation in both process and outcome that can occur. By designing research
programmes featuring a range of cases showing significant variation of key
outcomes, there is the possibility of developing better-founded knowledge of
the nature of mechanisms and their properties. One way of thinking about
comparative case design is that it helps to clarify the extent to which outcomes
are attributable to a mechanism or its context or their interaction. Where a
common mechanism can be identified a better approximation to scientific
explanation is achieved. If some features of an operative mechanism are partly
identified, more general knowledge may be sought through the consideration
of more data or comparison of a number of instances.

There are numerous comparative case studies that implicitly or explicitly
reflect realist principles (Edwards and Scullion 1982; Burawoy 1985; Delbridge
1998; Taylor and Bain 2005; Kirkpatrick, Ackroyd, and Walker 2005). Cases
have to be selected because they exhibit or are likely to exhibit variations in the
mechanism under scrutiny or its context. Comparative work is more effective
if something is already known about the generative mechanism(s) involved.
With intensive studies, it is assumed a generative mechanism is more formative in shaping outcomes than is the context. However, the actual interaction
between context and mechanism is often unknown, and fixing the relative
contribution of these components is part of the object of enquiry. It is the purpose of this design to raise the level of precision in the causal priority attributable to any identified mechanism.

A useful example of comparative work is Burawoy's (1985) comparison of the
labour process in factories in the USA, the UK, and Hungary (Burawoy 1985).
This exercise in comparative analysis features the labour process as part of the
generative mechanisms examined, which is taken to be substantially similar
in the three different locations. Burawoy makes comparisons between his own
work on the Chicago-based Allied Machine Shop, that of Lupton (1963) at
Jay's, a British engineering firm, and that of Haraszti (1977) about a Hungarian
tractor factory. Burawoy's principal finding is that, despite similarities in the
labour process and factory regime in all three countries, the political and economic context are relevant to the experience of the workers. The experience
of workers was in fact found to be quite different, industrial discipline being
much stronger in Hungary than in the UK or USA. This was because of the
broader institutional relationships outside the factory itself (which included
in Hungary political control of management decision-making and over the
labour market). These augmented managerial power. Despite the absence of

any unemployment in Hungary, workers were under tighter managerial control than was found in Burawoy's own research.

There is a temptation to regard comparative designs as naturally occurring experiments, in which circumstances serve up cases for comparison where everything is the same except for one crucial aspect. The causal effect of such a factor is then exposed. Such a chance variation would, it is true, allow for a rigorous test of the causal properties of a factor. Unfortunately, such a chance would be an extreme rarity and most comparative studies do not meet the requirements of experimental designs in this way. The cases used in comparative work differ from each other in multiple ways and are not to be thought of as approximations to experimental designs (Siggelkow 2007).

In realist comparative research it is accepted that much is different between the cases. It is not that everything bar one crucial variable is the same, as deductive logic requires. There is instead the argument that there is a generative mechanism at work that has distinctive properties, working itself out in particular circumstances. What indicates that the mechanism is there and how the process works itself out may vary a good deal. However, identifying the mechanism is largely a conceptual matter. It is not, therefore, a surprise to find that, even where there are opportunities for realist researchers to get directly comparable data from different sites, they may choose not to. For example, Edwards and Scullion, who undertook comparative analysis within their own research project, did not always seek comparable quantitative measurements of worker attitudes in different plants or similar data relating to forms of misbehaviour. In this work, evaluative comparisons are being made, but deductive reasoning is largely absent. In short, the logic of this design is little different from the single case. The end of the research is also the recasting of our understanding of the nature of the phenomenon under study. The logic of the design is basically abductive as with the single case (see also Danermark et al. 2002: 79).

Generative Institutional Investigations

As we have seen above, comparative case studies can be combined with general studies of the context, such as the institutional context, and comparisons made of their effects. Burawoy's work includes such material, as does Edwards's work following his studies of different factory regimes. Edwards explores temporal sequences in the development of capitalism as a different kind of context for the consideration of factory regimes (Edwards 1986). He considers the connection of change in the economy with forms of collective protest. This is a shift from looking for similarities and differences in the interaction of context and mechanism synchronically (that is, a cross section at one point in time), to searching for causal sequences diachronically (in which causal sequences are seen to work over time). Causal connections are sought suggesting the typical way generative mechanisms and contexts have connected historically to produce unique outcomes. Such research has to be historical as well as analytical and, in order to be accomplished at all, has to fall back on secondary sources or on the interpretation of data in a documentary record. However, this research is guided by ideas about generative mechanisms occurring in a context in which other processes are at work. In these examples movement takes the form of change in specific combinations of generative mechanisms and their contexts so that sequences of cause and effect can be seen to work over time.

like mine

Though few, there are important studies of linked generative processes. As realist-informed research develops, more may be expected. In addition to the later work of Edwards, other recent research may be cited: Smith (2005), Smith and Meiksins (1995), Clark (2000), and Mutch (2007). Peter Clark (2000) has perhaps done most to set out ideas about the temporal links between generative processes. His work combines discussion of temporal and geographical sequences and connections, and is accordingly complex. Another example of extensive research is the work of Chris Smith. This investigates three analytically distinct generative processes (which he calls 'system', 'societal', and 'dominance' effects) and considers evidence of all three working themselves out over time. Smith shows that reference to all three processes may be necessary to explain current strategies and practices of firms.

A focused study by Mutch (2007) illustrates this type of research. (The same author uses documentary content analysis to produce chapter 12 in this volume). Mutch looks at the practices of an individual entrepreneur in the transformation of the management of the production and sale of brewery products in nineteenth-century Liverpool. He identifies A. B. Walker, a nineteenth-century provincial businessman, as exhibiting the personality type called the 'autonomous reflexive' (Archer 2003), combining the capacity to monitor his own actions and business performance, but also so respecting his own judgement to be able to persist with his innovative behaviour in the face of adverse opinions about the likelihood of his business success. Fortuitous circumstances also aided his rise, such as being already the owner-manager of a brewery, and having earlier business experience in Scotland. The latter suggested to Walker the relevance of introducing new practices in pub management in Liverpool, and extending his brewing interests into the retail trade. Mutch argues that a key factor allowing the successful introduction of new forms of management of tied public houses by Walker was also due to his possession of the autonomous-reflective self-identity which allowed him to emerge as one of the first brewers to diversify successfully into retail trade. This secured the conditions for the profitability of his business, and provided a template copied and adapted in other British businesses. This study is more modest in its objectives than other research of this genre; but, as a generative mechanism, the process of organizational development described by Mutch is of interest because it shows the origin of what became a widely reproduced and influential business innovation.

This design does not make reconceptualization of research subjects central, though it may rely on other work that allows what seemed to be familiar processes to be reinterpreted. In this approach the conditions for existence of the generative process are given attention. Thus, research not only looks at specific generative processes, but they are also used as the basis for further enquiries. To the extent that this work involves characterizing generative mechanisms, it is abductive. But it clearly also extends into the consideration of the historical conditions and sequences of change leading to the emergence of a given generative mechanism. It investigates how developments followed each other in time so that one set of outcomes emerged historically and not others. Because research of this kind enquires about factors that gave rise to mechanisms and the conditions of their existence, it is essentially also retroductive in its logic.

Designs Employing Large-scale Quantitative Data Sets

Many realists make use of quantitative data (Sayer 1992; Danermark et al. 2002; Layder 1998) but most consider some instances of this to be highly suspect. For most CR researchers, for example, the results from surveys should be considered with extreme caution. The reasons are several. Firstly, realists are sceptical about the possibility of measuring attitudes effectively. Attitudes are inherently variable and are highly reflective of the context in which they are expressed. Secondly, how attitudes relate to behaviour is complex and unpredictable. Because of this, realists tend to prefer close observation to pin down the outlook (and its relation to the behaviour) of any group of people. Thirdly, realists are sceptical of the applicability of inductive logic to human behaviour—it is easy to apply but does not mirror the processes it is designed to assess. Realists often see problems with data collection and recording in interviews (Pawson 1989), data handling and analysis (Marsh 1982, 1988), and the unsocial and unreflective basis of positivist research practice (Bateson 1984).

The root of the problem is that complex, open systems studied in social science are not appropriately conceptualized by the positivist assumptions underpinning quantitative research (Karlsson 2011). Byrne (2004) pursues the criticism of traditional methods as far as proposing new ways of analysing quantitative data relating to populations arguing that population data can only be appropriately analysed by abandoning variable analysis and substituting 'multilevel modelling'. This procedure requires innovations in survey data recording, moving to the collection of information about the groups in which respondents are located in addition to recording their individual responses. Byrne is correct that standard research practices entailed in survey work are profoundly individualistic and that more theoretically adequate procedures for the quantitative modelling of data sets need to be developed. However, there is some way to go before these methods are readily available and widely used in organizational studies.

However, quantitative data collected from representative samples or whole populations can be revelatory about contexts in ways that allow connections to be made with known or conjectured generative processes. If key features of a mechanism(s) have been postulated, further insight into them may arise from considering data describing the context of their operation. A common feature of the quantitative research undertaken by realists is its interest in obtaining descriptive statistics on whole populations. Such statistics may be seen as describing the context of generative mechanisms. Thus, statistics on income inequality may be relevant to understanding changed attitudes and changed responses of employees to their employers. To the realist, quantitative research can be a way of contextualizing and even of re-framing organizational processes. It is economical in estimating population values to use samples to estimate population characteristics. Descriptive statistics in themselves may explain rather little. To know that 64% or so of the Swedish population have an instrumental attitude to work is one thing. However, to know also that this is an extremely low figure compared with many other advanced countries, and that this figure is moving up quickly, is to know much more. These observations, taken together, say something about workplace change in Sweden and stimulate further research into the processes that could be involved.

The design of several large-scale research projects has included collection of information on populations. An example is research into employment practices of transnational companies in the UK (Marginson et al. 1995), where the numbers of such companies was estimated. Focused work making good use of population data is also possible. To illustrate the possibilities here the work of Ackroyd and Muzio into change and reorganization of the legal profession in the last twenty years is considered (Ackroyd and Muzio 2007). Legal firms have been studied largely through intensive studies of a small number of firms, and especially of single case studies using ethnography. The leading model of contemporary professional firms, the managed professional business (MPB), originated in relatively small-scale studies of Canadian law firms. In other countries too, research into particular law firms had brought to light evidence of decline in working conditions and employment prospects of employed lawyers, leading some to argue for the de-professionalization of the occupation. On the other hand, it seemed clear that solicitor firms had been growing in size and importance in the UK and the USA, with very large firms and highly profitable firms emerging. A feature that was thought to unite these two trends was the rise of professional management. A key feature of the MPB model was the suggestion that the management of law firms was a growing phenomenon somehow implicated in the pattern of change. By considering general trends provided by data relating to the whole legal profession in England, however, Ackroyd and Muzio were able to find little evidence for any rise of a managerial cadre. Figures relating to the total of people employed in English solicitor firms actually showed a steady decline of administrative employees and sustained rise of the numbers of employed solicitors. Professional hierarchies were growing, with longer promotion intervals and a more complex professional division of labour. As a result, the understanding of the generative mechanism explaining change in the organization of the legal profession was revised, and an alternative model of solicitor firms, this time constructed around the idea of professional reorganization, was put forward (Ackroyd and Muzio 2007).

Similar considerations apply here as in generative studies: this design does not simply involve reconceptualizing the subject of the research. This research sets well-researched situations, in which there are already known generative mechanisms, against measured aspects of the context and compares the two. It considers possible links between the two areas of knowledge. Hence, both abduction and retroduction are involved. It is not difficult to see that a closer alignment of these perspectives would benefit our general understanding.

DESIGNS INVOLVING ENGAGED RESEARCH

As we have seen, many realists place emphasis on the emancipatory possibilities of social science and, of course, the knowledge produced in the detached mode of social research can be used and applied. However, it usually is applied by groups other than the researchers, such as professionals, policymakers, and activists in social movements. Given the commitment to emancipatory change, we might expect critical realist researchers to use their ideas and knowledge in direct ways actively to produce change themselves in directions they see as valuable, and so many of them do. In the following sections we consider the ways realist researchers have adopted an engaged mode of active intervention as part of the research process. We distinguish two types of engaged research. The first is research which actively intervenes in organizations and situations and tries to produce positive change. Examples are action research (in which the research effort is led by external agents and supported by participants) and 'barefoot research' in which research efforts are undertaken principally by internal participants themselves. The other type of engaged research considered here is evaluation, in which the efficacy of existing policies and attempts to produce change are thoroughly assessed.

When they undertake actively engaged research, realists attempt to influence social practices on the basis of theoretical generalizations concerning structures and mechanisms they know about or propose are operating in the places of research. As was argued in the introductory chapter, theoretical generalizations are important results from realist research. These take the form: 'wherever this structure can be found it possesses this/these mechanism/s and this/these tendencies'. However, outcomes are not reliably read off from the existence of specific mechanisms. The social world is open, and, as has been discussed in the previous sections of this chapter, what follows as the outcome of a mechanism may be modified by the context. The context of a mechanism includes other mechanisms. Ideas for social action and planning have to try to take into account changing contexts. For these reasons, realists tend not to write prescriptions for change, nor do they propose recipes for producing good social outcomes. Too much is unknown and contingent for this. Instead they provide practitioners with knowledge of structures, their mechanisms and tendencies that practitioners can apply to their specific contexts. Positivist advice to practitioners is based on empirical generalizations formulated as recipes saying 'if you do A, B will follow' independently of context. Realist advice is much more complex but also more practical in handling change. They can for example be like this (Pawson 2006: 100):

> 'Remember A'; 'beware of B'; 'take care of C'; 'D can result in both E and F'; 'Gs and Hs are likely to interpret I quite differently'; 'if you try J make sure that K, L, and M have also been considered'; 'N's effect tends to be short lived'; 'O really has quite different components—P, Q, and R'; 'and S works perfectly well in T but poorly for U;…'little is known about V, W, X, Y, and Z'.

Against the background of a need to take into account what is known of generative mechanisms and the relations between mechanisms and contexts, engaged realist research—when it is undertaken—is far from predictable or easy. Our discussion of designs in this mode is therefore more tentative and exploratory. Engaged research has a long history in some forms; but in these areas realists are behind the game. Compared to detached realist research, the engaged mode is still rare, although growing in importance. Much of this type of research, realist or other, tends not to be reported in journals and books— the action takes over and becomes the point of the activity, as opposed to publication of results being the end point.

Action Research

Action research is the best-known type of engaged research project. In it the researchers seek to produce change in the behaviour and practices of a group under study. The procedure usually involves a work group, often with the help of an outside 'consultant', formulating a diagnosis of its own behavioural patterns, deciding what needs to be done to produce change, and then undertaking the change. It can be thought of as another type of case study, in which the research involves attempts to induce significant change in pre-planned directions. Experience shows that action research can induce change in small groups in favourable circumstances, but it cannot easily prevail against the generative mechanisms already in operation in the workplace. There are considerable forces working against the possibilities of emancipatory workplace change, for example.

Because orthodox researchers believe significant change is difficult if not impossible (realists) or not desirable (positivists) there is frequently tension between action research and 'traditional' academic research where both exist. Disdain for 'mainstream' social science can be found almost everywhere amongst practitioners of action research (Gustavsen 2004: 154). Action researchers accuse academic researchers of living in an ivory tower, while academic researchers have regarded what action researchers do as lacking intellectual weight. However, to our minds the important divide is not between mainstream and action research but between realist and anti-realist approaches in both types of research. Most of the research is heavily influenced by positivist or constructivist ontology, but there are some realist strands. (An excellent account of critical realist action research is to be found in ch. 11 of this volume by Monder Ram and others.)

As yet, we do not think that we can talk about a distinctive critical realist type of action research, as we can of evaluation research (see next section), but there are examples of cases in which researchers do not present practitioners with prescriptions and rely more on theoretical knowledge. An example from Norwegian action research illustrates the difference (Rolfsen and Knutstad 2007). The project was carried out at a company delivering automotive supplies. It had just won a contract with a big car producer which required advanced technological changes, introduction of lean-production strategies, and implementing team organization. Two external action researchers became involved, being active at the highest management level and on the shop floor. Despite the protests of the researchers, management wrote a prescription for a change process based on lean-production ideas. Finally, they emphasized their expectation that employees follow the changes set down in the guidelines.

The researchers claimed this prescription would not work, especially the last point; but management implemented teams and appointed team leaders anyway. In practice there were many problems in the teams. In the forge team, for example, the skilled workers were accustomed to a high degree of autonomy. However, instead of trying to implement the lean-production prescription, the action researchers arranged a series of team meetings in which the members discussed what goals the team was to have. Supported by theoretical inputs from the researchers, the team members arrived at a plan for change in which the work group was to become a cooperative unit with shared goals; it would also share knowledge about the work process and eventually develop towards an autonomous unit without a team leader. The assembly-line team were unskilled, but they also, within certain limits, were used to having a degree of autonomy. Now they had to learn new skills and many doubted their capacity to do so. In this team there were theoretical contributions from the researchers and the members decided that the team should be organized as a learning arena, which meant that anyone could ask any question without being regarded as stupid and they divided learning tasks among them. 'The team', concluded the researchers (p. 352), 'strongly desired to be responsible for its own learning'.

The logic of discovery in realist action research envisages the possibility of reconstructing the generative mechanisms in which workgroups are implicated; this means identifying what is already happening in terms of mechanisms and, by collective endeavour, redesigning this. Active intervention is part of the research process. The recipe of making people work according to lean-production guidelines could hardly be more different; but in this case that objective was effectively replaced by the researchers introducing conceptual discussions in the teams. In critical realist terms the teams started to investigate and evaluate which mechanisms they wanted the team structure to have and ordered the team accordingly. The two teams built up diverse structures which fitted into their respective contexts. The difference between the detached and the engaged mode is thereby not concerned with the context—in both these cases it is given—but in the way of treating the mechanisms involved. In the detached mode the question is: what is the mechanism in this context? In the engaged mode: what mechanism do we want to install in this context? A formative new mechanism is an abduction, but one made not by researchers but by participants. The critical realist trait in this action research results in creating new mechanisms, not in moving the same prescription between contexts.

Intensive Realist Evaluation

A change programme is a political strategic plan to transform some problematic social phenomenon for the better, and an evaluation is made to compare the plan to the actual outcome. Positivism-inspired, method-driven experimental and quasi-experimental evaluations are common but theory-driven realistic evaluations are growing in importance, for example, in the fields of healthcare (Marchal et al. 2012) and social work (Kazi et al. 2002) programmes.

Quasi-experimental design leads to the problems associated with implementing recipes for reform without regard to context, which we flagged up as problematic in earlier sections. The critical realist alternative takes the complexity of interventions seriously and builds on the question 'what works for whom under what circumstances?' What is studied is the interplay between context and mechanism in producing the outcome of the programme, which is called the context-mechanism-outcome (CMO) configuration. As Pawson and

Tilley suggest, 'causal outcomes follow from mechanisms acting in contexts' (1997: 58). There is a move from asking whether an intervention works to asking what makes it work. Critical realist evaluation is therefore theory-driven, producing theoretical generalizations. It is through mechanisms that programmes and interventions work and that is where realist evaluation starts. Greenhalgh in this volume develops these fundamental ideas.

When an intervention is made it is introduced into an already existing social context and it is in the relation between the mechanism it initiates and the context that the explanation of the outcome can be found. As we have seen the same mechanism can have different effects (or none) in different contexts. The context can enable or constrain the effects of the mechanism, which of course makes the success or otherwise of the programme. Interventions are directed at the existing mechanisms creating problems and trying to install mechanisms that can block the problem mechanisms. Thus it is the effects of such CMO configurations which critical realist evaluation studies.

The following example illustrates the principle of not writing prescriptions but providing practitioners with complex conceptual knowledge and theoretical generalizations. It is an intensive evaluation of Internet-based medical education (Wong et al. 2010), based on existing studies of this field (cf. Pawson 2006b). An earlier meta-analysis along positivist lines found that the Internet is often used in education for medical students and that, on average, Internet education was equivalent to non-Internet education in important respects. However, there was substantial heterogeneity in response to similar provision which was difficult to understand. A technologically based course might be valued positively by one group and negatively by another. The critical realist evaluators, however, took this variation as their point of departure and among their initial aims was to '(a) explain what sort of Internet-based medical education "works", for whom, and in what circumstances; (b) produce pragmatic guidance that could be used by developers to optimize the design of their courses and by potential learners to evaluate whether a particular course is right for them' (Wong et al. 2010: 2). After an elaborate search and exclusion process the evaluation included 249 studies of medical Internet-based education and a number of candidate theories were selected as explanations of (a). They were then tested against data from all the included studies, some were modified, some excluded and more theories were added.

This process of searching theories about mechanisms and outcomes in different contexts led to two types of theories being chosen as explanatory candidates. One dealt with technology acceptance and led to the evaluators formulating a number of questions—not recipes—that they suggested course developers and prospective learners could ask, as guides for their actions (p. 5). These included how useful the prospective learners perceived the Internet technology to be, how easy the prospective learners found this technology to use, and how well this format fitted in with what learners were used to and expected. The other theory concerned interactive dialogue as a central mechanism, leading to two additional questions for practitioners to consider: how might high-quality human-human (learner-tutor and learner-learner) interaction and feedback be achieved, and how might high-quality human-technical interaction and feedback be achieved?

In this research there are important elements of abduction, as basic to it were theoretical conjectures concerning the nature of effective interactions to facilitate effective learning in the new context of a virtual learning space. The realist evaluation built upon and extended the results of the earlier positivist meta-analysis. It did not provide those interested in medical Internet courses with recipes to be applied independent of context, but with questions to think through as guides for actions for different groups in different contexts or different groups in the same context.

Barefoot Research

Barefoot research is a kind of research which encourages employees to research their own circumstances, exploring their company and industry from their own point of view and drawing their own conclusions. When Carl Ryant, one of the academic proponents of this approach, discusses the role of oral history in business history writing (1988), he finds it has very little presence. One way of correcting this, he says (p. 654), is 'to view the history of an industry as the history of its workers and to have the workers write the history of their own workplaces'. This is not classic action research in the sense of research being undertaken by researchers with practitioners, nor do researchers appear as teachers as in intensive realist evaluation. Instead, such an approach has been called 'barefoot' research, because it is a journey undertaken with very little support. We propose this definition of the research idea—academically untrained people doing research on their own circumstances. If this is a research design it is so in a minimal sense of the term.

Barefoot research in the UK has gone under the name of history workshops, but what Ryant principally has in mind is the Swedish 'Dig-where-you-stand–movement' (Lindqvist 1978, 1979). Business history, Lindqvist claims, has always been written for its owners and directors, written by researchers and authors selected and paid by representatives of the companies and approved by them. After reading all the available histories of cement companies in Sweden, Lindqvist summarizes their message as follows (1979: 24): management has never made a mistake and has never been morally at fault. It is a background assumption also that, as providers of capital, the contribution of the shareholders to the production of cement has been vastly more important than that of the workers, whilst the contribution of the worker has been mainly to receive benefits from the company and occasionally to make unrealistic demands.

In reaction to this, Lindqvist suggests that business history should be written by the workers and that a good place to start is their own workplaces. He has written a handbook for workers to do research on their own working life—in other words to dig where you stand. Lindqvist has high expectations that such research will uncover alternative accounts of the development of industry and lead to changed attitudes in the employees undertaking the (re)writing of their history. As an illustration Lindqvist considers the limited use made of electrostatic dust collectors in the cement industry in Sweden. Despite the efficiency of this technology in reducing health hazards, it was in fact slow to be installed. The principle of the electrostatic dust collector was discovered in Britain in 1884 but the first one was not installed until 1906 (in California) under acute pressure from the owners of adjoining land. In 1909 it was shown statistically that cement dust involved serious health hazards to anyone coming into contact with it. Both the health problems and the solution in the form of the dust collector were soon well known to the Swedish cement industry, but it was not until 1969 that all Swedish companies had installed the technology. Lindqvist comments that collecting information on the failure to implement this technological change, a failure that saved money at the cost of the workers' health, could well radicalize the ideas of employees (1979: 28–29):

> The abstract notion of the relation between Capital and Labour suddenly becomes concrete and tangible, almost touchable and breathable, through historical investigation of the particular circumstances in a particular place of work.

In the handbook for non-professional researchers Lindqvist discusses thirty ways of studying jobs and workplaces with the assumption that no professional researcher is a better expert on a worker's job than the worker herself.

It is, of course, very difficult to specify in advance what will be the logic of discovery employed in barefoot research. However, this type of research is allocated a place towards the extensive end of the intensive/extensive dimension because, initially at least, it is likely that background information on the workers' company and industry is what will be sought by them. In the Dig-where-you-stand–movement, employees have tried to find out more about the context of their experience as workers. They are intimately aware of their own work experience, but relatively ignorant of the context. Their first choice has often been to think retroductively by asking what has made their work possible.

Lindqvist suggests that minimal advice (concerning which archives, libraries, collections of historical statistics, etc. are available) will be all that is needed to develop this kind of research; but of course it is not known how far concern for gathering historical and contextual information will lead to discussions of theory and to the consideration of possible causal processes in history. In his example of the Swedish cement industry, workers' questions led naturally from fact-gathering to theoretical analysis, however. Lindqvist suggests that findings are placed without difficulty in the theoretical socio-economic per-spective of capitalism and wage labour. Hence he suggests thereby that both abduction and retroduction are put to use.

Extensive Realist Evaluation

As we have seen, many realists are sceptical about statistical techniques, espe-cially inductive techniques, if they are used to infer causal connections. For this reason, realist evaluation has usually been performed in the form of inten-sively designed case studies, which practically rely on the ontological claims of the openness of social systems and the epistemological demands that follow from them. However, some realists now use such techniques in evaluations of change programmes and thereby turn to the extensive end of the scale.

We take our example of extensive realist evaluation from the experience of a project organization called Shield in which a non-profit organization and a local social services department cooperated in a programme for children who sexually harm others. In this example, evaluators combined qualitative and quantitative methods and intensive and extensive design (Kazi 2003: chs. 6–8). The extensive design was only possible because it could build on results from the intensive part of the study. Kazi's account of this realist evaluation is in parts highly technical, concerning measures and statistical techniques; we refrain from discussing this, concentrating on the principles underlying this kind of evaluation. In this research each child was regarded as a case and followed longitudinally over time, thus making possible both synchronic and diachronic analyses. Here we focus on the latter, in this consideration of the extensive parts of the evaluation. The combination of intensive and extensive designs is discussed in detail by Scott Hurrell in this volume.

Earlier studies in the field had tried to identify risk factors for children who sexually abuse others. The Shield project aimed to find ways to reduce the likelihood of children in the programme committing these types of offences again. The procedure involved the by now familiar realist injunction to be concerned about which interventions work with what type of young people. In this project there was an action research ingredient in the evaluation in that practitioners discussed and learned the theoretical basis of the evalua-tion; they also registered data for it. The evaluator found that earlier, positivist, research, which included meta-analyses and evaluations, provided inconclu-sive and contradictory results on the factors which influenced children who sexually harm others. In this example the aim was to build an account of the mechanisms involved in the reproduction of offending behaviour.

In the intensive part of the evaluation a number of contexts, content, out-comes, and mechanisms were identified for each child in the programme. The first step in the extensive analysis was to aggregate the data from the intensive phase on contexts, mechanisms, and outcomes and to consider the possible shape of the CMO configuration at work in the cases. Thereafter the relations between the elements of these CMO configurations were studied with the help of quantitative methods. In the extensive analysis correlations between variables in the CMO configuration were measured through significance tests, measures of effect size and of statistical power. Among the patterns was that whether the intervention was completed or not was correlated with the engagement of the child, which in turn was associated with the engagement of the parent. Three mechanisms were especially important for the outcomes: parent's relationship with each other; the child's ability to engage in the assessment; and improvement in cooperation with other professionals.

The final step of the extensive study was to use regression analysis to map the interaction between the mechanisms and the contexts to produce outcomes. The most important results were that the programme mechanisms were triggered to block problem mechanisms in contexts of family trauma, especially domestic violence, and that the odds of the child being engaged in the work were much higher when the parent was engaged—and this was the case even when other mechanisms in the child's social context were disabling.

If the above exercise had been a positivistic evaluation, the focus of the work would have been on whether the intervention group fared better than a control group, whilst relations between the circumstances of the clients and components of the intervention would have been variables subject as far as practicable to control. In the realist evaluation of the Shield project, postulated mechanisms at work were central to understanding the outcomes for children in different contexts. Instead of a prescription saying what works and what does not, the advice to practitioners was more nuanced and fruitful.

> The Shield model assessment can be developed by focusing on engaging with the child/young person, and either parent, as well as with other professionals involved, even in the most difficult circumstances. However, with regard to these circumstances, there appear to be a number of choices. First, the Shield Project's model of assessment could be targeted at clients where the multiple problems highlighted above exist, for example, previous history of trauma. Second, the model could be developed in such a way that it could engage better with the others where such conditions are not present. Third, both of these strategies could be followed, targeting at the most needy, at the same time developing ways of engaging those that appear not to have these complex historical problems. (Kazi 2003: 156)

To many critical realists this type of extensive analysis, which goes beyond descriptive statistics into the use of inferential statistics, is controversial. However, as it has been executed here to examine the properties of the context of intervention, there seems to be few grounds for the realist researcher to object to it.

CONCLUDING COMMENTS

The applicability of realism to organization and management studies is obvious, and has a growing following. But, in the area of methodology, realist practitioners are well behind the game. There is a serious lack of appealing and accessible material on CR-informed methodology to set those new to these ideas off on a path to accomplish interesting and insightful research. It is hoped that the examples arrayed in the remainder of this book will make a contribution here and find a receptive audience. Perhaps the most important result of the present mapping exercise, and indeed from the collection of papers which follows, is that they show that many types of research project are possible, and also how underutilized they are. This area offers many possibilities for researchers to develop new procedures.

Directly or indirectly, positivist ideas have dominated the area of research methodology in social science, of which organization and management studies are part. These ideas have a firm grip, such that more insightful and interesting research—as that which is conducted under CR auspices—often does not make headway. Supplanting the positivist paradigm with one which has limited capacity to produce objective knowledge can hardly be considered an advance. On the other hand, it is surely difficult not to regard the challenges embodied in the need to develop realist research protocols as stimulating and exciting. This chapter is a contribution to developing the perception that there are valuable research procedures for the realist-inclined researcher to use, which have a clear rationale and which allow insightful research to be undertaken.

3

Employing a Form of Critical Realist Discourse Analysis for Identity Research

An Example from Women's Talk of Motherhood, Childcare, and Employment

Wendy Sims-Schouten and Sarah Riley

In this chapter we describe a method for doing critical realist discourse analysis (CRDA). We offer this method as a way for researchers to contextualize people's accounts of themselves, enabling links to be made between subjectivity, culture, and materiality. Below, we explore the epistemological issues of combining discourse analysis—a typically social constructionist approach—with critical realism, before outlining in detail our method. This chapter is therefore mainly a methodological piece, designed as a starting point for researchers interested in contextualizing how people explain themselves to others—a common experience in qualitative research. We offer worked examples using data from a study on mothers and their childcare decisions when returning to work, but the method we showcase could be applied to a range of identity research in management and organizational studies.

DISCOURSE ANALYSIS AND CRITICAL REALISM

Discourse analysis is a relatively new approach in psychology that developed in the 1970s, with seminal texts subsequently published from the 1980s (e.g. Parker 1992; Potter and Wetherell 1987). Discourse analysis is an umbrella term for a group of approaches that share a focus on analysing language because they generally conceptualize language as constituting reality, not neutrally describing it. Unlike other aspects of psychology, discourse analysts therefore focus on language in its own right rather than as a vehicle to understanding people's inner worlds or cognitive processes. Discursive psychologists, might, for example, examine the features of someone's talk that allows them to avoid blame.

Discourse analysis is grounded in social constructionism, although recent moves in psychology have led some discourse analysts towards a more agnostic stance in terms of epistemology. Social constructionists take a critical stance towards taken-for-granted knowledge, and understand knowledge as socio-historically specific and produced through social processes, which are then linked to social action (Burr 2003). From this standpoint, the ways in which we experience the world and the people we understand ourselves to be are produced through social processes, 'the process of understanding is not automatically driven by the forces of nature, but is the result of an active, co-operative enterprise of persons in relationship' (Gergen 1985: 267). For example, the pain of childbirth might seem to be an unequivocal natural truth, but social constructionists could point to a popular book that rejects the term 'contractions' in favour of 'rushes', so reconceptualizing the experience of childbirth and perhaps making it a different experience (Gaskin 2002).

As O'Mahoney and Vincent argue in the introduction of this volume, advocates of critical realism and social constructionism agree that claims to objectivity and truthfulness can have negative consequences, and place value in understanding the social world as concept-dependent and produced through discourse. Where the similarity ends is in critical realists' assertions that the social world is also made up of non-discursive structures that directly impact on our experience and understanding of the world (Bhaskar 1989; Harré and Bhaskar 2005). For example, Bhaskar's (1989) call to critical realism drew on the constructionist notion of the role of social processes in constituting the social world, and the realist position that people's actions will be influenced by personal and societal mechanisms that are independent of their thoughts or impressions.

The issue of what is 'beyond' discourse evokes critical debates between critical realists and social constructionists. For example, Harré (1990), accepts that there is a 'real' world beyond the text, and argues that what we can know of this real world is a sub-world he calls Umwelt. This world is restricted by the physiological, sensory apparatus of the human species. Yet, within those restrictions, he argues, our world is always socially constructed—*primarily through language*. But, in response, Bhaskar argued that this social constructionist tendency to reduce all the dimensions of social existence to discourse is fundamentally flawed:

> Does the food depend just on the cook? No. It depends on the utensils he/she has, it depends on the building he/she lives in, it depends on the amount of resources

that he or she is given by the authorities. It is obvious that he/she is constrained insofar as what he/she can cook. (Harré and Bhaskar 2005: 29)

Critical realism then, is an epistemology that uses elements from both social constructionism and realism, identifying extra-discursive processes and structures (such as the embodied and material) with the power to shape and form phenomena (history, culture, and individual experience) that are capable of being experienced and observed (Bhaskar 1998; Lauber and Schenner 2011; Willig 1998). As such, critical realists argue that social constructionism with its strong emphasis on language ignores the influence of embodied factors (such as missing limbs and colds), as well as personal and social histories (e.g. child abuse) upon social situations and activity (Cromby and Nightingale 1999). From a critical realist position, these factors are not reducible to discourse.

This call to the 'extra-discursive' has been heard by various members of the discursive community in psychology. Some discourse analysts have been content to argue that discursive and material practices inform each other, for example constructing gender equality in particular ways, can lead to particular kinds of legislation that subsequently impact on employment opportunities (Riley 2002). This allows discourse analysts to focus on the discursive while arguing that such talk has a direct impact on the material (and vice versa). But within this position the relationships between discursive and material practices remain under-theorized, and for some discourse analyst psychologists the focus on text was too reductionist, resulting in psychoanalytic moves (e.g. Parker 2002; Walkerdine, Lucey, and Melody 2001) or attempts at critical realist discourse analysis (e.g. Cromby and Nightingale 1999; Cromby and Harper 2009; Gómez-Estern et al. 2010; Kral et al. 2011; Nightingale and Cromby 2002; Sims-Schouten, Riley, and Willig 2007).

In their chapter 'What Is Wrong with Social Constructionism?' Cromby and Nightingale (1999) argued that social constructionist psychology should loosen its almost exclusive focus on language and discourse, and include other elements, such as embodiment and materiality without reducing them to discourse. Since then a range of attempts have been made to include the extra-discursive in discourse analysis. For example, Cromby and Harper argue in their analysis of accounts of paranoia that 'we experience a world suffused by the materially and socially shaped anxieties, hopes, fears, and desires that currently co-constitute our subjectivity' (2009: 346). They conclude:

> Consequently, by examining relational dynamics, social structures, and material factors, we might begin to construct an explanation for the empirical association between paranoia and social inequality. (p. 353)

Critical realist discourse analysts argue that the advantage to theorizing the material world as having an external existence outside discourse is that it can do justice to research participants by locating their talk in its wider context, showing how relational influences, embodiment, social structures (such as class), and material environments play a constitutive role in people's accounts (Cromby and Harper 2009; Gómez-Estern et al. 2010; Sims-Schouten et al. 2007). The fact that discourse has the potential to structure knowledge is an important part of the essence of discourse (O'Mahoney 2011). Yet, if we are to accept that important aspects of human experience are also located outside of language, accounts of identity and resistance are inadequate without reference to a non-discursive reality (Burr 1999).

This leads to the question whether one can make a distinction between discursive and extra-discursive aspects in talk. Despite various moves towards critical realist discourse analysis three problems have emerged that have reduced the efficacy of these attempts, namely, difficulties distinguishing the discursive from the extra-discursive, clashing epistemologies, and the lack of a systematic method. We discuss these points in more detail below.

First, is that a robust enough rejection of the question 'how do you decide what is "real" and what is "discourse"?' has not been forthcoming. It has been argued that critical realists do not have a systematic method of distinguishing between discursive and non-discursive factors, that these distinctions come down to individual choice driven by the researcher's political standpoint and that what is presented as extra-discursive can in fact be analysed from a relativist perspective (e.g. Edwards 1995). These issues are neatly summarized by Kaposi (with our elaboration in square brackets):

> Thus, a pattern appears to have been repeated in the debates between constructionist researchers over the years. As one side [discursive psychologists] claimed analytic rigour (and was still mostly denied broader/deeper relevance) and the other side [critical realists and other discourse analysts] claimed extra-discursive relevance (and was mostly denied analytical rigour), an integrative empirical perspective on discourse and identity remained elusive. (Kaposi 2011: 3)

In relation to the second criticism we note that combining critical realism and discursive psychology does involve mixing two more or less clashing epistemologies. The purpose of this chapter is not to significantly engage with this issue, other than to suggest that research is messy and on occasion theoretical in/coherence can be useful in helping researchers think about their topic through different lenses (Lather 2007). The purpose of this chapter is thus not to solve the epistemological problems between the two, but to outline a method which presents a starting point for researchers interested in doing critical realist discursive work because they want their work to have a dialogue between discourse and embodiment, materiality, or social structures. Our purpose in this chapter is therefore to address the third stumbling block with critical realist discourse analysis—a lack of systematic methodology, since few discursive methods have been devised with a view to also being able to analyse extra-discursive influences on talk (Sims-Schouten et al. 2007).

THEORETICAL FRAMEWORK

Our method for critical realist discourse analysis draws on the tradition of 'synthesized' discourse analysis. There is a body of work that supports synthesizing forms of discourse analysis (e.g. Edley and Wetherell 1999; Riley 2002; Riley, Thompson, and Griffin 2010; Wetherell 1998; Willott and Griffin 1997). Advantages include being able to draw on discursive approaches that analyse the interactive accomplishments of talk, such as managing facts, interest, and accountability; and locating these accounts in the socio-historic context in which the discussion is situated, either in terms of the common-sense ways that we have about talking about objects and events in the world and/or wider discourses that are often associated with institutions, such as government policy (Riley, Thompson, and Griffin 2010). A synthesized analysis offers analytical advantages through emphasizing the situated nature of meaning-making, as well as positioning discursive practices within a genealogical context (Riley 2002).

Our conception of subjectivity is that people draw on a set of (multiple, contradictory, and culturally specific) common-sense discourses (ideas out there in their social world that they can draw on to make sense of themselves [see Billig et al. 1988]). These discourses gain their explanatory power by being located in wider institutionally oriented discourses and through the specific ways in which they are deployed in interaction. But this talk and the wider discourses that support its sense-making occur within the boundaries of embodied, material, social structures and institutional practices that have an extra-discursive element to them that works to make certain understandings/ accounts more plausible than others (Sims-Schouten et al. 2007).

Our first standpoint then is that language does not independently constitute our world, rather language discursively co-constitutes the realities we experience (Nightingale and Cromby 2002). In addition to this, we argue that extra-discursive aspects, such as our embodiment (from colds to postnatal depressions), materiality (e.g. family income), and social structures and institutions (e.g. class, educational systems, employer's maternity-leave policies) shape and form the kinds of constructions we can 'choose', live through and with. Third, we take the point of view that critical realist discourse analysis has the potential to incorporate and theorize both the discursive and extra-discursive aspects of our being (Nightingale and Cromby 2002) through comprehensive analyses of the discourses available to groups and individuals, as well as analysis of the conditions that gave rise to these discourses (see also Willig 1999). Such conditions do not necessarily determine discourse; rather they mediate such accommodation. Conditions could be *macro-level* conditions, such as governmental policies and the power of multinational corporations, as well as *micro-level* conditions, such as the personal circumstances, family budget, age, and educational background of the participant (Sims-Schouten et al. 2007; see also Cromby and Harper 2009 for a discussion of 'realist' aspects in relation to mental health; and Lauber and Schenner 2011 for an application of CR in relation to environmental politics and social practices). As such, while we may choose from an array of discourses when positioning ourselves, this is by no means a boundless range. Instead, the ways we account for ourselves are stimulated by personal, psychological factors and social and institutional mechanisms and materiality (Houston 2001; Sims-Schouten et al. 2007).

Our aim is therefore to be able to offer a method of making sense of our participants' accounts that includes a wide range of factors including both the discursive and 'extra'-discursive. We do this through a layered synthesized form of critical realist discourse analysis, which analyses:

- the rhetorical strategies participants employ that allow them to do certain interactional work such as locate blame (in an interview or other form of communication);

- the wider discourses participants draw on to make sense of themselves, and the possibilities and limitations that these discourses produce (e.g. psychological discourses of maternal attachment); and

- how participants' material, embodied and social-structural/institutional contexts (e.g. the availability of institutional childcare in a geographical area) may provide the conditions of possibility that allows their sense-making to make sense, and to thus be treated as legitimate accounts, both by the speaker and the person(s) hearing the speaker.

Our focus is on how people account for themselves, which includes the interactional effect of these accounts (e.g. avoiding blame), and how the logic of these accounts can be made sense of through an analysis of discursive and material conditions in which participants are located. This focus assumes a 'stratified ontology', which refers to CR's distinction between the 'real' (structures with their associated causal powers), the 'actual' (events and processes), and the 'empirical' (the part of the real and actual that is experienced by social actors) (Fairclough 2005). Note that the relationship between the 'real', 'actual', and 'empirical' is not linear and predictable, instead various mediating entities and social processes are at play here.

For us, the non-discursive does not 'cause' a participant to draw on one discourse and not another, rather we see the non-discursive (e.g. a physicality of a building) and wider discourses (e.g. those linked to government policy) creating a kind of scaffolding milieu—the conditions of possibility—from which it makes sense for a participant to account for themselves in particular ways and not others. In critical realist terms our aim is thus to identify the discursive and non-discursive entities (things that make a difference) that 'combine to form generative mechanisms or a constellation of forces which come together to affect regularities in patterns of events' (O'Mahoney and Vincent, ch. 1, this volume), in this case patterns around women's decisions regarding childcare and employment.

Our approach works at what Bhaskar (1998) calls the 'causal level' (exploring mechanisms which generate events), seeing these mechanisms as discursive, material, embodied, and institutional. But we do not make claims that our method can identify direct causal relationships between one factor and another. Instead, our model for a critical realist discourse analysis is one in which discourse, embodiment, materiality, and social structures (which we conceptualize as produced through discourse, embodiment, and materiality) interact in complex, iterative ways, and in so doing, create the conditions of possibility for sense-making.

To explain our model with reference to our study on women's decisions regarding childcare: examples of embodiment might include the age of the mother (older women are more likely to use childcare) or the learning difficulties of a child (that increase the likelihood of drawing on discourses that construct childcare as a site for professional developmental support). In terms of discourse, we refer to both common-sense understandings and wider discourses linked to institutions. For example, psychological and educational discourses may scaffold an understanding that a child with learning difficulties needs professional, non-maternal support. And in terms of materiality, mothers who consider themselves to have limited resources in terms of space, gardens, or parks, may turn to childcare as a way to provide these.

We place social structures in the middle of our Venn diagram (Figure 3.1), since social structures are often produced through combined aspects of discourse, embodiment, and materiality. For example, the 'psy-complex' (the varied institutions and discourses associated with psychology) articulates developmental psychology discourses in which there is an expectation for children to develop and 'progress', creating the context for social institutions and other social structures that create a role for childcare and other government institutions to monitor and facilitate this progress. And these forms of monitoring/facilitation will differ depending on the embodied aspects of the child (for example, fully or partially sighted children may be given different expectations or levels of support).

How this might be played out can be seen in the example of a woman considered an 'older' mum, with one child who lives geographically far from grandparents who might have otherwise offered child care (three aspects of embodiment identified by surveys that are linked to an increased likelihood of using childcare). Her institution gives her one year relatively well-paid maternity leave and the offer of a full-time nursery place attached to her work when she returns, with tax relief of £243 a month from the government (material and discursive factors since tax relief has a material effect of increasing family income and is motivated by government policy that places importance on returning to work over maternal nurturing). In choosing to return to work and use these facilities, the woman might make sense of her choice through a 'career woman' common-sense discourse and perhaps through wider discourses that orient to neo-liberal subjectivity, that constructs a good citizen as economically active (Riley et al. 2010). But, given that in any society there are always multiple and thus contradictory discourses, the mother might also have to negotiate the psychological discourse of maternal attachment, that constructs her child's healthy development as contingent on the mother being the primary carer (Bowlby 1990). Thus in an interview she might account for her childcare decisions by orienting to the benefits her child, and not her, with the interactional effect of warding off any critique produced through an attachment theory discourse. Our analysis would not be that attachment theory discourse *causes* the participant to justify herself in this way, rather it is part of the conditions of possibility that produce a discursive milieu in which it makes sense for her to do so. And, as analysts, if we are as aware as we can be about the discursive (and material, embodied, and institutional/social) milieu in which our participant is located, we can start to make some tentative claims about the nature of what it's like to be a mother in these circumstances—the limits and possibilities of what she can say, think, and do. Our method is thus, in part, about identifying a process for developing this awareness, from which we can locate our participants' accounts of themselves.

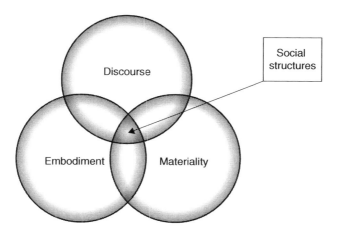

Figure 3.1 Model for the Interactions between Discourse, Embodiment, Materiality, and Social Structures

METHOD

Our critical realist discourse analysis method is operationalized in three phases. This multiphase approach allows us to identify a range of material and immaterial entities (things that make a difference) and explore how they may interact to create generative mechanisms that affect regularities in patterns of events (O'Mahoney and Vincent, ch. 1, this volume). Our method is described as a linear process below, but with the expectation that, as with most qualitative research, an iterative standpoint is required as information at one stage of a project may require the researcher to return to earlier stages and re-evaluate these in the light of the new information garnered.

The aim of the first phase is background work: to identify the common-sense and wider discourses and the embodied, material, and social structures that may be important factors in creating the conditions of possibility for the accounts that participants may use. This allows the research to identify some of the more common discourses available to individuals and the discursive and material conditions that give rise to these available discourses (Willig 1999), enabling us to list some of the entities that may combine to form generative mechanisms.

In our second phase, we developed ways of measuring these factors in participants' lives, as well as tools for accessing their accounts. This included developing both quantitative (e.g. questionnaires) and qualitative (e.g. interviews) methods. We note that integrating quantitative measures of extra-discursive variables into discourse analyses is a relatively novel practice, but is not unique. See for example, Cromby (2012), for an argument for this practice as a method for enabling consideration of the wider societal and material context of experience. Using multiple methods is also appropriate for critical realism research, since using a range of methods is considered useful for exploring the complexity of generative mechanisms (see O'Mahoney and Vincent, ch. 1, this volume).

Our final phase involves a synthesized discourse analysis, in which the participants' accounts are analysed using (a) discursive psychology (to explore the interactional accomplishment of participants' accounts such as locating blame); (b) a social constructionist analysis of the discourses they draw upon that allows their talk to sound plausible culturally; and (c) a critical realist analysis of the material, embodied, and institutional factors that may produce the conditions of possibility of the accounts our participants employ to make sense of themselves and their decisions. We describe these phases in detail below using an example from our research on parental decisions on childcare in the UK and the Netherlands, which is then followed with a worked example.

Phase 1: Identifying Factors that may Scaffold Participants' Sense-making

Our aim for phase 1 is an examination, as inclusively as possible, of what might be relevant to our study, so that we can later locate our participants' talk/sense-making within their wider material, embodied, institutional, and discursive context, allowing us to identify the conditions of possibility that scaffold this talk. To do this we adopt a form of analysis that focuses on 'discovery', with an aim to 'get inside the thing which is being researched' so that the analysis arises 'from', 'with', and 'after' the data creation processes (Olsen 2004b: 15). This 'discovery' process is also referred to as abduction (Levin-Rozalis 2004) in terms of the notion that research seeks to develop as broad as possible an understanding of what factors might be relevant, and then to test these, iteratively, against new information (Levin-Rozalis 2004). As such, our method was not to explicitly test hypotheses (see Levin-Rozalis 2004, for an example of this), instead rather than take a cause-and-effect standpoint, we were more interested in identifying as broadly as possible potential factors that we might use to read our participants talk in ways that allowed us to say something useful about the topic of our study (in this case women's decisions around childcare). Following the introduction to this book, societies and organizations form open, complex systems, which, whilst possessing tendencies, are not either constantly predictable or determined. It follows that the task of the researcher, therefore, is to develop fine-grained explanations for these patterns of events via the development of more adequate accounts of the generative mechanisms which created them. For example, we chose to look at mothers in both England and the Netherlands, since data from two different countries would increase our ability as analysts to identify, compare, and contrast the various discursive and extra-discursive factors at play.

To start phase 1 a thorough and focused literature review on relevant literature and research was conducted from as wide a perspective as possible. In this case, government policies on child care, national and local childcare provision availability, and academic and government research on childcare provision, parental childcare choices, and theories of childcare and child development were conducted in order to examine the discursive, embodied, institutional, and material elements that may impact on mothers' experience of motherhood, female employment, and day care. A range of differences between Dutch and English contexts were identified, allowing us to identify the most common reoccurring elements of embodiment, institutions, and materiality that impacted on childcare provision and uptake, which we theorized as extra-discursive factors in Dutch and English parental childcare decisions in line with our model described above (see Figure 3.1).

We also identified reoccurring ideologies and discourses in academia, government, and other relevant institutional bodies (e.g. in the UK the National Childcare Trust) that fed into these extra-discursive factors. For example, the neo-liberalism of successive UK governments has constructed ideal citizenship in terms of being economically autonomous and not reliant on the state (Hall 2011). This ideology informed government policy, so that childcare was constructed as a private parental responsibility to be addressed through private solutions, including the private provision of childcare. This policy resulted in a range of quality of provision with little consistency.[1] By contrast, Dutch childcare was constructed by the government as an employment responsibility, leading to systematically high-quality childcare being offered to its citizens (Daniel and Ivatts 1998; Tavecchio 2002). Institutional discourses of childcare responsibility also created differences in maternal leave and day-care policies between the countries. As well as the availability and quality of local day-care facilities and governmental policies that drove this, the literature review also helped us identify other extra-discursive factors in relation to day-care decision-making, including the age of the mother, number of children, and living space (e.g. flat versus house with garden). It was also found that governmental policies interacted with psychological theory, with John Bowlby's theory of attachment and maternal deprivation being particularly influential in the UK (see Sims-Schouten et al. 2007 for a more detailed discussion). Phase 1 thus allowed us to identify multilevel factors that might be relevant to our participants.

Phase 2: Developing Measures and Methods of Data Collection

Once we had identified key factors in the discursive and extra-discursive context of our topic, we then developed measures and a research design for exploring these factors. First we created quantitative indices of the extra-discursive variables discussed above. For this purpose we created questionnaires to be completed by the participants that included information about their age, income, local childcare facilities, and other extra-discursive factors that might be relevant to the research topic. For information that we could not assume participants would know (for example, the quality/number of all the day-care facilities in their area, or national and regional government policy regarding these) we employed observation and other research methods. Combined, these approaches allowed us to create a fact sheet of the material, institutional, and embodied conditions in which our participants lived. Using this fact sheet

---

[1] Note that significant improvements were made to day care in England, after the current study took place, see also Sylva's EPPE (Effective Provision of Pre-school Education) study (Sylva et al, 2010).

we were able to do justice to our participants, viewing them as individuals with their own materialities and personal histories, and not merely subjects that reproduce the dominant constructions of motherhood, day care, and female employment in their society.

We also drew up interview schedules for semi-structured interviews with mothers, which allowed the interview to cover topics identified in the literature above, as well as space for mothers to introduce topics that we may not have considered. Again, this fits with our abduction approach outlined above. We used interviews to collect participants' accounts of themselves (20 interviews with Dutch and 20 with English mothers), but other qualitative data could also be used. For example, researchers interested in parents' childcare decisions could look at how requests for after-school provision are made at parent teacher association meetings.

Phase 3: A Synthesized Discursive Analysis of Participants' Accounts of Themselves in Relation to the Research Topic

We analysed our interviews through a *three-level synthesized discourse analysis*:

First, drawing on discursive psychology we examined the rhetorical strategies participants employ that allow them to do certain interactional work such as locate blame. The aim of this phase of analysis is to explore what the talk is 'doing' in relation to the interactive effects it enables with others involved in the conversation (Hepburn and Wiggins 2007; Potter and Edwards 2001). This approach draws heavily on the theoretical ideas and analytic approach of conversation analysis and differs from Fairclough's Critical Discourse Analysis (CDA) in the sense that CDA tends to adopt functional analyses that attempt to connect textual structures to social structures, whereas in drawing on discursive psychology, we are more concerned with activities done through talk and texts (Hepburn and Wiggins 2007). In CDA discourse is treated as a thing, something that can be counted, whilst discursive psychologists focus on accountability, stake, and interest, and how people draw on psychological concepts such as personality, so that transcripts of talk are analysed in terms of how participants' talk achieves certain interactional effects, such as avoiding blame (Wiggins and Riley 2010).

Our second level of discourse analysis focused on the wider discourses participants drew on to make sense of themselves, and the possibilities and limitations of using these discourses in relation to what the participants could say, think, and do. These included common-sense discourses (e.g. 'career woman') and more institutionally oriented discourses such as the psychological discourses of maternal attachment. This work is informed by discourse analysts such as Billig (2001), Wetherell (1999), and our own work (e.g. Riley 2002).

Combining these two forms of discourse analysis involved an iterative process in which transcripts of the data were read repeatedly, to familiarize the
researchers with their content. They were then read with an eye for discursive
psychology analysis and/or a wider discourse analysis perspective, again iteratively, until a coherent analysis was developed that allowed us to construct
a reading of the talk that we felt was fruitful and met quality criteria of good
discourse analysis, in which that text is analysed for what it is constructing
and the functions of these constructions. For example, when a participant
says 'I don't know' a discourse analyst would not see this statement as a neutral description of lack of knowledge/information, but examine its interactional effect (for example, it might allow the participant to avoid answering a
question, or locate what they are about to say next as not their own position
and thus position themselves as unaccountable for their statement (see for
example, Wetherell and Potter's [1992] discussion of racist discourse). In our
study, this kind of analysis allowed us to see what some of the key identities at play are for these women, for example, the sacrificial mother or the
mother as primary childcarer; as well as how and who was held accountable
for childcare.

The third level of our synthesized discourse analysis, introduced the critical realist aspect of our work, by examining the talk in terms of how participants' material, embodied, and institutional contexts (e.g. the availability
of institutional childcare in a geographical area) may provide the conditions
of possibility that allows their sense-making to make sense, and to thus be
treated as legitimate accounts, both by the speaker and the person(s) hearing
the speaker.

Taking up extracts that articulated some of the core patterns in our discourse analysis we then examined these extracts to see if participants oriented towards the embodied, institutional, and material factors identified
in phases 1 and 2, and how their talk might be located within the logic of
these factors. Thus, rather than look at how stake or interest was being managed, as in the discursive psychology approach, or what wider discourses
were being drawn on (e.g. the 'career woman'), we explored any orientation
to the extra-discursive in the participants' talk, where by orientation we
mean 'when a participant explicitly or implicitly makes relevant a category
or issue' (Sims-Schouten et al. 2007: 109). For example, if, in discussing
the benefits of day care a participant stressed the fact that her local nursery had a big outdoor space, when she lived in a small apartment with no
garden space.

Our synthesized critical realist discourse analysis thus allowed us to explore
the context in terms of the discursive and the 'real' and 'actual' (to use critical realist terms) that provide some of the scaffolding for our participants'
sense-making in the context of this interview. See Figure 3.2 for a summary of
the three phases.

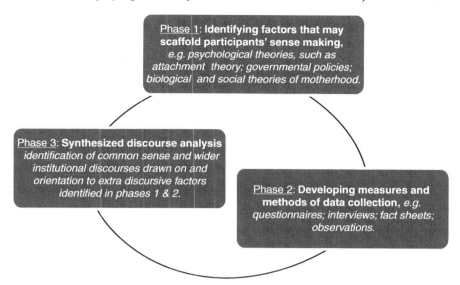

Figure 3.2 Critical Realism in Discourse Analysis in Three Phases

CRITICAL REALISM IN DISCOURSE ANALYSIS—EXAMPLES OF ANALYSIS

The extract below is an example of an analysis that included materiality in terms of physical space available to the participant and the number of children the participant had. The extract comes from an interview with a 44-year-old British mother, a former secretary, with one son aged two. The participant was not in paid employment and her husband was a computer programmer. The extract comes after a question on what form of childcare this mother would consider (see Appendix for conventions used in transcribing speech). Note 'P' stands for participant and 'W' the initial of the interviewer.

1 W: Talking about daycare.hhh what form of childcare would you consider
   if any
2 P: A nursery, I I think, because (1.0) the::, the reasons for my,
3 P: considering childcare, (2.0) are, are driven by:: (1.0)
4 P: >the fact that I think he might<, gain from being with, with other children,
5 P: ermm (1.0) doing things with other children, (1.0) perhaps in::,
6 P: in a location that, that I can't provide at home.

The main argument is that childcare has advantages in terms of being able to do things with other children. An analysis drawing on discursive psychology can be outlined as follows: describing the benefits of childcare this mother uses a three-part structure to characterize how her son might benefit from childcare (first, 'being with, with other children'; second, 'doing things with other children'; and, third, being in a different 'location' that she cannot provide at home). It could be argued that this mother uses a category-bound activity[2] (CBA) in which mixing with other children in a different location from home is defined as an activity that takes place in childcare (nursery), and is what makes it beneficial. An analysis drawing on wider discourses might consider this CBA as a common-sense ideology. This is evident from the fact that this mother has no personal experience of using childcare. Yet in her three-part structure she treats these benefits as given. As such she could be drawing on constructions that possibly come from the media and popular psychology. For example, the Daycare Trust (2001) in the UK argues in one of their publicly available brochures 'Daycare promotes children's development' (p. 3) (compare with line 4: 'he might<, gain'). So in this extract we can see how interactively the mother works up the advantages of childcare and that these advantages are accounts that are culturally available to her. Our next step is to explore the extract drawing on our CRDA level, and involves looking for any orientation to the extra-discursive factors that may be salient in this example. There are two factors that may be considered here. First, the participant does not have other children, nor does her family home have a garden. From this material position, then, it makes sense to argue that childcare is advantageous in terms of providing a social environment that has other children and additional amenities.

The following example comes from a Dutch interview with a 28-year-old council worker with two children, aged two years and nine months. This mother shares the childcare with her husband who is an activity therapist; relatives also provide childcare on occasion. Both parents work part-time. The extract starts after the participant has been asked if she'd currently like to be a full-time mother.

1 P: nn↓ee, ik ben er met zw↑anger*schaps*verlof ben
ik drie maanden th↑uis geweest
1 P: no, when I was on maternity leave I was at home for three months (1.0)
2 P: en daarna ouderschapsverlof heb ik anderhalve *dag* ge↓werkt maar dan=
2 P: and then I used parental leave and worked a day and a half and then=
3 P: = vind ik het *toch* wel weer leuk, het con*tact* met, collega's in ieder geval=
3 P: again I really enjoyed it, the social connections, with colleagues especially=
4 P: = het con*tact* met andere mensen, en *dat* heb ik heel erg gemis=
4 P: the socializing with other people, I really missed that a lot=
5 P: = in de periode dat ik gewoon heel erg veel *thuis* was
5 P: during the period that I was just at home a lot

Discursively analysing this talk we note how the participant indicates that her personal needs of socializing were fulfilled by returning to work. In the extract

---

[2] This is an example of social action within talk, when certain activities are automatically linked to certain events or people, e.g. to hear a report of someone crying may be heard as the activity of a baby (see Silverman, 2001 for more information).

she provides details creating an objective, factual account of times and lengths of work/leave, before constructing work as an enjoyable activity because it provides social interactions (lines 3 and 4). The importance of social connections is constructed through repetition and emphasis, allowing her to conclude that it was something she missed and that maternity leave was a limited home-based activity (line 5).

Her talk reinstates the traditional discourse of motherhood (i.e. the stay-at-home mother) as a negative point of reference (Knijn 1998) in which full-time motherhood is constructed as a category-bound activity of not socializing with other people. In this extract the participant thus works up the advantages of being a working mother in terms of socializing that orient to wider discourses of full-time motherhood as isolating and limiting. However, she is vulnerable to other available discourses (identified in phase 1) that construct good mothering in terms of sacrificing one's own needs and staying at home to look after your children. Later in the interview, the participant argues that the social element of work makes her happy, and in turn this happiness makes her a better mother. By doing this, she successfully inoculates herself against any charge of putting her own needs ahead of her child's.

The ability to argue that work provides a social life can only be supported if the speaker cannot be successfully challenged that there are opportunities for full-time mothers to socialize; and here our critical realist approach in exploring the embodied, institutional, and material context throws up relevant issues to contextualize this talk. Our phase-1 analysis showed that there are significantly fewer mother and child groups in the Netherlands than in the UK, so that Dutch mothers have fewer opportunities for the kind of semi-public social interaction that this Dutch participant described as available through work. In this example, the lack of mothers' social groups in the Netherlands could therefore be considered to be part of the 'actual' context (see introduction to this volume) that helps structures participants' sense-making and decision-making in relation to childcare and mothers' management of their own and their child's needs.

Not all our participants who used formal childcare were employed, and the following extract comes from an English 'full-time' mother, aged twenty-seven, with two children; a boy aged two and a girl of eleven months. Before she had her children, this mother worked in an office, her husband was a refrigeration engineer and at the time of interview this family was on a relatively low income making childcare costs a significant part of their household expenditure. The oldest child was delayed in his development and had attended a nursery two mornings per week from the age of eighteen months.

1 W: what is your perception of the *benefits* of childcare for the *child*?
2 P: (1.0) I think there's *loads* of benefits
3 W: right
4 P: erm, *mainly*, >I think<, it gives him more *confidence* (1.0)

5 P: *helps* them, if they're not talking very w↑e:ll, erm,.h helped=
6 P: = him to talk *more*, helps, *just* helps them *socially*.h
7 W: hm
8 P: I think, *also* (1.0) erm, the *child* places can *ac*tually, or the=
9 P: = *nur*sery schools can, spend *more* time, on, like I said,
10 P: >*arts* and crafts<
11 W: hm
12 P: a:nd (1.0) they they've got, I mean, they're *specifically* there,
13 P:.h j↓ust, to look *af*ter the chil↓dre:n, play with the child↓ren:
14 P:.hh and, *teach* them things (1.0) erm, *help* them to play to↓gether,
15 P: and >teach them about< *sha*ring
16 W: hm
17 P: whereas at h↑ome, you can *do* all of th↓at, *but* you've *still* =
18 P: =got to make the t↑ea, you've *still* got to cook din↓ner
19 W: yeah
20 P: =you've *still* got, y↑ou kn↓ow (1.0) *house*hold things to d↑o

In line 2 the participant responds to a request from the interviewer to account for the benefits of childcare, which she does by arguing that there are '*loads* of benefits'. This stress on '*loads*' constructs childcare as significantly beneficial, which works to reject a possible unsympathetic or sceptical hearing (Hutchby and Wooffitt 1998), and it potentially also buys the participant time to formulate a reply, one that perhaps is needed since it's not until line 4 and a prompt from the interviewer ('right') that the participant articulates what these benefits might be.

As the participant lists these benefits she shifts from talking about one of her own children (her two-year-old son) to children more generally; this bolsters her account: arguing personal benefits for her child serves as a warrant against doubt or disagreement since it's difficult to argue that someone's personal experience hasn't been experienced (Edwards 1997), while her talk of other children allow her claims for childcare to be generalized. In relation to her child she lists the benefits as giving him confidence and of helping if 'they're not talking well', a generalized claim that she rearticulates as one relevant for her own child in line 6–childcare helped her son talk more.

The participant continues then to list a range of benefits for childcare, allowing her decision to use childcare to be justified; constructing her as a mother who puts her child's needs first and inoculating against being portrayed as a bad mother who uses childcare to avoid engaging with her children. In this extract the participant constructs nurseries as professional childcare institutions, that are specifically there to help the child in any way, giving them confidence, helping them developmentally and socially. There is a caveat (line 17) where the participant notes that she too can 'do all of that', this is followed with a description of domestic labour associated with the traditional mother role of the participant, which is constructed as competing with her ability to facilitate her children's development. This caveat thus allows the participant to support her list of the benefits of childare while inoculating against being labelled an inadequate mother for not doing, or being able to do this herself.

Discursively then, we can see how this participant negotiates her family's decision to use childcare, both to the interviewer and in terms of wider discourses about good mothers. The participant's talk of childcare also introduces other institutional discourses: a psychological developmental discourse (that children need to learn cognitive and social skills) and a specialist discourse in relation to childcare workers and their ability to facilitate this development. From a critical realist discourse analytic perspective we would therefore argue that this participant's talk of the specific benefits of childcare (such as speech development) are produced through issues of embodiment (a child with learning difficulties); wider discourses on children's development and expert specialists on development; and the material and institutional conditions of a country that funds public health care professionals who bring developmental problems to the attention of mothers. See Figure 3.3 below for a simplified summary of the categories and content of what the analysis reveals, drawing on phases 1–3.

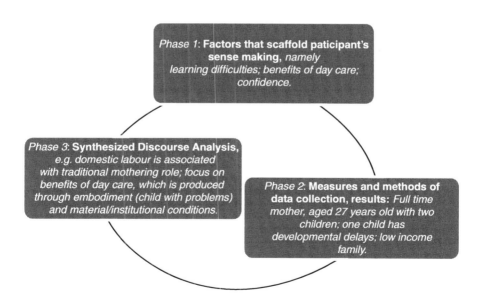

Figure 3.3 CRDA in Action

CONCLUSION

In this chapter we have offered a method for exploring aspects of the discursive, embodied, institutional, and material contexts which we argue can be understood as providing the scaffolding for how people account for themselves and make sense of their decisions and experiences. Since critical realists seek to develop analyses that explore some of the underlying factors or 'entities' behind empirical analysis, we call our approach a 'critical realist discourse analysis', theorizing that our analysis of the contexts from which our participants speak can help us better understand their talk.

In producing a critical realist discourse analysis our approach conceptualizes talk as a rhetorical accomplishment enabled in part by the discursive, material, institutional, and embodied circumstances of the speaker. These circumstances include material facts (such as lack of a garden), which, from a critical realist perspective, create tendencies (such as seeking play space for children elsewhere) under certain conditions (e.g. in societies where 'space' is constructed as important for child-rearing). At a wider level, this reflects causal relations between material poverty, discourses of childcare and state-sponsored opportunities.

Our synthesized critical realist discourse analysis thus allows us to locate participants' sense-making within their socio-historic-economic-linguistic community/ies, which in turn are informed by institutional structures that create both discourse (e.g. constructions of a good mother through attachment theory) and material/environmental structures (e.g. number of private/government-funded nurseries for under-school-aged children). As such, we are able to conceptualize our participants' talk of motherhood and employment as constituted from multiple lines of influence and produce an analysis that conceptualizes an agentic participant who is simultaneously structured by their social context since 'structural conditions constrain, without determining, the agents' room for manoeuvre' (O'Mahoney and Vincent, ch. 1, this volume).

Like other critical realist discourse analysts, taking a critical realist standpoint to make a connection between our participants' talk and our participants' lives, gave us a sense of doing justice to our research participants. In the context of this study for example, it allowed us to explore how mothers make sense of their childcare choices within the context of the complex material and discursive contexts in which they lived. In doing so, we were able to show the tensions women have to negotiate and the pressures on mothers when the contexts in which they live so often construct them as failing (as a good mother) whatever they do (Sims-Schouten et al. 2007). Since we first started writing about this our method has been applied by others on issues of mental health, identity, and environmental politics (see for example, Lafrance [2009] and Lauber and Schenner [2011]). The attraction of this method is, we think, because it allows researchers to put the person into their context, an approach particularly useful for organizational studies that often need to explore how people negotiate and manage themselves within an organization/ social context that is materially, embodied, and institutionally and discursively structured. We therefore hope it supports the readers of this volume who too are looking for ways to analyse their participants' talk in context.

APPENDIX: TRANSCRIPTION CONVENTIONS

o o	*Encloses speech that is quieter that the surrounding talk*
(1.0)	*Pause length in seconds*
- hyphen	*Word broken off*
↑	*Rising intonation*
↓	*Lowering intonation*
CAPITAL LETTERS	*Talk that is louder than the surrounding talk*
<u>Underline</u>	*Stress/emphasis*
> <	*Encloses speeded-up talk*
()	*Encloses words the transcriber is unsure about. Empty brackets enclose talk that is not hearable*
.hhh	*In-breath*
[ ]	*Overlapping speech*
[	*Onset of overlapping speech*
{ }	*Clarification, referring to tone or gesture, e.g. {laughs}*
:::	*Extended sound*
=	*Marks the immediate 'latching' of successive talk, whether of one or more speakers, with no interval*

Sources: Edwards 1997; Jefferson 1985; Ten Have 1999.

4

Researching Identity
A Critical Realist Approach

Abigail Marks and Joe O'Mahoney

INTRODUCTION

This chapter is slightly different from the others in the book because it deals with a substantive topic of investigation (identity) rather than a type of research method (say, interviews or ethnography). There are two reasons for this. First, the prominence of identity as a topic in (especially critical) management studies has led to methodological polarization between those who see identity as a rational, cognitive, and objective artefact and those who see it as a highly fragmented construct of language. Thus the (re)definition of identity that we attempt first in this chapter has strong consequences for the methods by which it is studied, which we tackle subsequently. Second, the nature of social research means that the identity of the researcher, in our view, must be considered in relation to the subjects which they themselves seek to study. A clearer understanding of identity will, we hope, support the researcher in assessing their own constructions when undertaking any form of study. Many of the methods that we later identify as suitable for the study of identity are covered elsewhere in the book; the present chapter connects them to a substantive approach.

From the 1980s onwards identity studies have been one of the most prolific movements in social science. We use the word movement instead of topic because, for the most part, its teaching and study has involved a transformation in thinking that has divided conservatives and liberals as to its utility (Bawer 2012; Windschuttle 2000). Much of the division has come down to ontological assumptions about what identity actually is (Morgan and Olsen 2007) and how consequently it can be researched and studied. We argue that the two dominant but polarized positions in this field—social constructionism and social identity theory (SIT)—have significant limitations which are based upon ontological weaknesses. We subsequently argue that a critical realist ontology can provide a strong alternative to these approaches and, illustrating this argument with an example drawn from recent research by one of the authors, draw out the methodological implications of our argument. In doing this, we do not seek to build a specific 'domain level' theory of identity (see O'Mahoney and Vincent, this volume) but instead seek to provide a broad sketch of how critical realism can be used to build bridges between seemingly incompatible positions, and assess the implications of this middle position for methodology.

DOMINANT POSITIONS ON IDENTITY

Within identity studies, two dominant positions can be traced. They are social constructivist, or postmodern, positions drawing on philosophers such as Foucault, Derrida, and Lacan, and empirical or positivist standpoints, in particular social identity theory (SIT) which builds on the work of Tajfel (1972) and Tajfel at al. (1971).

The former, those which give primacy to the constructive power of discourse, are now dominant. These studies, which deny a non-discursive reality (in their 'strong' form) or refute any possible knowledge of such reality (in their 'weak' form), have done much to highlight and question the power relationships which generate and sustain social categories such as 'disabled', 'immigrant', or 'terrorist' and the meanings with which they are associated. For post-structuralists, who embrace an ontology which rejects either the existence or the possibility of knowledge of a non-discursive realm, there are three philosophical issues for a critical analysis of identity. First, in seeking data about identity, constructivist accounts need only rely upon describing discourses, primarily through interviews with the subjects. As constructivism is incapable of judging between the validity of different texts, interviews are necessarily taken at face value. The possibility of subjects being incorrect, or untruthful, about their own identities is logically impossible under an ontology which puts terms such as truth, objectivity, or reality in inverted commas. Second, an account in which all conceptual tools must ultimately be reducible only to discourse weakens the theoretical potential of social constructivism in explaining how identity is created, altered, or destroyed (Bhaskar 1989: 60). Third, as a strong discursive approach dissolves all notions of the individual into language games, it generates an anti-humanism which is impotent in explaining how resistance is possible in the face of discourses generated by organizations, professions, or governments. As a consequence, the emancipatory potential of constructivist identity studies is diminished by a failure to engage with, or even recognize, the embeddedness of identity in social structures, such as class, where distributions of power can, according to realist positions, limit the resources available for building stable or ethical identities.

On the other hand, understandings of identity from a social identity tradition are also subject to limitations. SIT (e.g. Ashforth and Mael 1989; Turner and Oakes 1986) looks at the degree to which people define themselves in terms of their membership of a collective and how their feelings of self-worth are reflected in the status of the collective. The approach was originally devised by Henri Tajfel who was seeking an understanding of discrimination and fascism. Tajfel et al. (1971) set up a group of experiments—the minimal group studies—using school children to examine the mechanisms through which people who were previously unaware of each other formed a collective identity. However, because SIT is derived from experimental studies rather than actual empirical phenomena, the body of work has focused less and less on the 'real life' instances of discrimination and fascism that were so close to Tajfel's heart and could be argued to have limited relevance to actual situations. The minimal group studies involved a particular experimental situation and therefore it is problematic to generalize sufficiently to form a theoretical position. As Brown and Lunt (2002: 22) note, 'the fact that a given phenomenon is tractable enough to serve as an example of a theoretical position does not in any sense lend weight to the theoretical argument, since it is likely that such a phenomenon may prove equally tractable to other opposing positions'. According to social identity theory and self-categorization theory, individuals can develop two principal identities. People possess a personal self, which encompasses unique, idiosyncratic information about themselves in addition to a collective self (or social identity), which encompasses information about the groups to which they belong (Tajfel 1972). Social identity is concerned with the extent to which individuals feel attached to a specific group in addition to the status and characteristics of this group relative to other social categories (Tajfel and Turner 1986). Despite the acknowledgement of these two identities social identity is viewed as the dominant driver for behaviour.

When discussing social identity, Tajfel and Turner focus on the collective properties of social identity and how activity within a social setting is determined by social identity. Yet, they take a rather confused position in suggesting that the individual then takes discrete action in terms of decisions to move between similar social groups based on individual choice. Whilst there is a clear position on the abstracted tendency for an individual to assimilate with collective forms of understanding, there is an artificial separation of the individual as a rational agent and the individual as a social actor within a group. SIT also tends to separate individual behaviour from the subtleties of the social context and fails to understand how processes of both individual and social categorization and representation are embedded in a complex context comprising wider cultural practices and material settings (Billig 1985; Condor 1996; Michael 1990; Wetherell and Potter 1992). Whilst SIT acknowledges the individual self, most action is described in terms of social relationships and membership of social groups. As Brown and Lunt (2002) suggest, an individual may leave an organization not only because of a discredited social identity, but also as a result of processes of globalization, flexibility, and temporal specialization as well as their own individual role and position within the labour market.

The weaknesses of both the constructivist position and the social identity approach to identity emerge, primarily, from their ontological commitments. In relation to post-structuralists, the failure to distinguish between ontology and epistemology (see O'Mahoney and Vincent, this volume) results in an 'invisible' self that can only collapse into discourse, resulting in explanatory weakness and emancipatory impotence (Fairclough et al. 2002). For SIT, individual identity appears to be solely determined by group membership with little variation in the individual characteristics held by group members. Hence, all that is left are essentialized properties. A critical realist (CR) account of identity addresses these weaknesses.

IDENTITY'S UNDER-LABOURER

In this section we do not seek to promote a specific CR model of identity and focus instead on illustrating the general implications of CR for identity research. We do, however, assume both a distinction between social and personal identity, and also promote the role of reflexivity in generating agency, both of which are consistent with CR (Archer 2003) and are accepted in a broad range of critical literature. Thus, in analysing identity, researchers will need to either develop their own domain-specific meso-level constructs or draw upon existing authors who have developed frameworks that are explicitly or implicitly consistent with a realist ontology—such as Goffman (1972), Archer (2003), du Gay (2007), Polanyi (1958), or Bourdieu (1977). Caveats complete, let us examine the principles of critical realism as they apply to identity research.

Stratification and Emergence

A stratified, emergent ontology allows realist researchers to conceptualize different levels or entities upon which identity construction may be dependent, but irreducible to (for example, memory or reflexivity), or levels or entities which may be dependent upon, but irreducible to, identity (for example, culture). Emergence is important for two reasons. First, such a position is conceptually more sophisticated because it avoids collapsing identity into discourse (downwards conflation) or assuming that identity is simply as assemblage of component parts (upwards conflation). Second, without the existence of identity as a distinctive entity, humanity (and the rights associated with it) becomes either an assemblage of parts or is 'disappeared' to mere fantasy 'suspended betwixt and between...subject positions' (Musson and Duberley 2007: 160). Second, through retroduction, emergence helps bridge traditional divides between disciplines which study different levels of reality. For example, one might feasibly ask 'what must the mind be like in order to help structure the dynamics of identity that we see?'[1] Even social constructionist accounts often imply that people have memories, emotions, interests, histories, and imagination (O'Mahoney 2011). What critical realism provides is an opportunity to retroduce such properties without the inconsistency of an ontology which denies the possibility of (the knowledge of) their existence.

Depth Ontology

Critical realism's depth ontology distinguishes real generative mechanisms[2] from actual empirical occurrences, and both of these from what researchers believe they observe. For research into identity, these distinctions are vitally important for two reasons. First, contrary to (constructionist) discourse analysis, a depth ontology allows for the possibility that a text (for example, an interviewee's account of their identity) is factually incorrect, either through mistake or deliberately. Second, a depth ontology allows 'actual' events to be associated with generative mechanisms that have real but contingent effects, an approach which, in turn, helps conceptualize how identities change. For example, if one represents discourse as a causal mechanism (Banta 2007), one can theorize its (lack of) effect upon identities at an empirical level as a tendency which is contingent, not only upon conflicting discourses, but also upon other mechanisms and entities, including the agency and interests of the subjects themselves (Marks and Thompson 2010) and social structures such as class or organizations (Sayer 2005).

This depth allows identities to be researched as embedded within wider class or economic structures. For example, Marks and Thompson (2010) use Thomas Frank's (2007) account of why many of the poorest citizens of Kansas vote for

---

[1] One might replace 'mind' with 'society' or even with a new term altogether. Indeed, the latter statement is an important consideration when assessing the epistemological relativism of critical realism (Al-Amoudi and Willmott 2011): one should be reflexive and critical of the language one uses in seeking to describe reality.

[2] The 'mechanism' language employed by many realists is unfortunate because it conjures images of a deterministic relationship between cause and effect. However, even a brief reading of realist texts show this to be a misunderstanding (Danermark et al. 2002: 199). We have reluctantly adopted this term for the sake of consistency with other chapters and the wider CR literature.

a right-wing Republican agenda. Frank argues that the conservative movement managed to turn class differences into a cultural war that involved a 'systematic erasure of the economic', providing a 'ready-made identity in which class is a matter of cultural authenticity rather than material interests' (p. 259). Conservatives won the 'heart of America' by convincing inhabitants of Kansas to vote against their own economic interests through a perception of the defence of traditional cultural values against radical bicoastal elites. Yet, it is argued that 'all they (the people of Kansas) have to show for their Republican loyalty are lower wages, more dangerous jobs, dirtier air, a new overlord class that comports itself like King Farouk— and, of course, a crap culture whose moral free fall continues, without significant interference from the grandstanding Christers whom they send triumphantly back to Washington every couple of years' (p.136). A simple constructionist position would have assumed a naive ideological acceptance of conservative values and ignored broader cultural and structural determinants of identity. A realist analysis may allow the extraction of the complexities of the interplay between interests and identity. So, whilst the people of Kansas held interests which could be argued to be in line with conservative voting, such as a belief in religious conservatism, there were other material factors which they had no control over: the media and the wealthy have the power and resources to mould interests or perceptions of interests as the less wealthy do not have the resources to oppose or resist.

Entities and (Potential) Powers

From a critical realist perspective, discourse and identities have properties and powers that can be retroduced from empirical observations. Analytically, this allows the researcher useful distinctions between entities, their properties, the potential powers they possess, and the actual powers that are exercised. With this framing, discourse has a number of properties, such as signs and meanings, and a number of potential powers, such as the ability to construct identities or create categories of meaning. However, due to the constraints of the empirical context, potential powers may not be exercised: identities might not be constructed because there are counter-discourses or because an agent chooses not to engage with that discourse, or because they believe a discourse is misleading or untrue.

The identification of entities and their properties enables critical realists to be more precise when specifying the distinctions and relationships between different parts of a system. For example, a common distinction that is made by realists concerning the entities of identity is that between personal identity and social identity (Archer 2000). Personal identity emerges from the embodied, reflexive self, in part forged through the interests[3] and actions of

---

[3] The critical realist account of interests is not one where they can be 'read off' from economic (or other) structures, and thus does not fall prey to the charges of essentialism or determinism which characterize the post-structural critique of Marxist interests (Marks and Thompson 2010).

that individual. Personal identity is shaped by the experience of being held accountable by others and is a result of conscious thought and reflection as well as practical experience and tacit understandings (Webb 2004). Realist interpretations of personal identity have a strong focus on internal process such as reflexivity, agency, habitus, or memory. Personal identity is often represented as a project to attempt to escape experiences of anxiety and uncertainty, where individual moral judgements result from personal preference or feeling rather than from external authority or positions (Jenkins 2004).

Such a perspective is closely bound to Marx's alienation or Durkheim's anomie—where norms (expectations on behaviours) are confused, unclear, or not present. Constructionist positions, however, would articulate that the autonomous self or subject is nothing more than an ideological notion that deceives individuals into misunderstanding their own domination as self-determined and therefore accepting their own subjugation. This presents a passive notion of man and of personal identity. Such a deterministic account of identity is inconsistent because it confuses organizational prescription with the diversity of practical experience and misreads the connections between macro-levels of political economy and the micro-level of everyday life and its meaning (Giddens 1991; Webb 2004). It is far more profitable to look at individual relations with and within organizational power structures and what Jenkins (2004) and Goffman (1983) call 'the interaction order' where the individual interacts with the macro.

Social identity, as articulated through a critical realist lens, is the navigated position between personal identities and the way in which people believe they should be perceived in a social setting. Social identity concerns the actual embodiment of the roles and categories that are generated in social structures which 'occurs at the interface of structure and agency' (Cruickshank 2003: 23). Whilst personal and social identities are separate, there is a dialectical relationship between them as the individual is constrained in her choice of personal identity by the social identities that society makes available, but by occupying, or acting out, a social identity, both the social identity and the individual are changed. The distinction between personal and social identity is an important one because without it what the individual understands and wants their identity to be becomes conflated with the opportunities that society offers.

Agency and Structure

Agency is central to the critical realist conception of the social world as it is the point by which the person and social structure, and therefore, personal identity and social identity are reproduced and transformed (Figure 4.1). Such an account enables a richer and wider explanation than might a purely discursive account. To take an example, Holmer-Nadesan's (1996) account of university workers

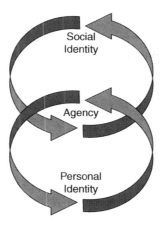

Figure 4.1 The Transformative Capacity of Agency

illustrates how the discursive controls experienced in their work generated acts of resistance, such as articulating alternative identities and dis-identification. Yet the focus on discourse, rather than social structure and the person, limits the wider implications of the workers' resistance. To take social structure first, we are not told how the workers' disidentification with their workplace identities affected their workplace performance, and thus their bargaining with their employers. Moreover, we are not told how their action (or absence of action) as a collective, or in relation to other collectives (for example unions), might influence the social rules and norms which govern their activities. In short, a focus on micro-politics and discourse elides the connection with structural power and the institutions which this might generate.

Further, the social constructionist derision of any personal properties as 'essentialism' also limits the consequences of the workers' agency for their current and future selves. For example, the workers' experiences of resistance, exploitation, or the effectiveness (or otherwise) of solidarity may have changed their plans, interests, and future strategies—concepts highly problematic for a constructionist position. Moreover, some workers also may have experienced stress, depression, or anxiety, again, concepts often derided as 'psychologizing' by constructionist authors.

Of course, the transformative capacity of agency[4] is a human potential, rather than an actuality, and the potential of that capacity to be actualized is constrained, not only by social structures but also the human's position in that social structure at their birth: 'we do not make our personal identities under the circumstances of our own choosing. Our placement in society rebounds

[4] Many critical realists adhere to Bhaskar's transformational model of social activity (TMSA). For more details on this, see Bhaskar (1989), Joseph (1998), and Collier (1994).

upon us, affecting the persons we become, but also, and more forcefully, affecting the social identities we can achieve' (Archer 2000: 10).

Historical Materiality

Contrary to constructionist accounts which 'deny the body' (Barnes and Mercer 2010: 68), realists adhere to an intransitive material reality which is independent of the transitive knowledge by which it is described. The material aspect of identity is not simply its physical performative aspects in the empirical world (such as wearing clothes, going to concerts, picketing corporations), nor even the material resources that enable and constrain identity construction (for example, wealth, freedom of movement, information architectures), but it is also the embodiment in a physical person: with a sex, a colour, or forms of disability. Such physical characteristics do not determine identities, either social or personal, but they are not simply social signifiers, the meaning of which is unconstrained and free for the writing. Our materiality is unavoidably packaged with our practice in the world.

The human body, like society, is held within a stratified, emergent reality. 'Our' neurons, and their relations, constrain and enable emergent properties such as memory, learning, imagination, and reflexivity, in a parallel manner to that in which our cells and their relations constrain and enable our actions. Moreover, these emergent properties have consequences for social identities through our agency which feed back into our personal identities through experience and reflexivity (Elder-Vass 2010: 89). For example, the poor memory and spelling of one of the authors led to a dyslexia diagnosis[5] which led to finding coping strategies which, in turn, facilitated their entry into academia.

The temporal aspect of materiality is also evident in the generative processes which (can) impact upon the body and its emergent properties (Williams 2001). This concerns not just the physical (children tend to grow and aging cells tend to deteriorate), but also the mental: memories, for example, tend to accumulate and fade. Statements which locate our selves as emergent from, but not determined by, our physical and mental structures are not essentialist, certainly less so than positions that assume these levels are constructed only through discourse.[6] Personal identities are rooted, partially, in our physical

---

[5] This is not to suggest that dyslexia, or the meanings associated with it, are not a product of twentieth- and twenty-first-century discourses and power relations, but that they cannot be disassociated with the practices of the embodied self.

[6] Some go further in this respect and argue that the body has emergent properties which respond to, and interact with some aspects of the (aesthetic) world, in a non-discursive (though not unmediated) way. For example, Radley (1995) argues that the body's response to music draws on 'pre-verbal' constructs—an argument developed by Burr (2003) to include art and sex: 'experience is primarily given through the body and not through language' (p. 121).

and mental structures, and, importantly, our reflections upon those structures and the discourses that seek to locate these in social identities. The inclusion of reflexivity in the transformational cycle means that the tendencies generated by our physiology cannot be framed as determinants. The self is a product of emergent historical processes, but its reflection upon these means that its future is not determined by them (du Gay 2007).

Criticality

Finally, a critical realist ontology provides greater scope for a critical, emancipatory agenda for identity studies than that provided by either constructionist or empiricist accounts. It does so in four ways. First, in distinguishing between the real, actual, and the empirical, researchers can differentiate between espoused and actual identities. For example, if, in 2009, an environmental activist was interviewed about their identity, a researcher may have assumed they had (inhabited, constructed, displayed, etc.) an identity associated with this position. However, when, in 2010, it was revealed that the activist was an undercover police informant this is not simply a matter of ironic juxtaposition or a collage of conflicting identities, but a discovery of an untruth—an important discovery in all but constructionist science.[7] Second, the location of identity in an emergent stratified ontology allows the consequences (and antecedents) of identity to be located and better described. In the example above, the policeman's identity (and claimed identity) has consequences for both the reproduction of state power and surveillance, and, perhaps, the psychological tensions which might emerge from maintaining two conflicting identities simultaneously. Third, by identifying the enablers and constraints of potential identities, critical realists can better describe the psychological and social barriers to the construction of emancipatory identities and the agency with which they are enacted. Finally, the location of discourse and identity within a framework of structural power and inequality allows critical realists to link the ideology of power relations with social and personal identities that emerge from that power. Of course, constructionist studies drawing on Foucault have successfully demonstrated how this is achieved at a micro-level, but they often forget that Foucault was a realist who sought to locate discursive effects in a wider structural framework of power (Al-Amoudi 2007; Pearce and Woodiwiss

---

[7] This is not to say that the earlier account was not important and did not have causal effects. In the recent case of this occurring (Evans and Lewis 2012), the police officer admitted developing sympathies for the activists.

2001). As such, 'critical realism shifts the direction of discourse analysis away from a single stranded focus on the symbolic representation and communication of constructed worlds towards a much broader concern with the political economy of discursive formation and its long-term institutional effects' (Reed 2000: 528). This commitment to structural positioning enables critical realism to reveal how interests of social groups might be the result of ideological conditioning without dismissing them as 'false' (Marks and Thompson 2010).

The critical potential of the realist position can be evidenced with reference to the debate around authentic identities. As many workplace studies have found, workers exposed to cultural or normative controls by management often 'act out' their roles (Collinson 2003), maintaining a cynical distance between their 'front stage' and 'back stage' selves (Goffman 1983). Yet, for many social constructionists, this smacks of an 'authentic' identity, which is, for them, just another form of essentialism (O'Dougherty and Willmott 2009). Thus, any claim by a worker to a real or authentic identity is necessarily 'imagined' (Costas and Fleming 2009) and, in any case, appropriated by organizations as another more insidious form of normative control, where workers are encouraged to 'be themselves' (Fleming and Sturdy 2010; Roberts 2005). As a constructionist ontology cannot distinguish between the validity of discourses, and cannot accommodate the distinction between a personal and a social identity, all identities are necessarily embedded in dominance relationships. However, the realist promotion of human agency and its distinction between personal and social identities enables a conceptualization of authenticity which is more sophisticated than the relativist version for two reasons. First, it allows the researcher to accept 'acting out' as precisely that—a refusal on behalf of the employee to engage their personal or social identities with workplace demands, even if their actions are strictly controlled. Second, it also allows the researcher to verify some of the claims of a participant as to the validity of their claimed authenticity. For example, if a worker claimed the identity of an anti-managerialist, left-leaning, unionist but consistently acquiesced in management demands and broke the picket line, then a researcher might reasonably suspect that their claims were problematic. It may, therefore, be assumed that there needs to be some degree of mutuality between acted-out and believed-in identities. Richards and Marks (2007) found several examples of cohesive teams which resisted managerial control strategies by enactment. Furthermore, Leary and Kowalski (1990) suggest that although impressions created by people may reflect internal thoughts (e.g. individuals who seek to be viewed as dedicated to their organization may truly be dedicated), on other occasions the impression maybe entirely false. Individuals can distance themselves from organizational scripts. So what they are feeling is separated, or can be separated from their performance.

THE CONSEQUENCES FOR RESEARCH

Research Questions for the Identity Researcher

A critical realist study of identity will concern itself with more than a description of identities and the discourses that describe them. Whilst this might prove interesting, empirical descriptions reveal little about the underlying mechanisms about why these identities and discourses exist, upon what they might be contingent, and the power relations which sustain them. Of course, many constructionist accounts have, de facto, been achieved by implying real constraints to the power of discourse; *de jure,* a constructionist ontology is incapable of making such statements (O'Mahoney 2011). The ontological precision of critical realism allows a clearer description of identity, which in turn, has implications for the types of questions a researcher can ask in seeking to understand it. Table 4.1 provides a summary of the key principles of critical realism, their implications for identity studies and the types of research questions that CR researchers might seek to answer when examining identity. The questions are not meant to be exhaustive and the categories overlap significantly; however, it is hoped that the table will provide a useful prompt for those tackling a relatively new area for critical realist research.

A final, important point, is the inclusivity of critical realist research agenda. It can ask 'traditionally' constructionist questions about the discursive effects on identity at the micro-level, and research these in a similar manner—but can locate these findings within a wider framework that retroduces information about both social structures and the self and the relations between them.

There are few specific consequences of critical realism for types of data collection because 'methods do not uncover reality (relativist epistemology) but rational analysis of phenomena can uncover it (realist ontology)' (Pujol and Montenegro 1999: 85). However, there are three general caveats to this statement. The first is the focus of data collection. Whilst critical realists might use the same categories of methods as any other research position, they will seek to move towards understanding the processes that enable and constrain identity construction and discursive activity. This means that within any method, say interviewing, the interviewer will focus on more than eliciting information about discourses, but, where relevant, will also seek to uncover biographical and structural information related to the questions in Table 4.1 (see also ch. 3).

The second and consequential caveat is that a realist study of identity will usually incorporate a multilevel analysis where identity construction is framed as an interplay between people, groups, organizations, political and economic systems, and social structures. Data collection, therefore, will not rely solely on interview data to either elicit descriptions of identities and

Table 4.1 Ten Realist Principles and their Consequences for Identity Research

Critical realist principle	Application to identity studies	Questions for empirical studies of identity
1. Causal mechanisms	Social structures, such as class relations, organizations, and cultures influence identity construction through various mechanisms, one of which is discourse. Identity construction mechanisms are enabled and constrained by empirical conditions. Humans engage in identity-seeking activities which draw on social identities to construct personal identities.	How are personal identities and social identities produced in this context? Which social structures relate to which discourses (semiotics, forms of language, descriptions)? What processes and mechanisms enable this production? Empirically, what enables and constrains the working of these mechanisms? How generalizable are these mechanisms? How might these be explored in other contexts? This concerns both the workings of a specific discourse (what mechanisms reproduce homophobic identities in Uganda?) and discourse more generally (how are discourses resisted?). How is discourse created, modified, and dissipated? How is discourse sustained? What material and social resources and structures enable this to happen?
2. Depth ontology	Talk about identities and actual identities are not necessarily the same thing. Empirical tendencies concerning personal and social identities are generated by causal mechanisms.	Do interviews and other methods of data collection elicit similar findings about social and personal identities? What might explain any differences? How are social and personal identities related in this context? What accounts for differences and similarities? What empirical tendencies are evident in representations of social and personal identities? Which empirical tendencies relate to which causal mechanisms? What are the transitive and intransitive features of your analysis?
3. Entities and powers	Personal and social identities are distinct, but dialectically and relationally intertwined. Entities have properties (which distinguish their nature) and (potential) powers.	What empirical and abstract properties and (potential) powers can be associated with your analytical categories (e.g. social identities, rules, organizations, discourse)? How and why do different entities interact in the ways they do? Are existing descriptive categories (entities) adequate in enabling explanation? If not, can you improve on them? What are the conditions under which an entity's power is exercised? Are the effects of this power contingent on contextual factors?

(Continued)

Table 4.1 (*Continued*)

Critical realist principle	Application to identity studies	Questions for empirical studies of identity
5. Emergence	Social identities are emergent properties of social structures. Personal identities are emergent properties of the self. Retroduction allows findings about identity to imply properties and powers of the self and social structures.	How are social identities constructed through discourse, rules, organization, or social structures? How do people construct personal identities? What other levels or entities are drawn, or relied upon, in this construction? How do memories, imagination, emotion, reflexivity, and action, for example, enable or constrain the construction of personal identity? What psychological or biological structures does such activity imply? Given the empirical findings concerning social and personal identity, what might researchers retroduce about the nature of the self and/or society, or the mechanisms that link society/the self to identity?
6. Agency and structure	Agency is an emergent property of humans which reproduces and modifies social structures. Reflexivity and agency are distinct from discourse.	What forms of agency are related to the generation, modification, and reproduction of social and personal identities? How does the agency associated with personal and social identities reproduce or modify social structures and power relationships? How and why do historical, long-term changes take place in social structures?
7. Materiality (embodiment)	Personal identity construction is enabled and constrained by the physical body.	How does the body enable or constrain the construction of personal identities or the occupation of social identities? How do physical (such as disability, race, or sex) or psychological (such as memory, imagination, or reflexivity) properties impact on the construction (or otherwise) of identities? Are traditional categories and descriptions of physical and mental structures sufficient explanation for the empirical findings?
8. Materiality (other)	Material and virtual structures, such as architecture and ICT enable and constrain social and personal identity construction.	How do material and virtual structures impact upon social and personal identities?

(Continued)

Table 4.1 (*Continued*)

Critical realist principle	Application to identity studies	Questions for empirical studies of identity
9. Temporality	Different emergent levels of identity are associated with different temporalities.	How does the social biography of individuals relate to the identities which they construct? How have personal and social identities changed over time? Why are these identities being constructed *now*? What types of time or lifecycle are associated with the identities that are constructed and the processes that enable and constrain them? What temporal dynamics characterize the activity of other structures, entities, or discourses at play in this environment?
10. Criticality	Power	What forms of power are exerted through the mechanisms (including discourse) which construct identities? How do humans seek to resist the discourses that might generate compliant or normative identities? How does this resistance modify the structures of dominance in the empirical context?

discourses, or understand the processes that underpin their generations, but instead seek a number of different sources of information to understand which entities or levels are important in identity construction and how they influence each other.

The third and final caveat is the relationship between the different methods used for data collection. Within a critical realist framework, multilevel and multiple methods of analysis have different intentions from 'traditional' mixed methods research. The conventional rationale for usage of mixed methods and the purpose of triangulation is to use a range of methods in order to validate findings (Erzberger and Kelle 2003). Originating in geometry, the view of triangulation is that a position is determined in relation to an objectively verifiable reference point (Modell 2009). Denzin (1989) presents crystallization rather than triangulation as an alternative metaphor for data 'validity' which demonstrates no single truth and the self-validity of different forms of data. Crystallization and triangulation each then represent the polarized positions of interpretive and functionalist paradigms respectively. If reality is multidimensional and subjectively constructed by those being researched then the meanings attached to different empirical phenomena will vary considerably; however, true to a critical realist position, the complexity of empirical phenomena could be compromised by attempting to find convergence (Modell 2009). As Fielding (2008) note, converging and diverging causal explanations originating from different methods may merely obscure or mirror the coexistence of competing accounts inherent in a complex and conflicting world.

In order to tackle these contradictory positions on triangulation, and to acknowledge openness to the idea of divergence of information from different methods (which can be argued is one of the reasons for using email data, below), Modell's (2009) critical realist interpretation of triangulation should be mentioned here. Modell argues that converging or diverging meanings informed by mixed methods enquiry should only be a starting point in interpretation. So, for example, organizational documentation and focus groups need to be viewed as distinct from any narrative created during a research interview or via a questionnaire, where a participant potentially has the time to present a position that they feel comfortable expressing.

Consequences for Data Analysis

A critical realist study of identity will seek to reveal the mechanisms that enable and constrain identity construction. This will involve implicating specific social structures and their influence on identity and, implicitly or explicitly, suggesting the properties of the individual that are involved in the production or alteration of these structures. Furthermore, the research might give an indication of the extent to which these entities and their powers are generalizable and the extent to which the empirical context is important in enabling or constraining these powers.

The most common route to achieving this is retroduction. Moving from empirical findings to causal mechanisms by asking 'what must the world be like in order for these findings to be possible?' However, in reality, such a step can be presumptuous or unrealistic. Depending on the research questions, a researcher might, from an inductive perspective, seek first to develop codes which provide some abstraction which can make retroduction easier. Others, taking a more deductive approach, might begin with a theorization that they find convincing, for example that of Bourdieu or Archer, and use this to provide an explanatory framework for their findings. Others still might compare their findings against an array of different theoretical explanations and abduct a 'best fit' for their data. Again, the specific methods by which data is analysed will rarely differ from those from other ontological perspectives, but their direction and purpose may differ significantly.

IDENTITY IN VIRTUAL TEAMS

This section will report on the process and outcomes of research that looks at identity in virtual teams (see Au and Marks 2013), with a critical realist approach to triangulation. This research examined four organizations and seven teams across seven different countries and followed forty-two employees. As this chapter is focused on methods rather than outcomes we only report on data from one organization. The company concerned is an international shipping firm based in Asia. The head office of the organization is located in Singapore. The employees within these teams operated between the UK and Singapore. In total, there were twenty-eight employees across the four teams, working on sales and marketing, trade, customer service, and fleet management. The organization was studied over a period of three months. Non-participant observation was undertaken in both the headquarters in Singapore and in the London office. This process involved sitting in meetings, listening to interactions between project members, and observing video conferences and teleconferences. Twenty-seven of the participants were interviewed and the full portfolio of email exchanges between the virtual team members was gathered, covering the three months of data collection.

One of the key tools in the process of triangulation was the analysis of email exchanges. Email can potentially reveal insights into informal interactions and concealed attitudes. Yet, email can also be a formal presentation of a position and deliberately constructed to be a written record of a particular event or action. This research employed email alongside other forms of data—interview and observation—so that the particular biases of each can be understood and compared. The analysis of the data looked at the presentation of identity and located key events to illustrate the enactment of identity for particular individuals and teams. There was no attempt at convergence of explanations, as is conventionally the case in triangulation, as such a process is incompatible with a realist position: triangulation views reality as unified, readily observable, and objective and hides important differences in situated meanings (Modell 2009). The interview process explicitly asked participants to discuss their identification with the virtual team. The responses to this question were generally positive. For example, Frank and Chris, team leaders on the same project attested to the unity of their working relationship and strength of the team during the formal interviews.

'I am happy and feel proud to work with (the organization) as now people like to work for us—they like to work for our ships. I have a good team now... they give us ample support so we can drive things' (Frank).

'I can identify with my (virtual) team because the team identifies with us' (Chris).

The interviews reflected a presentation of identity which appeared to be as the interviewees wished to present themselves or a perception of identity that would be favoured by the interviewer. A social identity perspective would take these comments as a literal account and, ironically, a constructionist account would also adhere to the truth of the text. Whilst there could well be a literal explanation for these statements, a critical realist interpretation opens up a number of possibilities which are hidden by the two dominant positions on identity. The team identity could be the presentation of a social identity that may differ from a personal identity and could be the product of collective interests being represented as a function of structural pressures. If the presentation of such attitudes is a reflection of personal identity, then it could be argued to be a product of the anxiety of moral judgements resulting from a personal preference. As a presentation of social identity there is the possibility of anxiety of the moral judgements placed by the researcher.

Importantly, by using multiple methods we can realize the critical realist potential for the analysis of a stratified, emergent reality. If only interviews or possibly interviews and an organizational survey had been used, there would likely have been a fairly positive display of identity with the virtual team. This was probably perceived as reflecting well on employees and the organization. Yet, by using Modell's (2009) position on triangulation and a variety of methods, we can see many potential levels of interpretation and account for phenomena. Observation notes taken in the Singapore office (and incorporating Chris and Frank) present a very different story to that presented during the interviews.

Abridged Observation Record from 12th September:

Frank (Project Two, Singapore Office) was engaged in a discussion with a UK colleague regarding the allocation of space in shipping vessels. Frank wished to fill the vessel and to maximize profit. However, Chris (UK Office) was looking for the lowest freight charge that he could offer to his customer.

Frank picked up the phone and it was Chris. Chris asked about reducing the quote from $1300 to $1100. Frank refused. Conversation ends abruptly. Frank rushes into his manager's office. After twenty minutes Frank emerges and rushes to the water cooler. He looks angry and frustrated.

When Frank was back at his desk I asked him what happened. He said he was 'frustrated'. 'Sometimes I wonder how come they cannot understand and we have to explain again and again. In the whole day I will get emails discussing the same thing again and again.'

After 10 minutes Frank opens his email and starts to reply to Chris. He mentions that 'our team guideline is "never put your emotion in email"'. When Frank finishes his email to Chris he states that he rejected Chris in a polite way. He says to me that replying to an email showing your negative emotions by writing in a sarcastic way is unprofessional.

When asked about electronic communication in an interview, a member of Frank's team from Singapore stated that 'Working with people from the UK, we face problem in communication. They are not following rules and procedures... They often change things without notifying us... I would highlight their shortcomings in two lines but they would come back with twenty lines. Maybe this is a cultural problem. My impression is that UK people are laidback so I have a bad impression towards them.'

Much of the data from this project revealed a gap between individuals' articulation of workplace relations in an interview situation and practice as identified by observation and via interactions over email. While some of the interview participants admitted that perceptions of cultural differences impacted on working relationships and importantly on identity, the majority claimed no such effect and maintained that virtual team identity was strong and salient. Yet, email exchanges were frequently tense. They further suggest that individuals, as a critical realist interpretation would allow, either present an impression that may represent internal thoughts or deliberately present an entirely false impression (Leary and Kowalski 1990). Either way, individuals are separating the presentation of identity from internal thoughts.

Below is an extract of an exchange between Tim (a Portuguese employee in the UK office) and Sarah (a local employee in the Singapore HQ).

> After waiting for some weeks for a special rate for *Customer X*, I had to say in the end to our customer that we are not interested in his cargo. It is now your turn to tell us where you need the boxes and the rates that you can offer. (Written by Tim, 19th December)
>
>   We can all be anxious to secure shipments but on the other hand I do appreciate email ethic where tone is concerned. Where there is urgent matter, there's always a phone. (Written by Sarah, 22nd December)
>
>   You are right! Ethic is quite important... But please explain to me why we have to wait for such a long period of time. Why do we have to send reminder and reminder? Is that ethic as well? We did call around, did friendlily ask our customer. On 09/01 we gave you the details. Today we are 14 days later.... Do you really think I can do this more often? I remember the last issue where you disappointed me as well and we did not get a reply at all... Maybe we should discuss ethics in the other way round? With very friendly greetings from a frustrated agent which will not be able to arrange bookings and to claim any commission which would be our income... (Written by Tim, 23rd January)

Nonetheless, it should be noted, that in the formal interview, Sarah was very positive about working with people from different cultural backgrounds and about her identity with her virtual team.

> When interacting with people from overseas I get to know their culture, working style and the experience gained broadens my knowledge. Also, I get a change to meet up with the members once in a while so to me, it is quite an eye-opening experience... I can identify with virtual teams as well as teams in the HQ.

This evidence points to a dialectical relationship between social and personal identity and suggests that social identity may be a result of either impression management or the pressures of social structures on identity formation and presentation. Through the research interview, the process of 'acting out' identity can be observed, not just for the sake of management but for the purpose of a more general 'front'. Yet, cultural differences mediated through ICT and other modes of remote working indicated high levels of conflict and limited identification with the team. If there had been a total reliance on one method, the outcome of the research would be very different. The interviews would have presented a corporatized self (constructionist interpretation) or a successful project of social identity creation (social identity perspectives). The use of multiple methods allows a context-specific analysis via attempts to position theoretical insights through variations in context-specific meanings.

CONCLUSIONS

This chapter has identified weaknesses in the two dominant approaches to identity studies and argued that they are, at root, weaknesses of an ontological nature. Subsequently, we argue that critical realism offers opportunities to promote a non-determinist, non-reductionist version of identity, which distinguishes between social identity, the roles in social structure which humans imperfectly inhabit, and personal identity, the individual's own beliefs. There is, we argue, a dialectical relationship between these two phenomena, mediated through agency. These are high-level commitments which researchers can draw upon to create their own, domain-specific models of identity.

The example we have offered here provides an insight into one of the authors' attempts to do just this. It highlights that a realist approach enables the researcher to identify claims of identity which might be 'front stage' or even misleading—an important commitment that constructionist approaches would find problematic. It also suggests an important distinction between the formal roles that organizational structures might demand and the individual beliefs and norms—a distinction that is difficult under social identity theory. In short, we hold that the sophistication and sensitivity of the concept of identity requires an ontology that is of equal rigour.

5

Critical Realism and Grounded Theory

Steve Kempster and Ken Parry

INTRODUCTION

In this chapter we seek to provide the methodological detail of critical realist-informed grounded theory. To help in providing the necessary detail of the *how* aspects we will illustrate our argument by application to a specific field of research—namely leadership learning—looking at how critical realist-informed grounded theory was undertaken. In unpacking these *how* aspects we will move through the research process looking at how critical realism informed the research approach including research strategy, data collection, and data analysis. The focus of the research was to explain how leadership learning occurs by identifying causal powers shaping such learning. Further, the research sought to develop contrastive explanations (Lawson 2003) of causal powers impacting on leadership learning between self-employed owner-managers and employed managers, employed managers within public sector and private sector, and between employed male and female managers.

The field of leadership studies generally and specifically leadership learning has been dominated by positivism. Recently a post-structural orientation has emerged as a consequence of the limitations of the positivistic approaches. The concern relates to an inability to address context and an almost exclusivity of agency over structure. The pendulum has swung (to a small extent) towards post-structural debates focusing on contexts and placing emphasis on structures in which leader-follower relationships occur. This see-sawing between empiricism and discourse overlooks the fundamental need in leadership to replace the competing either/or and explore both: leadership as a malleable interaction of structure and agency. Further we have argued in our recent publication (Kempster and Parry 2011) that leadership studies needs to develop an integrated understanding of leadership emergence and the causal powers shaping such emergence occurring within the real, the actual, and the empirical reality. To achieve this we sought to encourage research to be retroductive and go beyond the restraints of empirical evidence associated with deductive and inductive approaches: to explore and suggest what might be the causal powers shaping leadership emergence.

The chapter outlines in detail how leadership learning was investigated through what we describe here as 'critical realist grounded theory'. A compound noun mouthful for sure but it does capture the essence of our approach: *to first understand and explain how leadership learning occurs* through examining the lived experience of managers; second *to identify causal powers shaping leadership learning*; and third to explain *how these powers operate in particular contexts*—identifying the contingent nature of causal powers shaping leadership learning. The findings of the research undertaken will not be reported here—rather we use the approach to illustrate how we undertook retroductive critical realist grounded theory. For the interested reader the findings and explanations of leadership learning are outlined in Kempster (2009).

The research approach seeks to establish coherence between the underpinning philosophy of critical realism, the approach in terms of data collection, and data analysis. The chapter is thus structured as summarized in Table 5.1. Although we will proceed through each of these aspects, in order to reflect our thinking and action that shaped the research, these need to be seen broadly as stages. In practice the application of extant theory and testing with respondents of emerging explanations did occur in an iterative manner. As a consequence it would be inappropriate to envisage the themes as necessarily producing outputs to be used as inputs in the next theme as often the themes ran concurrently. Accordingly we suggest the stages outlined in Table 5.1 as a structure or guide.

The first theme, the subject matter—assumptions related to researching leadership learning—has been introduced in the opening of the chapter. We now move to theme 2, the ontology of critical realism. In this section we will outline: the causal powers assumed to be operating in Bhaskar's three domains of empirical, events, and the real; how this relates to notions of internal and external relations in the context of leader-follower relationships; and the development of the notion of causal tendencies and how these modify by causal relationships in specific contexts.

ONTOLOGY: CONTEXT AND CAUSAL POWERS

We are seeking to explain what causal powers shape leadership learning and explain how context affects such causality. We have broadly framed our approach to causality and context through Pawson and Tilley's (1997) argument that critical realist ontology is understood and explained through

Table 5.1 Structure of the Chapter

Theme	Theme	Assumptions
1. Subject matter	Leadership learning	Learnt through lived experience shape by causal powers. Assume limited awareness of causal powers.
2. Ontology	Critical realism	Stratified reality: causal powers operating in real, actual, and empirical.
3. Methodology	Retroductive grounded theory	Applying theory to the data to illuminate and/or suggest generative causal powers as well as context-specific causal powers.
4. Data collection	Exploring lived experience through interviews	Designed to assist respondents to elicit recollections. Assumption of limited awareness of causal powers in the actual and real stratified levels.
5. Data analysis	Retroduction	Applying theory to the data to illuminate and/or suggest generative causal powers as well as context-specific causal powers.
6. Theory development	Retroductive explanation	Explanation provided of generative causal powers that explain leadership learning. Contrastive explanations of causal configurations between contexts.
7. Testing theory	Discussion with respondents prior to theory propagation	The retroductive explanation needs to be tested with respondents from where it has been derived. Subsequent variation through discussion can then be put forward for researchers to question and test in alternative contexts.

[handwritten margin notes: "Mechanisms", "Context", "Outcome", "yes but not..."]

identifying one or more mechanisms (causal powers), the context in which it is working and the outcome. Although the simplicity of the model is helpful, it is rather unclear what the difference is between mechanisms (as causal powers) and context. For example, is a context not a result of structures that reflect outcomes of historic causal powers interacting with current causal powers? In this way context can be seen as a complex nexus or configuration of causal powers.

This notion of causal configuration (Fleetwood 2004) is central to our explanatory approach. We are seeking to reveal causal configurations shaping leadership learning and how these may vary between contexts. Extending the interpretation of context as a causal configuration is Harrison and Easton's (2004) suggestion that context is constructed from a set of internal and external relations. They draw on Sayer's (1992) useful distinction of these two relations:

> The relation between yourself and a lump of earth is external in the sense that either object can exist without the other. By contrast the relation between a

master and slave is internal in that what the object is [is] dependent on its relation to the other. A person cannot be a slave without a master (1992: 89).

In the context of our case research, internal relations exist between leader and followers. The axiom that you cannot lead without followers captures the essence of this internal relationship. However, the individuals in this relationship exist independently from each other in other contexts but draw on the impact of external relations from other contexts to inform this internal leader-follower relationship. Thus internal relations of the leader-follower context exist in a temporal moment as a result of context. Thus, context can be seen to be constituted from a set of relationships and embedded practices which, in realist language, are real if they have the power to cause an effect (Fleetwood 2004). The internal and external relations of a causal configuration impact on an individual; yet the individual also sustains and elaborates the embedded practices and relationships (Archer 1995; Fleetwood 2004). From this perspective context is constituted by (Kempster 2006: 7):

- structures—a nexus of embedded practices and relationships that pre-exist agents (that have been formed from historic causal configurations);
- agents—who are enacting practices and relationships;
- therefore structures causally affect agents' actions and, in turn, structures are causally effected by them.

Context then is created through an interaction of structure and agency as the complex causal configuration (Fleetwood 2004) developed over many years and reflects the antecedences of structure-agency interaction of groups, organizations, sectors, and countries (Archer 1995).

Thus we suggest that all entities be they mechanisms, internal and external relations, structure and agency, or simply the holding position of 'context', are referring to a number of causal powers having an effect at a particular point in time in a particular situation. Drawing together all these perspectives on context, Figure 5.1 outlines a framework that illustrates how causal powers form a causal configuration that produces a tendency to create outcomes; in the case of this research, the outcome being explored is leadership learning. The tendency is influenced by external relations, as is the causal configuration.

Figure 5.1 illustrates two patterns of contextual causality. The two sample sets share the presence of generative causal powers, while additional causal powers are seen to be prevalent in one sample-set context and different in another. The outcome of these variations is seen to create a causal tendency. The tendency can appear similar at a high level of analysis; yet at a lower level of analysis variation can be explained by the effect of internal relational context-specific causal powers; and/or variation in the effect of external relational causal powers. For us a most fundamental principle that has guided the case-research approach is that what is known can only be explained as

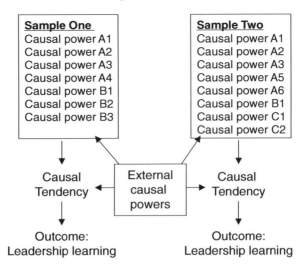

- *A = Generative causal powers present in a particular context*
- *B&C = Additional causal powers present in particular contexts changing or inhibiting the effect of generative causal powers*
- *External causal powers common to both contexts effecting the internal relationship and the causal tendency – for example media discourses*

Figure 5.1 Causal Configurations of Two Contexts

a tendency for causal powers to produce a similar outcome. The approach in Figure 5.2 (page 99) reflects Lawson's notion of 'contrastive explanations' (Lawson 2003: 146). Each sectoral perspective can be explained as a causal configuration (Fleetwood 2004) where the generative causal power(s) (for example, the influence of notable people on leadership learning is shared by both examples) have greater or lesser influence dependent on the presence and strength of other causal power(s)—more on this later in the chapter.

We have thus established the nub of what we are seeking to identify and explain. We seek to identify causal configurations that shape leadership learning and develop contrastive explanations of managers' leadership learning between men and women, employed and the self-employed, and between public and private sectors. The remainder of this chapter seeks to apply methodological rigour to the identification and explanation of these causal powers (in the variety of contexts) by utilizing Bhaskar's four stages of retroductive argument complemented by our recommended steps for critical realist grounded theory (Kempster and Parry 2011). We now move to theme 3 and the development of the methodology of retroductive grounded theory.

METHODOLOGY: RETRODUCTIVE
GROUNDED THEORY

Retroductive argumentation involves suggesting a theory that seeks to provide causal explanation of what has not necessarily been empirically deduced or induced, but has been synthesized and inferred from available empirical data and related concepts (see Introduction, this volume). As such, retroductive argumentation is most relevant to the development of critical realist grounded theory when there is the assumption of causal powers within a stratified reality. Going beyond the empirical grounded evidence has a sense of discomfort—particularly from a positivist frame of reference. For example how could such grounded theory be reliable and valid? We suggest a clear and robust method gives such comfort when moving beyond the empirical data. We summarize our synthesis of the four stages of the retroductive argumentation within the context of our case research:

1. Description of a phenomenon—a human-agency perspective of the lived experience of managers' leadership within a range of contexts.

2. Description of causal powers that produce the phenomenon—leadership learning—or are a condition for it.

3. Theories and concepts are developed to explain how causal powers shape events at the level of human agency.

4. Theories are tested in reality against a pragmatic common referent—a manager's experience of leadership learning. Do the causal explanations make sense? Are they practically adequate and do they provide epistemic gain to our understanding of how leaders learn how to lead?

The four stages strongly resonated with our goal to identify causal configurations as explanations of leadership learning and test the relevance of these explanations with managers. The last point regarding testing is significant. Bhaskar (1978) argues for the need to 'test' theories in reality, against a pragmatic common referent, in order to satisfy a central pragmatic critical realist goal that the theory seems to fit the practice of experience. In essence, the explanations are able to 're-describe' the familiar in ways that enlighten understanding of phenomena (Fleetwood 2004). Simply put, do explanations make sense in light of a manager's experience? This is for us a central tenet shaping both data collection and data analysis in terms of validity and theoretical generalization. You may recall that the testing element is suggested in Table 5.1 as the seventh and final theme. Yet as described when introducing the themes in Table 5.1 we placed emphasis on the iterative nature of testing. As a consequence emerging explanations from respondents occur throughout the research process and testing is both continuous with respondents, as well as tested by other researchers as a result of publication (more on testing in the final section of the chapter).

A significant challenge for us in our research project was to develop a qualitative methodology that could draw out from managers their tacit knowledge on leadership learning. This has been a major restraint on leadership-learning research to date, that of going beyond the data. On the one hand an epistemological restraint—why would we want to go beyond? Surely that is not good science! On the other hand how to go beyond? How would we know how to do this? How would we justify reliability and validity? We argue (in Kempster and Parry 2011) that grounded theory has suffered by this restraint. We assert that grounded theory is most suited to providing the opportunity to do this. We hope to give researchers the confidence to go beyond the empirical data using grounded theory by outlining here the detail of how the complementary retroductive approach and critical realist informed steps of grounded theory can be undertaken through our case example.

The key principles of grounded theory are to move in a systematic way from categorizing data related to a phenomenon (open coding), to linking categories about the phenomenon (axial coding), from which an integrative picture or story is developed that seeks to explain the phenomenon (selective coding) (Glaser and Strauss 1967). Ken Parry has utilized a similar method of grounded theory development in the context of research into leadership learning (Parry 1998). We have outlined how these methods can be integrated together within our article in *The Leadership Quarterly* (Kempster and Parry 2011) to form 'critical realist grounded theory'. We summarize the key characteristics here (2011: 118):

1. Place an emphasis on context-rich qualitative data collection. This direction is in contrast to the context-free objectivity that presently drives much grounded theory research.

2. Awareness of a stratified reality and that the empirical data may be influenced by underlying mechanisms.

3. Draw on the ideas and theories of extant knowledge (whether related or unrelated) in order to [extract and] analyse the data.

4. Generate explanations that are either drawn explicitly from the empirical data or are postulated to be occurring.

5. A grounded theory is suggested that seeks to understand and explain social processes...within a particular context. It would test the usefulness of the emerging explanation with respondents from the context...This involves a test for the practical adequacy of the emerging theory from the perspective of the people closely involved with the context from which it was derived.

6. Be 'offered up' for other researchers to critique for its usefulness in other contexts. The aim is not to prove or disprove but rather compare

explanations for similarities and differences. At high levels of abstraction there may be some convergence of explanation related to intransitive underlying power.

We suggest that this framework for critical realist-informed grounded theory provides a clear structure that can demonstrate the logic of the development of the retroductive argument; a transparent process (and audit trail) of theory-building. It provides a scientific basis for the development of theory and retroductive argument as it seeks to address issues of reliability and validity. In regard to generalization it is explicit in seeking to draw from the validity of the context in which the theory is drawn. Further, by explicitly suggesting generative causal powers these can be tested to see if such powers become manifest in other contexts, and have impact in other contexts, or if the impact is contingent on other causal powers manifest within a specific context.

With our frame of critical realist-informed grounded theory established we now outline how this approach shaped data collection.

DATA COLLECTION: LEADERSHIP LEARNING LIVED EXPERIENCE

We have outlined the intention, shaped by retroductive grounded theory, to identify generative and context-specific causal powers of leadership learning by examining the lived experience of experienced managers. This is easy to suggest, yet significantly more difficult to do. The process of extracting the lived experience of tacit leadership learning was problematic. This was illustrated by the pilot interviews. These interviews showed the necessity of an ontological commitment that the emergence of a phenomenon (in this case leadership learning) is more than the empirical recollections of the phenomenon. As such there was an expectation of needing tools to help explore and reveal (if possible) the stratified reality of causal powers shaping leadership learning. Previous leadership research has been content that the empirical data is the reality of leadership learning. Drawing on the notions of Kempster and Parry (2011), expectations of critical realist-informed grounded-theory researchers would be to go beyond, to assume a deeper reality. Furthermore, CR researchers would not automatically bracket out related literature within the process of data collection. This would be a source of insight and reflection. To illustrate our experience of this dynamic we outline the journey of data collection—with particular attention to the pilot process, stimulation of related and unrelated literature, and the development of research tools. All of which enabled us to explore all three levels of reality to allow for a retroductive critical realist grounded theory to be formed.

The Pilot Study

The purpose of the pilot study was to develop techniques for exploring and revealing leadership learning. The pilot study consisted of four interviews— very much a convenience sample! Two of these people were alumni of an MBA programme that Steve Kempster had taught; the first working in the not-for-profit sector and the second an owner-manager. The other two interviewees were senior colleagues at the university, John and Rick.

The first pilot interview was significantly unsuccessful. The approach was informant-led with minimum intervention in order to let the interviewee express his views on leadership. There were only three questions (Kempster 2009: 109):

- How would you define and characterize leadership?
- What are the key incidents that have influenced your thinking about leadership?
- What rules of thumb guide your approach to leadership?

These respondent questions were designed to be open in style to enable expansive discussion in three broad areas along the lines of an informant, non-directive interview (Wengraf 2001). 'Answers to the first and last question were lucid but seemed disconnected, rather abstract. The middle question was very difficult for the interviewee and the discussion lacked depth. He could not clearly recall much that had influenced his thinking' (Kempster 2009: 110). Concerns were on depth and reliability. When we speak of reliability we are seeking to obtain data that gives insight into the stratified reality and the causes within this that shape leadership learning. We are not questioning the truthfulness of the comments received.

In light of this disappointing interview, the second interview with a senior colleague, Rick, was much more structured. A framework known as repertory grid (Kelly 1955) was introduced to help the interviewee think through his biography related to leadership learning. Kempster had used this in his teaching and found that it had generated student reflection in a manner that seemed to help express tacit awareness. Rick was asked to identify significant people from his lived experience that shaped his thinking about leadership. The repertory grid was useful in terms of eliciting depth of how he understood leadership, but Rick described a feeling of frustration that he was inhibited in discussing his experience in a more integrated and holistic manner. In a sense the constructs developed did not enable exploration of the journey of his leadership learning. The tool of the repertory grid nudged us toward the stratified reality illustrating the potential; but a better tool was needed.

A television programme came to the rescue: *Parkinson*. Watching this programme Kempster was struck with the way the interview was able to draw out considerable reflection from the interviewee as a result of following a timeline approach that built up a story. An emergent process for constructing and using a timeline narrative technique was subsequently used with the third pilot interview, Carol, an MBA alumnus who was keen to assist. 'The timeline created both depth and holistic meaning to the interviewee that enabled Carol to make sense of the phenomenon of leadership learning in a manner that appeared to elicit aspects of her tacit knowledge' (Kempster 2009: 111).

This approach helped address the issue of trustworthiness (Bryman and Bell 2003) through the use of hidden research questions. At no point did Kempster explore these questions. There was no hint that he was seeking to make sense of a stratified reality and illuminate/suggest causal powers shaping leadership learning. Reliability and truthfulness within the interview was anchored in the narrative that the manager wished to provide and that makes sense to the manager. Kempster sought to generate respondent triangulation (Janesick 1998): the emerging narrative of the lived experience provided insight and illumination to the respondent—this was the first priority. This point on respondent triangulation relates to the importance of testing emerging themes with respondents (theme 7 from Table 5.1). The interview discussion was an opportunity to help the manager understand their lived experience. At this stage Kempster would probe, question, and explore emerging issues; offer up ideas and themes. The key was to ensure any emerging issues/themes resonated with the manager's experience—if it helped them surface and make sense of the experiences then respondent triangulation was seen to have occurred. Kempster was not seeking to retrieve data isolated from the manager engaging with the emerging learning. Rather there was an overriding assumption that the data sought of causal powers operating in a stratified reality would emerge from this narrative of lived experience.

The fourth pilot interview with Ian, another MBA alumnus, helped to refine the narrative method for illuminating lived experience of leadership learning. The interviewee had limited experience of being in a managerial leadership role within an employed context. The nature of Ian's self-employed context revealed a very different orientation and manifestation of leadership learning. This was very striking. An emerging insight (albeit perhaps axiomatic) was that context greatly enabled and disabled the presence and influence of causal powers on leadership learning—in a sense, illustrating the presence of the deep reality and causal powers operating transfactually.

Towards a Stratified Reality

The pilot experiences identified that a narrative approach was useful but the process needed to go further. Narratives are seen to have significant benefits in enabling respondents to describe their tacit knowledge learnt through experiences that may not be immediately retrieved or capable of being articulated in response to direct questions (Spradley 1979). To assist such narrative articulation, greater structure was required and the following stages were piloted with the third manager and refined with the final pilot interview. The technique was outlined in Kempster's 2006 article and we draw on this here (Kempster 2006: 9):

- *Pre interview*: Interviewees were asked to prepare a timeline diagram identifying influences that have shaped their leadership learning (Kuhnert and Russell 1990) from the youngest age to the present.
- *Stage One*: Interviewees were asked to describe their view (or definition) of leadership.
- *Stage Two*: Biographical data on leadership learning—interviewees were asked to talk through their timelines from the earliest influence to the present date. Reflections were given on experiences and learning both during and at the end of the interview.
- *Stage Three*: Identify interviewees' heuristics of leadership—the interviewees were asked to think of rules of thumb that they use in action or would describe to someone else to illustrate their approach to leadership. These heuristics were then discussed and compared to the biographical data.
- *Stage Four*: Final reflections on the definition of leadership given at the outset in light of the discussion through the interview.

The stages appeared to enable respondents to establish for themselves a triangulated understanding of how their lived experience shaped leadership learning. For example often the definition of leadership became amended as a result of developing and organizing their narrative—revealing more and more tacit detail. Furthermore, following these stages helped to bracket out preconceptions of the interviewer (Glaser and Strauss 1967) or limit interviewer assertiveness to address interview questions. Rather, the interview questions remained subordinate to the primary outcome of interviewee self-understanding. A fundamental assumption of the interview process was that the research questions would be implicitly addressed if the interviewees had a successful conversation in terms of understanding their lived experience. The importance of this aspect is in regard to seeking to illuminate the stratified reality—that is the empirical, the actual, and the real. Often in the interview process Kempster interrogated the interviewee so she/he would become highly reflexive of her/his experience.

In traditional grounded theory (Glaser and Strauss 1967) there is an espoused desirability to bracket out theory. For critical realists (arguably also with other practising non-CR researchers) this is not necessarily the case. Rather the use of theory and metaphor is arguably essential to help explore beyond the empirical domain in search of causal powers that may not be recognized by either respondent or researcher without theorizing possible causes.

The argument for bracketing out theory reflects a desire for value-free analysis and to avoid bias in data collection and data analysis (understandable from a positivist perspective). Certainly the use of theory contaminates both interaction with managers and subsequent interpretation. It is accepted within critical realism that there is no neutral, value-free language and that all knowledge of the real world is socially constructed and theory-laden (Sayer 1992). In essence, the construction of knowledge through an interview conversation is inevitably biased; the key principle is that the data reliably reflect and confirm the interviewee's understanding of leadership and the events and processes that have shaped this understanding. An awareness of bias and recognition to reflect on such affects is arguably the CR maxim.

Furthermore, from a critical realist perspective causal powers either exist and have impact, exist and do not have impact, or do not exist. Our steps 4 and 5 require researchers to ensure that the explanation of causal powers speak to the reality of the respondents. In critical realist language—does the explanation make sense and resonate to a common referent—a manager's lived experience? Hence Kempster's interrogation to create respondent reflexivity of her/his experience was not neutral and theory-free. Kempster's questioning was informed through extant theory. He was seeking to go as far as he could on exploring aspects to reveal possible causal powers. Either they existed and had impact or they didn't. However, bias was limited through the process focusing on the respondent learning about themselves—the primacy of respondent triangulation previously outlined.

Implicit within these interview conversations are causal explanations and it is the purpose of the final section on data analysis to draw out, through retroductive argument (Bhaskar 1989) at the agency level, causes that shape leadership learning and contingent explanations that lead to contextual variety.

DATA ANALYSIS: CONSTRUCTING CRITICAL REALIST-INFORMED GROUNDED THEORY

The critical realist notion of identifying socially real phenomena through retroductive argument (Bhaskar 1989) is the meta-theory that integrates the structure of the research analysis to be described here. We repeat the abridged process adapted to the focus of our research:

1. Description of a manager's perspective of leadership learning.
2. Description of causal powers that produce leadership learning or are a condition for it.

3. Theories and concepts are developed to explain how 'real' causal powers shape a manager's lived experience of leadership learning.

4. The theories are tested in reality against a pragmatic common referent—other managers' conceptions of lived experience.

This then is the meta-framework that shaped the research. Within this frame we situate grounded theory. Parry's method of developing grounded theory (Parry 1998) seeks to create a meta-explanation drawn from a comparison of case interviews. Using the coding principles of grounded theory (Glaser and Strauss 1967; Strauss and Corbin 1998) it builds up from case chronology to intra-case analysis and finally to theory generation. The method describes theory-building as higher levels of abstraction.

For Kempster the coding steps were not helpful in terms of accessibility to interview analysis, creating the personal impression of 'not seeing the wood for the trees'. The coding steps reflect an underpinning philosophy and guiding practice of bracketing out theory. As mentioned earlier retroductive argumentation encourages the utilization of theory and metaphor to enable exploration of the stratified reality. A phenomenological orientation, drawing on Moustakas (1994), is sympathetic to this and places central attention to lived experience—the central focus of Kempster's research in terms of leadership learning. This led to the identification of Hycner's alternative yet complementary method of 'phenomenological' data analysis (1985). Kempster felt this approach to be significantly more intuitive to the research process to enable retroductive grounded theory-building related to lived experience. The use of a technique drawn from a phenomenological standpoint does not cause a concern of mixing methods drawn from different philosophical traditions. Critical realists place primacy on ontology and reflect a sense of bricolage—using a variety of methods to help reveal the real.

We now move to step 4 to 'generate explanations that are either drawn explicitly from the empirical data or are postulated to be occurring' in order to build 'a grounded theory... that seeks to understand and explain [leadership learning] within a particular context'.

GENERATION OF RETRODUCTIVE EXPLANATIONS THROUGH GROUNDED THEORY

Kempster had interviewed thirty-seven managers from the sectors of not-for-profit, profit, and self-employed. Transcripts of these interviews and notes taken during the interviews were the data on which the retroductive explanation of causal powers shaping leadership learning was built along with contemporaneously reading extant theory.

Kempster's approach to both the interview notes and the transcripts was to reduce the volume down to the core meaning. Such meaning is represented both as 'clusters' and 'themes' (Hycner 1985). Kempster used diagrams (encouraged by Miles and Huberman 1994) drawn from the clusters of meaning. This had the effect of synthesizing the data into a systemic whole—rather than a list. The diagrams complemented the narrative analysis. First we wish to illustrate in Figure 5.2 the process of building a grounded theory through Hycner's technique (1985: 280–94).

- 1. Transcription—transcribe interview tapes

- 2. Bracketing and the phenomenological reduction—understand the meaning of what a person is saying from their word-view

- 3. Listening to the interview for a sense of the whole—often a number of times to get a feel of the gestalt

- 4. Delineating units of meaning—a word, sentence, paragraph or significant non-verbal communication

- 5. Delineating units of meaning relevant to the research questions

- 6. Training independent judges to verify the units of relevant meaning—to ensure bracketing of presuppositions and verify the rigour of the study.

- 7. Eliminating redundancies—identifying the number of times a unit of meaning is mentioned as well as differentiating between meaning in context of the same unit of meaning mentioned more than once

- 8. Clustering units of relevant meaning— seeking natural groupings of units that have similar meaning; overlapping is seen to be inevitable as the clusters are part of the whole phenomenon

- 9. Determining themes from the clusters of meaning—central theme(s) which express the essence of clusters and the gestalt of the interview

- 10. Writing a summary for each individual interview—reflecting on the whole of the interview in light of the clusters of meaning and themes(s)

- 11. Return to the participant with the summary and themes—validity check to see if the interview agrees with the clusters and themes(s) and whether additional information is required

- 12. Modifying themes and summary—in light of additional information from (11) and repeat stages 1-10

- 13. Identifying general and unique themes for all interviews—looking across interviews for common themes and unique themes

- 14. Contextualisation of themes—placing the common themes back into context to enrich and validate meaning

- 15. Composite summary—the phenomenon in general as experienced by the participants

---

Figure 5.2 Hycner's 'Phenomenological' Analysis

Not all the steps were undertaken, and certainly not undertaken in the pre-scribed manner as outlined above. For example the use of independent judges to verify units of meaning was not employed as the focus was on ensuring that the units and clusters of meaning made sense from the respondent's per-spective—that is, Janesick's (1998) notion of respondent triangulation. A fur-ther departure from the list was the use of extant theory during the process of data analysis. Kempster used theory, concepts, and metaphors through-out the period of analysis. As a result of this clusters of meaning were gener-ated that may not have been drawn directly from the transcribed interview. Guided by an explicit expectation of a stratified reality and, as a consequence, an expectation that respondents may not be able to recall or recognize the impact of causal powers and when these may have had impact, Kempster made suggestions to explain leadership learning drawn from an individual's lived experience. We describe various literatures and theories applied further on in this chapter. If these explanations did not reflect the respondent's per-spective then, in line with guidelines 11 and 12, these were amended. The tran-scripts were analysed in the same way as the interview notes but at different points in time, providing useful comparison and re-evaluation of units and clusters of meaning as well as themes. This process often provoked significant reflection on different perspectives between immediate post-interview analy-sis and a more analytic approach using significantly more detailed transcript analysis.

A passage reproduced in Figure 5.3 from Kempster's 2006 article illustrates the process. It shows the movement from units of meaning, to the develop-ment of clusters of meaning and finally to the emergence of themes.

Kempster applied this process with each manager within each data set. In this way the lived experience of each manager formed a grounded theory that explained her/his leadership learning. This process is captured in Figure 5.4 (adapted from Kempster and Parry 2011: 116).

Figure 5.4 highlights the stratified reality associated with different aspects of the process. It gives emphasis to retroductive dynamic within the analysis of the themes. In practice an iterative dynamic occurs during this process: first to make sense of data generating a possible theme; second to read extant litera-ture that suggests possible themes; third to revisit the data and question ini-tial interpretations—looking afresh at the clusters and sometimes the units to see what other aspects might be occurring to explain the manifestation of the events that form the lived experience of leadership learning. This then is the retroductive movement of going beyond the data in order to derive themes as causal powers to explain leadership learning enabled by theory. For example, Figure 5.4 suggests an explanation at the highest level of abstraction as appren-ticeship. This was not mentioned in the data. It is a concept introduced as a result of reading Lave and Wenger's (1991) influential argument for situated learning—an anthropological orientation. Similarly the development of the

Units of Meaning

Below is an extract from Joe talking about someone he worked with:

"He was a very hard task master. Heused to reduce half the staff, and particularly his secretary, into shivering wrecks. I often found myself in a position of translating what he meant into something slightly more palatable…he just had a very hard view on life and was very driven. Not surprisingly he was a project director by achieving goals and milestones"

The above example highlights units of meaning, coded by font, to match the clusters below. The actual transcripts were colour-coded and were assimilated through constant comparison with emerging clusters of meaning evolving out of the whole transcript. A similar process occurred with the interview notes and both were compared to create a composite list of clusters of meaning.

1. Clusters of meaning: Drawn from the above text, and reinforced in the remainder of the transcript, the following clusters of meaning emerged that became significant to the interviewee:

1. Notable people

2. Task-driven

3. Abuse of power – bullying

4. Supportive / considerate

5. Social Identity

This list of five clusters of meaning eventually totalled 15 clusters of meaning for the whole transcribed interview with Joe; however, these fonts became representative of an identified cluster of meaning and were used for the whole interview.

Themes: Working iteratively between the clusters and the transcribed interview and reflective notes, a set of dominant themes emerged as central features shaping the lived experience of leadership learning. These themes suggested underlying power shaping leadership learning. For this interviewee they were:

a. Clarity of beliefs about effective leadership driven from experience

b. Impact of notable people and critical episodes on his understanding of leadership

c. Social context shaping leadership perspectives

d. Abuse of power – bullying

e. Value of task-driven behaviour]

f. Importance of teamwork

Figure 5.3 Building a Grounded Theory

notion of apprenticeship resonated with Bandura's (1986) argument for observational learning being prominent in social learning theory—a social psychological orientation. In essence, using insights from wherever they can be found that can give insight and explanation of causal influence. These two different theories had not been connected before in the field of leadership learning. This lack of connectivity is in part because the field of leadership learning is divided (often by the Atlantic Ocean!) between the North American studies rooted

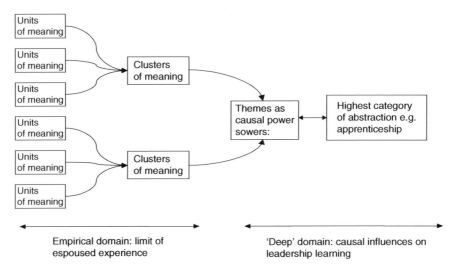

Figure 5.4 A Retroductive Grounded Theory of Leadership Development

in positivistic approaches drawing on a prominent psychological orientation, and the North European sociological orientation reflecting constructivist and post-structural approaches. Also in significant part the absence of awareness or desire to adopt a retroductive approach and look beyond the empirical data. Thereby drawing on both related and perhaps unrelated extant theory as well as metaphors to enrich and liberate data analysis and theory-building (Bhaskar 1989; and Sayer 1992).

In this research Kempster went beyond the data of the clusters to seek out themes as causal powers through a number of literature frames of reference, for example:

1. Social learning theory (Bandura 1977, 1986)—identifying causal powers connected with notions of self-efficacy, and observed and enacted learning.

2. Situated learning (Lave and Wenger 1991; Wenger 1998)—causal powers associated with legitimate peripheral participation, and the importance of career pathways and situated curriculum (Gherardi et al. 1998).

3. Identity development—'becoming' (Gergen 1971; Markus and Nurius 1986; Ezzy 1998; Ibarra 1999)—most revealing was the investment of oneself into potential and possible selves related to aspirational identities.

4. Salience (Gergen 1971; Ashford and Mael 1989; Hogg and Terry 2000)—having the influence to shape attention towards phenomena of prominence and significance to an individual.

5. Structure-agency relationship—the notions of morphostasis and mor-phogenesis (Archer 1995) as causal dynamics.
6. Informal learning (McCall et al. 1988; Jackson and Parry 2001; Hill 2003; Conger 2004; Janson 2008; Kempster 2009). All of these works closely cohered around the prominence of informal naturalistic learning, most notably observing others and role enactments in a variety of contexts—linked with (1) above.

Viewed through the respective lenses of the above bodies of work, the data took on a new appearance. Through numerous iterations of conceptualizations the themes became distilled into an emergent set of causes influencing leadership learning.

It is important here to amplify the connectivity of themes with causal powers because the generative properties of anything comes from the description of its powers as opposed to its properties. So for example, the social identity associated with leadership might have properties such as the type of identity or its strength, but it might also have powers, such as the power to influence self-identity of the leader someone wants to become, or the power to influence others' perceptions of leader identities. In this way the identified clusters and themes of leadership learning were seen as causal powers by their influence to shape leadership learning—contingent to contextual influence. Thus, for a theme to be a causal power it will need to indicate the powers associated with it that indicate its ability to cause an effect on something else (context allowing).

We have found the representation of emerging themes as causal powers placed onto causal diagrams to be most helpful in order to illustrate causal relationships between phenomena of interest. Just naming and classifying what is out there is usually not enough; 'we need to understand the patterns, the recurrences, the whys' (Miles and Huberman 1994: 170). A number of prominent commentators strongly suggest that to build theory researchers need to develop diagrams to help synthesize explanations into holistic patterns (see for example Glaser and Strauss 1967; Bhaskar 1989; Strauss and Corbin 1990; Miles and Huberman 1994; Parry 1998). A technique familiar to Kempster is that of causal maps (Eden 1992; Huff 1990; Jenkins and Johnson 2001). The process reflects cause-and-effect relationships drawn into a holistic map or picture and it is argued that it is a simple method (Clarke and Mackaness 2001) that provides a pattern of relationships without losing detail (Jenkins and Johnson 2001). The process utilized in this research adapted the cause-and-effect process to create a holistic map rather than a directional cause and effect, advocated by Eden, Huff, and Jenkins and Johnson. This holistic orientation reflects arguments of Checkland and Scholes (1990) who advocate the use of system 'holons' as verb descriptions of activity systems to summarize and simplify complexity and sustain understanding.

A further and significant strength of a causal map is its ability to simplify and summarize complex detail through the use of verb descriptions, in this case clusters of meanings, that signal and remind a respondent of experiences and knowledge that sit behind a particular heading. Interviewees were readily able to access and interconnect these verb descriptions, thus creating a systemic picture or mapping process of their leadership learning through lived experience.

In this research Kempster constructed causal maps from the clusters of meaning of each case interview. Kempster sent the causal maps to the interviewees and they were asked to comment. Following telephone conversations, revisions were then incorporated, as required, into the maps. The managers have found the causal maps a useful summary and helpful in terms of reflecting on their learning from the interview conversation. The accessibility of the maps and clarity of the cause-and-effect relationships are seen as highly informative. In relation to our framework for critical realist grounded theory this verification with the managers reflects step 5–ensuring resonance of an explanation with respondents. As a consequence we have found the accessibility of the causal maps to be a useful tool for verification and central to ensuring validity of the arguments being drawn from the analysis.

With the retroductive analysis undertaken and themes with associated causal powers suggested for each individual manager we now move on to building an explanation of the phenomenon—suggesting the critical realist grounded theory that *explains the social processes occurring within a particular context.*

THEORY-BUILDING: EXPLAINING THE PHENOMENON WITHIN A PARTICULAR CONTEXT

Critical realism is not guided by a particular approach to causal explanations. Rather critical realism provides a framework of guidance, structured around the need for generalization, methods of inference, and descriptions of how explanations manifest themselves under particular conditions (Danermark et al. 2002). Inference from a critical realist standpoint is oriented around moving from the empirically observed to generalized universal concepts and arguing how they causally explain the empirical observations on a contingent basis.

Unlike the modes of deduction and induction there are no rules or validity criteria to structure and examine retroductive argument. This is why we suggest the necessity to take the explanation drawn for the grounded theory to respondents. In this way we seek to ensure resonance of the postulated explanation is linked to the common referent from whence the theory has been drawn—the experiences of the managers. The resonance seeks to explore and in a sense 'test' a very basic notion—'does that makes sense?'

There is a limitation to this approach of seeking respondent resonance to the suggested explanation. The respondent managers may not recognize the causal explanation as it may lie at the deep-stratified level of reality and there may be a tendency to be sceptical of the deep-stratified suggested causal powers. Rather than modify the explanation due to a lack of recognition, in this research Kempster gave the managers examples of how the causal powers in the explanation may relate to episodes in the managers lived experience. In particular the causal maps were useful in this respect. The explanations that are presented are not seeking to be judged as absolute truth. Rather, we advocate what Dean et al. (2006: 53) see as a continuum of truth—obviously correct, evidence to believe, plausible, evidence to disbelieve, obviously incorrect. This allowed us to explore with a manager the grounded theory of leadership learning and link this to her or his lived experience. In essence we are moving from their lived experience and towards the identification of causal powers—both generative and context specific—shaping the emergence and manifestation of the phenomenon—in our case leadership learning—through contrastive explanation.

The comparative process seeks to provide an empirical foundation for the retroductive argumentation by being able to compare causal explanations from contingent and idiosyncratic experiences and infer, through retroductive argument, broad universal concepts that may not have been discernable from the individual case. The comparative method of retroductive argumentation moves from the empirical towards generative causal powers in order to create causal configurations at the level of universal concepts for a specific context.

For Kempster's research he wanted to explore the similarity and difference of causal configurations of leadership learning between managers in public and private sectors, employed and self-employed, and men and women managers. He wanted to explain why some causal powers have impact in one context and not in another, as well as identifying causal powers common to both.

We earlier described context as a system of causal powers having a collective effect, captured in the notion of causal configuration (Fleetwood 2004). A framework was outlined in Figure 5.2 which enabled causal configurations of leadership learning of each sample-set to be compared to the other three sample-sets in order to illustrate similar and distinctive patterns of causal power. Such configurations have been able to show not only variations of causal powers, but also insights into the varying relationships with leadership associated with different contexts. An example of such a contrastive causal configuration is illustrated in Figure 5.5. This compares self-employed owner-managers and employed managers and is used in the article written with the late Jason Cope (Kempster and Cope 2010).

The detail of these causal powers is outlined in Kempster and Cope (2010). We will not elaborate here on the content issues of Figure 5.5, save to comment that the causal powers identified in the private sector box above as observed,

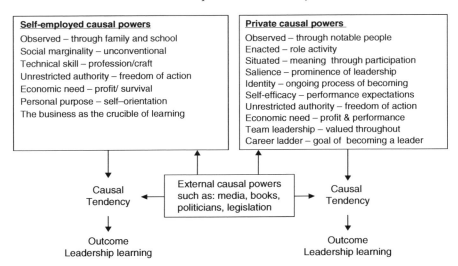

Figure 5.5 Example of Contrastive Causal Configurations

enacted, situated, salience, identity, and self-efficacy are the suggested generative causal powers of leadership learning. These reflect the discussion earlier
captured in Figure 5.4 as themes and are elaborated in the narrative describing the creation of causal powers through retroductive grounded theory using
extant theory. Rather, we wish to highlight the contrast between the contexts.
It shows a different combination of causal influences for each context that con-
figure to create a different tendency of causal influence on leadership learning. The contrastive approach allows for the identification of generative causal
powers and how the effect of these is contingent on the presence of other
causal powers.

We suggest that viewing contexts as causal configurations anchors centrally
to critical realist research. It provides a useful frame through which causal
powers at specific contextual levels of analysis can be examined—for example
individual, team, organization, sector, regional, and national, as well as aspects
such as ethnicity or gender. It enables the notion of generative/universal power
to be made explicit alongside context-discrete causal powers. Yet it also allows
for explanation about why in certain contexts generative powers have effect
and not in other contexts. We suggest that the notion of contrastive causal
configuration is most useful to grounded theory. This is primarily because
grounded theory is a context-specific method (Fassinger 2005). The need to
move towards theoretical generalization of social processes and practices is
the scientific goal of grounded theory research (Kempster and Parry 2011).
Through a critical realist frame such generalization requires explanation of
contexts at particular levels of analysis. At a local level no two contexts can be

the same—but causal powers may be present and their effect can be contingently explained. Through contrastive comparison we can build up explanations at different levels of analysis of generative and contextual causal powers impacting on social processes and practices at these different levels of analysis.

TESTING THEORY

The final theme has been touched on a few times in the chapter. We spoke earlier about notions of truth—drawing on Dean et al. (2006) and viewing such as a continuum rather than an absolute. This clearly has direct implications on the nature of testing. Rather than a positivist orientation of proving is disproving in search of causal regularity, within critical realist-oriented research there is an acceptance of emergence; emergence reflecting re-configuring combinations of causal powers producing effects. As a consequence a satisfactory 'test' of a grounded theory would, of necessity, seek to achieve two outcomes: firstly, connecting with respondents—does the explanation seem plausible/implausible, strong evidence to agree or perhaps strong evidence to disagree; secondly, testing the presence of generative causal powers contributing to the emergence of the phenomenon. The second test reflects the traditional notion of publication of results for comment by peer researchers in the related field. We argue in our article published in *The Leadership Quarterly* (Kempster and Parry 2011) that this issue of testing is a central aspect of the argument for critical realist-informed grounded theory in that grounded theorists have not made salient the need to engage with respondents to test and develop the emerging theory. The testing of other researchers is not to prove or disprove the explanation; after all the explanation is a retroduced grounded theory and is thus drawn from a specific context. Rather the explanation is tested to see whether the postulated generative causal powers occur in other contexts; whether the generative powers need to be re-described; or whether different unidentified generative causal powers appear to explain the emergence of the phenomenon under investigation. Of course all explanations are contingent on contextual influence of specific situated causal powers on the generative causal powers. The contingent nature of explanations reinforces the different notion of testing within a critical realist frame.

CONCLUSION

We hope the quasi 'co-constructed autoethnographic' approach we have used to examine Kempster's research design under-laboured by critical realism has enabled a rich insight into key aspects of critical realist grounded theory. We have sought to illustrate an example of critical realist grounded theory research that embraces a desire for generalization and contextualization. In this way we seek to reflect Bryman's (2004a) call for social science research, and specifically leadership research, to be both *contextualized* and *generative*.

Applications of grounded theory have long advocated the use of metaphors and of the thesaurus to help to articulate the processes and phenomena that emerge. However, the implicit warning has always been to not get too far away from objectivity when explaining leadership and the resultant theory. For these people, the risk with critical realism (rather than a limitation) is precisely that: that we get too far away from objectivity and comfort and safety. On the contrary, we suggest that this is not a risk at all. Indeed, it is a strength to be developed by grounded theorists. One thing that grounded theorists have not advocated is the use of respondents in validating the plausibility and practical adequacy of emerging theory. We emphasize that respondents are not generating explanations of reality and they are not testing theory. That is all still the task of the researcher, and the emerging theory is richer for it.

Critical realist grounded theory, drawing upon retroductive argument, seeks to build an explanation of social processes and practices by first identifying generative causal powers that shape such processes and practices; and second to explain how such generative causal powers are contingent upon local emergent causal powers. Probing into the plausibility of emerging explanations is one way to achieve this, as is the implementation of extant theory into the evolving analysis. Our use of Lawson's (2003) notion of contrastive explanation has been helpful in allowing us to outline how generative and local causal powers can be embraced through a critical realist approach.

By suggesting all this, we have not sacrificed the anchor-points of good grounded theory. Functions such as theoretical sampling, theoretical coding, iterative data-gathering and analysis, hierarchy of abstraction, causes and consequences are still as important as ever. It is just that we have posed a richer way to explain the phenomenon and process that emerges.

Critical realism gives us a richer grounded theory. We advocate that it enriches any methodology, not just grounded theory. In the past, grounded theorists have found phenomena that have worked there and then, for them. But still they wonder how these emergent phenomena will work here and now, for us. To be both contextualized and generative, good researchers must be able to pose such answers to their readers. A critical realist approach to grounded theory will help to achieve such an insight.

6

Critical Realism and Interviewing Subjects

Chris Smith and Tony Elger

INTRODUCTION

Interviews probably represent the commonest method of social research, though they can take many forms, from highly structured questioning to informal conversations, and from one-to-one exchanges to focus group discussions. As a result there is an extensive literature on the organization, process, and analysis of interviews which provides considerable insight and instruction for researchers wishing to use this approach to gathering data. However, there are also significant disagreements across this literature regarding the most appropriate and fruitful ways to conduct interviews which are often linked to different approaches to social research more generally, usually with distinctive philosophical underpinnings. For example, in their wide-ranging discussion of ethnography Hammersley and Atkinson (1995) identify positivist, naturalistic, postmodern, and realist approaches to social research and more specifically to interviewing. At the same time they register the recent dominance of post-structuralist and postmodern sensibilities in discussions of the qualitative interview, against which they advocate a realist approach.

This provides the context for the present chapter, which addresses what might be distinctive about a critical realist (CR) approach to the design, conduct, and analysis of social research interviews. This means that we focus on what appears to differentiate CR from positivist and postmodernist characterizations of such interviews, but we also consider whether, and to what extent, some of these different approaches might also share commonalities in their approaches to this form of social research. This is the focus of the first section of the chapter, the sub-sections of which look at influential constructionist, realist, and CR accounts of the social research interview and seek to map out critical similarities and differences between them. Our second section then

builds on our evaluation of these three approaches, by tracing the ramifications of a CR approach for the actual process of conducting interviews and
the sorts of data that this generates. This involves consideration of three main
themes. The first sub-section addresses the selection of interviewees in relation to differentiated patterns of respondent expertise. The second considers
the interview as a tool for investigating the reflexivity of human agents. Finally
the third sub-section discusses the scope for using interviews as resources for
understanding different aspects of a layered social world.

Towards the end of the chapter we are particularly keen to reflect on concrete
examples drawn from our own experiences of research. But in this regard we
should immediately admit that in designing and conducting such research our
commitment to critical realism was generally rather diffuse, helping to define
an overall orientation that was neither positivist nor postmodernist, rather
than furnishing well-defined guidelines for the research process. Indeed, our
assessment is that this has been a common pattern among social researchers
interested in realism or critical realism and one that is reflected in a relatively
sparse literature when it comes to addressing the ramifications of critical realism for particular research methods such as the interview (important exceptions are Hammersley and Atkinson 1995; Pawson 1996; and Pawson and
Tilley 1998, considered further below). An important implication of these
observations is that this is an exploratory chapter, but one premised on the
notion that unpacking such ramifications is a valuable undertaking because it
will contribute to a richer appreciation of the options and choices involved in
conducting social research interviews.

POSITIVIST, CONSTRUCTIONIST, AND REALIST APPROACHES TO INTERVIEWING

The central attraction of the interview as a form of research inquiry is that
it appears to offer the researcher direct access to the *point of view* of interviewees, both in terms of the attitudes they hold and their accounts of their
experiences. As such it is a key method that is not available in natural history,
where the voice of research subjects, such as a bird's call or a whale's song, can
only be interpreted externally from a pre-established repertoire of theories,
for example about defending territory or attracting mates (Birkhead 2008).
Theoretical interpretations of the sounds of animals are *imposed* on their utter-
ances, whereas interviews are an *interactive* method—a dialogue where the
meanings, explanations, and emotions articulated by interviewees are taken
seriously by researchers. Thus the interview as a process of human interaction
involves the mutual construction of meanings and the possibility of the joint
construction of knowledge about experiences, events, and activities.

There has been considerable controversy within the social sciences about the form and status of such interviews, especially between positivist and constructionist approaches. Positivists have generally argued that the dialogical process of interviewing must be tightly controlled, using a uniform structure and standardized questions posed by neutral interviewers, as this is the only way in which to elicit unbiased and replicable responses (O'Connell Davidson and Layder 1994: 117–21). Furthermore they focus primarily on aggregating such responses in terms of statistical distributions as a basis for developing law-like generalizations about social phenomena. Thus they regard qualitative interviews that seek to capitalize on mutual constructions of meaning as inferior to such structured surveys and quantitative analyses (Goldthorpe 2000: 84–9).

In contrast the interpretive tradition celebrates the mutual construction of meanings within interviews as a basis on which researchers can gain access to their informants' subjective understandings of events, social relations, and social contexts. At the same time some feminists and other standpoint theorists have argued that divergences in the social characteristics of the interviewer and interviewee, in terms of gender, ethnicity, or class, are likely to facilitate or negate such joint-meaning construction. Finally contemporary constructionists have often developed these approaches into a position which emphasizes that such subjective understandings involve the play of varied narratives, and these coexist but cannot be assessed against an external or objective social reality.

As the earlier chapters have underlined, critical realists recognize the significance of meaning construction and communication among human actors, both as a topic of investigation and as an essential medium of research and theorizing. In these respects they share some common ground with the interpretive approach to interviewing. However, critical realists also emphasize that social action takes place in the context of pre-existing social relations and structures, which have both constraining and facilitating implications for such action. This means that critical realists seek to utilize interviews and other social research methods both to appreciate the interpretations of their informants and to analyse the social contexts, constraints, and resources within which those informants act. This entails a non-relativist conception of these social relations and structures, and thus an evaluation of the adequacy of competing accounts of this social reality, albeit one that often emphasizes its layered and complex character.

We will now examine the implications of some of these positions by discussing three specific characterizations of the social research interview that explicitly locate their discussions in these terms. While we recognize that there are different strands to the broad interpretive tradition, Holstein and Gubrium (1995, 1997) provide an exemplary exposition of the implications of this tradition for conducting active interviewing. We then consider two different treatments of the implications of realism for the process of interviewing and the analysis of interview data. The first of these, Hammersley and Atkinson (1995), present a realist conception of ethnographic interviewing whilst remaining unconvinced about some of the specific claims of critical realism (see especially Hammersley 2009). Meanwhile the second, Pawson and Tilley (1997; also Pawson 1996) adopts an explicitly CR approach to data collection through theory-led interviewing. Comparing these approaches provides us with a firm basis for assessing their similarities and differences, drawing out their strengths and weaknesses, and finally identifying the options and dilemmas they suggest are faced by social research interviewers.

The Active Interview: A Constructionist View

Holstein and Gubrium develop their conception of active interviewing in opposition to a positivist model in which neutral interviewers simply extract information from interviewees, seen as mere carriers of opinions, sentiments, and 'the unadulterated facts and details of experience' (1997: 116). Instead they emphasize the 'constitutive activeness of the interview process', involving 'give and take' by both interviewer and interviewee as they interact and collaborate in the construction of meanings and narratives (1997: 114). This involves the interviewer in 'activating, stimulating, and cultivating' the subject's 'interpretative capabilities', just as those subjects actively draw upon their 'stock of experiential materials' (1997: 122).

Thus, social research interviews do not involve passive recording, but rather active drawing out, and represent a distinctive sort of *communicative interaction*. They therefore have many parallels with 'naturally occurring talk', but remain distinctive because they allow researchers to encourage narratives and 'provoke interpretative developments' which might rarely be articulated in other settings (1997: 126).

For these authors the active interview has a dual character, involving both the process of meaning construction and the substantive meanings that are so constructed, and they wish to address the process but also to 'harvest' those meanings for 'narrative analysis' (1997: 115). This distinction is not always clear-cut but the focus on process involves the ways in which informants position themselves and/or are positioned by the interviewer; how such positioning and associated interpretative resources or narratives may be switched; and finally how such positioning may be explicitly reflected upon during the interview process. At the same time Holstein and Gubrium celebrate the capacity of the interview to 'incite the production of meanings that address issues relating to particular [substantive] research concerns' (1997: 122).

Against this background they provide further guidance on what is involved in being an active interviewer:

The consciously active interviewer intentionally provokes responses by indicating—even suggesting—narrative positions, resources, orientations, and prece-
dents. In the broadest sense, the interviewer attempts to activate the respondent's
stock of knowledge…and bring it to bear on the discussion at hand in ways that
are appropriate to the research agenda. (Holstein and Gubrium 1997: 123)

Thus the active interviewer/social researcher brings the research agenda to
bear within the interview in a light and non-directive fashion, as 'the objective
is not to dictate interpretation, but to provide an environment conducive to
the production of the range and complexity of meanings that address relevant
issues, and not be confined to predetermined agendas' (1997: 123).

Meanwhile the respondent remains an active agent, who 'not only holds
facts and details of experience, but in the very process of offering them up
for response, constructively adds to, takes away from and transforms the facts
and details' (1997: 117). In this context these authors highlight the scope for
respondents to refuse to give priority to any one position on a subject, but
rather to register or even embrace narrative complexity.

Treating the interview as active allows the interviewer to encourage the respondent to shift positions in the interview so as to explore alternate perspectives and
stocks of knowledge. Rather than searching for the best or most authentic answer,
the aim is to systematically activate applicable ways of knowing—the possible
answers—that respondents can reveal, as diverse and contradictory as they might
be. (1997: 125)

Nevertheless the interviewee is not given free rein, since 'the active interviewer
sets the general parameters for responses, constraining as well as provoking
answers that are germane to the researchers' interest.…It is the active interviewer's job to direct and harness the respondent's constructive storytelling to
the research task at hand' (1997: 125).

Finally these authors argue that this joint process of meaning production
should characterize each stage of the interviewing process, from the formulation of a research topic, through selection of interviewees, and the interchange
of questions and answers to processes of interpretation and analysis, though
clearly most of these phases give more scope to the researcher than the informant in this regard and this asymmetry is not really addressed. Meanwhile
interpretations of both substantive meanings and processes of meaning construction are sharply counterposed not only to the usual positivist criteria of
replicability and validity but also to any critical assessment of the adequacy or
accuracy of the substantive accounts involved.

Holstein and Gubrium's conception of active interviewing as an interactive social process offers some important insights for all social researchers,
and it is certainly more adequate than the positivist 'straw man' that they critique. However, their approach has a strong tendency to deny the existence of
any social reality other than that which exists in and through the interactive

process. Thus from a realist perspective their conception of active interviewing does not go far enough. It does not address the scope for critical evaluation of the adequacy of rival narratives, either within the interview or through post-interview analysis. Furthermore, its focus on the construction of narratives emphasizes the story-like structure of actors' accounts in a way that risks glossing over the uncertainties and dislocations of recollection that arise from the layered, contradictory and contingent character of experience. Finally it neglects the role of theorizing in guiding the design, execution and analysis of interviews, and in particular efforts to theorize structures and processes that are only partially understood by those involved. Such considerations underpin the accounts of interviewing considered in the next two sub-sections.

The Ethnographic Interview: A Realist View

Hammersley and Atkinson (1995) discuss the interview as a research method within a more wide-ranging commentary on the principles and practice of ethnography. In particular they embrace an explicitly realist conception of qualitative ethnographic research, which is formulated in opposition to both positivism and the anti-realism of radical constructionism and postmodernism. From this position they appreciate the force of the argument that ethnographies are socially constructed and thus the importance of reflexivity on the part of researchers. They insist, however, that this:

> Only undermines naive forms of realism which assume that knowledge must be based on some absolutely secure foundation.... But we can work with what 'knowledge' we have, while recognizing that it may be erroneous and engaging in systematic inquiry where doubt seems justified; and in so doing we can still make the reasonable assumption that we are trying to describe phenomena as they are, and not merely how we perceive them or how we would like them to be. (Hammersley and Atkinson 1995: 17–18; see also Hammersley 2009a)

This means that research findings cannot simply be taken at face value, but it also implies that patterns of data can be identified and alternative interpretations of processes can be explicated and subjected to critical scrutiny. It is worth adding that Hammersley's (2009b) sceptical appraisal of the philosophical and analytical bases on which critical realists develop their more radical claims to critique existing social structures and practices helps to explain why they prefer to characterize their overall position simply as realist.

Against this background Hammersley and Atkinson (1995, chapter 5) see the qualitative ethnographic interview as an active process of listening and asking questions to gather 'insider accounts'. From a realist perspective such accounts provide access to both 'information'—knowledge about events and processes that we wish to analyse—and 'perspectives'—concerns, discursive strategies, and cultural frameworks. Compared with other ethnographic research methods such interviews do have distinctive weaknesses, largely because of the uncertain relationship between talk and action. But they also have considerable strengths, in terms of access to forms of information and perspectives that may otherwise be very difficult to obtain, such as reflections on alternative lines of action and accounts of decision-making processes.

Their realist orientation emphasizes that the validity of such knowledge cannot be taken for granted but demands critical scrutiny, but they also suggest that an understanding of the preoccupations and standpoints of informants (their perspectives) can help in this process of scrutiny. Thus they argue that drawing out both 'information' and 'perspectives' from the accounts offered by interviewees represents two complementary ways of reading such accounts, while together they offer leverage for their critical evaluation: 'the more effectively we can understand an account and its context—the presuppositions on which it relies, who produced it, for whom and why—the better able we are to anticipate the ways in which it may suffer from biases of one kind or another as a source of information' (Hammersley and Atkinson 1995: 126).

In turn this overall argument frames advice about the process of ethnographic interviewing. Like many other commentators they recognize the importance of building rapport, facilitating a dialogue, and pursuing the interview agenda in a flexible manner which takes account of the interviewee's responses. And like others they also underline the need for the researcher to retain some control over the course of the interview: 'they are never simply conversations, because the ethnographer has a research agenda and must retain some control over the proceedings' (Hammersley and Atkinson 1995: 152). Nevertheless their distinctive commitment to realist ethnography is reflected in the nuances of their conception of such control. In particular they suggest that the interviewer's research agenda may warrant probing questions, such as asking the respondent to discuss specific incidents, offer further details, comment on alternative accounts, or respond to the interviewer's attempts at precis or explanation. Furthermore, it may also involve persisting in asking questions in order to overcome initial resistance or vagueness, or (carefully) posing leading questions or expressing doubts or puzzlements to clarify respondent's claims, or more bluntly it may mean directly challenging misleading superficialities or apparent untruths. Their overall objective in all such interventions and interactions is to obtain a 'frank and substantive interview' (Hammersley and Atkinson 1995: 142, quoting Ostrander).

Thus Hammersley and Atkinson show that active ethnographic interviewing in realist guise involves a process of joint meaning *and* knowledge production, and this means that the parameters set by the researcher's agenda include a critical appraisal of the adequacy of informants' accounts and explanations. Placing their discussion of interviews within their overall discussion of ethnography also highlights the wider context of such

Probing
+
Comparing
with other
interviews
+
Comparing
with info
from other
research
methods

evaluation. It not only involves probing and questioning within specific interviews but also comparing and assessing the information gathered from different interviews and from other research methods, in order to develop a more adequate understanding of social structures and processes. At the same time they emphasize that any such analysis is itself a social construct and remains corrigible in the face of a combination of fresh evidence and new theorizing. On this basis they provide a powerful overview and justification of realist ethnography, including interviewing, whilst remaining open to quite diverse styles of analysis and ways of presenting those analyses (Hammersley and Atkinson 1995, esp. chs. 8 and 9). In this sense they present the case for a relatively weak form of realism compared with the arguments of Pawson and Tilley (1997) to be considered next.

Theory-Driven Interviewing: A Critical Realist View

Pawson and Tilley (1997) make their distinctive contribution to a 'realist theory of data collection' in the context of a particular interest in policy evaluation studies. In addressing this topic they take issue with conventional models of evaluation, strongly influenced by positivist accounts of scientific procedures, and instead draw directly on Bhaskar's (1975, 1979) CR conception of investigation and theorizing in both the natural and social sciences as the basis for an alternative approach. They codify this CR approach to evaluation (and hence to data collection) in terms of investigating relationships between underlying causal *mechanisms* (including actors' understandings and rationales for action), the varying *contexts* in which such mechanisms operate and the resultant *outcomes,* anticipated and unanticipated. This formulation builds on the CR premise of 'ontological depth' by highlighting the multi-layered character of social reality, and thus seeks to address the ways in which 'social events are interwoven between [these] various layers' (Pawson 1996: 301).

This provides the framework for Pawson (1996) and Pawson and Tilley (1997) to develop an explicitly CR conception of interviewing which, they argue, transcends the polarized rationales of quantitative positivism and qualitative phenomenology on the basis of a coherent alternative rather than mere methodological pragmatism. In particular they converge with Hammersley and Atkinson in recognizing the active roles of both the interviewer and the informant in addressing a range of aspects of experience and subjectivity, but draw on their 'mechanisms, contexts, and outcomes' formula to offer a stronger specification of their respective roles:

> People are always knowledgeable about the reasons for their conduct but in a way which can never carry total awareness of the entire set of structural

conditions which prompt an action, nor the full set of consequences of that action...In attempting to construct explanations for the patterning of social activity, the researcher is thus trying to develop an understanding which includes hypotheses about their subjects' reasons within a wider model of their causes and consequences. (Pawson 1996: 302; also Pawson and Tilley 1997: 162–3)

On this basis Pawson and Tilley argue that interviews should be explicitly 'theory-driven', in the sense that the subject matter of the interview is the *researcher's theory* rather than the informant's 'thoughts and deeds'. Thus the interviewer remains the expert about the issues being investigated (see Pawson and Tilley 1997: 164, on the 'hierarchy of expertise') and the interviewee 'is there to confirm or falsify and, above all, refine that theory' (Pawson 1996: 299).

This clearly puts the researcher/interviewer more firmly in the driving seat than our other accounts, but it is not intended to suppress the active role of the interviewee. After all, at one point Pawson (1996: 307) presents the research interview as a negotiation and dialogue in which 'I'll show you my theory if you'll show me yours'. The theory-driven interview therefore hinges upon a characterization of the interviewer and the interviewee as possessors of different types of expertise, which together frame how their communicative interaction is negotiated. The researcher/interviewer is seen as having particular expertise in characterizing wider contexts and the outcomes of action, so discussion of these features 'should be led by the researchers' conceptualizations' (1996: 303). Meanwhile the expertise of the interviewee is likely to be greatest in relation to explanatory mechanisms that focus on 'reasoning, choices, motivations', so 'the researcher will often assume that the balance of expertise lies with the informant in describing the detailed way in which reasoning contributes to social change' (1996: 303).

This 'division of expertise' influences different aspects of the dialogue between researcher and informant in distinctive ways. Firstly the researcher/interviewer is involved in a 'teaching-learning' process, which shows respondents how to bring their awareness and understanding to bear on the researcher's theory, especially in regard to contexts and outcomes:

> What I am suggesting here is that the researcher/interviewer play a much more active and explicit role in teaching the overall conceptual structure of the investigation to the subject, for this in turn will make more sense of each individual question to the respondent. In practice this means paying more attention to 'explanatory passages', to 'sectional' and 'linking' narratives, to 'flow paths' and 'answer sequences', to 'repeated' and 'checking' questions and so on. It also means being prepared to take infinite pains to describe the nature of the information sought and thus a sensitivity to the struggles the respondent may have in using what are ultimately the researchers' categories. (Pawson 1996: 305)

Pawson and Tilley (1997: 166–7) emphasize this is not just about the clarity and intelligibility of specific questions (highlighted by advocates of structured interviews) but also involves addressing informants' puzzlements about how specific questions relate to an overall research agenda.

When interviewees have particular expertise, through 'privileged access' to attitudes, motives, and reasons, a different dynamic of interaction results, revealing 'how their thinking has driven them to particular actions' (Pawson 1966: 306). Still the interviewer retains an active role (highlighted by Pawson's terminology of 'conceptual focusing') by offering different accounts of such attitudes and reasons for the informant to accept, reject, or better, reflect upon and refine. Hence 'the respondent is offered a formal description of the parameters of their thinking followed by an opportunity to explain and clarify this thinking' (Pawson 1996: 306) or, put slightly differently, the researcher helps focus the ideas of the interviewee in relation to specific contexts, by 'carefully contextualizing the domain in which subjects reflect on their own thinking' (Pawson and Tilley 1997: 168).

Pawson and Tilley present a strongly didactic account of the interview process which sometimes glosses over the insights of earlier commentators. Though they acknowledge the 'tentative' status of some theorizing, their model of theory-driven interviewing tends to overstate the clarity of the conceptual framework deployed by researchers and underplay the challenges involved in moving between that framework and informants' accounts. It may also pre-empt the use of more indirect queries where a more overt research agenda risks biasing responses or alienating informants. However, their arguments can be formulated in rather more open and flexible terms by saying that they mandate the interviewer to help the respondent to appreciate the different aspects and the distinctive layers of the social processes the researcher is seeking to understand, and to do this in terms that both can recognize so that interviewee responses can throw maximum light on these features.

This certainly requires the interviewer to coach the informant on what is relevant through the character and sequencing of questions and the elucidation of areas of interest. For example, researchers might pursue focused discussion of specific, apparently pivotal, processes and their different interpretations within the research setting. Such recommendations highlight the importance of connecting analytical agendas with actors' own experiences and reflexivity, but suggest that this is a less didactic process than Pawson and Tilley imply. In this context they themselves acknowledge that several established elements of the interviewer's repertoire, such as the scope for elaboration in semi-structured interviewing, the use of vignettes to invite comments, and interviewee reviews of pilot interview questions, may all be deployed within their remit of the theory-driven interview.

DEVELOPING THE CRITICAL REALIST
APPROACH TO INTERVIEWING

The three accounts of social research interviewing outlined above all share the idea that it involves more than 'recording' views as a checklist of objective features to set against a fixed reality. For constructionists, realists, *and* critical realists such interviews involve interviewer and respondent engaging in a fluid interactive process to generate a set of responses which formulate perspectives, observations, experiences, and evaluations pertinent to an overall research agenda. Furthermore, they all recognize that this interaction is critically influenced by that research agenda, though this is given more emphasis by the realists than the constructionists. However, constructionists make quite narrow claims about the status of the resulting accounts, emphasizing that such interviews remain bounded spaces which generate their own local narratives, and should not be seen as referencing a wider reality in the form of an independently existing social realm. For example, Alvesson (2011: 19) emphasizes the local and situated character of the 'knowledge' generated in such interviews, as 'people are not reporting external events but producing situated accounts, drawing upon cultural resources in order to produce morally adequate accounts'.

For realists, however, interviews provide *one* route for gaining access not only to the attitudes and emotions of informants but crucially to richly textured accounts of events, experiences, and underlying conditions or processes, which represent different facets of a complex and multi-layered social reality. From this vantage point interviewers should always be interested in listening to and exploring the subjective experiences and the narrative accounts provided by their interviewees, but this does not mean that they should suspend their critical analytical faculties in the process. Knowledge about events and processes, let alone causes and underlying conditions, is not simply the transparent product of a conversation between interviewer and interviewee.

For interviews to yield insights into these features, then, the interchange between interviewer and interviewee has to be informed by an appropriate analytical framework, which can guide questions, frame answers, and suggest probes and directions for further discussion, so as to enhance the depth, texture, and complexity of the accounts being developed. This is the critical implication of Pawson and Tilley's conception of theory-led interviewing, albeit with the reservations about didacticism mentioned above. Furthermore, informants' accounts need to be subjected to critical scrutiny not only in their own terms but also in relation to other sources, including observation, documents, and other interviews. This is one important implication of Hammersley and Atkinson's conception of the ethnographic interview and its relationship to other research methods.

It is also important to recognize that these features of realist, theory-led, ethnographic interviewing have a wider salience beyond the process of interviewing itself. Firstly they can also inform decisions about the overall research design, including preparations for interviewing, the selection of informants to interview and the ways in which different research methods are to be combined. Secondly they can be carried through into the processes of analysis and writing up. In particular, the accounts generated by such interviewing should not simply be treated as a series of discrete but equivalent narratives. Instead they should be contextualized in relation to other sources of data, assessed in terms of their comparative adequacy or completeness, and on this basis used to test and develop explanatory theories.

Informant Expertise and the Selection of Interviewees

In their CR approach to evaluation research Pawson and Tilley (1997) distinguish between the forms of expertise of two categories of informants: 'practitioners' and 'subjects', and we take their distinction as a starting point but elaborate it to explore the varied expertise possessed by different potential informants. For Pawson and Tilley practitioners are seen as having expert knowledge about the ways in which particular policies have been implemented, the challenges and opportunities involved, and immediate influences on the outcomes, including putative successes or failures. Thus they can be expected to be able to offer their own accounts of what researchers may formulate as the mechanisms, contexts, and outcomes implicated in efforts to implement specific policies—a characterization that appears equally applicable to management informants who have the responsibility to formulate and/or implement management policies. At the same time these authors argue that practitioners/managers are unlikely to be able to offer a full and systematic account of these analytical features, because their experience is embedded in specific contexts, much of their practice will be taken for granted, and their evaluative horizons may be quite narrow.

Furthermore we should not assume that senior managers are the most knowledgeable about the substance of management policies: as Macdonald and Hellgren (2004: 265) remark, 'top management may not know most about what is going on in the organization'. Indeed different locations within the wider practitioner/managerial division of labour are likely to be characterized by distinctive perspectives and priorities, ranged both horizontally and vertically across the organizational division of labour, so the researcher is likely to be involved in drawing out the specific insights of these differently located informants while also seeking a critical distance from the terms in which they are formulated.

However, this argument depends upon the capacity of the researcher/interviewer to see beyond the horizons of specific interviewees. This cannot be taken for granted, though it may be enhanced theoretically by insights derived from a wider analytical literature and methodologically by access to multiple informants and sources of local knowledge. Furthermore, we should not overstate the contrast between practitioners and researchers. Some managers/practitioners become acknowledged experts, albeit with varied levels of involvement in academic research and publication. Finally, however, some powerful figures, such as top executives or consultants, may also be very experienced in addressing public media and providing polished but strongly edited accounts of their views and activities. All these features represent challenges for CR interviewers, who will be concerned to do justice to the accounts of their respondents, but also to subject such accounts to critical scrutiny whilst sustaining the impetus of their own analytical agenda. In our research for *Assembling Work* (Elger and Smith 2005) we found it helpful to interview such people more than once, and to schedule one of those interviews late on, after exposure to other relevant sources, within and sometimes beyond the organization. It also helped to have two researchers present, with a division of labour between active discussion and a 'listening brief' to take stock and pose queries.

Pawson and Tilley regard the expertise of 'subjects' as much narrower, primarily focused on their immediate experience and orientations to policies developed by others. In particular they argue that 'subjects are invariably in a good position to know' the impact of policies designed to 'motivate' them (Pawson and Tilley 1997: 160). In some respects this matches our experience of interviewing workers in British subsidiaries of Japanese companies (Elger and Smith 2005) as their attitudes towards management policies were often explicitly grounded in pertinent details about their day-to-day experiences of those policies. In other respects, however, this remains a rather narrow conception of the knowledgeability of such informants. True, workers who had not participated in the formulation of management policies had no direct knowledge of this process. Nevertheless, they were often aware of official accounts and informal rumours about these matters (e.g. Elger and Smith 2005: 138–40, 326–9, and 346) in ways that could enrich our analysis.

Furthermore, the argument that such informants had 'a rather personal view of choices made and capacities changed within an initiative and so [would] not be able to speak of fellow participants' encounters' (Pawson and Tilley 1997: 160) also needs qualification for our research setting. Some people, particularly newcomers, knew little about the longer evolution of policies or the wider patterning of employee responses, but others spoke about such features in a more informative manner. Often they could report their experience of fellow workers' responses, and sometimes they could claim to speak for a wider constituency. For example, one of our interviewees was recognized as a spokesperson for other workers and another came to our interview armed with results from her discussions with workmates. We should add that these were interviews among workers who were not participants in formal collective representation, and in other circumstances discussions with workplace union representatives may throw particular light on work relations as well as the dynamics and dilemmas of collective organization (as exemplified in Beynon 1973).

Overall, then, this discussion vindicates Pawson and Tilley's attention to different categories of informant, with implications not only for selection but also the formulation of interview agendas and interpretation of transcripts. However, it also questions the sharpness of their contrasts, perhaps skewed by their focus on public policy evaluations where subjects are 'processed' through programmes. Thus these insights need to be developed and adapted in some of the ways we have suggested, not least in relation to specific research settings.

The Interview as a Tool for Investigating Informant Reflexivity — *Archor*

As many of our earlier comments suggest, critical realists see interviews as valuable forms of social research, but they also recognize that they have significant limitations, associated especially with the preoccupations, vantage points, and interests of specific informants. This recognition of the limitations of interviews has sometimes been (mis)interpreted to suggest that critical realists believe interviewing informants does not reveal much about the social world. For example Alvesson (2011: 5) quotes leading exponents of critical realism to claim that: 'Critical realists... argue that "actors" accounts are both corrigible and limited by the existence of unacknowledged conditions, unintended consequences, tacit skills, and unconscious motivations' (Bhaskar 1998: xvi)'. But there ought to be a '...' here, as Alvesson does not finish the quotation from Bhaskar, who goes on to complete the sentence with 'but in opposition to the positivist view, actors' accounts form the indispensable starting point of social enquiry' (Bhaskar 1998: xvi). He is similarly cavalier with Archer: 'learning through talking with people is marginalized if not dismissed by Archer through a reference to broader and deeper elements of society: "we do not uncover real structures by interviewing people about them" (Archer 1998: 199)' (Alvesson 2011: 5). But what Archer was saying in this passage is that with a layered ontology, actors' accounts give a way into structure, but not the whole account or access to deep structure. Interviews, from a CR perspective, are necessary for accessing human thought, meaning, and experience, but they are not by themselves an adequate basis for analysing the multiplicity of causal factors in play in social relations. Surprisingly, Alvesson makes no reference to Archer's more recent work (Archer 2003, 2007), a series of books on reflexivity which draw on interviews with working people and students in Coventry. Having underlined the distinct causal powers of social structures, cultural repertoires, and human agents in her earlier work, Archer's primary concern in this recent work is to explore different forms of reflexivity and their role in the efficacy of human agency. Thus she repudiates reductionist accounts of human conduct, whether biological, social, or cultural, as none allows that her subjects are doing what they think they are doing.

Taking one of her informants as an example, she shows that he is 'reflecting upon himself in relation to his circumstances—as two distinct parts of reality with different properties and powers. In saying what he does, he endorses a belief in his own subjectivity and that his reflexive deliberations affect his actions within the objective social situation [in which] he finds himself' (Archer 2003: 14). On this basis she emphasizes the autonomy of human agents, with interior thoughts that belong to themselves alone, but also that such agents reflect upon themselves in a relational fashion, in relationship to others and to society. Indeed, she celebrates the 'mental capacity of all normal people to consider themselves in relation to social context and social contexts in relationship to themselves' whilst also developing a typology of varied forms of reflexivity and the capacities they make possible (Archer 2012).

For Archer, then, one important role of the interview is to draw out and analyse human reflexivity, individual reasoning, and their grounding in the 'inner conversation'. Furthermore an informant's explanations of thoughts and actions are significant because such inner conversations 'have powers that can be *causally efficacious* in relation to himself and to society' (Archer 2003: 14). In these respects Archer's protocols for interviewing are rather limited but nevertheless telling. In particular her extended analysis of different modes of reflexivity was the product of what she calls 'conversational collaboration' with her informants. This involved 'attempting to remain receptive and never intentionally to be evaluative'; being 'quite ready to participate in non-directive exchange' on features of everyday life (such as child care or sport); and making 'no attempt to play the role of interviewer-as-cipher', not least because detachment would have been impossible in relation to the eight informants she knew, whilst she characterizes the remaining twelve as 'dialogical partners' who 'deserved human reciprocity' (Archer 2003: 162).

This suggests that, on occasion, the theoretical agenda pursued in CR interviewing may prompt a largely non-evaluative conversational approach. This, alongside the differences between Hammersley and Atkinson and Pawson and Tilley outlined earlier, serves as a valuable reminder that critical realists have not embraced a strongly defined uniform view on the implications of their philosophical stance for social research interviewing. At the same time, however, Archer's analysis of the reflexivity of human agents explicitly remains one strand of a layered account of both the distinctiveness and the interplay of structural, cultural, and agential dynamics. And in this regard Archer's discussion of the relational character of reflexivity returns us closer to the Pawson

agenda, as it implies that for many projects interviewers will also ask informants to review and comment on different features and competing accounts of
the wider relationships and contexts within which they act.

INTERVIEWS AS RESOURCES FOR ANALYSING
ASPECTS OF A LAYERED SOCIAL WORLD

As we noted in our introduction, our explicit interest in the implications of
critical realism for social research methods, including both interviewing and
the overall conduct of case-study research (Elger and Smith 2005; Elger 2010),
largely post-dated major research projects in which one or both of us were
involved. However, we had already been influenced by CR arguments more
generally, and were informally exploring their implications as we designed and
conducted some of this research, and here we seek to highlight some of these
possibilities. Our first and most substantial interview excerpt is taken from
fieldwork for *Reshaping Work* (Smith, Child, and Rowlinson 1990), an analysis of the emergence and outcomes of a corporate strategy for the substantial
reorganization of the confectionery division of Cadbury-Schweppes. These
changes were contextualized using a 'firm-in-sector' approach, not simply in
terms of wider contingencies but also in terms of strategic options and choices
(Child and Smith 1987). This placed management agency at the centre of
decision-making, but within a structure where choices were being suggested
through wider corporate networks and market relations, and the excerpt below
documents how interviews can throw light on some of the nuances of this
interplay. Shorter interview snippets from our later joint research, *Assembling
Work* (Elger and Smith 2005), are then used to highlight some further features
of CR interviewing and analysis.

The research for *Reshaping Work* used a combination of in-depth interviews with 'key informants' and a range of documentary sources (such as
management committee minutes and reports) to investigate how and why the
changes had been accomplished, identifying the main actors and the processes
involved. Interviews were targeted, focused on gaining informants' accounts
and viewpoints on salient issues and events, and also had a cumulative character as earlier interviews helped to identify features that needed further investigation or clarification. The researchers were generally aware of these issues
and events, but were interested in how they were understood and explained by
the various actors involved and especially in their accounts of their own roles.
In seeking to understand management decision-making they were also concerned to discover any other strategies that were advocated but not pursued.
Thus interviews with key actors recounted their involvement in the change
process, but also touched on options that were considered but not followed

through: these included closing the giant Bourneville factory for relocation to more management-friendly greenfield sites, or pursuing a strategy of enhanced worker participation, building on existing legacies within the Cadbury story (Smith et al. 1990). In the present context this is important because these interviews gave the researchers access to strategy discourses and accounts of the politics of decision-making that were otherwise largely unavailable, but were crucial resources for addressing both how and why change occurred.

The excerpts below are from an interview with a former director of Cadbury's main manufacturing site and consider the appointment of a new personnel manager, whose remit was to force through change with the trade unions following a major strike in which management were perceived to have lost. In dialogue with the interviewer this key informant recollects and discusses the implications of this pivotal appointment, and in so doing rehearses both management debate and his own 'internal conversation' about agency, in relation to some of the challenges and constraints they faced but also some of the resources they were able to develop as part of their reorganization strategy. Thus in CR terms it provides important though partial evidence (to be compared and combined with other research materials) for understanding pre-existing organizational structures and relationships, the sorts of individual and collective agency that this informant and his colleagues mobilized to seek to change these structures and some of the consequences of these efforts.

Interviewer: So he [new personnel manager] had a record which was probably associated with running down manning and implementing that kind of change? In a sense I'm asking what the criteria were for taking him on.

Respondent: I didn't know him well. I reached the conclusion after the '77 strike that we needed to take a tougher line, needed to be more determined... [Question was] who to succeed him with? I didn't know Will Jones [the new personnel manager] intimately. As an old Bournville hand I knew him and had played cricket with him about ten years previously and things like that, but our careers had gone separate ways for a long time. I hadn't had a great deal to do with him. I knew he was a person—his favourite definition of himself was 'shit shoveller'—and I knew that he had a reputation of climbing mountains, and inventing mountains if there weren't any and climbing them. He wasn't a diplomat and all the rest of it and I obviously talked to a lot of people. I talked to Martin Kenny [manager who had worked with WJ] particularly. I think his recommendation was most influential of any that I received, both because of the job that he was doing, because he has known Will a long time and therefore when Martin said 'I think he has many qualities that you need at this time' that was pretty influential. After all one doesn't have too many choices in this kind of situation.

He was initially seen by the unions as an enormous improvement... It didn't last very long. But Will gave line management a belief in themselves

again.... [But] in many ways he was his own worst enemy, but I would go
through most of it again. I mean I would, that one would, do a good deal of
it a lot better—but the contribution which Will made, and he's a funny guy,
because it wasn't in the thinking at all—because I found actually that given
time and patience you could point him in almost any direction once you'd
learnt what his particular style, prejudices, and attitudes were. You know,
I'm not trying to suggest that I'm a great manipulator, I hope I'm not—but
he was capable of being manipulated. If Carol Challenger [deputy personnel manager] was honest she would certainly tell you, he's a very instinctive
person and you have to play on his instincts. If you played on the right
instincts you got the right results.

It wasn't for the power of his thinking, it was for the basic management attitudes that he personified.... I mean there are comparisons with
Mrs Thatcher in a kind of way. Now David [previous personnel manager]
gave them support, intellectually more consistently, though no doubt with
perhaps a touch of world-weary understanding of the limits of his power
and the managers' power and the ultimate need for compromise and all
the rest of it, which are not words in Will's vocabulary. And nothing suc-
ceeds like success in a sense, a few examples of practical, sharp, and speedy
support couched in their own terms, in their own idiom, really did won-
ders. It's nothing which the convoluted Oxbridge intellectualism of David
or myself or Walter [previous factory director] could ever supply them
with. It was earthy directness. That really epitomized his kind of contribution. The detailed working through of policy was nearly all done by Carol
Challenger. (Interview transcript, see also Smith et al. [1990: 206–7])

How, then, might this account inform the broader analysis of strategic options,
constraints and choices involved in management policy formation and implementation at Cadburys and, potentially, elsewhere?

Through the process of the interview the respondent is both recollecting
and thinking through past actions, including options not taken, and to some
extent anticipating criticisms and justifying the actions he took. As such he is
rehearsing his own 'project'—how he fitted into the actions taken, as well as
the outcomes of the struggle between Cadbury management and unions. On
this basis the excerpt throws particular light on one key aspect of the dynamics
of change, namely the leverage afforded to senior management by their capacity to move managers around, and especially to appoint people as agents of
change. In this regard it documents how, ultimately, the new personnel manager was seen as capable of playing a role that was both different from that of
his predecessor and necessary in the new circumstances.

In more detail this involves, firstly, a valuable characterization of the conditions that management confronted ('we needed to take a tougher line, needed
to be more determined', to make uncomfortable decisions 'for the sake of the
business'). Secondly this appointment was the topic of significant deliberation

among senior managers, and as such was informed by considerable personal knowledge about the style and personality of the new man and his capacity to play that role ('he has many qualities that you need at this time'). This invoked indicators such as his career trajectory and associations (he was 'an old Bournville hand') and his personal management style (a 'shit shoveller'), which were buttressed by a range of comparisons with other Cadbury managers (the 'convoluted Oxbridge intellectualism' of the respondent and others) as well as external figures ('Mrs Thatcher in a kind of way'). Furthermore, the excerpt provides a brief but illuminating meditation on the scope and character of the 'manipulation' that may be exercised as senior managers seek to mobilize the capacities of their appointees. Finally, however, the informant also exposed some of the uncertainties that had been involved. The scope for selection was limited ('there were not a lot of options'), and the new man's approach carried risks ('he was his own worst enemy... one would do a good deal of it a lot better'), but nevertheless his actions restored line management's belief in itself ('It wasn't for the power of his thinking, it was for the basic management attitudes that he personified'). In all these ways this interview contributed to a fuller understanding of the form, scope, and limits of management agency, and placed the micropolitics of corporate strategizing within the wider context of employment relations and sector developments.

Similar issues were also addressed in *Assembling Work* (Elger and Smith 2005), our joint research on Japanese subsidiaries in the UK—adopting a theory-driven comparative case-study approach (see Kessler and Bach, this volume). This study was informed by labour process theory and the system-society-dominance framework (Smith and Meiksins 1995), and again utilized a combination of semi-structured interviews and documentary sources to investigate the evolution of management strategies and management-worker relations, this time in three large and two smaller Japanese-owned companies. Both our theoretical orientation and our assessment of existing literature (see also Elger and Smith 1994) made us sceptical about many conventional accounts of the character of such subsidiaries, so in our interviews we deliberately avoided treating their Japanese character as our starting point. Instead we pursued an agenda about management policies and shop-floor relations where this issue could emerge and/or be problematized as the discussion proceeded.

As with the Cadbury research, we also treated our interviews as cumulative and iterative rather than simply discrete indicators of attitudes or sources of narratives. Within the limits set to protect the anonymity of our informants, later interviews were self-consciously informed by insights we had gained from earlier findings, especially from the same setting or organization. This enabled us to identify and explore contrasting accounts and gaps in our knowledge; ask more focused and meaningful questions; elicit comments on views expressed by others; and probe matters that might be glossed over. Our interviews therefore had a dual aspect, documenting the spectrum of experiences and viewpoints found in each setting, but also contributing to the iterative development of an analysis of the social relations and processes addressed by our research. This was not simply a smooth cumulative process, as sometimes earlier analyses had to be radically revised in the light of later interviews, while the coexistence of contrasting accounts could itself become a focus of explanation. It nevertheless allowed us to develop, test, and revise our initial analyses and explanations over the course of the research project.

Such an approach allowed us to trace the ramifications of changes in wider circumstances and policies for the orientations and commitments of particular managers. When informants were asked to reflect upon their own past experience, they sometimes highlighted 'revelatory moments' that dramatized patterns of constraint and opportunity, as a revised sense of agency came to terms with changed circumstances. In one such account a young but senior British quality manager recalled how he had been encouraged by top management to embrace a major reorientation in his approach to quality, away from that of his original Japanese mentor. His earlier expectation of rapid promotion was initially unfulfilled:

> That was the big shock for me.... I was then asked to go away and make a plan for the next six months and it would be reviewed. I had to think very long and very hard... it was such a radical cultural change that I was being asked to make... [as a result] I had to work very hard re-establishing different relationships with local management, becoming more co-operative, not banging their heads with a stick but more looking to areas of support. (Elger and Smith, 2005: 293, see also 136–7)

Such accounts focused and clarified our understanding of the competing agendas *and* the power relations associated with mentoring and career advancement in our case-study firms.

But the reflections of one manager in Nichols and Beynon's (1977: 41) classic study of Chemco, on responsibilities for redundancies, emphasize that cross-pressures on managers can sometimes generate bemusement rather than resolution:

> The thing is I don't think they think it's *me*. I don't think they think it's *my boss*. They think it's '*them*'. But we're '*them*'. But it's not *us*. It's something *above us*. Something up there.

And in our own research the pressures besetting both workers and managers were sometimes recounted as insidious and persistent, with little sense of effective agency. For example, a manager in one of the smaller sub-contracting companies reported that:

> [The operators] are being pushed. Changeover times, machine breakdowns, deadlines to keep. They've short-circuited the procedure. Everybody's happy until it goes wrong. They've actually been told to short-circuit the procedure sometimes.

It's not a problem until it goes wrong, then they get a warning. (Elger and Smith 2005: 197)

Furthermore, our sequence of interviews with the small cadre of managers in this firm also revealed sharply divergent diagnoses and responses to such pressures, which we eventually interpreted as symptomatic of the escalating challenges and limited resources besetting this factory, which later closed (Elger and Smith 2005: 185–202).

Meanwhile our interviews with workers were also able to trace how their views were related to distinctive patterns of experience over time. On some topics, such as the use of quality circles to involve workers in problem-solving, widespread scepticism was underpinned by details about perceived gaps between management rhetoric and practice.

Quality circles are a good thing, you can get some brilliant work done, you can get the team going, but if the people on the shop floor don't see the involvement from above they don't care either... [Management] started cutting corners on our hour a fortnight, so during that hour we would have to do rework rather than QCs, and it's just failed. (Team-leader; Elger and Smith 2005: 139)

But direct experience of other policies sometimes overcame deep scepticism grounded in earlier experiences, as in the realization that some Japanese firms were serious about enhanced job security:

Every time there was a rumour [of redundancies] they'd [Japanese management] stand up and say 'no'. By the end of it you knew they weren't going to make anybody redundant....I was pretty impressed actually, because I thought they were under quite a bit of pressure. (Production worker; Elger and Smith 2005: 147)

Such excerpts again illustrate the scope for interviewers to elicit and analyse accounts of events and experiences that in different ways address the relationship between structure and agency and thus illuminate the complex and stratified character of social reality.

So far we have argued that interviews do not simply generate narrative accounts, but can provide insights into substantive events and experiences and thus form the basis for analysing the interplay of social contexts and generative mechanisms. Here we wish to add that this does not preclude giving attention to narrative tropes or ideological themes, so long as their coherence and efficacy are problematized and their relationships to other facets of social relations are addressed. These are key implications of Fairclough's (2003, 2005) programme of 'critical discourse analysis', in which he calls for:

A clear and coherent account of the difference and the relations between discourse and other elements of the social....Change in discourse may for instance be rhetorically motivated, to do with persuading others without necessarily implying change in one's own beliefs. Or even if it is not rhetorically motivated it can be ephemeral, without durable effects on beliefs or habits of action. Whether it does or does not have such effects is contingent on other factors. (Fairclough 2005: 930)

In our research, for example, we attempted to map the prevalence of the argument that Japanese management techniques were 'just common sense', a widespread characterization among British managers but especially among those in our smaller sub-contractor case studies. In particular we explored the uneven salience of this argument among such managers and sought to understand its strengths and limits as a diagnosis and guide to action (Elger and Smith 2005: 295–8), though we did not carry this very far. One way in which this could perhaps be pushed further would be to theorize the relationship between the use of such formulae and the embedded practices of managers in terms of their insights ('penetrations') and 'limitations', as in Willis's (1977) classic study of 'the lads'.

CONCLUSION

The discussion above focused on the multi-faceted character of the respondents' accounts, whilst leaving the interviewer's role largely implicit. But it is important to underline the importance of the active, investigative, and analytically informed orientation of the CR interviewer in helping to generate such data. As we have suggested, this involves keeping an initial focus on specific events and examples rather than generalities; encouraging respondents to compare their experiences of different settings and episodes; probing for details and implications; raising queries about puzzles and inconsistencies, including those arising from other data sources; challenging the adequacy of the accounts where appropriate; rehearsing provisional analyses with informants; and attention to the 'positions' from which respondents choose to speak. We have also suggested sequencing interviews in ways that help ground the interviewers in the contextual reality of their fieldwork site, prior to interviewing key practitioner/management informants. Knowing about empirical and actual events in the workplaces meant Elger and Smith (2005) could probe more deeply into the managers' accounts. Naive, stand alone, or passive interviewing would not do this. As we have also acknowledged, discussion of many of these features of interviewing predates recent explicit advocacy of realist interviewing, but our argument has been that critical realism provides a particular mandate and clearer guidelines for pursuing such interviewing.

Five further points are worth adding by way of conclusion. First, there remains scope to continue to draw on fresh insights from the wider literature on interviewing and to use these to further enrich the practice of CR interviewers. An example would be Layman's (2009: 226) argument, as an oral historian, for the 'interpretive value of analysing reticence rather than simply dismissing it', which led her to explore the significance of hesitations, terse responses, and avoidance of topics in understanding both hegemonic culture and workplace social relations. Secondly, our discussion emphasizes that CR interviewing will be most valuable when it is conducted and analysed as part of a wider research design, both in terms of iterative interviewing and other research methods (see Ackroyd 2009). In this context the widely used concept of 'triangulation' becomes relevant, so long as it is recognized that this may involve many different sorts of data comparison (within and beyond a corpus of interviews) and that it is the task of theorizing to both recognize and integrate the apparently divergent or contradictory implications of such comparisons. Thirdly, critical realism suggests theories should be developed 'in process' during data collection as this allows development of theoretically informed data and is less likely to create divisions and disconnections between empirical data and theoretical analysis—something which is very common to ethnographic and case-study research. Realism would suggest that post hoc applications or grafting of theory to data post-fieldwork are problematic, as this can take data into idealized narratives from the analyst which become separate from the fieldwork setting and actual agential development. Fourthly, we have also shown that debates about critical realism and interviewing do not resolve into a narrow orthodoxy but exhibit a degree of pluralism, as in the different emphases of Hammersley and Atkinson, Pawson and Tilley, and Archer. In particular, there is scope for different emphases in conducting theory-led interviewing, especially in negotiating the relationship between social theorizing and the language of respondents and in remaining open to unexpected or contradictory findings. Finally there are many aspects of social research interviewing that we have hardly touched on here. These range from lessons in the art of interviewing, such as recording detailed notes of themes and reflections immediately after each interview (see, for example, Wilkinson and Young 2004), to the very important ethical issues associated with access, confidentiality and the protection of informants (see especially Hammersley and Atkinson 1995; Macdonald and Hellgren 2004). This is because of space limitations rather than insignificance, and it remains appropriate to consider whether critical realists would have a distinctive contribution to make on these matters.

7

Critical Realism and Ethnography

Chris Rees and Mark Gatenby

INTRODUCTION

This chapter has two aims. The first is to explain how ethnographic enquiry can be strengthened through recourse to the ontological assumptions of critical realism. The second is to look in the other direction and show how critical realist researchers might benefit from utilizing ethnography as a means of initiating the 'retroductive journey'. We thus argue that critical realism and ethnography can have a mutually beneficial relationship. We provide a broad overview of the core tenets of ethnography, consider how particular developments in the ethnographic tradition—from phenomenology and postmodernism—have challenged some of its founding principles, argue that ethnography now needs to find a way to deal more adequately with social structure, and suggest that critical realism offers a fruitful way forward in this respect.

Our contention is that ethnography is most usefully seen not merely as a *method* of data collection but rather as a *sociological practice*. This involves linking rich individual ethnographic accounts to various layers of context and social structure, and attempting to *explain* rather than merely describe social phenomena (Watson 2012). Seen in this way, the well-established core principle of ethnography—to 'get inside the heads' of individuals and their 'subjective understandings'—is insufficient. Rather, ethnography must reveal the links between these subjective understandings and their structural social origins. We believe critical realism is well equipped to provide this 'connective tissue', and we illustrate this with reference to the study of work and organizations. Ethnography remains crucial for exploring and explaining the world of work, whilst critical realism offers a robust philosophical grounding for ethnographic enquiry.

DEVELOPMENTS IN THE ETHNOGRAPHIC TRADITION

The term ethnography has been used since the early nineteenth century to describe some manner of anthropological investigation, but it was during the last century that it gained far wider currency in social science. It can be defined as 'a family of methods involving direct and sustained social contact with agents, and of richly writing up the encounter, respecting, recording, representing at least partly in its own terms, the irreducibility of human experience' (Willis and Trondman 2000: 5). It is a research process based on fieldwork using observational diaries and the collection of cultural artefacts. The eventual written product—an ethnography—draws primarily from fieldwork experience, and consequently emphasizes descriptive detail (Davies 2008).

The roots of ethnography are usually traced to European cultural anthropology. During a period of rapid 'New World' colonization, ethnography, as the study of race and comparative human culture, became part of a colonial enterprise of travel, exploration, and record-keeping. In a world without Google Earth, 24-hour TV news and geography teachers, there was no easy way to find out about non-industrialized societies, so the obvious approach for those with time and resources was to visit first-hand and personally document what it was like. 'Document' meant using whatever technological tools were available at the time, which in the 1910s and 1920s included pen and paper, early photographic equipment, and perhaps a phonograph sound recording device. The first person to elaborately describe the method of ethnography was Bronislaw Malinowski, a Polish-born anthropologist affiliated with the London School of Economics between 1910 and 1930. His detailed study of New Guinea, published in *Argonauts of the Western Pacific* (1922), gave him the title of 'father of social anthropology' among many commentators. Malinowski was influential for conducting a lengthy period of fieldwork, writing up detailed cultural descriptions along with theoretical generalizations and, most importantly, including extensive reflections on his methodological experience and tactics.

Early ethnographers like Malinowski offered little reflection on or sensitivity to their philosophical beliefs. We might describe them as 'naive realists' who considered immediate sensory experience as enough to precisely record the truth—after all, seeing is believing—and indeed there remained much anti-philosophical empiricist thinking in ethnographic literature until relatively recently (Hammersley 1992). If Malinowski provided the foundations of ethnography, it was the Chicago School of sociology, under the leadership of Robert Park and Ernest Burgess, that re-energized the approach to study 'society as it is' (Park and Burgess 1921: 210) within the context of industrialized societies. The Chicago School was hugely influential in the early twentieth century, by some approximations training over half of all sociologists in the world by 1930. A hugely productive period of ethnographic work followed, with studies of slums, brothels, communities, professions, and later workplaces. The Chicago researchers, like the early anthropologists, did not propose any systematic philosophy of social science, but they did develop an approach that placed sociology (a relatively young field at the time) at the theoretical and empirical centre, locating an open *relational* understanding of society at the core of social science. It was obvious to the Chicago researchers that 'good social science' required getting outside and seeing the world, and they contrasted what they saw as this courageous enterprise with others who sat in their armchairs quantifying the world by manipulating an arbitrary mix of variables or producing philosophical categories without empirical insights.

Despite the fact that intimacy with local space and time was necessary and straightforward to the Chicago researchers, this perspective became oddly lost in subsequent ethnographic reportage (Van Maanen 2011). More recent developments moved ethnography away from the confident approach of its originators, and in so doing threatened to undermine its credibility. In a recent overview of the broad applications of ethnography, Davies (2008: ix) suggests that it has in many respects become 'scarcely more than a legitimizing label for activities that bear little relation to…ethnographic research…as it is understood in the discipline in which it was first developed'. In particular, we can identify how the combined influence of two significant strands of work—firstly phenomenology and, more recently, the so-called 'postmodernist turn'—has led to 'the erasure of structure from the ethnographic imagination' (Porter 2002: 53). Following Porter, we contend that a solution to this impasse is offered by critical realism, in that it grounds ethnographic enquiry within a robust and convincing conception of social structure.

Phenomenology gives primacy to the idea of a socially constructed reality created through interaction among people, who use symbols to interpret one another and assign meaning to perceptions and experiences. It is the study of what Alfred Schutz (1973) called the 'life-world', consisting of the taken-for-granted stream of everyday routines, interactions, and events. In essence, the significance of Schutz's ideas for ethnographic sociological research lay in encouraging ethnographers to rely exclusively on uncovering the subjective interpretations of individuals without paying attention to how social structures and processes influenced those interpretations. As Porter (1993, 2002) explains, this emphasized the subjective at the cost of recognition of the *causal effects* of the wider social world upon the subjectivities of individuals. Smith and Elger (this volume) remind us that social structures such as class, gender, and race have causal powers over such things as resource allocation, privileging and punishing people in ways that they do not alone determine. Micro-level ethnography on its own is thus insufficient, and purely interpretive accounts of social action are inadequate for generating a full understanding of the reality of social phenomena.

Porter cites an example of an ethnographic study informed by the phenomenological standpoint, namely Hockey's (1986) study of British soldiers on combat duty in rural Ireland, which, in good ethnographic tradition, described their everyday lives in rich detail, but stopped short of asking *why* the soldiers were acting in the way they were (and thus included no consideration of how political, social, and economic relations between Ireland and Britain have been historically structured). As Porter puts it, the problem here is that 'the restriction of the interpretation of behaviour to the subjectively intended meanings that immediately generated it obviates the possibility of deeper analysis of the social situation encountered by the ethnographer... While understanding the interpretations of the social actors is a necessary condition for sociological knowledge, it is not a sufficient one' (2002: 57). If ethnography is to be an effective method of social research it therefore needs to be grounded in an ontological, epistemological, and methodological position that can provide a deeper understanding than subjectivism is capable of, one which is able to link the subjective understandings of individuals with the structural positions within which those individuals are located. Critical realism offers such a position.

A second direction which ethnography has taken in recent years was influenced strongly by the postmodernist philosophy of science. This arose from a critique of the classic tradition of anthropology in which the ethnographer is in a position of authority, with the Western researcher presuming to explain various non-Western cultures according to his or her own preconceptions. The critique of the construction of the non-Western 'other' within this paradigm led many to radically question the authority of the ethnographic author, and here we see what Porter calls 'a full swing across the spectrum of epistemological confidence—from the point where ethnographers assume unproblematically the validity of their authorial position, to the point where ethnographies are seen as nothing more than the inventions of their authors' (2002: 58). Postmodernism allows us little or no confidence to assume that one interpretation of the social world can claim epistemological superiority over any other. As Porter points out:

> The difficulty with such a position is that, if ethnographies are simply authorial inventions, rather than reflections, of greater or lesser accuracy, of social reality, then what is the point of ethnography?... If absolute uncertainty and relativism are accepted, there is little else for ethnographers to say about the social world, for what they say can claim no superiority in terms of adequacy over that which anyone else says. (2002: 59)

Although each is problematic, we would not contend that the phenomenological and postmodernist critiques of ethnography can be easily dismissed. As Porter (2002) acknowledges, phenomenology reminds us of the importance of understanding subjective meanings as the basis of social action, and postmodernism makes us aware of the dangers of making absolute claims about those understandings. On the latter, Davies suggests that ethnographers should 'utilise creatively the insights of...postmodernist perspectives—insights that encourage incorporation of different standpoints, exposure of the intellectual tyranny of meta-narratives, and recognition of the authority that adheres in the authorial voice—while at the same time rejecting the extreme pessimism of their epistemological critiques' (2008: 5–6). In other words, ethnography needs to 'incorporate these insights, while at the same time going beyond them, in order to take into account the patterning of social behaviour' (Porter 2002: 59). And this is where critical realism comes in. An adequate philosophical underpinning to ethnographic enquiry must be one which 'accepts that there is a reality beyond individuals, but which does not over-extend its claims about how much we can know about that reality (in response to postmodernism) or about the degree to which external reality controls the decisions of individuals (in response to phenomenology)' (Porter 2002: 60). Effective ethnographic research 'requires both an ontology that asserts that there is a social world independent of our knowledge of it and an epistemology that argues that it is knowable' (Davies 2008: 18). Critical realism provides a philosophical basis for such an integrative position.

CRITICAL REALISM AND ETHNOGRAPHY

We have suggested that ethnography should avoid being diverted from studying the connection between the actions of people in social settings and the social, economic, and political structures within which those actions occur. In this we echo Watson's (2011) view that the behaviourist and psychological uses of ethnography simply to tell 'stories' and describe individuals' feelings are insufficient. As Davies (2008) argues, we can neither take behavioural observations as simply representative of some given social world nor fully reveal or reconstruct the social through our understanding of actors' meanings and beliefs. Rather, explaining observable events requires a consideration of the *conditions that enabled these events*, and she quotes Margaret Archer on this point: 'Observing a cherry tree in England depends on its prior importation from China, just as experiencing educational discrimination is posterior to a given definition of achievement being institutionalised' (Archer 1998: 196, quoted in Davies 2008). This introduces a necessary historicity into explanation, along with recognition of the layering of social phenomena.

Since chapter 1 of this volume provides a full outline of the core principles of critical realism, we stress here only those aspects of the realist position which are relevant to its potential as an effective 'under-labourer' to ethnographic enquiry. It is clear that critical realism takes a stance against both positivism, on the one hand, and relativist approaches such as constructivism and postmodernism, on the other. With regards to postmodernism, we need only note that once particular 'agential discourses' become the objective elements of social structure, through a process of institutionalization across time and space, they are then *ontologically prior* to individual human agency, and therefore constrain its capacity to change the underlying conditions of action. As Searle (1995: 190) powerfully observes, 'we do not "create" social structure, we reproduce and transform it', and as such 'a socially constructed reality presupposes a *non*-socially constructed reality'.

This brings us to the heart of what critical realism offers to ethnography. Crucially, it holds to the existence of underlying structures and mechanisms. Human action is conceived as both enabled and constrained by social structures, but this action in turn reproduces or transforms those structures (Leca and Naccache 2006). Critical realism thus offers a meta-theoretical paradigm for explaining the underlying 'generative mechanisms' that shape human agency and the social relations that this agency in turn reproduces and transforms (Reed 2005). Importantly, pre-existing material and social structures are considered to have an independent ontological status irrespective of their recognition by social actors, causality referring to the inherent powers or *capacities* of mechanisms or structures to generate tendencies or regularities which *may or may not* be contingently observed in empirical events or outcomes (Collier 1994; Danermark et al. 2002). However, whilst deep structures and generative mechanisms are not readily apparent, they can be observed and experienced through their *effects*. Accordingly, the objects of social research are those 'persistent relations between individuals and groups, and...the relations between these relations. Relations such as between capitalist and worker, MP and constituent, student and teacher, husband and wife' (Bhaskar 1989: 71). And it is these relations that ethnographic research is particularly well suited to examine.

Considering generative mechanisms as 'tendencies' with sets of 'potentials' that may or may not be realized draws our attention to the *indeterminacy* of causal powers. Rules, norms, and institutions develop logics independent of the choices of individual actors, and causal powers are not necessarily activated. It is thus the task of social science to establish the necessary structural conditions given for conscious human activity. This is the 'transcendental question' (Banfield 2004). As Davies notes, critical realism thus proposes a subtle and complex view of society in which human agents are neither passive products of social structures nor entirely their creators, but rather are 'placed in an iterative and naturally reflexive feedback relationship to them' (2008: 26). Ethnographic writing involves the adoption of intensive field-research observational practices, and a critical realist ethnography would seek to provide a grounded and contextualized account of 'how the social world works' (Watson 2011), setting out from the premise that subjects' own accounts are the *starting point*, but not the end, of the research process. A critical realist ethnography would aim not only to describe events but also to *explain* them, by identifying the influence of structural factors on human agency. Specifically, its objective would be to elucidate the specific, contingent manner in which a certain mix of causal powers has been formed and activated.

IMPLICATIONS FOR METHOD

Having considered, in principle, what critical realism can offer in terms of a robust philosophical underpinning to ethnography, what does a realist basis for ethnography entail in methodological terms? Given that critical realism assumes necessary and contingent relations among objects, its methodological goals are primarily descriptive and explanatory (Morais 2011). Causal explanation requires 'finding or imagining plausible generative mechanisms for the patterns amongst events' (Harré 1975: 125), leading to 'the postulation of a possible mechanism, the attempt to collect evidence for or against its existence, and the elimination of possible alternatives' (Outhwaite 1987: 58). A critical realist explanation will thus involve a gradual transition 'from *actions* through *reasons* to *rules* and thence to *structures*' (Sayer 1992: 112). Beginning with actions, these constitute the phenomena under study, presupposing conditions in terms of which reasons are formulated. Reasons, in turn, are inferred from actors' accounts as to why the actions have taken place. Such reasons are made intelligible in terms of the rules they invoke, through the identification of structures or objects responsible for such rules. As Morais (2011) explains, a critical realist explanation will thus be complete with the identification of the set of circumstances in which the causal powers of objects and structures are exercised.

Following this process, however, presents a real challenge to the researcher. Since underlying structures and mechanisms are not directly accessible to sense experience, they have to be theoretically constructed and modelled, through a process of conceptual abstraction, which critical realists call 'retroduction'. The retroductive research strategy and design contrasts with the deductive form characteristic of positivism and the inductive form typical of constructionism and postmodernism, with the objective being to *explain*— rather than predict, describe, or deconstruct—social behaviour. Applied to the study of work organizations, for example, the key is to uncover why it is that certain persistent relations or features of the organization have certain effects or observable outcomes in some settings and not others, and what the factors are—for example, management strategy, employee resistance, sector, nation— that may explain this. Research strategy thus focuses on the complex interplay between social structure and managerial agency over time and place, linking local changes in organizational forms and control regimes to deeper structural changes within the political economy of capitalism. As Reed (2005) explains, methodologically this requires identification and exploration in painstaking detail of each historical case, revealing the complex interaction between relevant corporate agents, structural conditions, and situational contingencies. Ethnography, entailing direct, detailed, and sustained contact with individuals over time, is ideally suited to facilitating this retroductive process.

In terms of how a critical realist ethnographer might collect data in a manner that is true to their philosophical assumptions about the world, we would expect their 'domain-specific ontology' (Elder-Vass 2010) or 'scientific ontology' (Bhaskar 1989) to be consistent with the meta-theory of transcendental realism. Elder-Vass (2010: 69) offers some guidance on how this might be achieved, suggesting that the researcher must identify:

1. the particular types of *entities* that constitute the objects of the discipline;
2. the *parts* of each type of entity and the set of *relations* between them that are required to constitute them into this type of entity;
3. the *emergent properties* or *causal powers* of each type of entity;
4. the *mechanisms* through which their parts and the characteristic relations between them produce the emergent properties of the wholes;
5. the *morphogenetic causes* that bring each type of entity into existence;
6. the *morphostatic causes* that sustain their existence; and
7. the ways that these sort of entities, with these properties, *interact to cause the events* we seek to explain in the discipline.

Successfully compiling this list is no small feat and completing it should perhaps be considered the 'holy grail' of critical realist social research. These activities are all part of the process of data analysis, with steps 5–7 being largely retroductive in nature. But these tasks also suggest particular techniques of data collection. For example, to achieve steps 1 and 2 the researcher will—as comprehensively as possible—map out the qualitatively distinct ontological entities relevant to the domain ontology.

The concept of the 'laminated system' is useful here (Bhaskar 1993; Elder-Vass 2010). This is the idea that structures in both the physical and social world are morphostatically and emergently made up of many different kinds of entities. For example, a biologist might describe the human body as being made up of an arrangement of organs, tissues, cells, organelles, molecules, atoms, and so on. These ontologically distinct entities can be identified and differentiated through a process of reduction and abstraction, but none of these layers can easily be eliminated if the biologist wants to understand the causal powers of the human body as a whole. Likewise in the social world we might identify organizations or industries as laminated systems of interest. In the case of an organization, the management researcher might identify relevant entities as human beings, physical buildings, technology and equipment, normative rules, hierarchies, job descriptions, and so on. These entities are consistent with the ontological entities of interest to the biologist but they operate at a different scale of lamination. In this case it is straightforward enough to differentiate the organization and the human body as distinct but related laminated systems, but this is not always the case. Using the relevant domain ontologies the critical realist ethnographer needs to identify the relevant scale of lamination and then begin collecting data on its constituent and emergent entities, parts, and relations.

Whatever kinds of data the critical realist ethnographer collects, they will need to begin the retroductive process by filtering this data into themes and categories. There are various approaches to doing this (e.g. Spradley 1980; Crinson 2001, 2007; Hammersley and Atkinson 2007). Crinson (2001) offers some guidance on a useful analytical schema, which starts with the coding of qualitative interview and focus group data set out in transcript form, after which the issues and ideas raised by respondents are interpretatively abstracted into 'themes' or conceptual categories, representing the perspective of social agents, as would be usual in an orthodox hermeneutic approach. As Smith and Elger (this volume) explain, layers of explanation of reality can be revealed through an informed and interactive dialogue between interviewers and respondents, in which the co-production of knowledge is possible. Subjects construct a story of events or actions, which an interviewer can record and challenge but fundamentally engage with as a realistic explanation of action.

These abstracted 'themes' represent only the first stage in the retroductive process. To leave the analysis at this level, as Crinson (2001) notes, would be adequate from a phenomenological perspective (because it is rooted in the actual discourses of the respondents), but is insufficient from a critical realist perspective, as it merely examines the 'domain of the actual' and as such 'cannot establish the hidden dynamics of the multi-relational stratified nature of shared discourse' (Crinson 2001: 11). Hence the next step will be to establish theoretically deduced categories, drawn from the literature, which might offer a structural context for the particular discourses. This 'theorization' reflects those hypothesized structural determinants of the discourse of social agents. As Smith and Elger (this volume) note, laying bare the reasons for action requires bringing in contextual knowledge acquired about a subject from theory and ideas. Once again, the problem with leaving the analysis at this 'theoretical-deductive' level would be that it is in essence merely a generalized conceptualization of a complex social phenomenon and lacks specificity. Finally, therefore, the process of inference (or retroduction) is attempted, in which the conditions for the social phenomena under investigation are explained through the postulation of a set of generative mechanisms which can account for, and contextualize, the discourses of the specific social agents being investigated (Crinson 2001). This interactive process searches for connections between subjective interpretations, actual events, and deeper causal explanations.

In the analytical schema developed by Elder-Vass (2010), the first step is to categorize data into entities and parts. Table 7.1 sets out one way ethnographers can approach this, using a framework provided by Spradley (1980), and we suggest illustrative examples of entities relevant to organization studies.

This process allows particular subject-specific questions to be examined against the wider framework. For example, in a study by the current authors (Gatenby 2008; Gatenby and Rees 2011) an intensive period of ethnographic fieldwork observed managerial attempts to transform a failing local government authority by introducing high commitment work practices, including

Table 7.1 Categories of Ethnographic Data

Categories of data (adapted from Spradley 1980)	Examples of entities for organization studies	Subject-specific entities for teamwork (adapted from Gatenby 2008)
Space (and boundaries)	Buildings, local geography	Office department layout
Actors	Managers, employees, customers	Chief executive, team members, audit inspectors
Activities (procedures)	Work processes and rules	Chief executive's 'private sector practices', HR practices, work tasks
Physical objects	Technology, resources, and documents	Computer technology, organizational reports
Language (acts)	Face-to-face communication, telephone calls, emails	Manager communication, briefing emails, group discussions
Events	Meetings, away days, lunch breaks	Team meetings, away days, quarterly business reviews
Time	Routines and cycles	Office routines and audit reporting cycles
Goals	Strategies, projects, and targets	Organizational transformation and Performance Indicator improvement
Relationships	Line manager–employee	Team members, managerial relations, inter-team relations
Feelings	Satisfaction, commitment, fears	Fear of change, disbelief, acquiescence
Symbols	Signs and uniforms	Old and new organizational culture

teamwork. Detailed participant observations were conducted for a period of three months across a number of workplace settings. Extensive fieldwork diaries were maintained, along with data from a series of face-to-face interviews and the collection of local artefacts. The ethnographic process revealed the difficulties that managers faced in trying to implement team-based quality circles and development meetings at the workplace level. These were analysed through a contrast method (Lawson 2009), by identifying entities as either morphogenetic forces (leading to transformation of the dynamics within the context, and restructuring of the laminated system) or morphostatic forces (which reproduce the dynamics of the context, and retain the social structure of the laminated system). The ethnographic data allow these entities to be identified and positioned within a theoretical framework of multiple determination. Figure 7.1 is an attempt to depict the causal mechanisms interacting with the major ontological entities and parts within the research setting.

The analysis suggested that the introduction of teamwork into an office environment within the UK public sector is unlikely to lead to changes in behaviour and routines if there is little need for task interdependence and employee interaction to accomplish work tasks. Employees belonged to departmental 'teams' but their work activities revolved around individual routines and external requirements. Employees did not know what to expect from their fellow team members and their relationships involved little peer control. Team members in this context had little past experience of using teamwork for their

Team development meetings

Morphogenetic forces

Chief Executive communication

Researcher observing

Service manager suggestion

Team briefing day

New weekly meeting added to team diary

Morphostatic forces

Team members remain constant

Team member expectations

Established routines

Asymmetrical working patterns within team

Isolated team initiative

Team development meetings abandoned after three weeks of following the new routine

Figure 7.1 Causal Mechanisms

(adapted from Gatenby 2008)

work tasks, their knowledge mainly deriving from new strategy documents and their immediate experiences of team 'away days'. Finally, team members had many other opportunities to communicate and interact informally, and the team meeting did not offer them anything more in this respect, and so was widely perceived as 'boring' and/or as merely a more formal version of their normal office interactions.

The subject-specific theory of interdependence (Thompson 1967) suggests that for teams to work together the social entities (the people and their relationships) need to fit or 'jointly optimize' with the technical entities (technology, resources, role demands, etc.). This was clearly not the case in this particular context. The symbolic entities at the organizational level were changed through interventions by the new chief executive and individuals representing the Audit Commission, but the social and technical entities of the workplace largely remained in place. Because the focus is on a specific routine behaviour (i.e. team meeting) it is relatively straightforward to identify morphogenetic and morphostatic forces in this case. The morphogenetic forces were clearly insufficient to lead to significant change within the workplace setting. The study shows the contrast between centralized organizational change through 'transformational leadership' at the organizational level and the morphostatic forces of routines, old rules and symbols, and persistent behaviour at the workplace level. The ethnographic data gave access to detailed work routines over time and the episodes of morphogenetic interventions. Some changes could be observed in language and documents, but physical boundaries, major work tasks, procedural requirements, and workplace routines and relationships remained very similar.

CRITICAL REALIST ETHNOGRAPHY AND ORGANIZATION STUDIES

The study discussed above illustrates how the critical realist focus on process enables a view of the organization as a 'political arena', in which social interaction, power, and political manoeuvring become more central in the analysis and understanding of organizational life. These processes are in turn shaped by the wider institutional context. This linking of micro-level data with abstracted social patterns has been a perennial challenge in the social sciences (Barley 2008), and there have been several recent calls from organizational scholars to re-examine the value of the structure-agency dualism and consider critical realism as a potential theoretical advance (Edwards 2005; Fleetwood 2005; Reed 2005).

However, although the explicit adoption of critical realism has until recently been relatively rare amongst management and organization scholars, Ackroyd and Fleetwood (2000) remind us that philosophical realism has been present, if often implicitly, in a wide range of organizational research for some time, and in fact has been the orthodoxy in several branches of this broad field over many years. Much of institutional theory, labour process analysis, as well as regulationist theory, is essentially realist in character. The particular field of industrial relations has a long and impressive tradition of materialist and realist-informed research (exemplified by one of the editors of this volume— see Edwards 1986, 2005). This research tradition draws on the rich streams of Weberian and Marxist social science, where it is acknowledged that *both* social structures (mechanisms, relations, powers, rules, resources, institutions) *and* the meanings that actors and groups attribute to their situation (along with the discourse used to convey these meanings) must be taken into account in any full and proper explanation of events (Ackroyd and Fleetwood 2000a).

There is thus historical depth to current substantive realist research, and contemporary applications of critical realism in organization studies are not merely a response to, or 'turn' away from, postmodernism—or indeed any other philosophical position—but rather emerge from specific and well-founded intellectual roots. Much of this work (e.g. Delbridge 1998; Taylor and Bain 2004; Elger and Smith 2005) focuses on issues concerning the control imperative within managerial capitalism, a causal mechanism shaping relationships between managers and workers (Thompson and Smith 2010b). As Smith and Elger (this volume) note, control remains central to capital-labour relations in capitalism as a system, though it is constantly refashioned for new circumstances and in new forms. This highlights the value of comparative case studies, which can uncover the varying and complex ways in which combinations of structural, historical, and operational contingencies interact. Once a mechanism or process is identified, generalization from case studies is possible if the same mechanism is recognizably operative in many similar situations. As Ackroyd (2009) explains, case study accounts of generative processes involve the conceptual interpretation of causal sequences, and comparative research can help pin down the way generative mechanisms and contexts have intersected historically to produce unique outcomes.

As a complement to comparative case studies, critical realist ethnography could also usefully be applied to analysing the dynamics of relations and processes within multinational enterprises (MNEs), as the current authors have recently argued (Rees 2009, 2012). Actions such as personal contacts in MNE headquarters-subsidiary relations are social events, which take place in the *actual* domain of reality. Such actions or events are observable as experiences in the *empirical* domain of reality by those who experience them and those who study them. Those who experience them are able to suggest conditions in which such actions or events occur, that is, reasons, which researchers may further examine in terms of objects in the *real* domain of reality (Morais 2011). Sharpe (2004, 2005) outlines the relevance of critical realist ethnography to an understanding of practices and processes within the MNE, and suggests that in the broad field of international management research the potential for ethnographic research has not been fully realized. As she observes, a large amount of research on MNEs has used surveys and structured questionnaires to address, for example, questions of what employment practices and work systems have been transferred from headquarters to subsidiaries within the organization. However, such surveys often are pitched at top management and require simply a tick-box acknowledgement of whether or not a practice has been transferred, and as such they are far less suited to 'an understanding of *how* management practices are introduced, received, responded to, adapted, resisted, or transformed in different contexts' (Sharpe 2005: 4). Ethnographic studies can provide a rich appreciation of the MNE as a social and political arena, and a critical realist framework provides a means of conceptualizing how actors' experiences within the MNE can best be examined 'by a macro regress to the social structures shaping and constraining individual action' (Sharpe 2005: 8). Critical realist ethnography can therefore illuminate the 'connective tissue' between the agency of individual managers and workers at the MNE level and the structured context of global, national, and sector-level constraints.

If a realist approach to work organizations has been well established over many years, this is certainly also the case for explicitly ethnographic studies of work and organizational life, which have a fine tradition. In a wide-ranging overview, Hodson (2004) finds 204 book-length ethnographies over the last century. Areas receiving the most coverage are the manufacturing assembly line, management roles and structures, healthcare, and low-skill service work. The earliest studies appear in the 1940s, such as Clawson's (1944) study of shipyard welders and Whyte's (1948) analysis of human relations in the restaurant industry. Classic texts from the post-war period include the *Boys in White* study of a medical school (Becker et al. 1961), the *Men Who Manage* study of managerial work (Dalton 1959), the 'Banana Time' study of work group behaviour (Roy 1959), and the *On the Shopfloor* study of factory life (Lupton 1963). This canon of work provided the inspiration for more recent ethnographic research such as Collinson's (1992) shopfloor study, Kunda's (1992) study of an American high-technology company, Delbridge's (1998) study of new manufacturing techniques and worker experiences in two factories, Watson's (2001) account of managerial work in a UK telecommunications manufacturing company, Down's (2006) study of entrepreneurship in a small business, and Ho's (2009) ethnography of Wall Street.

There have been periodic calls to 'rediscover' or reinvigorate the ethnographic study of work and organizations, the latest exemplified by the recent launch of the *Journal of Organizational Ethnography* (Brannan et al. 2012).

Critical realism provides 'a viable ontology of organizations and management' (Fleetwood 2004: 49), and in our own research we found a realist-informed multilevel analysis to be particularly useful in understanding public sector organizations, illuminating the relative pressures for change and/or continuity at different levels (sector, organization, and workplace). As Kessler et al. (2006) have similarly argued in this context, the theoretical resources provided by critical realism, conceiving of social agents as purposeful if constrained actors, can be fruitfully combined with an account of negotiation and resistance at the workplace level to provide a richer understanding of the dynamics of workplace restructuring.

CONCLUSION

The core argument of this chapter has been that ethnography is most useful when located explicitly within a realist framework, utilized not merely as a method of data collection but rather as a sociological practice of linking observed accounts to context, and explaining rather than merely describing social phenomena. The full value of the detailed micro-level data gathered through ethnographic studies can only be realized if they are situated and interpreted in their historical, economic, and social contexts. Critical realism is well placed to provide this 'connective tissue' and act as an effective 'under-labourer' to ethnographic enquiry.

Moreover, not only is the ethnographic method strengthened by recourse to critical realism, but at the same time we have suggested that critical realists can benefit from utilizing ethnographic techniques. As Ackroyd observes, certain forms of data collection 'recommend themselves as ways of gaining insight into causal mechanisms' (2004: 158), and he refers to ethnography and, in particular, participant observation in this respect. Ethnography provides a well-established way of clarifying patterns of relationships between participants, based upon the sustained observation of behaviour to reveal emergent patterns of interaction, and can potentially make a significant contribution to the conceptualization of causative mechanisms at the societal level. Ethnographic enquiry, if analysed within a realist framework, can thus 'expand our understanding of the interdependence of social structures and social interaction' (Crinson 2001: 2).

The critical realist emphasis on contextualizing social phenomena by reference to social mechanisms operating below the surface and contingent upon specific historical, local, or institutional contexts is highly resonant of Marx's (1852) classic dictum that 'men make their own history, but they do not make it... under circumstances chosen by themselves, but under circumstances directly encountered, given and transmitted from the past'. Bhaskar expresses this same principle when stating that people 'do not create society... it always pre-exists them and is a necessary condition for their activity... Society does not exist independently of human activity (the error of reification). But... [neither is it] the product of it (the error of voluntarism)' (1989: 36). The dynamic relationship between the generative potential inherent in social structures and its contingent realization through human agency thus stands at the ontological core of critical realism (Fleetwood 2005).

Following Banfield (2004), these arguments imply that critical realist ethnography will have certain core tenets: (i) it will hold to a stratified emergent ontology, with a materialist view of history as its foundation; (ii) it will take structures and generative mechanisms as its objects of inquiry; and (iii) it will understand events as the outcome of multiple causal processes. We have suggested that, based on these philosophical principles, critical realist ethnography will require a particular methodological framework, one that enables qualitative data to be integrated into an analytical process resulting in a concrete conceptualization of a set of interactive generative mechanisms. This means moving from specific observations, through thematic conceptual categories, and on to a more causal analysis, going beyond the micro-interactions of social agents and 'towards an explanation of the way in which social discourses arise out of the interaction between agency and structure in a particular material context' (Crinson 2001: 13).

Finally, we have briefly considered how critical realist ethnography might contribute to the particular area of management and organization studies. Ethnographic studies in this area already have a fine tradition of examining the realities of how organizations work, continually testing intuitive understandings, challenging conventional wisdoms, and questioning taken-for-granted or ideologically-grounded assumptions (Watson 2011). Critical realist ethnography in particular can help to explore beyond and below the surface appearance of organizational strategies and practices, something of increasing worth in a field ever more dominated by managerial fads and fashions. As Down (2012: 9) observes in the opening volume of the *Journal of Organizational Ethnography*, we should 'be wary of... expedience and of a fixation on the most novel organizational and employment trends'. Critical realism offers ethnography the promise of moving beyond a phenomenology of surface appearances, insofar as it offers a theory of hierarchical stratification and ontological emergence, where organizational 'reality' is understood to comprise the concurrent operation of multiple mechanisms rooted in, and emergent from, lower ontological strata.

8

Critical Realism and the Organizational Case Study

A Guide to Discovering Institutional Mechanisms

Steve Vincent and Robert Wapshott

INTRODUCTION

This chapter explores how critical realists can develop organizational case studies (OCSs) in order to explain the *institutional mechanisms* they contain. It starts by differentiating realist OCSs from other approaches before exploring realist approaches in more detail. A framework for dissecting the causal powers that affect institutional mechanisms is introduced and illustrated. Subsequently, using examples from labour process analyses, three approaches to developing explanations through OCSs are considered: *exploratory, exceptional,* and *qualifying* cases. In the final sections, data analysis is discussed. The chapter concludes with a summary case, taken from one of the author's own research projects, which is used to draw ideas together by demonstrating how theoretical generalizations can be achieved through a single case.

BEYOND SOCIAL CONSTRUCTION AND EMPIRICISM

Realist OCSs are substantively different from both social constructionist and empiricist approaches. Stake's (2005) approach illustrates the former. It has much in common with 'thick description' in ethnographic practice (Geertz 1973): the goal is to articulate the subjective meaning systems of those studied so that they become accessible to the reader. Cases are worth knowing because they facilitate more informed interpretations of particular social realities. Cases communicate the multiple and frequently conflicting perspectives of diverse social agents. Social processes become reduced to subjective systems of meaning and how these lead people towards particular activities. Causal forces disappear because outcomes are 'multiply sequenced, multiply contextual more often than causal...interrelated and context bound, purposive but questionably determinative' (Stake 2005: 449). As a result, structural processes are reduced to mere epiphenomena of subjective realities.

CR scholars would assert that his approach is guilty of *upward conflation* (see Archer 2000). This is because social structures are entirely determined by the social constructions of the actors they contain: the possibilities of developing knowledge about independent organizational structures and how these affect behaviour is effectively denied. Whilst realists are certainly interested in subjective meaning systems and how these emerge, they are also interested in how these combine to inform collective social processes, as entities or *institutional mechanisms* in themselves.

An alternative but no less limited approach is the empiricist perspective, which has been substantially developed by Yin (2009). For him, OCSs should be developed with specific and instrumental purposes or 'tests' in mind, with the data simply confirming or repudiating the theoretical postulate(s) examined. Each case becomes akin to an experiment where the goal is to deduce and, subsequently, test theory through a rigorous exploration of the data collected about a case or class of cases. If the deduced theory appears to be inadequate, the researcher is invited to abduct or infer a new explanation, after which further data-gathering and analysis is prescribed to test the new explanation.

This approach bears some similarity with that of CR scholars (see also Ackroyd and Karlsson, this volume): all researchers are, after all, interested in cases or classes of cases that are inherently novel or under-researched. In these circumstances, outcomes are less likely to fit with existing theories and models, indicating opportunities to develop new forms of understanding. In these situations, we must reconsider or abandon our original frame(s) of reference in order to account for the novelty we observe (see also Burawoy 1998). However, Yin's approach is limited because there is nothing beyond abduction and nothing to know beyond what we confirm through the data themselves. *Deeper* levels disappear from view and retroduction disappears as an analytical device.

Realists are attracted to OCS research not only because they can help us abduct novel theories, but also because they want a better explanation of broader social mechanisms (class-based, racial, religious, sectoral, national, cultural, etc.) that operate through a case or class of cases. Knowledge of these mechanisms often requires retroduction: establishing the contextual conditions that give rise to the particular mechanisms we are observing (for a more complete exploration of abduction and retroduction, see O'Mahoney and Vincent, this volume). These mechanisms may not be obvious or explicit within the case itself and must be worked out theoretically from a broader analysis of the setting, often through comparison (see Kessler and Bach, this volume). There is no empirical 'test' that can act as absolute confirmation. Rather, and as will be demonstrated, the theory and data must be 'fitted together' as an explanation of what is observed.

STUDYING ORGANIZATIONS

When developing explanations of the antecedents, causal powers, and potentials of institutional mechanisms it is useful to start with ontological assertions about what organizations are and how they are formed. Here, the realist concept relational emergence is particularly useful. This concept has been developed by Elder-Vass (2010), who applies it to causal powers of all *entities*. For him, an entity is '*a persistent whole formed of a set of parts that is structured by the relations between these parts*' (Elder-Vass 2010: 17, original emphasis). Relations are how the parts interact to become causally efficacious. Put another way, they have causal powers because they are articulated, combined, or configured to form particular wholes. Finally, emergence is both the process by which something comes into being and, subsequently, the 'relation amongst the parts of an entity that gives that entity as a whole the ability to have a particular…causal impact' (Elder-Vass 2010: 23). Organizations, then, are made of people, who form the 'parts' of emergent organizational structures. The specific configurations that they form and roles (norms of behaviour) that they embody structure the relations they contain in ways that ensure that the organization reproduces itself, as otherwise the organization would cease to exist. In other words, it is particular configurations of norm-based activities that define the distinctiveness of specific institutional mechanisms.

Whilst it is possible to develop OCSs that trace the conception and development of an organization, most studies are of organizations that already exist. As a result we must abduct and retroduct the causal powers and antecedents that are relevant to the organization(s) studied. To do this, research designs must be sensitive to the history of the case(s) examined (see Mutch in this volume), in order to understand the emergence of causal powers of the 'parts' of organizations and the broader context(s) within which they reside. For example, if we are exploring the causal properties of a team we need to understand how and why the team came to be constituted in a particular way, the abilities and preferences of the people they contain and the organizational system (production unit, corporation, economy) that they reside within. Alternatively, if we want to explore the production unit we need to understand the teams, offices, workshops (etc.) that constitute the production unit, as well as the organizational system (corporation, value chain) that they reside within. In short, our research designs need to be sensitive to the temporally stratified nature of the world. Analysts must look 'upwards' to the complex array of context(s) that act through and influence patterns of behaviour in the organizational entity studied and 'downwards' for how they are constituted of complex sets of interacting subunits.

CLASSIFYING CAUSAL MECHANISMS

In order to undertake such a stratified examination of cases, identifying the significant types of causal influence that affect organizations is a useful starting point. In this area, the work of Elder-Vass (2010) is, again, particularly useful because it argues that relational emergence is affected by causal processes across various dimensions. Firstly, and as outlined above, causal powers of different levels interact, so it is important to distinguish *upwards causation* and *downwards causation*, as well as how an entity affects others that reside at the same level. Secondly, there are also separable causal influences associated with norms and rules (*normative powers* and *potentials*), on the one hand, and organizational configurations (*configurational powers* and *potentials*) on the other. In Figure 8.1, these types of powers and potentials are combined to

	Normative Powers and Potentials	Configurational Powers and Potentials
Upwards Causation	Upwards normative causes Internal normative routines active within and affecting the institutional mechanism observed. *(e.g. Taylor and Bain 2003)*	Upwards configurational causes Internal organizational configurations which articulate the institutional mechanism observed. *(e.g. Barker 1993)*
Downwards Causation	Downwards normative causes Extra-organisational norms which shape outcomes within the institutional mechanism observed. *(e.g. Muller 1999)*	Downwards configurational causes Higher level organisational systems affecting the institutional mechanism observed. *(e.g. Thompson 2003)*

Figure 8.1 Significant Types of Causal Mechanism

types or Forms of causal powers

suggest that four forms of causal process are particularly common in organizational research.

    — norms + rules

①   Normative powers and potentials emerge from enduring patterns in the activities of agents who constitute specific institutional mechanisms. For example, employees tend to have specific levels of absenteeism and turnover, intensity in work activity, skill use, and patterns of social interaction. These activities, which constitute the habitual patterns of everyday life that continually recreate and, potentially, transform specific institutional mechanisms, can be considered in terms of their antecedents and causes. It is useful to consider this normative dimension of institutional mechanisms because analysing typical behaviour facilitates a better understanding of participant actions, how these are affected by broader or external contexts and the internal motivations people have as they engage with particular routines.

②   Configurational powers and potentials, on the other hand, are those that owe their existence to specific spatial distribution of people, where 'there is a sense in which the members of the organization work together like parts of a machine to produce collective effect' (Elder-Vass 2010: 157). The archetypal example is Adam Smith's pin factory: rather than each individual producing whole pins, the factory method breaks down the production of pins into a series of specialized roles, the combination of which produces substantially more pins. Here, it is the specific combination of effort, rather than the powers of atomized individuals, that is a causal property of the group or institution. It is useful to consider this dimension because differently ordered and sized institutions have different powers and potentials, even if actors constituting them reproduce similar norms and values (observing a game between unevenly matched team usually demonstrates this point).

③   In upwards causation, the causal powers of the parts interact to affect the causal powers of the whole (*superconstruction*). For example, changing interpersonal relationships at the level of teams can affect the speed of production at the level of the production unit. ④ In downwards causation, the emergent relations are altered as a consequence of transformations within a 'higher level' organizational entity or system, of which the case is partially constitutive (*intrastructuration*). For example, when an individual joins an organization she typically agrees to act in accordance to an assigned role (as an employee, treasurer, team member, etc.). In effect, the role incumbent is altered as a result of accepting the role. In this case, 'the higher level entity... acts *through* the individual; those properties that the individual acquires by occupying the role are essentially properties of the organization localised in the individual' (Elder-Vass 2010: 158, original emphasis).

Examining adherence to organizational roles, such as the behaviour of an employee in a corporation, facilitates exploration of normative powers and potentials. These powers and potentials are also apparent within broader social fields (see also Mutch in this volume), such as national systems, and a good example of a study that considers this type of power and potential is that of Muller (1999). He studied the uptake of human resource policy and practices within a class of cases (corporations within the German organizational system), and found that some human resource practices (job security, sophisticated training, and employee involvement) occurred automatically and without the activity of human resources departments because the legal and regulatory rule system demanded or encouraged certain institutional practices within German employers. When human resource departments attempted to implement other practices (notably appraisals and performance related pay) these did not happen automatically and met with resistance because they conflicted with cultural norms (such as those concerning equity, autonomy, and trust) and other institutional mechanisms (such as trade unions) that operated within the same organizational system. Here, normative dispositions that were reproduced within a specific national regulatory regime and culture led to specific patterns in the reproduction of human resource practices at lower organizational levels.

The powers and potentials of norms act in both directions—the normative logics of local groups can have particular consequences for institutional mechanisms at levels above. One study that reflects this logic is that of Taylor and Bain (2003), who analysed workplace humour and collective identity in a call centre in the UK. In what was described as a rather oppressive organizational regime, workers used informal humour and cynicism about managerial motives to find space to 'be themselves' despite their negative experience of work. Subsequently, trade unions tapped into these local norms and, in doing so, engendered more formal acts of resistance to managerial prerogative. In this case, local joking rituals came to have organizational consequences well beyond the levels at which they emerged: they became collectively articulated to challenge the dominance of management ideas.

As with normative powers and potentials (and whilst recognizing that the two are empirically interrelated) configurational powers and potentials also act in two directions. Causal influences in both directions and of different types can be observed in Barker's (1993) exploration of 'self-managed' teamwork. He explored how the devolution of authority to teams transformed local norms which, in turn, had broader organizational consequences. Initially, a specific configurational change, in which supervisors were removed and responsibilities devolved to teams, was imposed 'top down' by senior managers who wanted to encourage cooperation at the level of the group. Subsequent to this configurational change, and what is, perhaps, most interesting about this case, novel 'bottom-up' developments ensued. Specifically, and in the absence of an authority figure, workers started sanctioning one another and became less accepting of 'slack' than the old supervisory regime: workers actually internalized broader organizational goals and norms more strongly. This stronger internalization of organizational norms had consequences at higher levels: self-control within the workforce led to reduced supervisory costs and increasing productivity. At the same time, power relations, which were highly visible within more bureaucratic supervisory regimes, were more obscure because teams disciplined themselves in the absence of an authority figure.

Finally, Thompson (2003) offers an example of a more configurational relationship that operated from the top down. His analysis, which focuses on what he calls 'financialized economies' such as the UK, considered how local employment institutions were affected by these systems. He argues that 'forms of financial competition reflect the requirement to meet the expectations of the capital market' (p. 366). Consequential forms of financial organization, such as high remuneration packages for senior managers, effectively tied their interests to those of organizational owners and shareholders, encouraging short-term strategies (such as divestment, delayering, and downsizing) to secure more immediate returns for owners and shareholders. Such organizational developments, which operate at the top of organizational structures, have direct consequences for management practice and experiences of employment. In particular, attempts to meet employee expectations, in terms of better jobs and remuneration, for example, are inhibited because these outcomes would be 'at odds under the interrelated impacts of globalization, the shift to shareholder value in capital markets and systemic rationalization across the whole value chain of firms' (p. 371).

It is notable that both Thompson and Muller do not extend their analyses using specific case studies, so they are more akin to the 'generative institutional analysis' outlined in chapter 2. However, both offer good illustrations of how broader normative rules transmitted through organized systems impact on institutional mechanisms at lower organizational levels. As such, these are studies of a class of cases and also demonstrate the interaction of levels: the higher level acts through the case(s) examined. Here our OCSs cease to be *of* the level being studied, and different classes of organization and types of case (governments, legislators, councils, corporations, etc.) constitute the broader organizational system examined.

These exemplar studies also illustrate the intimate interconnectedness and practical inseparability of normative and configurational powers and potentials: the dimensions always come in combination. The distinction is purely conceptual. The human resources outcome in Muller's study depended on a combination of normative and configurational powers and potentials at national and local organizational levels; local normative behaviours in Taylor and Bain's study transformed organizational capabilities at higher organizational levels; organizational changes in Barker's study transformed how actors embodied norms and this had broader organizational consequences; and, in Thompson's analysis, patterns of organization at the level of the financial system limited what managers could deliver at a local level. In all these studies a particular organization of norms was configured in a particular way to inform the institutional mechanism observed. Despite this, we assert it both possible and useful to distinguish between configurational and normative powers and potentials that constitute institutional mechanisms.

DEVELOPING NOVEL INSIGHTS

When using OCSs to develop new knowledge about institutional mechanisms, it is particularly useful in the design phase of the research project to reflect on existing theory and knowledge. At this stage an effort can be made to ensure that the research is aimed at something new or under-explored. Where existing theory fails to explain what is observed there is an opportunity to abduct and retroduct new forms of understanding. It should be noted, however, that the research process is not typically a linear progression from identifying novelty to abduction and then retroduction. It is usually quite messy and is likely to involve false starts as the researcher oscillates between exploring what we know, on the one hand, and considering that which is 'out there' but inadequately explained, on the other.

There are, however, specific tactics we can employ in the effort to maximize our chances of developing novel research, which are explored in this section. To illustrate these tactics, examples will be drawn from research that uses Labour Process Theory (LPT). LPT has been chosen, in particular, because it is a well-established body of theory and related research, so there are many studies to draw on. It has also been argued to be generally consonant with critical realism (see Thompson and Vincent 2010). Initially, a little space is dedicated to exploring this theoretical tradition because this will create space to consider the particular role of theory in realist OCSs.

Labour Process Theory

LPT aims to explain how conditions within and beyond workplaces interact to affect emergent labour processes at any specific institutional level. Downwardly, the capitalist system is seen to possess particular causal imperatives within institutional mechanisms. Specifically, firm survival depends on the creation of value within production and the appropriation of this value by the firm's owners (profit or valorization). This is because, in cases where firms are unproductive and profits are inadequate, owners and managers are impelled to transform their businesses and investments, or they may lose both. In an upward direction, human effort at the point of production is essentially indeterminate (prosaically, the effort we put into the working day is not constant) so that the firm is also faced with the problem of converting human *potential* into actual effort in order to ensure capital is extracted from labour at a rate that is comparable with competitors—as outlined above, the alternative induces the potential for firm closure (see Littler 1990). That is, if the conversion is not successful at local level, implications are felt higher up the system. Jaros (2010: 71, emphasis original; see also Edwards 1986 for the origin of 'structured antagonism') succinctly summarizes the theoretical propositions that follow from this as:

> Capital's need to *control* labour; a logic of *accumulation* that impels refinement of technology and administration; a fundamental, *structured antagonism* between capital and labour; and because it is the place where labour is valorised, the 'labour process', the point of production, is *privileged* for analyses.

Edwards (1990) also suggests that, as labour processes are bound within specific institutional mechanisms (such as teams, divisions, firms, conglomerates, and supply chains), they are also relatively autonomous. In CR terms they are institutional mechanisms in themselves which evolve according to their own logics.

In summary, LPT uses a set of general abstractions about the nature of both the human condition *and* capitalist competition to make assertions about how these combine to inform particular tendencies within institutional mechanism (hierarchical organization, 'structured antagonism', etc.). Subsequently, the researcher is left to explore how these tendencies play out within specific organizational settings. Ultimately, and pretty much as soon as the researcher enters the field, she is presented with a bewildering array of opportunities to explore how the labour process is manifest in a particular situation, exceptions to its assertions, and areas in need of qualification. There are, as a result, ample grounds for a range of case-based analyses, which have become a methodological mainstay within this line of research.

Exploratory and Exceptional Cases

In *exploratory case studies* the goal is to discover the consequences, at a specific level, of a specific organizational development. These can either be known changes within the context (governance structures, legal regulations, strategic positions, etc.) or constituents (internal structures, normative practices). The key point is that the researcher is or becomes aware of a change that has occurred or is occurring with the case study being undertaken to see what happens as a result of the change. The research of Barker (1993), outlined previously, offers a good illustration of this type of logic. As we saw, he was interested in the consequences of self-managed teams which were a relatively novel organizational development at the time of his study. He identified a manager from a firm who had recently implemented self-managed teams and used this relationship to develop an ethnographic case-based analysis of the organizational consequences of this change. In doing so, he articulated how this innovation had consequences at the level of the subject, the team, and the broader organization within which the team resided.

One does not have to identify any specific novel variance in the conditions of an organization before one enters the field: it is possible to select a case simply because it seems to be different from other cases, and it is often possible to discover a case which you thought typical to be exceptional in some unexpected way. The logic of the argument by Stake (2005) is that all organizations are unique and therefore exceptional to an extent, but they also share features within particular groupings (see also DiMaggio and Powell 1983). Where there are marked differences within an organization when compared to that which is thought to be normal for that field or class of cases, it is possible to explain the novel mechanism that impelled the observed difference. Such *exceptional cases studies* have the analytical purpose of working through the combination of forces (both within and beyond the organization investigated) that provide a more adequate account of why the case does not do what we might expect. The orientating question is 'why is my case exceptional or different and what can this tell us about the world?'

A good example of this logic is the research of Jenkins et al. (2010). They explore the case of 'VoiceTel', a call centre that had been particularly successful and was expanding. Existing labour process research suggests that call centres in the UK operate with relatively oppressive regimes of surveillance and control which render them sites of tension and resistance (see Taylor and Bain 2003). However, there were very few observations of worker malcontent at VoiceTel. Workers said they enjoyed their jobs and followed the rules. Indeed, they internalized the rules, with the owners of the firm benefiting greatly 'from the value that emanated from hiring women who were capable of utilizing their socialized selves to provide quality customer interactions' (Jenkins et al. 2010: 561). The problem was to understand why relationships at VoiceTel were cordial when similar organizations were generally characterized as negative working environments.

Whilst Jenkins et al. (2010) do not, themselves, assert that they abduct a novel generative mechanism, this is implicit in their account. For example, they describe how the observed consensual behaviour was 'informed by multiple influences beyond management prescription' (p. 546). More specifically, they describe how the general conditions of the local labour market (in which there were few 'good' jobs), the hiring policy (which created a convivial atmosphere by using recommendations and workers' social connections), and the form of work organization (which gave the workers control over their relationships with clients), all marked the VoiceTel environment as 'different'. As such, they demonstrate that it was the particular conditions within and surrounding this labour process that rendered it exceptional.

The Qualifying Case

Whilst theory has an essential role in our explanations, it is important to recognize that theories are partial and necessarily so. Arguably, the best theories are relatively parsimonious to the extent that they are not seeking to explain the sum of all causal forces but, instead, elucidate the particular connectedness of specific levels where these either have not been assessed (a deduced inference) or are difficult to assess locally and empirically (associated with 'deep' causes). Given the partial nature of all theory and the complex, open, and multiply determined nature of reality, theories will inevitably need to be *qualified* in relation to particular circumstances. We make such qualifications in order to understand the intersections of different causes that may operate at different levels and combine to affect the particular events we observe. Here, the effort is to develop a better causal explanation of institutional mechanisms by exploring the interactions between powers of different types.

LPT is, quite explicitly, developed from a limited set of theoretical resources (see Thompson 1990). Whilst it extends from a limited range of assertions about the human condition and capitalist competition, it is rather looser and vaguer about specific manifestations of labour processes (which are left open to the empirical and theoretical assertions of the researcher). It does not, for example, say much about other phenomena (whether ideological, technical, gendered, racial, emotional, regulatory, etc.) which transcend labour processes and also affect outcomes. From the point of view of supporters of LPT, these influences are important and which is important in any location and how will be a matter for empirical analyses. Equally, however, they are also a matter for other theoretical resources (theories about politics, technology, gender, ethnicity, and so on). As a result, there is often a need to combine different theoretical lenses (*theoretical pluralism*) to build better causal explanation of the range of generative mechanisms that most adequately explains the institutional mechanism observed.

A good example of a qualifying case is offered by Cockburn (1983). She analysed the intersections of gendered, technological, and organization within the labour processes of the printing industry. Her analysis of the labour processes revealed, as LPT might predict, that managers used technological and organizational developments in the effort to increase their control (see also Braverman 1974). Alongside this, she also observed how a group of skilled men maintained their position as 'skilled' workers, despite the apparently negative labour process context. They did this, specifically, by distinguishing their work from that of women and preserving their masculine approach and values. From a CR point of view, the causal mechanisms explained within the analysis combined gendered processes and workplace processes, which intersected within a particular institutional mechanism. In demonstrating the significance of this mechanism, Cockburn accounts for an important general tendency towards male dominance at work.

ANALYSING DATA

As the goal of any case study is to explain something new, the outcome of the research will not be known in advance. However, some projects are easier to guide and develop than others. Targeting one's efforts can be relatively straightforward when the goal of the research is to explain something quite specific, such as 'what are the consequences of policy X for organization Y?' However, targeting one's attention may be less easy where the researcher is motivated by a more general interest, such as 'why is firm X unsuccessful?' In order to encourage movement towards a better understanding when one has less defined interests or an unknown set of causes, this section explores modes of data analysis and tactics for using theory in developing understanding of institutional mechanisms. Here, we develop the point in chapter 2, that realist research designs typically start in a more expansive and exploratory phase before targeting what seems to matter most in explaining the specific mechanisms observed.

As we have seen, causal powers do not have to be actual or manifest to be real: they can be deep and hidden from view. Abducting the mechanisms apparent and retroducing their antecedents and causes can thus be difficult. However, and in the effort to explain institutional mechanisms, researchers may engage with specific analytical tactics to unpack the configurational, normative, and broader contextual conditions to which they relate. These are (1) analyses of how actors and groups are articulated and positioned—*configurational analysis*, (2) analyses of how the people tend to respond to their situations –*normative analysis*, (3) analyses of how broader contextual conditions manifest themselves within the case—*field analysis*, and, (4) analyses of how (1), (2), and (3) can be combined to explain the genesis of causal powers and potentials of the emergent institutional mechanism—*institutional explanation*. Below a brief section is dedicated to each of these types of analysis. Subsequently, the final section offers a summary case, which describes how these analytical stages worked themselves out in a specific research project.

Configurational Analysis

From the early stages of an OCS project it is useful to start developing an analysis of any institution's configuration. This involves a kind of 'thick description' of the structure of activities that inhere within the case. The objective is not to elucidate, in detail, why behaviour is meaningful to the actors involved (cf. Stake 2005) but to set the scene in such a way as to account for the articulation of the particular institutional mechanism that interests us.

There is no prescription as to which data are needed to undertake this ana- lytical process, although interviews, organizational charts, and other docu- ments are likely to be particularly useful. The goal is to abduct a basic outline of the specific powers and potentials of the institutional mechanism observed by describing where people are, the subunits they form (if this is the case), the technologies they use and/or develop, what their (and the technologies') capa- bilities and potentials are, how people tend to behave, and how these things tend to combine to produce particular outcomes (levels of growth, productiv- ity, happiness, conflict, or whatever other regularity takes one's interest).

This account may also explore the normative expectations generally associ- ated with particular roles, or how the organization is supposed to work, as this is often quite different from what is actually the case. The overall goal is to identify the size, shape, and general pattern of activities associated with a particular institutional mechanism, which can subsequently be explored and refined. The outcome can be likened to a road map of the institutional mecha- nisms explored. As the map is constructed and the data exhausted, a point of *configurational saturation* is reached (see also Glaser and Strauss 1967). After this point, no new data about agents' various locations and activities will be discovered, and a specifically articulated set of actors will have been described.

Normative Analysis

The second but by no means separate or independent type of analysis is *normative analysis*. Here, in a manner congruent with social construction- ist approaches, the objective is to explain how and why actors and groups of actors behave as they do in specific situations. The goal is to explore their *projective tendencies*: their behavioural norms and expectations, as well as the extent to which norms are followed consistently. Matters are particularly inter- esting where there is a gap between *normative expectations* (such as manage- rial orders, operating procedures, legal requirements, which are often defined as part of the field analysis) and *normative tendencies* (or how organizational members actually behave in specific contexts). Observations of difference highlight areas of tension that are likely to be significant. Alternative norma- tive pressures coexist, such as where one's peers and one's superiors have dis- tinctive orientations to the content and nature of work. Understanding which norms take precedence, when and where, as well as how they are incongru- ently related, creates space to explore social dominance and conflict within local experiences.

Interviews and observation are particularly useful for normative analyses. It is usually impossible to interview and observe everyone within a given field, but one should try to canvass a diverse cross section of different types of respondent in the effort to ensure a broad palette of norms and values is covered. Some theoretical replication, in which similar samples are taken from compared cases, may also be employed to work out how similar mechanisms play out in different settings (see also Yin 2009). As a rule of thumb, it is important to try to interview respondents from all the social groups within the field(s) examined, although practical matters often prevent this happening so that one must also be led by the regularity one is seeking to explain and the resources available (see also Stake 2005).

THEORETI-
CAL
REPLICATION

The goal is to develop an effective appreciation of how the projects of different groups vary and to invite participants to reflect on how they frame their own situations. This stage of the analysis is complete at the point of *agential saturation* (see also Glaser and Strauss 1967), when the normative tendencies of all the groups within the institutional mechanism are known and understood from the point of view of the participants.

Field Analysis

In field analysis an effort is made to describe and explain the conditions of the broader organizational system and the other organizations to which our case relates in order to better explain how these are causally implicated in the patterns of events we observe. This broader analysis can be guided by existing theories that purport to explain something about the empirical markers we come to be interested in. In effect, existing theory can be used to assist the retroductive step 'backwards' from the empirical regularities observed to the contextual features that help better explain why matters are so and not otherwise. So, and reusing an example introduced above (Jenkins at al. 2010), if we become interested in the apparent lack of tension and conflict in a call centre, various conditions are likely to affect actor choices. Some of these, such as the tightness (or otherwise) of the local labour market, may suggest themselves as more salient or important causes of local outcomes than others, such as the availability of broadband from a local Internet provider. Whilst the availability of broadband may say something about conditions of existence of the call centre, the analysis of the labour markets allows one to make a connection between levels that appear to have implications for workers' opinions about their own work: labour market theory suggests that where labour markets contain fewer opportunities people may be more likely to look positively on jobs that are viewed more negatively where there are more opportunities available. As we (theoretically) explore potential causes of specific patterns of events it becomes possible to assemble a range of contextual features that can be combined to better explain patterns of activity in the specific institutional context.

It is usually important to undertake field analyses, even where researchers are more narrowly interested in explaining the particular consequences of a known change (of the 'what are the consequences of policy X for organization Y?' type). As demonstrated within the analysis of Muller (1999), the implementation of specific human resources policies was, in practice, mediated by norms and regulations that were properties of a broader organizational system (the German national economy) rather than any specific organization. As such, it is important that researchers immerse themselves within the minutiae of the case and the environment that their case forms part of, because only with intimate knowledge of the constitution and external conditions of the case is the researcher able to retroduct which contextual conditions have a significant impact on local activities (either through comparison or recourse to existing theory).

Institutional Explanation

An important goal of realist OCSs is to understand how micro-level normative practices condition the causal powers of institutional mechanisms through an analysis that also accounts for broader context(s), which affect the possibilities for action and actor choices within our cases. The previous three forms of analysis concentrate on different elements of this equation: configurational analysis reveals more about *what* institutional mechanisms are, their powers and potential; normative analysis reveals more about *how* the institutional mechanisms are routinely reproduced; field analysis reveals more about *why* the institutional mechanisms are as they are and not otherwise by revealing how their specific manifestation is affected by conditions that operate at other levels. In short, by combining our configurational, normative, and field analyses we can build better institutional explanations of the specific mechanisms we observe and the causal forces that affect their specific manifestation.

As these forms of analyses are combined, the researcher's task is to refine their accounts and descriptions to distil the separable but interacting influences of the various significant causal powers apparent within their cases. As we saw above, at least four types of causal power are significant for the purposes of revealing the causes of institutional mechanisms (see Figure 8.1). When developing institutional explanations, these become useful as targets for description:

1. *Downwards normative causal explanation.* Descriptive analyses and theories combine to explain how normative expectations within the broader context (cultures, laws, ideas, strategies, etc.) have an impact on the causal properties of institutional mechanism studied (see Muller 1999).

2. *Upwards normative causal explanation.* Descriptive analyses and theories combine to explain the ways in which normative practices within the organization studied have an impact on the causal properties of the institutional mechanism studied (see Taylor and Bain 2003).

3. *Downwards configurational causal explanation.* Descriptive analyses and theories combine to explain how the properties of broader organizational systems (possibly at multiple levels) interact to have an impact on the causal properties of the institutional mechanism studied (see Thompson 2003).

4. *Upwards configurational causal explanations.* Descriptive analyses and theories combine to explain how subunits are articulated to have an impact on the causal properties of the institutional mechanism studied (see Barker 1993).

As multiple causal influences interact to shape outcomes in any institutional mechanisms, the explanatory accounts we generate will necessarily employ these causal targets variously to illuminate the peculiarities and commonalities of the case(s) at hand.

ILLUSTRATIVE CASE *(their example)*

In this final section, an effort is made explore how these forms of analysis and explanation-building were developed in a single case study that sought to explain a particularly complex institutional mechanism (Vincent 2008). The case study was a 'Strategic Partnership' between Govco (a large and bureaucratic government department) and Futuretech (a multinational business software development specialist). The Partnership was established so that Govco could access Futuretech's stock of in-house technology and expertise, which could be used to improve on Govco's unique proprietary IT systems. As well as making a profit from the arrangement, Futuretech would benefit from having a large and high-profile client who could act as a referee with prospective clients. The Partnership emerged to manage the distinctive ways that each organization depended on the relationship.

The Institutional Mechanisms as a Configuration of Norms

Configurational analysis revealed the existence of a group of senior managers from both organizations (the Strategic Partnership) who worked together through a series of meetings and committees in the effort to achieve the objectives of both organizations. This group was originally constituted by IT experts, employed by either Govco or Futuretech, who knew a great deal about technological possibilities, capabilities, and susceptibilities within both organizations. They were given responsibility, firstly, for defining the work Futuretech would deliver and, subsequently, ensuring that it was delivered. At a basic level, the Partnership was an institutional mechanism that sought to understand Govco's needs, Futuretech's capabilities, and how these could be brought together for the benefit of both organizations.

The managers of the Partnership had a particular ability to act, which gave them a good deal of latitude to decide what 'good performance' looked like. They could define the 'scopes of work' undertaken, and some technologies were much easier to deliver than others. As a result, where performance dipped below expectations any underperformance could be reconciled against easier-to-deliver work. Contractual targets, which stipulated that the price per unit of technology delivered would decline over the five years of the contract, were consistently delivered. So, in some ways the relationship was effective: it hit contractual targets and IT user surveys showed improved perceptions of performance. However, there was also evidence to suggest this cooperation was less than effective—some less senior respondents complained about the effectiveness of the technologies delivered and suggested that, over time, Futuretech became able to deliver increasingly 'off-the-peg' rather than 'bespoke' technologies for its partner. Ultimately, it is likely to have been more generally recognized that the institutional mechanism was failing to deliver as effectively as it might: the contract was not renewed after the five-year term ended.

This view of failure was not shared within the Partnership: the normative analysis suggested that members of this Partnership organization believed in its success. They conformed to particular values and norms. They boasted that it was difficult for outsiders to tell who was from Govco and who was from Futuretech. They saw the value of 'working in Partnership' (in practice, this meant Futuretech should be allowed to make a profit, with the proviso that Govco should also have access to better and cheaper technology). All those within the Partnership had a strong interest in the organizations being a success (future careers depended on it!), and despite apparent failings, both sides extolled the merits of the relationship.

This brief description suggests that a combination of configurational and normative analysis may be used to produce what can be described as a *level-abstracted* view of an institutional mechanism (Elder-Vass 2010: 49), or one that considers the impact of the whole entity in isolation from its context. The existence of an institutional mechanism (the Partnership) works itself out as (1) a particular set of local enablements and constraints, which defined the Partnership's 'room for manoeuvre', and (2) a particular constellation of people with specific agential potentials (skills, forms of knowledge, attitudes, etc.). However, this description throws up as many questions as answers. For example, why did the Partnership have so much latitude to determine its own 'successes'? And, why could Futuretech get away with delivering apparently more shoddy and less customer-focused technology as the relationship developed? Answering these questions involves taking retroductive steps 'backwards' to consider the antecedents that pre-formed relations and the possibilities manifest within the institutional mechanism itself. At this point, field analysis and existing theory became an invaluable tool.

Theorizing the Significance of Field Forces

As part of the development of this case analysis, the research questioned how others theorized the structure and operation of similar cooperative inter-organizational forms, resulting in a trawl of the available literature. In order to develop a better causal explanation (one which could account for the questions that remained unanswered in 'level-abstracted' configurational and normative analysis), various theories were considered and combined in the effort to provide a more effective insight into the antecedents that conditioned the Partnership. Three theories, in particular, appeared to be useful. These were *transaction cost economics*, which highlights how inter-organizational contracting can be affected by the type of product developed and exchanged, and how this relates to the organizations involved in the exchange; *resource dependency theory*, which invites us to consider each partner's relative dependency on the other's resources and abilities and how this affects relations; and, *institutional theory*, which suggests that broader ideological trends and norm-enforcing mechanisms shape local behaviour. There is not space here to do justice to the complexities of these theoretical frameworks or why they were selected. Instead, we explain *how* these theories were incorporated within an explanatory framework for the institutional mechanisms observed.

An important first step in developing CR models of the generative processes that cause specific institutional mechanisms is to interrogate any theoretical resource which claims explanatory power over our class of cases from the point of view of a CR meta-theory. The goal is to establish the extent to which it is consonant with and can be assimilated into CR explanations in general. As the vast majority of theories are constructed by people who are not realists, there are numerous opportunities for qualifying exactly what a CR explanation may take from *any* theoretical resource (indeed, this is an explicit objective of Vincent 2008). In short, theoretical assimilation creates opportunities to develop novel explanations of specific event regularities by incorporating insights from the various theories available.

For some theories (in the case of this research project, resource dependency theory and institutional theory), this can be a relatively unproblematic endeavour because the theories in question are relatively parsimonious in specifying the things they can account for (even if the theory's protagonists are not always aware of their specific limitations). However, transaction-cost economics is based on an economist's view of human agency (wherein all that matters is the personal utility-maximizing behaviour of atomistic agents), which is incompatible with the richer view of human agency advocated by most realists (see Marks and O'Mahoney, this volume). Some theoretical reframing was thus necessary to redeploy this conceptual resource within an overarching critical realist explanation.

This was considered important groundwork because the theory seemed to talk to the data itself: our particular choice of theories is not arbitrary but results from establishing an intimate relationship between a theory that more adequately explains *something* about the antecedent causes of the institutional mechanisms explored, on the one hand, and data from the case, on the other. Specifically, transaction-cost economics suggested that, where contractual mechanisms govern complex, uncertain, changeable, and idiosyncratic tasks or undertakings, the actors involved will necessarily have greater autonomy in determining their own ends. Data from the field confirmed that technologies were developing quickly within the market and that Govco's IT systems were so idiosyncratic that few outside the Partnership could tell what good performance looked like (benchmarks were used, but none was considered adequate). So, the technologies in the field that surrounded the Partnership were found to be complex, uncertain, changeable, and idiosyncratic. This helped within the theoretical model developed by Vincent (2008) because it helps account for the relative autonomy that senior managers enjoyed within the Partnership.

In this case, the theory is rooted at a particular level (in the field of technology that transcended the Partnership). These were not part of the Partnership as an institutional mechanism in its own right; but they were a consequential condition of the technologies the Partnership was obliged to deal with.

Suffice to say, a similar story can be told for resource dependency theory. The processes of the Partnership accrued knowledge on the side of Futuretech as it developed new technologies for its client. This resulted in a temporally emergent imbalance in the expertise of Govco's and Futuretech's agents, who constituted the Partnership. Futuretech's agents thus became increasingly powerful in asserting their own technological imperative and interests, even if these did not meet Govco's needs exactly. This analysis of dependency relationships helped account for a particular tendency in the Partnership, in which the value for money Govco received seemed to decline as the relationship endured.

Finally institutional theory, which suggests institutional mechanisms are conditioned by dominant organizing logics that operate across broader social formations, contributed to the explanation by connecting the Partnership's tendency to extol its own successes with local career interests and the broader public sector policy regime. At the time of the Partnership's inception, private sector provision was prioritized over public sector provision as a matter of policy prescription, owing to a generalized ideological faith in the relative efficiency of private sector providers (even where transactional considerations suggested this may not actually be the case). In these circumstances, it is unsurprising that few were shouting about the Partnership's failures.

Developing Transferable Explanations

The analysis of the Partnership was used to develop a theoretical model of the generative mechanism that could account for the specific empirical tendencies observed within the case. Having trawled the literature for explanatory theories and considered these in relation to the data available, three sets of ideas were used to enrich the explanation of the Partnership. These theories added richness to the explanation by rendering more explicit the causal dynamics that existed between the Partnership and its antecedents, including the material (e.g. technology/resource) and ideational (norms, discourses) phenomena to which it related. Ultimately, this combination of theories provided a new supporting model, which made it easier to understand how the context of the Partnership affected its actors' patterns of behaviour.

In conclusion, theoretical models developed in OCSs become a transferable resource in themselves that can be reapplied in similar analyses of similar institutional mechanisms. More specifically, and in relation to the Partnership, the combination of insights about idiosyncratic technical conditions, mutual resource dependencies, and a supporting institutional rule system, which inhered within this case, are likely to be present in cooperative inter-organizational forms more generally. This model can, then, be used as a basis for building alternative explanations of the particular configuration of contextual determinants that shape other similar structures. Knowledge obtained about a single case study is, as a result, not confined to the boundaries of the case itself (Stake 2005) but is theoretically transferable across a class of cases. Thus, the theoretical models we develop through our OCSs, as we explain the peculiarities of our cases, also help articulate the specific conditions that makes a class of cases classifiable in terms of their common antecedents. It is this form of theoretical generalization that realist OCSs should seek to extend and develop.

9

Comparing Cases

Ian Kessler and Stephen Bach

INTRODUCTION

The tenets of critical realism encourage a particular interest in the case-study approach to exploring managerial and organizational issues. This is largely related to the emphasis placed by both on context and causation. As an open, non-deterministic paradigm, sensitive to the interaction between structure and agency in stratified entities, critical realism views context or situational influences as crucial to an understanding of processes and emergent outcomes. Presenting the critical realist framework, Elder-Vass (2010: 21) quotes with approval Holland's observation that 'emergence is above all a product of coupled, context-dependent interactions'. It is this capacity to explore issues in context which defines the case study as a distinctive methodological approach. In one of the most widely cited texts on this method, Yin (2009: 18) charac- terizes a case study as 'an empirical inquiry that investigates a contemporary phenomenon in depth and within its real life context'.

At the same time, critical realism has a strong interest in causation, and more particularly underlying generative mechanisms which explain a process or outcome. As Sayer (2000: 14) notes, 'explanation depends on identifying causal mechanisms and how they work and discovering if they have been acti- vated and under what conditions'. This is mirrored in the case-study approach's interest in searching out explanations. As Geering (2007: 45) stresses: 'Case studies, if well constructed, may allow one to peer into the box of causality to locate the intermediate factors lying between some structural case and its purported effect'.

There is, however, some tension between the weight placed upon context and causation within critical realism. There have, for example, been sugges- tions that a matching-case approach, where entities with shared features are purposively selected, is not sensitive enough to those context-specific or situ- ational characteristics which might influence process and outcomes (Locke and Thelen 1995; Edwards 2005). While such concerns are clearly raised as a means of seeking more nuanced explanations, there is a danger that an emphasis on context drives the researcher into an ever deeper engagement with the locally contingent, running the risk of overlooking broader patterns and, in particular, losing sight of cross-cutting causal mechanisms. As Thompson and Smith (2010: 20) note in reviewing numerous workplace case studies of the 1980s, 'whilst this opened a space to see distinctive workplace dynamics, when the "relativity" became the dominant focus, it created the potential, if unintended, legitimation of a narrow frame of analysis'. They stress 'the danger is that the research programme can disappear into micro-level case studies whose causal chain ends at the office door'.

For critical realism, the case study needs to balance the lure of context, which recognizes the influence of specific situational factors, with a broader perspective, acknowledging and seeking to locate wider patterns and generative mechanisms. This chapter argues that the value of the comparative case approach lies in its capacity to identify these broader tendencies or demi-regularities (Lawson 1997), and underlying causal mechanisms, locating them at the appropriate 'door', whether that 'door' is to be found in an 'office' or beyond it. The capacity of the comparative case approach in this respect rests in part on generic features of the case methodology: certainly some sensitivity to context, as well as in-depth, intensive fieldwork generating different types of data. But its contribution to critical realist analysis, particularly relative to the single case, derives from moving beyond locally contingent processes and outcomes to tease out and examine wider patterns and their generative forces. It is argued that this project is advanced by the careful selection of cases on the basis of whether they are likely to reveal patterns of similarity or difference, and a tentative but plausible a priori narrative which explains these patterns and their causes. In presenting this argument the chapter is divided into three main parts. The first outlines generic features of the case-study approach and how they support critical realist analysis. The second outlines the distinctive contribution made by the multiple-case design to this analysis, drawing in the main on examples from the authors' own field of study, employment relations. The third part illustrates the link between multiple-case research and the critical realist approach by presenting a detailed example of research which sought to examine and explain patterns in the shape of the healthcare assistant role in the English National Health Service.

As a prelude to exploring the relative analytical value of the comparative case approach, it is worth (re-)stating the principal tenets of critical realism. These tenets have been set out elsewhere in this volume, so they are presented briefly and in schematic terms. Critical realism is predicated on the capacity of researchers to engage with the 'real', typically assuming the form of observable and knowable structures which constrain but do not determine agency in the realm of the 'actual'. These structures are susceptible to influence or elaboration by agents across space and time, the latter being captured by the notion of the morphogenetic cycle (Archer 1995). Agency is not only exercised in structural elaboration. It is also apparent in morphostasis, the preservation or ongoing maintenance of structures. Indeed both morphogenesis and morphostasis are based on the assumption that structures have emergent properties, which plausibly affect agents, and function in a cascading fashion at different levels. As an open paradigm, critical realism views the realization of these emergent properties as highly contingent and uncertain. Nonetheless they are likely to yield tendencies or demi-regularities which need to be explained. The search for causation is core to the critical realist project but remains problematic: generative mechanisms are not always readily and easily grasped, often underlying the 'real' and the 'actual'. Indeed the covert nature of causation encourages retroductive reasoning techniques which rely on inference and further exploration rather than on abstracted and deductive forms of modelling.

CRITICAL REALISM AND THE CASE-STUDY APPROACH

A distinction is typically drawn between research approaches which rely on a single case and multiple cases. This distinction can reflect profound ontological and epistemological differences (Yin 2009: 53), which rule out the use of one or the other approach: for example, meaning can be seen as closely tied to context, encouraging a focus on the singular case, and challenging the validity of the comparative approach (Gomm et al. 2000). More prosaically, the choice of approach might be related to the nature of the research question under consideration. Looking beyond these differences, there are shared, generic features of single- and multiple-case methods which support critical realist analysis. They are presented in brief because they provide the foundation for the more specific contribution made by multiple cases to critical realism; in other words, while comparing cases has added-value to a critical realist analysis, this still rests on the scope to draw upon these generic elements of the case approach.

The case approach is based on in-depth analysis of a limited number of entities. It is this in-depth analysis which allows for a focus on causation. Harrison and Easton (2004: 195) note: 'The role of the researcher is to keep in mind the question 'why?' when working with the data. The use of case studies allows a researcher to attempt to tease out ever-deepening layers of reality in the search for generative mechanisms and influential contingencies.' As implied, in-depth analysis facilitates a thorough examination of the case as an internally stratified entity, but this form of analysis also relates causation to the case as holistic and embedded. Ackroyd (2009: 535) makes a distinction between extensive and intensive case studies, the former a holistic perspective which 'describes all major processes at work and their interactions', the latter presenting 'no claim to holism' and 'focusing on particular generative mechanisms and making expedient use of the organisational context'. It is a distinction, however, which needs to be treated with some care. While understanding is certainly rooted in context, it is the very interaction between the parts of a case as a holistic entity which often creates a generative mechanism. Indeed critical realism views parts as typically combining to create structures with distinctive emergent properties to constrain or empower agents.

The in-depth analysis associated with the case approach can also be related to its multi-method research design. On occasion, the case study has been viewed as solely founded upon qualitative data (Miles 1979) and the research techniques needed to collect such data including observation, focus groups, and interviews. However, it is more generally acknowledged that the case approach is a research strategy or design which, depending on the nature of the research questions being addressed, seeks qualitative and quantitative, including survey, data (Yin 1981: 58; Bryman 2004b: 49; Swanborn 2010: 13). This is not to suggest that cases invariably draw upon both data sources: cases can exclusively be based on qualitative or quantitative data. However, it is the use of multiple methods which has particular value to the critical realist. In part such value derives from the scope to triangulate data (Teddlie and Tashakkori 2009). The use of complementary data sources establishes a more assured basis for the identification of tendencies or demi-regularities. But perhaps more significantly these different data sources become the basis for retroductive reasoning as attempts are made to infer patterns and causation from them. As Downward and Mearman (2007: 77) note, 'mixed methods triangulation can be understood as the manifestation of retroduction, the logic of inference espoused by critical realism'.

Such retroduction might well be at its liveliest when there is a disconnect between qualitative and quantitative case data: this inevitably prompts inquiry into the reasons for data misalignment. For example, our own research on how registered nurses viewed and used healthcare assistants (HCA) in a number of case-study hospitals revealed a marked difference in outlook depending on different data sources: interview data suggested that nurses saw the HCA-contribution to their working lives as extremely positive, while survey data presented a much more qualified picture (Kessler et al. 2012). Such a finding might well relate to the character of the research techniques: there is an extensive literature on how techniques influence subject responses (Teddlie and Tashakkori 2009). However, linked to debates on the development of the nursing profession, this data-disconnect might plausibly be seen to reflect genuine nurse ambiguity about HCAs: on the one hand, routine tasks could be delegated to HCAs allowing nurses to advance their professionalization project by acquiring and deepening specialist, technical skills; on the other, the very divestment of such tasks ran the risk of undermining traditional nurse claims to professional status based on the holistic provision of care (Doherty 2007).

THE DISTINCTIVENESS OF THE COMPARATIVE APPROACH

Selecting and Theorizing

The analytical and theoretical value of a comparative approach rests on the retention of the generic features of the case-study method highlighted in the preceding section. Given resource constraints and the likely trade-off between intensity and breadth, this might well be problematic, placing limits on the scale of comparative case design. While clearly much depends on the nature of the case—its size and complexity—and the resources available, Pettigrew (1997) suggests that six to eight cases represent a manageable number at any given time. On the assumption, however, that the comparative case approach retains its context sensitivity, mixed methodology, and intensity, the key question remains as to whether and in what ways it makes a distinctive analytical and theoretical contribution, particularly within a critical realist framework. Some commentators, and indeed researchers, remain vague on this issue. As Harrison and Easton (2004: xx) note, 'the use of multiple cases more often results from the nervousness of the researcher rather than from any profound concerns about epistemology or methodology'. Bryman (2004b: 53) asserts that a comparative case design helps researchers 'understand social phenomena better', but still leaves open how and why it does so.

Rational for multiple cases For the critical realist, the choice of more than one case helps to identify cross-cutting patterns or demi-regularities, while at the same time signalling possible causes and the opportunity to follow them up through deeper analysis. The value of the comparative approach in these terms is predicated on the careful selection of the cases, but this inevitably begs questions as to what constitutes careful selection and how it yields benefits for critical realist analysis. There has been some debate on the design of multiple case studies which *Rationale for selection of cases* helps address these questions. Eisenhardt (1989), for example, suggests three mutually exclusive rationales for the selection of multiple cases: to replicate previous cases; (2) to extend emergent theories; (3) or to fill theoretical categories. Indeed she challenges random case selection as 'neither necessary nor even preferable' arguing that the inevitable limits on the number of cases that can be studied at any one time encourages a more direct focus on, say, extreme or polar types (p. 536). Yin (2009: 54) is also supportive of a directed approach to case selection, but places particular emphasis on replication. Framing his views in positivistic terms, Yin suggests that case replication might be seen as analogous to multiple experiments, with cases chosen to 'either predict similar results (literal replication)' or 'predict different results for anticipated reason (theoretical replication)'.

Eisenhardt and Yin raise two important issues, which need to be considered in carefully selecting cases: the techniques of comparative case selection and the contribution of any selection technique to the explanation of a phenomenon. Both commentators conflate these issues. For example, in viewing her three rationales for case selection as mutually exclusive, Eisenhardt implicitly rules out the possibility that emergent theory might be advanced by using replication. Similarly, Yin makes a false distinction between his sampling techniques—literal and theoretical replication: so if an anticipation of *different* outcomes requires an a priori explanation, it might be argued that an assumption of *similar* outcomes also requires an a priori explanation. Notwithstanding the conflation of these points, Eisenhardt and Yin direct attention to two features of a careful multiple-case design which might support and further a critical realist analysis which focuses on revealing patterns and their underlying causation.

As implied, the first of these features is the case-selection technique, and in particular the purposeful selection of cases. Certainly such an approach to the choice of cases raises practical issues, not least given difficulties in achieving research access, and the temptation to select cases on the basis of convenience (Bryman 2004: 33–3). Purposeful sampling does not negate the possibility of choosing for convenience, but it does suggest that there needs to be some rationale underpinning the sample frame of cases finally selected. This rationale might emerge from some directed, purposive selection process or from retrospective review of cases chosen on the basis of convenience. Whether prospective or retrospective, this rationale might be labelled a 'light theorization' and is the second essential feature of the multiple-case design. 'Light theorization' is a tentative but plausible account of similarities or difference that might be revealed by the case comparison. For the critical realist, it is likely to rest on a narrative which centres on how structure and agency interact at different levels to produce these similarities or differences.

Selecting for Difference and Similarity

While critical realists will baulk at Yin's positivistic language, particularly the suggestion that a multiple-case design equates to an 'experiment' founded upon or generating firm 'predictions', his distinction between different forms of replication, selecting-for-difference and selecting-for-similarity, are useful in highlighting the close relationship between case-selection techniques and light theorization.

In broad terms, selecting cases for difference is lightly theorized as likely to reveal divergence in process and outcomes related to the structural or institutional features which characterize the cases selected. If, counter to the theory, there is a convergence in processes or outcomes, it would suggest greater scope for agency and the weaker influence of these shared emergent properties. By the same token, selecting-for-similarity is lightly theorized as suggesting a convergence in process or outcome which derives from the influence of common case features. Where findings depart from such expectations, it would again encourage re-evaluation of choice and constraint. (For further, more detailed discussion on the method of similarity or difference see Saka-Helmhout in this volume.)

A number of studies, mainly from the field of employment relations, can be drawn upon to illustrate these multiple-case designs based on selecting-to-similarity and selecting-to-difference. While few, if any, have been framed in critical realist terms, they have still aimed to explore the interaction between structure and agency at different levels: country, industry, and organization.

Locke and Thelen's (1995) characterization of the typical methodological design in comparative labour politics provides a useful example of selecting-to-difference. The authors suggest that this design rests on exploring a single process, for example, the restructuring of pay bargaining, in response to shared external pressures, in a range of countries. In this instance, selecting-to-difference involves choosing countries with contrasting institutional arrangements in relation to such issues as corporate governance and employer and worker collective organization. These institutional differences are 'lightly theorized' in that they might plausibly be seen to moderate the impact of external pressures to restructure pay bargaining, leading to variation in the process and outcomes of this restructuring between countries. Indeed, different approaches to restructuring direct attention towards generative mechanisms in the form of properties emerging from a nationally distinctive configuration of institutions, suggesting that national actors might be constrained by embedded local institutions in ways which lead to country variations. Of course, such a case design might reveal similarities in the restructuring of pay bargaining despite national institutional difference, suggesting the potency of external pressures to force convergence.

Edwards's (2004) study of company-level restructuring provides a specific example of this country-based selecting-to-difference approach. Based on a light theorization which suggested that the institutional features associated with distinctive national business systems, not least their industrial relations arrangements, might influence such a corporate restructuring process, Edwards selected four country cases: France, Germany, the Netherlands, and the UK. Using secondary data, the study was able to confirm the importance of national differences in corporate approaches to restructuring, and the impact of national business systems in generating these differences.

Studies have also selected-to-difference according to industry. Here the light theorization relates to the emergent properties associated with the sector and how they might constrain or empower in contrasting ways. Thus, sectors will vary in a number of respects—their technologies, exposure to national and international competition, profitability, and regulation—leading to differences in managerial processes and outcome. As a means of exposing the influence of these features, cases would be selected from various sectors: where sector-based differences in process or outcome emerge they would provide a clue to such industry influence. Where a pattern cut across and remained unrelated to sector, this would suggest a weaker industry influence. Marginson et al.'s (2008) study of variable pay schemes (VPS) and union engagement with them provides an example of selecting-to-difference by industry. The study used a matched sample of six companies in two sectors, retail banking and machinery and equipment. Similarities between sectors, in terms of shared managerial rationales for VPS, were revealed, but also important differences in practice by sector. These differences were meticulously traced back by the authors to variation in industry features: the sectors contrasted in international market exposure, profitability, and work organization. For example, given high profitability and the direct interaction between worker and customer in banking, organizations in the sector 'have been better placed to use bonuses to drive their culture change initiatives and to incentivize and reward staff without adding to fixed costs' (p. 334).

Other studies have selected-to-difference as a means of exploring the relative influence of country *and* sector. In this instance the theorization is more open than one based on country or sector. It suggests that both nation and industry might plausibly be influential, with cases selected in ways which might reveal their relative influence. Such designs have taken slightly different forms. There are examples of studies which have selected-to-difference by country, but held the industry constant. The study by Caroli et al. (2010) on the use of different forms of workforce flexibility selects-to-difference in choosing seven French and six British case organizations, while ensuring these thirteen companies are drawn from the food processing industry. In finding that there were indeed national patterns in the use of different forms of flexibility, with French companies more likely to pursue functional and British numerical flexibility, the authors could more confidently attribute these to country influence having controlled for the industry. Indeed the in-depth case approach allowed the researchers to explore the emergent properties which produced these national differences, highlighting the importance of contrasting legislative frameworks in the domain of employment protection.

A somewhat more sophisticated multiple-case design has selected-to-difference along both the country and industry dimensions, in the hope or expectation of revealing the relative potency of these two factors in generating patterns. This selection is grounded in a light theorization which suggests three plausible possibilities: differences in process and outcome by country; differences by industry which cut across country; differences by organization regardless of and not obviously linked to either country or industry. Marginson et al.'s (2004) study of European Works Councils (EWC) and their impact on managerial decision-making was designed to explore these possibilities. Its comparative case-study design was based on eight multinational companies from the US and the UK across three different industries: engineering, chemical, and food/drink. As no clear pattern of EWC influence by country or industry was revealed, the authors were able to suggest the importance of organizational contingency and the distinctive configuration of structure and agency at this level: whether the company had a European structure; whether they had an industrial relations platform upon which EWCs could build; and whether and how company management and unions were prepared to engage with the EWC.

Finally, a number of studies provide examples of selecting-to-similarity. These have often been sector studies, the multiple-case design drawing upon organizations from the same industry, and privileging a theorization which suggests convergence by sector. For example, Greer and Hauptmeier's (2008) study of labour transnationalism was based on four case organizations—VW, Daimler-Chrysler, Ford, and GM—in the same industry: vehicle manufacturing. The authors explicitly based their comparative case design on the possibility that there would be similarities in labour transnationalism related to characteristics of the auto industry: its domination by a few powerful multinationals competing with each other on price. However, the dominant pattern was one of significant organizational differences in the nature of such transnationalism which, given the focus on a single industry, they suggested reflected the relatively autonomous relationship between structure and agency at this level. Thus, these differences were seen to 'depend on the interaction of management labour strategies in the context of the company structure' (p. 91).

We have argued that comparing case studies supports and furthers critical realist analysis by seeking both to identify patterns and reveal their underlying causation. A careful approach to case-study selection has been presented as crucial in taking forward this analysis, with the need to consider the relationship between case-selection technique—whether cases are selected on the basis of difference or similarity—and 'light theorization' which provides a tentative but plausible rationale for the potential similarities and differences. The findings from such a research design establish a starting point for the development and strengthening of explanations: the light theorization either finds some confirmation or if confounded points to other possible causes. In the next section we provide a more detailed illustration of this approach to multiple-case design.

A MULTIPLE-CASE DESIGN: THE NATURE OF
THE HEALTHCARE ASSISTANT ROLE

The multiple-case design underpinned a research project conducted by one of the authors into the role of a particular occupational role: the healthcare assistant (HCA), a worker supporting registered nurses in British National Health Service (NHS) acute hospitals (Kessler et al. 2012). This project analysed the shape and nature of the HCA role: its contours, tasks, and responsibilities. This section illustrates how the features of multiple-case design sought to reveal and then explain patterns in the distribution of tasks and responsibilities to HCAs by reference to the interaction between structure and agency within the NHS. The section comprises three parts which respectively set out: the research strategy, outlining the process of case selection and how it was underpinned by a light theorization; the research findings, which highlighted patterns in the character of HCA role; and the search for the causative mechanisms generating these patterns, which drew upon various data sources intrinsic to the research design.

Research Strategy

In terms of light theorization, the shape of the HCA role was viewed as plausibly related to structure-agency interaction at different levels: the NHS, the hospital, the clinical directorate, and, possibly, the ward. As a means of exploring such interaction, the research selected-to-difference, choosing four case-hospitals or acute trusts located in various regions of England (North, South, Midlands, and London) and within each of these hospitals, general medical and general surgical wards.

The selection of the cases was founded upon plausible narratives connected to how the HCA role might be shaped by emergent properties at these levels. In choosing the hospital trust as the case, the broader NHS became the context both for the functioning of the hospital and for the development of the HCA role. More specifically, it was possible to view the four case-study hospitals as susceptible to the standardizing influences emanating from the NHS. There were 'real' NHS systems and policies designed to regulate hospital activity both in terms of general services' delivery and the management of local workforces. The Department of Health was the source of NHS funding, and a range of NHS policies and practices continued to cover NHS hospitals and their workforces. Interestingly HCAs were unregistered workers, not subject to national statutory regulation governing NHS professionals, opening up some discretion within the four hospitals as to how they shaped the nurse support role. In terms of the 'real', there were, however, other NHS policies covering hospitals and this group of workers, such as the Agenda for Change (AfC) pay agreement establishing a national pay and grading structure and placing HCAs in pay bands 2 and 3. Closely associated with AfC was the Knowledge and Skills Framework (KSF) designed to manage staff performance and to regulate pay progression at the upper end of grades. Indeed there was evidence to suggest that policy shifts at the national level had profoundly influenced the role of the HCA. For example, the extension of the European Working Time Directive to junior doctors was widely seen to have led to re-calibration of nursing tasks, allowing HCAs to assume a more prominent bedside presence (Kessler et al. 2012). Such national policies and practices were the product of agency: policymakers, managers, and union officials at this level formulating, negotiating, and sanctioning them. Once in place, however, they acquired an objective reality with real emergent properties affecting the pay and performance management of HCAs and other NHS workers. To what extent did these system practices constrain or empower hospitals to shape the role of the HCA?

Certainly there was scope for structure and agency to play themselves out at various levels within the hospital and in ways which might lead to a differentia-tion of the HCA role between and within trusts. The selecting-to-difference, in choosing four regionally differentiated hospitals, was rooted in a light theoriza-tion which implied possible differences in the shape of the HCA between the trusts. The hospital was, after all, the HCAs' employer. As employers, hospitals had scope to develop their own job descriptions and policies for HCA recruit-ment, development, and training within the context of AfC and the KSF, a dis-cretion enhanced by the HCAs' unregistered status. At the time, it was equally plausible to postulate differences in the shape of the HCA role by clinical area, in particular according to whether HCAs worked on general medical or general surgical wards; in other words, the shape of the HCA might be similar across all four trusts according to clinical area. Naturally, patient conditions varied by clinical area, generating very different needs with implications for work organi-zation and the role of support workers as well as registered nurses. In choosing to focus on wards from these two clinical areas, it was felt possible to pick up differences in the shape of the role generated by these distinctive features.

In short, the comparative design provided an opportunity to explore differ-ent patterns in the HCA role, and at the same time to uncover their generative mechanisms: similarities between the four different case-hospitals in the shape of the HCA role would suggest the standardizing influence of the NHS, and a constraint on agency at the level of the trust; differences between trusts would imply a degree of agency on the part of trust actors, and the possible influence of locally devised policies and practices on the HCA role; similarities in the shape of the HCA role by clinical area across the case-hospitals would point to the emergent properties of general medical and general surgical wards as an influence on the distribution of tasks to HCAs.

Adopting a multiple-methods approach, the research comprised two main phases. First, qualitative data were collected from each trust, based on over 200 interviews with key stakeholders (HCAs, nurses, managers, and patients) and over 200 hours of on-ward observation of nurses and HCAs performing in their roles. Given the emphasis placed on the hospital as an internally stratified entity, this phase had to be carefully designed to ensure data were collected at different levels: interviews were held at trust, clinical directorate, and ward levels. However, given the weight placed on the 'actual' shape of the HCA role, and how this might emerge within the context of 'real' NHS and trust policies and procedures, much of the fieldwork was conducted at 'shop-floor' level, on some thirty wards across the four hospitals. Second, three surveys, all with response rates of around 50 per cent, were completed in each of the four trusts, covering HCA, nurses, and patients (a total of twelve surveys).

Tendencies and Patterns

The first phase collection of qualitative data served three main purposes. First, it provided an opportunity to explore and clarify the interaction between structure and agency, particularly at the levels of the hospital, the clinical area, and the ward as it affected the shape of the HCA role. In so doing, these data began to feed into competing narratives which underpinned the light theorization, lending support (or not) to the various tentative explanations. Second, these data provided a reservoir of material to be drawn on retroductively in seeking to explain patterns as they emerged from later research findings. Third, and more specifically, this phase allowed the range and nature of the tasks performed by HCAs to be more fully and sharply distinguished. Thus, four sets of tasks were revealed: direct-care tasks addressing patients' hygiene needs, for example feeding, making beds, and washing patients; ward-centred tasks such as maintaining stock cupboards; lower level clinical tasks including taking blood sugars and observations; and higher level technical tasks covering the taking of blood and taking ECGs.

Clarifying the range of tasks performed by HCAs was crucial to establishing the shape of the HCA role. Surveyed HCAs (750 across the four trusts responded) were asked how frequently they performed the different tasks (daily, weekly, monthly, annually, or never). It was then possible, using cluster analysis, to distinguish different types of HCA role. Five such roles, based on a different configuration of tasks, were revealed and labelled by the researchers as follows:

- The Bedside Technician: the most common role, regularly performing both direct-care tasks and low level technical tasks such as taking observations and blood sugars.

- The Ancillary: a role mainly confined to regularly undertaking more routine-care tasks such as changing and making beds.

- The Citizen: concentrating particularly on the provision of ward-centred tasks such as transporting patients and stocking cupboards.
- The All Rounder: a niche role undertaken by only a few HCAs, performing across all sets of tasks with some frequency.
- The Expert: also a niche role, primarily focusing on the delivery of high level clinical tasks.

In important respects these five HCA types might be seen to represent the 'actual' allocation of tasks and responsibilities to HCAs in the four trusts. Against the backdrop of the 'real' in terms of formal NHS polices and practice, patterns had emerged from the interaction of structure and agency at trust level. Indeed, the 'actual' clearly departed from the 'real' in a number of ways. In particular while AfC provided for two HCA grades, in practice HCA roles had coalesced around five types. Moreover these types did not map onto the two AfC HCA bands in a straightforward way. Certainly the influence of AfC was to be seen: the more diverse and technically sophisticated All Rounder and Expert role types were more likely to be in band 3, but this was not invariably the case—some HCAs performing these roles were at band 2 level. Similarly, many of those in the less diverse and complex role type—the Ancillaries—were in band 2. Again, however, this was not uniformly the case: a noteworthy number were at the higher band 3 level. Clearly the 'real' in the form of AfC systems and structures was influential, but the 'actual' painted a more nuanced picture, and encouraged the search for causes in the distribution of HCA types within and across the four hospital trusts. A ward manager in one the case trusts noted:

[The HCA role is] different wherever you are and dependent on the skill sets of the individual. And then I think it's also down to how the individual's motivated and in terms of what they want to take on. Sometimes it's being clear what is the role, and that's different everywhere you go in relation to if you talk to somebody about a health, a nurse assistant in one place, a nurse assistant somewhere else, they're different. I think it's fine them being different if they're different for a reason, but you can be different in one medical ward to another, it can be the whim of the ward sister, those types of things. And that's where some of the things Agenda for Change and having the Knowledge and Skills Framework started to say well what is this role about and what sort of person do you need...what sort of skill do they need, what quality do they need, all those type of things?...[But] it is still done in an ad hoc way.

Causation

In seeking to uncover mechanisms generating the 'actual' patterned allocation of tasks and responsibilities to the HCAs, the value of the multiple-case design re-emerges. The starting point was the distribution of these five HCA role types across the four hospitals. A shared or standard distribution of these types between the trusts might point to the potency of generative mechanisms across the NHS. However, differences in distribution between or within trusts would suggest generative mechanisms at the level of the trust or the clinical area.

The survey data did reveal some similarities in the use of HCAs across the four hospitals, which suggested the standardizing influence of emergent properties from the NHS. For example, in exploring the distribution of HCAs by band, it was clear that in all four trusts the overwhelming majority of HCAs, typically close to 80 per cent, were to be found in band 2 rather than band 3. This was perhaps indicative of external pressure encouraging the hospitals to use HCAs as a 'cheap resource' and a means of cost minimization. However, when it came to the distribution of the five HCA role types, Table 9.1 indicates there were marked differences between trusts. Such differences point to the permissive nature of the 'real' in the NHS structure, allowing structure and agency to play themselves out in a relatively autonomous way at trust level, so producing hospital differences in the organization of nursing work and the distribution of tasks to HCAs. Differences in the prevalence of the Bedside Technician between trusts were particularly striking: it can be seen that in Trusts 3 and 4 around a half of HCAs fell into this type, while at Trusts 1 and 2 it was barely a quarter; at the same time Trust 1 appeared to be a much higher user of Ancillaries than other trusts.

These findings suggested that there were generative mechanisms at trust level which gave rise to these patterns. This then encouraged consideration of what these mechanisms might be and how they might operate. The pursuit of causation prompted a return to the qualitative data, which provided some help in this respect, supporting a retroductive process. The use of this qualitative data is illustrated in two examples:

- In seeking to explain the higher incidence of the Ancillary HCA type at Trust 1, qualitative material on trust-level policies and practices was drawn upon. Thus, it was clear that Trust 1 had deliberately abandoned

Table 9.1 Distribution of HCA Roles by Trust

	Trust 1%	Trust 2%	Trust 3%	Trust 4%	Sig.
Bedside Technician	29	26	55	46	***
Ancillary	34	18	2	17	***
Citizen	25	36	13	25	***
All Rounder	9	5	9	5	ns
Expert	4	16	21	7	***
Total	100	100	100	100	

*** p< 0.001.

the national NVQ accreditation system for HCAs. The relatively significant presence of Ancillaries at this Trust might therefore be related to the
absence of transparent forms of accreditation: there were few devices at
this trust to signal the competence of HCAs, perhaps forcing post holders
into a narrow range of basic activities.

- It was also possible to trace the relatively higher incidence of Bedside
Technicians in Trusts 3 and 4 to local market conditions: in both cases
local labour markets were relatively loose, with high levels of unemployment allowing hospital managers to be selective in recruitment, choosing
individuals to HCA posts with the kinds of background skills needed to
perform as Bedside Technicians. In exploring the career backgrounds of
HCAs in interview, we were able to map career pathways, and reveal that
HCAs from these Trusts 3 and 4 were more likely to have work experience
in health and social care than those from the other trusts.

Analysis of the survey data also revealed differences in the distribution of HCA
type by clinical area which cut across the four trusts. For example, as Table 9.2
shows, the Bedside Technician was much more likely to be found on medical
than on surgical wards, while Citizens were more prevalent on surgical wards.
The qualitative observational data could be drawn upon to support this finding: it suggested that across the case-hospitals HCAs on medical wards were
involved in more sustained bedside care over a shift than HCAs on surgical
wards. These findings suggested that while trusts might vary in their use of
the different HCA role types, there remained some cross-cutting similarities
based on clinical area. This finding confirmed the influence of emergent properties associated with clinical area as an influence over the distribution of tasks
and responsibilities. Again we could draw upon qualitative data to reveal the
emergent proprieties associated with clinical area which might shape the HCA
role. Patient needs were found to vary by clinical area: those patients on medical wards often had chronic conditions which required intense bedside care;

Table 9.2 Distribution of HCA Roles by Type of Ward

	Medical %	Surgical %	Sig.
Bedside Technician	43	28	**
Ancillary	20	15	ns
Citizen	20	33	**
All Rounder	5	12	**
Expert	12	12	ns
Total	100	100	

** $p < 0.01$.

surgical patients generated a greater range of ward-centred or team tasks for HCAs to undertake, such as the transportation of patients to operating theatres. This in turn generated different patterns of work organization and the need for HCAs to perform different types of role.

SUMMARY AND CONCLUSIONS

The case-study approach has particular attractions to critical realism with its capacity to explore entities in context and to reveal underlying causative or generative mechanisms which reflect the interaction between structure and agency at different levels. Some care is needed, however, in balancing this interest in context and causation, with implications for methodological approaches. Thus, while the singular, context-sensitive case study might provide insights into the influence of local contingencies or situational factors, there is a danger that broader, cross-cutting patterns and generative mechanisms might be missed or obscured. This chapter has argued that the comparative case design has a distinctive contribution to make in uncovering these patterns and their causation. This contribution was still seen to rest on generic features of the case-study approach: the in-depth focus on holistic entities, not least reflected in a multi-methods research strategy, allowing the retroductive pursuit of 'how' and 'why' questions. However, it was the careful selection of more than one case which allowed similarities and differences to be distinguished and prompted a concomitant search for their causes.

The value of the comparative case design was seen as heavily dependent on two intimately related design features. The first was selection technique. Following Yin (2009) it was suggested that cases might be selected on the basis that they would reveal patterned differences or similarities in processes and outcomes. The second was a light theorization which provided a tentative but plausible explanation of potential patterned differences or similarities. To the extent that such theorized similarities or differences were revealed through fieldwork, they provided clues to generative mechanisms to be further probed. To the extent that expected patterns were not revealed, it suggested the search for alternative causes. This purposeful approach to the choice of cases was in part illustrated by reference to a range of studies selecting-to-difference or to-similarity. These studies had selected cases as a means of exploring country and sector effects on organizational policies and practices. By controlling for industry, a study was able to reveal the importance of country effect on the use of functional flexibility by French and British companies in the food processing industry. At the same time, by controlling for country and sector, studies suggested the residual importance of agency: thus trade union and managerial strategies within shared structural contexts pointed to the choices and options

184 Ian Kessler and Stephen Bach

still available to actors whether in relation to labour transnationalism or the development of variable pay systems.

This comparative case research design was more fully illustrated by reference to a study, explicitly drawing upon the tenets of critical realism, which explored the shape of the HCA role in an acute healthcare setting. Selecting four case-study hospitals and examining the distribution of tasks and responsibilities to the HCA role within their general medical and general surgical wards provided an opportunity to explore the interaction of structure and agency at different levels: NHS, trust, and clinical division. The influence of emergent properties at each of these levels on the HCA role was lightly theorized: 'real' NHS-wide systems perhaps encouraged some standardization in the nature of the HCA role; against this backdrop, the 'actual' of the trust acting as an employer might have been expected to lead to hospital differences in the tasks performed by HCAs; at the same time the different needs of patients might equally have generated similarities in the HCA role according to different clinical area across trust.

2 The use of different data sources illustrated the capacity of this multiple-case design to reveal and explain patterns. The first phase collection of qualitative data provided an opportunity to sharpen quantitative techniques seeking to further expose patterned similarities and differences, while providing a reservoir of material which might subsequently be used to explain these patterns. Indeed the survey data revealed the pattern distribution of HCA role types by trust and clinical area, with attempts retroductively to consider how they might have emerged.

10

Critical Realism and International Comparative Case Research

Ayse Saka-Helmhout

INTRODUCTION

The field of international business (IB) has traditionally had a rich qualitative research foundation (e.g. Wilkins 1974; Prahalad 1975; Bartlett 1979). This has shifted, over time, to quantitative methods to establish legitimacy, mirroring the move towards more positivistic methods in the social sciences (Birkinshaw et al. 2011). In spite of the IB field's multicultural, multidimensional and dynamic nature and the broad range of methodologies that it lends itself to, the dominant view is the positivistic paradigm (Morais 2011). This philosophical stance drives the efforts of many IB scholars to discover 'natural laws' that determine human behaviour. Such scholars aim to capture objective reality through scientific tools that are employed independently of the investigators' values. The role of case studies within this paradigm is one of exploration, which follows Yin's (2009) assumption of case studies serving the purpose of developing hypotheses or propositions for theory-testing. Although there is an increasing appreciation of the explanatory power of case studies (e.g. Piekkari et al. 2009), the prevailing positivistic stereotype about the case study still calls for further confrontations to demonstrate its alternative role—a role beyond exploration for theory-building as is commonly understood in IB—that is, explanation. This alternative role of case studies is manifested in the paradigm of critical realism. My objective in this chapter is to present a practical application of critical realism in IB research, in particular in cross-national transfer of knowledge, to show its potential use in causation, explanation, and generalization.

I discuss the critical realist view of explanation and the formalization of its principles in comparative historical analysis (CHA) in the following section. In the third section, I demonstrate how a comparative case study can be conducted through CHA. The fourth section concludes the chapter by sum-marizing the key arguments on ways of enhancing the explanatory power of case studies and outlining the implications for IB research in general.

CRITICAL REALISM AND COMPARATIVE
HISTORICAL ANALYSIS

The fundamental assumption within critical realism is that reality is not sim-ply constructed. Rather, there is the existence of an objective reality independ-ent of our interpretation (Bhaskar 1986). A critical realist perspective views social phenomena as concept-dependent, and the production of knowledge as a social practice (Sayer 1992). Its ultimate goal is to develop deeper levels of explanation and understanding than what is offered by the positivists who focus on generalizable laws and the interpretivists who emphasize the lived experiences or beliefs of social actors. This is achieved through the logic of retroduction, which involves moving from the level of observations and lived experience to postulating about the underlying structures and mechanisms that account for the phenomena involved (Mingers 2003). It implies a retro-spective inference of unobservable causal mechanisms from actors' accounts of observable experiences (Morais 2011). The perspective relies on theoretically guided analysis of relationships among mechanisms, contexts, and outcomes to identify combinations of conditions as causes of events. It is recognized that the addition of contextual factors can change a contributing cause to a counteracting one, or vice versa (see George and Bennett 2005). The approach taken to cause-effect relationships is one of configurational logic, that is, one of seeking specific combinations of conditions that produce a given outcome of interest. Such logic conceptualizes variables as interdependent and often complementary and operating as a cluster in the context of a particular case (Saka-Helmhout 2011). The aim is to gather in-depth data from different cases and to capture their complexity at the same time as producing generalization (Rihoux and Lobe 2009). It contrasts a variable-oriented approach where gen-erality is given precedence over complexity by testing propositions derived from general theories (Ragin 1987). A correlation between a variable and an outcome may be insufficient to explain the given activity since the effect of one variable may be altered by other variables (Easton 2010).

A method that formalizes the logic of retroduction and pursues causality in a handful of cases is the CHA. This method offers control over unwanted causal inferences in case comparison and facilitates a case-oriented approach to data analysis. Although the method has been used extensively in political science (e.g. Luong 2002) and historical sociology (e.g. Dixon et al. 2004), its applica-tions in the field of management (e.g. Kogut and Ragin 2006; Greckhamer et al. 2008; Fiss 2011) and international business (e.g. Pajunen 2008; Schneider et al. 2010) are more recent. The aim of this chapter is to demonstrate the potential of the method in improving generalizability of cross-case comparisons by identifying patterns of causalities.

CHA serves the function of (1) building a typology of differing cases, (2) describing the various conditions present at the occurrence or nonoccurrence of a phenomenon, (3) testing various existing theories against empirical observations, and (4) going beyond mere observation to build middle range theory through the use of logical cases (potential combinations of causal conditions) (Rihoux and Lobe 2009). Although it offers a broad range of strategies of causal assessment (see Mahoney and Rueschemeyer 2003: 338), I focus here on the nominal strategy of causal analysis. This technique of causal assessment is designed to identify the necessary and sufficient conditions for an outcome. It differs from the causal logic employed by most large-N investigators who seek linear associations and rarely test for necessary and sufficient conditions. Nominal or categorical comparison relies ideally on mutually exclusive and collectively exhaustive categories. In other words, cases cannot be classified in terms of more than one category, and one of the categories should apply to each case. For instance, a national case can be classified in terms of its regime as authoritarian, democratic, or totalitarian, as well as its state as conservative, liberal, or social-democratic welfare for a nominal comparison.

The aim here is to identify the presence of causes that exhibit, in at least certain aspects, invariant associations with outcomes within a specified domain of cases. In other words, the investigator seeks to capture which conditions or combinations thereof are 'necessary' or 'sufficient' to produce a given outcome. A condition is *necessary* for a given outcome if it is always present when the outcome occurs, that is when the outcome cannot occur in its absence (Rihoux et al. 2009). A condition is *sufficient* for an outcome if the outcome occurs when the condition is present, but it can also result from other conditions. 'Only when a given factor is a necessary *and* sufficient cause will the outcome *always* be present when the cause is present and *always* absent when the cause is absent' (Mahoney and Rueschemeyer 2003: 341).

A notable nominal technique that enables the identification of necessary and sufficient conditions is John Stuart Mill's method of agreement and method of difference ([1843]/1967). These methods provide a logical foundation for eliminating conditions that are not associated with an outcome (Berg-Schlosser et al. 2009). The method of agreement can be used to eliminate potential necessary causes, whereas the method of difference can be used to eliminate potential sufficient causes.

The former method assumes that where two or more outcomes across cases are common, there will be similarities in bundles of conditions that, at least in part, account for that outcome. It involves initially identifying instances of the phenomenon under investigation, and subsequently determining which conditions precede its appearance. The condition that satisfies this requirement is taken as the cause. This approach uses a Boolean algebra to determine which combinations of conditions combine to result in the outcome in question (Boswell and Brown 1999). For instance, organizational performance has been associated with organizational structure defined by formalization, centralization, complexity and size (Miles and Snow 1978), firm strategy (e.g. Miller 1986), and environmental context characterized by the rate of change and uncertainty (e.g. Miles and Snow 1978). If all the potential conditions prevail in the first case, then the method of agreement would require the investigator to analyse other cases of high-performance configurations in an effort to eliminate some of the explanatory conditions. If a case of high performance lacking environmental uncertainty was found, this condition would be eliminated. The process of elimination would continue until the investigator reached a cause or a set of causes. If the cases agreed on all of the conditions, these conditions would be taken as significant. Essentially, a hypothesized cause that is not shared by the cases cannot be necessary for the outcome's occurrence (Mahoney and Rueschemeyer 2003).

By contrast, the method of difference compares cases with different outcomes to confirm the absence of a common cause. It requires that cases in which the outcome is absent also be included in comparisons with the expectation that the cause will be absent in those additional cases (Skocpol and Somers 1980). For example, if cases displaying both high organizational performance and low-cost firm strategy also display high centralization and formalization, then some of the cases displaying an absence of both high organizational performance and low-cost firm strategy should also reveal high centralization and formalization for this potential explanation of performance to be eliminated. In effect, the method of difference rejects competing single-factor explanations through paired comparisons (Ragin 1987). Essentially, a hypothesized cause that is shared by all cases cannot by itself be sufficient for the outcome if the outcome is present in some cases and absent in others.

The two methods serve as powerful techniques for eliminating rival causal explanations, even when only a small number of cases are sampled, as a single deviation from an expected pattern of regularity is decisive (Mahoney and Rueschemeyer 2003). This power is unleashed when the methods are used in combination where positive cases (in which outcomes are present) are compared to negative cases (in which outcomes are absent). For example, the observation that high organizational performance occurs simultaneously with firm strategy does not necessarily suggest a cause-and-effect relationship between high organizational performance and firm strategy. An unidentified condition such as labour market conditions in the country that can limit the prerogative of employers in setting incentives and compensation (e.g. Siegel and Larson 2009) may be the cause of both firm strategy and organizational performance.

Hence, the method of agreement is best used in combination with the method of difference to circumvent the risk of 'false positives', that is, attributing causal significance to the conditions that seem to be associated with the variance in outcome when in fact these conditions may not be present in other cases with the same outcome (George and Bennett 2005). Control is sought by defining boundaries around the measurement of conditions through theoretically sampled and comparable cases. In other words, cases must resemble each other in many respects except in the phenomenon of interest so that unwanted causal inferences can be controlled (George and Bennett 2005).

It is worth noting that methods of agreement and difference generally will have difficulty assessing the net effect of any single condition. An organizational structure by itself is neither a necessary nor a sufficient condition for organizational performance, that is, high organizational performance can occur in the absence of large size, formalization, centralization, and complexity (e.g. Fiss 2011), and not all instances of large size, formalization, centralization, and complexity produce high organizational performance. Hence, CHA allows for equifinality, that is, several different combinations of conditions can be causes of an outcome (Ragin 1987).

CHA IN ACTION: UNLEASHING AGENCY IN INSTITUTIONALLY DIVERSE SETTINGS

The above ideas are illustrated by a study addressing the extent to which institutional and organizational conditions influenced 'projective agency' in the full implementation of continuous improvement programmes at three subsidiaries of two large—Dutch and British—MNEs in the chemical industry. MNEs that were close rivals in the chemical industry were sampled to minimize the effect of sectoral variation on the phenomenon of observation. Although Yin (2009) requires at least four cases for theoretical replication, the investigation was focused on three subsidiaries as the fourth subsidiary—British MNE's local subsidiary—failed to meet our sampling criteria. It was a lean plant that was characterized by an absence of an institutional gap between home and host countries. Our intention was to select subsidiaries on the basis of a small or large institutional gap between home and host institutional contexts and the similarity of practices to be implemented.

The host institutional setting either reflected the German collaborative national business system or the UK compartmentalized national business system, as discussed below. A large institutional gap was evident in the national cases of Dutch Chem operating in the UK and British Chem operating in Germany. Germany and the Netherlands emphasize cooperation, commitment, and participation, in contrast to formal mechanisms and strong separation of strategic and operational management in compartmentalized systems such as the UK (Whitley 1999, 2007).

The three subsidiaries displayed similar characteristics in terms of the transferred practice and key organizational features (see Table 10.1). Similar new procedures and systems in production were introduced to all subsidiaries between 2002 and 2003. The transfer content was similar in terms of instilling a continuous improvement culture and a team-based structure in addition to key metrics such as cost per litre and the right-first-time, and techniques for improving manufacturing such as the 5S housekeeping principles [sort, set, shine, standardize, and sustain]. The subsidiaries were of similar size and form of ownership, and displayed comparable skill levels and technology.

Table 10.1 Key Subsidiary Characteristics and the Nature of Transferred Practice

Subsidiary characteristics	Dutch Chem's German subsidiary	Dutch Chem's UK subsidiary	British Chem's German subsidiary
Size (number of employees at the time of data collection)	411	324	131
Form of ownership	Acquired in 1998	Acquired in 1994	Acquired in 1998
Skill levels	Largely semi-skilled workers with an average of 18 years of employment in the subsidiary	Largely semi-skilled workers with an average of 15 years of employment in the subsidiary	Largely semi-skilled workers with an average of 22 years of employment in the subsidiary
Technology	Semi-automated mixing and filling units	Semi-automated mixing and filling units	Semi-automated mixing and filling units
Change effort			
Transferred practice	Continuous improvement programme called Star Trek, including operational improvements such as quality, cost per litre, and stock levels, continuous improvement culture and team-based structure (2003–2007)	Continuous improvement programme called Star Trek, including operational improvements such as quality, cost per litre, and stock levels, continuous improvement culture, and team-based structure (2003–2007)	Continuous improvement programme called [Chemical] Plant of the Future, including operational improvements such as efficiency, cost, and cycle times, continuous improvement culture, and team-based structure (2002–2004)

As the interest was in performing a controlled comparison of contextual influences on the orientations of subsidiaries to implementing new practices, data were analysed using CHA. The Dutch Chem's German site and the British Chem's German site served as positive cases, in which the outcome proved sufficiently similar; that is, subsidiaries displayed projective agency (i.e. engaged in imaginative generation of possible future trajectories of action that transforms or challenges existing practices) in the implementation of new practices. The Dutch Chem's UK site served as the negative case where there was iterative agency (i.e. reliance on past practices). Cases were selected on instances of outcome where our gatekeepers at the Dutch and the British MNEs indicated clearly which subsidiaries were good examples of firms that made the continuous improvement programme work in a given host context. In addition to specifying institutional settings, MNE coordination structures were considered as enabling or constraining agency. This was based on the assumption that actors' engagement in divergent change where there is a contradiction in institutional demands (e.g. Herrigel 2008) is contingent on the presence of complementarity between an MNE coordination structure and host context demand that can offer some stability for actors to instantiate change in their response to institutional contradictions.

Drawing on Bartlett and Ghoshal's (1989) criteria and relying on company document- and interview-based evidence, we categorized the Dutch MNE as operating a multi-domestic structure and the British MNE as having an international structure. Consequently, the conditions at the institutional level and the nature of MNE coordination structure at the organizational level were derived from the literature. The remaining conditions were identified during the course of the fieldwork through open and axial coding (Strauss and Corbin 1998). This is elaborated in the section on identifying patterns of regularities. *[margin annotations: DOCUMENTS; Fieldwork: open + axial coding]*

The field study drew on 23 semi-structured formal interviews (13 at the Dutch MNE and 10 at the British MNE) that were held between 2002 and 2003 at the British MNE, and between 2006 and 2007 at the Dutch MNE, a week-long participant observation at each subsidiary involving on-the-job discussions with 28 shop-floor operators and team leaders, and company documentary data such as operation manuals, division production newsletters and organization charts. The broad aim was to understand the ways in which the local workforce at UK- and German-based subsidiaries participated in the process of constructing alternative modes of operating and how this participation was realized. The research questions addressed the strategic and operational goals underlying continuous improvement initiatives, resources that were made available by headquarters, the manner in which changes were implemented, the extent to which UK- and German-based subsidiaries accepted practices, and the degree to which the parent company was involved in this process. Observations and interviews provided material upon which to base the emerging organizational conditions of 'employee relations' and 'leadership style'. Orientations described in interviews and observed in fieldwork were categorized as 'projective' agency where subsidiaries aimed to change practices through local interpretations of continuous improvement programmes. Iterative agency was characterized by subsidiaries' inclination to rely on past practices. This did not involve any fundamental changes to existing practices. The motivation to break away from institutional constraints was manifested in the implementation of new practices, which was coded as (1) 'full implementation' where there was full adherence to the formal rules implied by a new practice, (2) 'compromise accommodation' where there was the balancing of expectations of multiple constituents, and (3) 'non-implementation' where there was full resistance (Ferner et al. 2005).

CROSS-CASE ANALYSIS OF BUNDLES OF CONDITIONS

Our findings, summarized in Table 10.2, demonstrate how a variety of strategic responses to overcome institutional contradictions arise within an MNE. They indicate that it is supportive host institutional arrangements rather than institutional incompatibilities between home and host countries that promote projective agency. Home and host institutional incompatibilities lose significance in explaining actors' capacity to formulate strategic actions in the presence of supportive host contexts and organizational conditions. In spite of similarities in subsidiary characteristics such as age, size, skills levels, and technology, the three subsidiaries differ considerably in their orientation to change and the manifestation of that orientation in the implementation of alternative practices. Furthermore, projective agency does not necessarily lead to practices being fully implemented. Full implementation also depends on whether there is an MNE structure that is aligned with the host context.

At the organizational level, the findings show that projective agency was facilitated by cooperative employee relations and participatory leadership, as at Dutch Chem's German site. Operators were encouraged to participate in continuous improvement practices through a suggestion scheme and direct initiative. The emphasis on people could be seen in the site's efforts to create solidarity through worker engagement: 'What have made their way to everyone are the guidelines. Workers were involved in their formulation. They find themselves and their ideas in them' (group advisor). The workforce respected the management team as most of them had apprenticeship or trade training in the company. The key assistant to the plant manager, the group advisor, had worked himself up from the shop floor and was a 'Meister'. The plant also used 'group speakers' who under the new structure headed groups of operators with the aim of reducing vertical gaps between operators and supervisors. The

Table 10.2 Key Institutional and Organizational Characteristics Related to Type of Agency

	Dutch Chem's German site	Dutch Chem's UK site	British Chem's German site
Institutional gap between home and host countries	Small between collaborative home and collaborative host NBS	Large between collaborative home and compartmentalized host NBS	Large between compartmentalized home and collaborative host NBS
Complementarity between MNE coordination structure and host context demand	Complementarity between multi-domestic structure and demand for collaboration	Non-complementarity between multi-domestic structure and demand for operational flexibility	Non-complementarity between international structure and demand for collaboration
Host context	Supportive of change efforts	Unsupportive of change efforts	Supportive of change efforts
Approach to employee relations	Widely available employee involvement systems; participation of Works Council members in new practices	Limited employee involvement systems; emphasis on formalization and explication	Employee involvement systems such as focused improvement teams; participation of Works Council members in new practices
Leadership style	Participatory: strong emphasis on people; functional similarity between the German manager and the local workforce	Non-participatory: weak emphasis on people, strong line of demarcation between operators and management	Participatory: emphasis on empowering people; 'Dutch openness'; respect for local capability
Type of agency in the implementation of new practices	*Projective agency Full implementation of continuous improvement programme*	*Iterative agency Non-implementation of continuous improvement programme*	*Projective agency Compromise accommodation*

group speakers had a very high acceptance by the workers as they 'knew their trade inside out' (operator). The participation in new practices also involved the Works Council members. The Works Council maintained favourable relations with management to the extent that they were perceived by some of the operators as belonging to 'them up there' (factory manager).

By the same token, the German site of British Chem encouraged involvement in the continuous improvement programme, for instance, by setting up focused improvement teams in both mixing and filling lines. Operators received on-the-job training and a series of off-the-job seminars to improve performance measurements and control. The transfer of responsibility from quality assurance and maintenance to operators in self-testing in improvement teams fostered the ownership of processes. Similar to the German site of Dutch Chem, some of the management team members had risen from the ranks of apprenticeship. A culture of 'it's not my problem', broken promises, and punishment was replaced with one that emphasized open communication, early warning of problems, and a 'can-do approach'. This rested on the principle that 'without openness and transparency, we know that we cannot enable and sustain change' (shift manager). The site also saw the involvement of Works Council members in its initiatives:

> The power of the Works Council is enormous in Germany. But I must say the way in which we work with our Works Council is very open-minded. We put things on the table as they are, probably due to the fact that my colleague and I are not Germans. His nature is more or less 'let us be friends. We do not need to compete with each other'. (managing director)

In comparison, the British site of Dutch Chem emphasized formalization and explication rather than employee relations that encouraged involvement. The implementation of Star Trek—a range of systems such as Kaizen, Six Sigma and Lean manufacturing and tools such as 5S and value stream mapping that subsidiaries could use to realize continuous improvement in production— remained largely in the hands of management and external consultants. Even though many operators participated in external training programmes, they were, largely, not involved in translating the continuous improvement principles: 'Many of the suggestions made by [an external consultancy firm] had already been made by other operators... but had not been acted on by management' (operator). Where conflicts emerged, management was perceived by the operators as siding unconditionally with the shift supervisors. Middle management was identified as hampering the introduction of continuous improvements at the site:

> In order to get managers like [X] out of their comfort zone, you need to create an environment that is challenging for them. It is by far more rewarding and effective to change the motivation of the majority of people who are mainly on the shop floor than help managers to be able to deal with this and support it... They are very traditional, political animals, not normally very good listeners. (European improvement manager)

An analysis was carried out at the national level, where macro-institutional dynamics could play a role in the agency displayed in the implementation of new practices. The institutional differences between home and host countries, the extent to which there was complementarity between MNE coordination structure and host context demand, and the extent to which the host context was supportive of change efforts were derived from the literature on cultural and normative differences between Germany and the UK (e.g. Aguilera and Jackson 2003). Collaborative institutional settings such as Germany encourage and support cooperation between collective actors through a variety of mechanisms such as networks, associations, and the state (Lane 1996). Employees are encouraged to participate in management's decision-making processes. This participation functions through employee representatives that take the form of Works Councils at the plant level and is backed by extensive legislation (Jacobi et al. 1998).

By contrast, the institutional context of the UK is defined by an emphasis on the reduction of agency costs through heavy reliance on formal mechanisms, strong separation of strategic and operational management, and the exercise of control via financial mechanisms (Aguilera and Jackson 2003). Limited collaboration among employers, unions, and other groups tends to discourage cooperation in the management of training systems (Whitley 1999).

Comparative institutionalism argues that misalignments between institutionalized rules and situational demands provide the space in which actors' choices may lead to innovative changes through mobilization of resources (e.g. Crouch 2005; Streeck and Thelen 2005; Hall and Thelen 2009). Subsidiaries in diverse institutional settings were thus expected to display different orientations to new practices. We focused on MNE coordination structure in relation to host country demands as a source of resource that could enable or constrain agency. Network forms of organizing within MNEs are widely recognized as enabling subsidiaries' ability to contribute to the creation, adoption, and diffusion of knowledge owing to the degree of normative integration of the subsidiary into the MNE through organizational socialization and dense intra-unit and inter-unit communication (Bartlett and Ghoshal 1989). By contrast, more centralized forms of organizing within MNEs tend to constrain the development and diffusion of knowledge by subsidiaries.

The UK subsidiary of the Dutch MNE displayed iterative agency despite a gap between home and host institutional contexts. The superficial transformation of the transferred knowledge that resulted in a strong focus on performance indicators such as service and stock levels could be related to (1) the multi-domestic structure of the MNE that failed to support the expectation on the part of the UK subsidiary for central directives, and (2) the institutional feature of the UK, such as management-worker separation, that left the subsidiary less supported than those in collaborative institutional settings. However, the operational flexibility granted by this MNE structure enabled local solutions at Dutch Chem's German subsidiary, and the German host institutional characteristics supported labour inputs to formulating these solutions. The highly regulated and strongly institutionalized labour market relations in Germany demanded a subsidiary initiative that addressed the local institutional pressure of collective bargaining and co-determination as well as the competitive pressure for quality improvements and cost minimization. This was achieved at the German site by engaging both Works Council members and operators in alternative practices: 'It [Works Council] receives information up-front and is more involved in decisions than would legally be required' (group advisor, Dutch Chem Germany).

British Chem's international MNE structure provided centralized authority that was not highly appreciated by the German subsidiary. The compromise accommodation of continuous improvement practices could be explained by (1) the relative lack of complementarity between HQ coordination efforts, and (2) the German institutional expectation of collaboration where learning across vertical divides is much more common than in the UK. Employee relations and leadership style at the site, which were supportive of developing a local vision, motivated actors to challenge old practices, that is, display projective agency. These local efforts of *bricolage* served, in part, to offset the central directives of the parent company that focused solely on operational and financial gaps. For instance, operators reduced cycle time of twenty hours to ten hours by shortening the distances that raw materials travelled in the manufacturing process. Similarly, test cycle times were reduced from six hours to four hours with some of the operators testing the product themselves rather than passing it on to the quality control department to pass or fail. Although 'a majority of people liked the new initiatives' (team leader), there was some resistance on the part of both middle managers and operators. A number of operators preferred to work the 'old way': 'We were told to do it and we did it' (operator). By the same token, the team leaders found it challenging to own quality control problems owing to the involvement of the parent company: 'All of a sudden, there comes a parent company, puts a foot on us and says "we will guide you through some of our standards. We have got company standards that you have to follow", people see that sometimes as pain' (team leader).

As the analysis at the organizational and national institutional levels indicates, Dutch Chem's German site and British Chem's German site were more successful in encouraging a future orientation to implementing new practices than Dutch Chem's UK site.

DEVELOPING EXPLANATIONS: CAPTURING PATTERNS OF REGULARITIES

The appeal of CHA is the control that it offers in comparing cases, allowing investigators to draw causal inferences between conditions and a clearly specified outcome where cases are comparable. The task is made easier where outcomes can be categorized a priori. However, more often than not, outcomes become apparent during data collection. In such instances, cases can be selected on the basis of theoretically justified causal conditions rather than the outcome. In the study reported here, there was a combination of both these approaches. We were informed of the differences in implementation outcomes by our gate-keeper. However, we were not aware of the types of agency displayed by each subsidiary. Hence, we also applied the sampling criteria of differences in insti-tutional contexts between home and host countries as well as variation in MNE structures. I outline below the analytical process followed, from initial coding to cross-case comparison, to delineate the necessary and sufficient conditions in the relationship between causal conditions and the outcome.

The first step was to scan interview transcriptions and observation notes to generate a list of tentative categories or conditions at the organizational level. Interviewees focused on organizational culture (openness to know-ledge sharing), managerial mindset (level of people orientation), training (classroom-based versus on-the-job), and involvement in change efforts. The examples given by the respondents indicated that managerial mind-set and organizational culture were associated with the 'style of leadership' at the site, which either encouraged or discouraged the full implementation of new practices. Employee involvement was illustrated in the translation of the continuous improvement programme into a local vision, and was sup-ported by the availability of schemes that encouraged participation in change efforts. This was elicited in response to the question on the manner in which changes were implemented. It was coded as 'approach to employee relations' as other respondents acknowledged it. Subcategories were identified on the basis of a category's properties and dimensions such as 'the participatory or non-participatory nature of leadership' (Strauss and Corbin, 1998). Table 10.3 provides an illustrative list of codes and their definitions as well as the state-ments denoting how these are related.

The emergent categories of 'approach to employee relations' and 'leader-ship style' were used to organize data as these aligned well with our interest in the way in which incompatible institutions enable actors to engage in pur-posive action in implementing new practices. A considerable body of work on agency has focused on organizational capabilities that help actors mobilize resources (e.g. Rao 1998; Lounsbury 2001). Within comparative institutional-ism, 'approach to employee relations' (i.e. the availability of collective and/or direct employee involvement schemes) and 'leadership style' (i.e. the manner in which the workforce is guided by managers to work with new practices) are distinctive organizational capabilities that can aid in developing process and product innovations. Central to the development of both of these capabilities is the willingness of employers to commit themselves to joint problem-solving through authority-sharing (Whitley 2007). Consequently, it was theoretically consistent for us to organize our data along these particular organizational capabilities.

Table 10.3 Illustrative List of Codes

(Open codes) Categories related to the type of agency in the implementation of new practices	(Axial codes) Subcategories	Dutch Chem's German site	Dutch Chem's UK site	British Chem's German site
MNE structure (i.e. the extent to which capabilities and decision-making are decentralized and high interdependency of work between subsidiaries and HQ exists)	International/ Multi-domestic form of MNE structure	'We just buy brands and we keep those brands. We build [our brand] next to a pre-existing brand.' 'Still, there is a lot of local decision-making about marketing, recipes they choose, assets they have… The [chemicals] business is very much a local business. [They] are not organized internationally, not even organized regionally.' (supply chain Europe director) 'There are so many different models in the business of [Dutch MNE], some are very local, some are very global. Decorative is much more local.' (supply chain Europe director) 'I refused to take one of these [5S, Six Sigma, TPS] and say this is what we are going to do. That's why I call it Star Trek, because Star Trek is new, you cannot read books about Star Trek… We are not going for TQM, CQM, or we are not going for Six Sigma. We say we have a very simple model, on top its results, you need to come to real results… That's also why I am very cautious of using level metrics like efficiency, productivity, cost per litre. In my opinion these are not real results. These are just ratios that you can use to track performance.' (supply chain Europe director) 'We have been quite successful I think in lowering our raw material cost by making absolutely sure that the quality of the batch of [chemical] is right on the middle of the spec. In the past, to be on the safe side, everybody was going for the top end of the spec to make sure that there would be no quality complaints whatsoever. But the problem is that the customer is used to that top quality. So we have actually said "let's go back to the centre of this pack. If we find the batch which has got too high viscosity, then we have got to dilute it". The customer still gets a good product, but you are saving yourself from material cost.' (operations director for the UK)		There is a very clear process where people sit down regularly, develop their new product plans and other product activities. We [HQ] identify when they need it, how we deliver it etc.' (general manager R&D Europe) 'Unfortunately, the acquisition of [Y] and [Z] in the US was not all that successful. [British MNE] followed the wrong branding approach. It introduced European brands such as [W] in the States. These did not sell as well, and that is now being recovered.' (senior VP global marketing and R&D) 'We do have a discipline, so there is a template, an operating system, that says that what is decided, where, which decisions are taken locally, which decisions are taken regionally, which decisions are taken internationally and what things you need to tell people about [operating] regionally, internationally.' (general manager R&D Europe)

Employee relations (i.e. the availability of collective and/or direct employee involvement schemes at subsidiaries)	Dual/High-road individualized/Low-road minimalist approach to employee relations	'The Works Council is perceived by some [workers] as belonging to "them up there".' (factory manager plant B) 'They have translated our whole Star Trek programme into their own programme with a vision, with how they operate, what they do, how they measure success.' (supply chain Europe director) 'What have made their way to everyone are the guidelines. Workers were involved in their formulation. They find themselves and their ideas in them.' (group advisor plant B)	'There should be more regular briefings and more investment in management training…At first, the push from above is big, but then it withers over time because people are busy. The target has been to get the service level up to 99%, which has reduced the focus on other principles' (blue shift manager)	'The power of the Works Council is enormous in Germany. But I must say the way in which we work with our Works Council is very open-minded. We put things on the table as they are, probably due to the fact that my colleague and I are not Germans.' (managing director) 'On-the-job training and off-the-job seminars are offered to empower operators.' (shift manager)
Leadership style (i.e. the manner in which the workforce is guided by managers to work with new practices)	Participatory/Non-participatory form of leadership	'There is a manager who really understands how to do this…much better than I do. If you want to get this continuous improvement in place, you have to change your style from being extremely directive to a completely different way of managing.' (supply chain Europe director) 'Whatever we do, we try to focus on our people, on behaviour, on culture, on getting their passion…It is all about people at the end and nothing else.' (group advisor plant A)	'Our improvement efforts are more or less a trial and error process. We need a firm strategy. There is a lot from HQ that is relevant but we are asked further questions like… "what is your local vision?" We do not know how these translate to the operational level.' (site manager) 'There has always been conflict between the implementation of continuous improvement and delivering results. With a lot of pressure on cost saving, the focus has been on head count.' (operations director)	'Productivity improvement teams were set up to create end-to-end responsibility with a particular focus. Operators were trained to become maintainers. We introduced a competency-based selection process, which was unique for Germany.' (managing director) 'Our operational initiatives focus on bottom-up changes in ways of working. Without openness and transparency, we know that we cannot enable and sustain change.' (shift manager)

The second step involved identifying the outcome conditions. The cases were classified as displaying projective or iterative agency, and as having fully, partly, or not implemented new practices on the basis of workers' attitudes towards a HQ-initiated continuous improvement programme. The selection of conditions at the organizational level was based on an inductive approach on the basis of case knowledge rather than on existing theories. Based on an in-depth knowledge of the cases and the literatures discussing the implications of institutional diversity and MNE structures for knowledge transfer, five conditions were identified with the use of a 'crisp set'. This refers to identifying the presence (denoted by the binary value of 1) or the absence (denoted by the binary value of 0) of conditions, or their membership or non-membership in sets of firms, that are associated with projective agency and full implementation of continuous improvement programmes.

The causally relevant conditions, as seen in Table 10.2, are as follows: (1) 'institutional gap between home and host countries': whether there was a large gap between a collaborative or compartmentalized home and collaborative or compartmentalized host country, (2) 'complementarity between MNE coordination structure and host context demand': whether the multi-domestic (offering operational flexibility) or international MNE (providing central directives) supported the expectation of the host country to harness the constructive or partnering role of collective arrangements or direct action from the HQ, (3) 'host context': whether the host country was supportive of change efforts, (4) 'approach to employee relations': whether there was the availability of collective and/or direct employee involvement schemes at the subsidiary, (5) 'leadership style': whether there was management engagement with workers.

The outcome conditions, that is, the type of agency and the level of implementation of new practices, take the value of 1 (present, represented by an upper-case letter) if they are observed to be projective agency and full implementation of new practices in comparison to the other cases. By the same token, an iterative agency and non-implementation of new practices take the value of 0 (absent, represented by a lower-case letter). Each of the three cases receives membership scores for each causal and outcome condition, creating seven sets (including the two outcome conditions and five causal conditions). These membership scores are presented in Table 10.4.

The combination of conditions associated with projective agency and full implementation of new practices at Dutch Chem's German site is aBCDE (where a = small institutional gap between collaborative home and collaborative host institutional contexts, B = complementarity between multi-domestic structure and host context demand for collaboration, C = supportive host context, D = widely available employee involvement schemes and Works Council participation in new practices, and E = participatory leadership). By contrast, British Chem's German site, which also displays projective agency, offers a different combination: AbCDE. What is absent is the condition of

Table 10.4 Truth Table Indicating Necessary and Sufficient Conditions

Case conditions	Dutch Chem's German site	Dutch Chem's UK site	British Chem's German site	Type of condition
Institutional gap between home and host countries	0	1	1	Neither necessary nor sufficient
Complementarity between MNE coordination structure and host context demand	1	0	0	Sufficient but not necessary
Host context	1	0	1	Necessary and sufficient
Approach to employee relations	1	0	1	Necessary and sufficient
Leadership style	1	0	1	Necessary and sufficient
Type of agency in the implementation of new practices	1 1	0 0	1 1	Outcome

'complementarity between MNE structure and host context demand'. Although this constitutes a different pathway to the same outcome, it needs to be analysed in conjunction with findings at Dutch Chem's UK site in order to identify necessary and/or sufficient conditions. Dutch Chem's UK site presents Abcde as combination of conditions associated with the outcomes of iterative agency and non-implementation of new practices.

The conditions that are always present when there is projective agency and implementation/compromise accommodation (hence are necessary) are the 'supportive host contexts', 'widely available employee involvement systems and Works Council participation', and 'participatory leadership'. 'Institutional gap between home and host countries', which is present when the outcome is absent, and 'complementarity between MNE coordination structure and host context demand' are not necessary conditions. Given that the outcome can occur in the presence as well as the absence of 'complementarity between MNE coordination structure and host context demand' (see Dutch Chem's and British Chem's German sites), this is only a sufficient condition. This causal configuration indicates the existence of only one path to 'projective agency and full implementation/compromise accommodation of new practices'. In other words, projective agency in the full implementation/compromise accommodation of new practices is a product of high membership in the set of firms with a supportive host context, widely available employee involvement systems and Works Council participation, and participatory leadership (see Table 10.4).

These conditions that are always present when the outcome occurs but do not necessarily always lead to the outcome (that is, are sufficient) are 'complementarity between MNE coordination structure and host context demand', 'host context', 'approach to employee relations', and 'leadership style'. Although all necessary conditions are also sufficient conditions, all sufficient conditions are not always necessary conditions. This is exemplified by the condition of 'complementarity between MNE coordination structure and host context demand', which does not necessarily lead to projective agency in the full implementation or compromise accommodation of new practices.

The analysis shows the importance of examining conditions in combination with others in a specific population of cases. Although some may criticize the analysis as not offering a perfect match between values on the causal conditions and those on the outcome condition, hence for failing to indicate causation, a perfect match between cause and outcome is not required to infer causality (see Mill 1967: 402–6). Furthermore, causality is context- and conjuncture-specific (Rihoux and Lobe 2009). The idea is not to specify a single causal model that fits the data best, but instead to determine the number and character of the different causal models that exist among comparable cases (Ragin 1987). As a general rule, CHA researchers, who follow Mill's standard, aim to have a moderate number of cases to avoid claiming relationships that are simply products of pure chance. The more positive cases (that display projective agency in the full implementation/compromise accommodation of practices) and negative cases (iterative agency in the non-implementation of practices) can be added to the sample to eliminate competing explanations and to further strengthen relationships. This would enable a closer examination of potentially omitted conditions, in particular, in contexts where the same values on causal conditions exhibit different values on the outcome condition (Ragin 1987).

As an approach and a technique, CHA should be considered as case-oriented even though it resorts to variables in its analytic phase. Cases need to be compared as wholes or as ordered and meaningful combinations of parts, including social structures, mechanisms, and agency, in conjunction with the search for competing explanations. In the context of the study reported here, we moved from the type of agency in the implementation of continuous improvement programmes to underlying MNE and national institutional structures that account for this agency. The causal conditions were inferred from actors' accounts of observable experiences, and confirmed by the relevant research literatures of comparative institutionalism and international business. Regularities in actors' experiences were sought across cases to attain leverage for generalization.

CONCLUSION

Although critical realism is essentially a philosophical approach and does not offer methodological tools, there are efforts to demonstrate the ways in which it can be applied to empirical research (e.g. Morais 2011). International comparative case research is, in particular, well suited to the critical realist aims of explanation and generalization through causal mechanisms. However, the view of causation in critical realism should not be confused with that in positivism. Reality is regarded by critical realists as stratified into a real domain of objective but unobservable structures with causal powers, an actual domain of objective and partially observable events, and an empirical domain of subjective but observable experiences (Bhaskar 1978). As is illustrated by the case study reported here, the causal mechanisms, or deep generative processes and structures, could not be understood directly as they were not open to observation. However, they could be inferred through a combination of empirical investigation and theory construction. This was enabled by the application of CHA to the case. Patterns of constant association were sought through methods of agreement and disagreement. The use of a combination of methods of agreement and disagreement enabled the identification of a plausible set of causes for a given outcome drawing on a set of theoretically sampled cases. However, it did not offer a closed explanation. In fact, the idea behind equifinality in CHA is openness to non-deterministic causalities. A similar outcome across cases can be explained by a different constellation of conditions. What makes a certain condition, a commonality, causally relevant in one setting and not in another is the fact that its causal significance is altered by the presence of other conditions, that is, the effect is altered by context. By the same token, different conditions can have the same effect depending on which other conditions they are associated with. Such contextualization of causality is the rule rather than the exception. It justifies examining cases as wholes to see how causal conditions fit together, or how relatively dissimilar cases experience the same outcome or how relatively similar cases experience different outcomes. In Sayer's (1992: 116) words, 'according to conditions, the same mechanism may sometimes produce different events, and conversely the same type of event may have different causes'.

Hence, attaining causality is very much an open systems approach where there are continuous cycles of data collection and reflection, and a dialogue between data and theoretical ideas. In fact, CHA is as much an inductive methodology as it is a deductive one. Its deductive nature is derived from the theoretical notions that serve as guides in the search for similarities and differences across cases. At the same time, the method is inductive as the investigator decides which of the similarities and differences are operative by examining empirical cases (Ragin 1987; Rihoux 2003). The initial theoretical ideas are enhanced through this induction. Each case is examined as a whole, as a relatively comprehensive situation resulting from a combination of conditions. This makes it possible to address causal complexes. Delineating such complexes is feasible where the number of relevant cases is small, that is four to eight cases. However, as the number of cases and conditions increase and the intimate familiarity with each case is reduced, it becomes more difficult to use a CHA. Hence, it is common for investigators to limit its use to small numbers of carefully selected cases. In spite of this limitation, CHA's contribution in terms of a controlled examination of cases is noteworthy. It combines deep understanding of cases with leverage for generalization. The traditional view that explanatory claims based on qualitative research have low validity may, therefore, be challenged from a critical realist perspective.

11

Pulling the Levers of Agency

Implementing Critical Realist Action Research

Monder Ram, Paul K. Edwards, Trevor Jones, Alex Kiselinchev, and Lovemore Muchenje

INTRODUCTION

Action research (AR)—a term invented by Kurt Lewin in 1944—aims to combine scientific inquiry with active participation in a situation with two views in mind: to effect change in the situation and to advance the stock of knowledge. The latter feature distinguishes it from consultancy. 'Classic' AR was often like a field experiment in that the researcher entered a situation, devised an intervention, and studied the effects; more recent uses place more emphasis on active engagement with participants, including addressing their self-perceptions and their processes of learning (Chisholm and Elden 1993). AR is consistent with a range of specific research techniques as discussed elsewhere in this volume (Bryman 1989: 179).

So why is action research (AR) relevant to the CR project? The two approaches have traditionally had a relationship of 'detachment' (Ackroyd 2009), reflecting AR's lack of interest in methodology and CR's distance from the very down-to-earth interventions that are the stuff of AR (Drummond and Themessl-Huber 2007). Yet not only is AR compatible with CR (Cassell and Johnson 2006); there are persuasive reasons for taking an interest in it. In particular, CR is interested in human emancipation. New knowledge based on CR would challenge existing power structures and expose misguided prior beliefs (Kilduff et al. 2011). AR claims to show how to put this into effect. It offers the opportunity to ask a retroductive 'transcendental question': in addition to CR's core question of 'what must the world be like for the existing state of affairs to exist?', 'how can better explanation inform alternative futures?' In this chapter, we draw on an action research study of new migrant enterprise and a business support intermediary (SUPPAG) to ask what levers enabled the intermediary to think differently about migrant business owners. We are, then, not addressing a concrete method such as interviewing but, rather, the application of such methods to concrete action.

A weakness of some forms of AR is that engagement often takes the form of 'egalitarian incrementalism' (Porter and Shortall 2009) where all actors' accounts meld together to form some free-floating consensus without a point of reference. As with constructionism discussed in chapter 1, real causal structures are neglected, and engagement operates at the level of the empirical. Harrison and Leitch's (2000) participatory action research study of organizational learning is perhaps indicative of this approach since it confines its analysis to a narrow group of elite actors rather than organization as a whole. Yet this is not a necessary feature of AR. One of its key architects, John Collier (1963, cited in Cooke 2006), advanced a socially engaged model of action research in which scientists are 'socially visible', with an obligation to engage with wider structural concerns and 'trace out' the implications of their interventions; the affinities with realism are clear. Greater attention to philosophical matters is being encouraged by contemporary practitioners of action research (Cassell and Johnson 2006; Winter and Munn-Giddings 2001) as a means of enhancing the validity and contribution of the approach.

Critical realism also offers action research a means of reconciling the tension between meaning-making and causality (Friedman and Rogers 2009). Some forms of action research focus on the lifeworld of participants, and see their ultimate goal as one of building 'consensus'. Structural impediments that may curtail scope for action are often underplayed, or even ignored. Yet explanation encompassing such broader constraints is a prerequisite for change (Rogers 2004). Critical realism has the potential to serve as a 'meta-theory' in that that helps researchers and participants to scrutinize their pre-existing views, or 'theories in use' (Argyris and Schön 1996). It also operates as a causal theory that connects participants' perceptions with hitherto unrecognized aspects of their reasoning, behaviour, and environment (Friedman and Rogers 2006). This focus on ontic depth helps action research to move beyond the empirical, and provides participants with an insight into the generative mechanisms that may not have been fully appreciated. It is a precursor to change since 'being able to perceive these forces is the first step in controlling them, rather than being controlled by them' (Friedman and Rogers 2006: 44).

Three more specific features of AR and CR suggest that they are compatible (Morgan and Olsen 2007, 2008). First, AR stresses the creation of knowledge in specific contexts and the fact that knowledge is not fixed. CR similarly insists on epistemological relativism. Second, a critical realist approach to objectivity is compatible with 'situated action', which is often seen as a defining feature of AR. CR sees all knowledge claims as corrigible, and encourages researchers to work with subjects who represent multiple standpoints; 'objectivity becomes significant as a lever of agency in the service of dialogue and debate and of transformations' (Morgan and Olsen 2008: 107). Critical realist action research offers the immediacy and practical context to realize this conception of objectivity. Finally, objectivity thus serves as a bridge between the subjectivities of subjects and the real world, which 'links philosophical work to the everyday work of realist researchers' (Morgan and Olsen 2008: 107). This has echoes with Lewin's oft-quoted refrain that 'there is nothing so practical as a good theory', and Friedman and Rogers's (2009:31) inversion: 'there is nothing so theoretical as good action research'.

THE ACTION PROJECT

This chapter sets out to describe how CR-informed action research works. In contrast to other chapters in this volume it tells the story of a particular project in some detail. This is in part because such an approach to AR is rare, so that there are few exemplars. It also follows the logic of AR in focusing on concrete engagement with practice in a very specific context: to see the point, you need to see the context. But the project was also unusual. Classic AR addressed such questions as how to improve the design of jobs, often using socio-technical approaches. This project was about a business support agency and its links with local businesses. It was not a 'typical' AR intervention, but it embraced some of the main aspects of CR-informed AR. These include the following. First, we engaged with people in SUPPAG to address their understanding of their aims and how these aims can change. Second, we helped to change their practice, drawing on relevant theory. Third, we assessed the effects of the changes.

We now consider how we enacted an explicitly critical realist approach to action research. The context for the study was the desire of SUPPAG—a business support intermediary—to engage with new migrant businesses in its catchment area. The term 'new migrants' is used to describe the increasingly diverse geographical origins of arrivals to the UK. We focus on new migrants arriving over the past decade or so, concentrating on entrepreneurs from twenty-five countries. This excludes newly arrived individuals coming to join settled ethnic minority communities. SUPPAG is a joint venture formed by local Chambers of Commerce to deliver the business support across a particular English region. It reflects the then English approach, where a regionally devolved decision-making structure allowed regional support organizations, called Business Links, to develop different local support strategies within a national policy framework (Mole et al. 2011); this structure has since been dismantled by the Conservative-led Coalition Government elected in 2010, wiping out the causal powers of bodies like SUPPAG. SUPPAG's core purpose, according to company materials, was to 'deliver the business support strategy of the region through its Information, Diagnostic and Brokerage (IDB) service'. Like many of its counterparts in other regions (Sepulveda et al. 2011) SUPPAG did not have a clearly articulated strategy for supporting ethnic minority and new migrant businesses; it lacked knowledge of the dynamics of the new migrant business community in the region, their business support needs, and practical interventions aimed at such groups. Our role was to work with SUPPAG on each of these areas. But 'to be situated is not to be trapped' (Morgan and Olsen 2008:108); we examine how the project objectives were addressed by pulling levers aimed at pursuing our interest in *critical realist* action research.

The remainder of the chapter examines the various levers that were pulled in order to realize a critical realist approach to action research. We first reflect on the background to the project, locating the researchers' role in shaping the project, and the variety of pressures that influenced the sponsor organization to become involved with the initiative. We next examine the tension of researching 'ethnic' minorities in the context of enterprise, and consider the ways in which we infused concrete research methods with CR ideas. This leads to a consideration of the difference that critical realist action research made to SUPPAG. We conclude with a discussion on the value of critical realist action research, and some reflections on the limits of emancipation in this context.

LEVER ONE: POLITICAL ANALYSIS AND ACTIONS

What gives rise to an action research intervention? Typically, accounts of action research commence with the intervention itself, and the ensuing 'political analysis' (Winter and Munn-Giddings 2001) is often confined to an assessment of the extent to which proposals for change can be effectively implemented. Hence, the emphasis appears to be on the 'possible alliances and potential opposition in the practical context' (Winter and Munn-Giddings 2001: 22). This is necessary, but arguably not sufficient for action research conducted within an explicit CR framework. Rather, the local flux of the intervention has to be prefigured by a 'causal history' that casts light on 'underlying mechanisms and structures, along with the human agency that reproduces and transforms these mechanisms and structures' (Fleetwood and Hesketh 2010: 233). This generates explanations of 'thick causality' (Fleetwood and Hesketh 2010), rather than the thin accounts of action research that confine themselves to surface interactions of a restricted group of actors (usually the sponsors of the intervention). In the present case, the genesis of the project stemmed from Ram's longstanding involvement with SUPPAG as a non-executive director of the organization. His role, to which he was appointed in 2006, essentially involved providing guidance on how SUPPAG could support ethnic minority businesses in the region.

Three sets of institutional pressures were germane to the evolution of the project. The first arose from SUPPAG's requirement to meet nationally imposed targets for engaging with ethnic minorities and other 'under-represented' groups (for example, women and young people). These performance targets were regularly discussed within the organization and at board meetings. 'Ethnic minority' effectively meant South Asian groups, African-Caribbeans, and Chinese communities; no information was kept on the region's growing new migrant communities. SUPPAG managed to meet the target in respect of ethnic minorities (although it struggled with other under-represented groups). However, these targets were often reached by contracting with a few specialist providers that worked with established minority communities (for example, South Asian and African-Caribbean groups). SUPPAG had appointed internal 'champions' to promote awareness of ethnic minority businesses; but they struggled to fulfil this role because of competing pressures on their time. Further, even the most basic information on new migrant communities was lacking, illustrating Vertovec's (2007: 1048) general contention that 'most areas of service provision have not caught up with the transformation brought about by the new immigration of the last decade'. Ram raised the matter of the lack of information on new migrant businesses at board meetings and more private interactions with officers at a variety of different levels of the organization. There was general acceptance that the lack of attention to new migrant enterprises represented a challenge. But there was little guidance from the literature on how to address this issue. Nor was funding available to support an exploratory exercise or intervention.

Secondly, SUPPAG was also subjected to pressure by very influential intermediaries purporting to represent ethnic minority groups. Two such intermediaries were particularly vociferous, and were very critical of SUPPAG's capacity to support ethnic minority-owned business. One group maintained that they spoke for 'Asian' businesses, and was continually trying to lobby SUPPAG for funds to support its activities. The other group claimed to represent *all* ethnic minority groups, and wanted SUPPAG to commission it as the prime contractor to support ethnic minority businesses in the region. Ram had considerable 'local knowledge' of both these intermediaries stretching over a five-year period. He often met the group representatives at events, initiatives, and engagements relating to enterprise and diversity. Moreover, he frequently clashed with them over interpretations of the 'needs' of minority businesses, how these perceived needs should be met, and the representativeness of intermediary bodies. Senior SUPPAG officers asked him to provide guidance on these matters on a number of occasions. In many respects, this bears out Kundnani's (2002) critique of 'ethnic fiefdoms', where community leaders with their own vested interests engage in a struggle for state funding.

Finding a way to handle this seemingly intractable problem was a continual topic of conversation between Ram and SUPPAG officers. His usual response was to stress the desirability of gathering evidence to examine the accuracy of such claims.

Ram's stance towards the putative project was also informed by his structural location as an academic responsible for a research centre on ethnic minority businesses; this is the third salient pressure that shaped the intervention. He genuinely believed that evidence on the context, profile, and business support requirements of ethnic minority firms would be helpful in devising more appropriate policy interventions for organizations like SUPPAG. Previous research (Ram and Smallbone 2002; Deakins et al. 2003) had pointed in this direction. Importantly, the approach of this research was informed by the perspective of mixed embeddedness (Kloosterman 2010), which shifts attention away from the cultural characteristics of ethnic minorities to a more considered analysis of the economic and institutional contexts in which their businesses operate. Mixed embeddedness is compatible with CR since the pursuit of ontic depth is central to both perspectives. The former emerged as a response to one-sided approaches to embeddedness which either stressed structural entrapment of minority entrepreneurs ('political economy' approaches), or focused primarily on the 'ethnic' resources that facilitated minority businesses ('culturalist' approaches). Mixed embeddedness acknowledges the social relations and ties that ethnic minority businesses utilize; but it assesses them against the political, institutional, and economic contexts in which they operate. Hence, mixed embeddedness and CR accord serious and separate attention to structure and agency, and are concerned with their implications for each other.

However, Ram was also acutely aware of the fact that the centre that he directs had undertaken only one previous study on new migrant businesses (Ram et al. 2008). He felt that the centre needed to engage more seriously in contemporary discussion with 'superdiversity' (Vertovec 2007) as it applied to new migrant businesses in order to be responsive to contemporary developments. His engagement with SUPPAG provided an opportunity to explore ways in which he might pursue the funding required to make this a reality.

It was against the backdrop of these pressures that, in late 2007, Ram mooted with SUPPAG the idea of submitting a joint proposal to the main social science funding body in the UK, the Economic and Social Research Council, to identify and respond to the needs of new migrant businesses in the region. This involved negotiations with SUPPAG on the focus, approach, and ultimate purpose of the research. Its principal concern was with the identification of new migrant businesses, intermediaries with whom they could work to deliver support to such businesses, and the recruitment of individuals to undertake these tasks. Ram wanted to ensure that the funds would be used to recruit workers with academic as well as business experience, pursue theoretical interests as well 'profiling' activities required by the funder, and enact a consciously critical realist approach to action research. SUPPAG jointly funded the project with the ESRC. The formal start date for the project was October 2008, ending a year later. However, project-related interactions between the researchers and SUPPAG continued into much of 2010.

The foregoing discussion highlights how interactions with stakeholders involved in action research can provide insights into the nature of mechanisms and the objective structures in operation in a particular context. Relationships with stakeholders involve 'dialogue and negotiation between the potentially conflicting forces which make up the situation' (Winter and Munn-Giddings 2001: 65). SUPPAG was evidently struggling to respond to state-driven policy to objectify ethnic categories in a way that could be easily understood and managed (Gunaratnam 2003). This was compounded by the actions of locally powerful 'ethnic brokers' intent on articulating the 'authentic' ethnic voice of minority business owners, regardless of other networks and webs in which these individuals might be engaged. In such circumstances, the role of research as a resource for 'knowledge-based arbitration' rather than 'arbitration on the basis of power' (Porter and Shortall 2009: 259) is potentially significant. This was the approach taken by the researchers to promote the idea of the project; but it too reflected the position of the investigators. In the next section, we examine how we attempted to bring our perspective to bear on the different elements of the intervention.

LEVER TWO: NEGOTIATING THE 'TREACHEROUS' BIND

Undertaking research on 'race' or 'ethnicity' inevitably puts researchers in a 'treacherous bind' which involves managing the tension of 'how researchers can work with inadequate racial and ethnic categories that are to hand, whilst also finding ways of identifying and disrupting the ways in which the same categories can "essentialise"' (Gunaratnam 2003: 29). Gunaratnam's response is to argue for a 'doubled-practice' that simultaneously challenges essentialist approaches to ethnicity, whilst also making links with lived experience, political relations, and the production of knowledge. This accords with Carter's (2000) realist analysis, which recognizes the importance of examining 'race' as an object of social scientific inquiry, but not the notion of race as a conceptual tool in such an inquiry. This perspective informed each of the techniques that we deployed as part of the action research intervention, which comprised: participant observation; the design of a survey of new migrant business owners; and focus groups. The key implication of critical realism for these methods is that data are seen as evidence for real phenomena and processes, rather than simply the 'constructions' of participants. Data are used to make inferences, which can be tested against additional data (Maxwell 2012: 103).

Participant Observation

The capacity of the research team to act as participant observers was vital in establishing SUPPAG officers' theories-in-use in relation to the ways in which minority businesses were constructed by the organization. This was not a stated objective of the project; but was nonetheless central to our approach. 'Race-thinking' took a variety of forms. As a non-executive director, Ram witnessed the way in which ethnic minority businesses were seen as a distinct category by virtue of their ethnicity. Figures were kept on the number of firms in such categories; but there was little information on other features, for example, their markets, networks, or internal resources. Two other members of the research team were participant observers by virtue of being part of the business advisor team (as well as researchers gathering data on new migrant businesses). They observed the implementation of actual practices and policies towards ethnic minority businesses, and were able to assess the approaches that advisors adopted to such enterprises. This revealed that an essentialized approach to ethnic minority businesses was being perpetuated at an operational level too. For example, SUPPAG had appointed internal 'champions' to promote awareness of ethnic minority businesses; their remit was to act as a source of information and to work with colleagues to promote greater engagement with such firms. The prime qualification of these 'champions' was that they came from ethnic minorities themselves (rather than having the experience and knowledge of the kinds of *businesses* owned by ethnic minority communities). This is a crude form of 'ethnic matching' which implies a direct correlation between phenotype and 'perspective' (Ratcliffe 2001).

We extended the participant observer role to the development of links with intermediary organizations that had been ignored or excluded by SUPPAG. This was again outwith the project brief. SUPPAG's principal interest in this element was to identify intermediary groups that worked with new migrant communities. Our stated task was to 'map' new migrant intermediary organizations with a view to identifying relevant networks to disseminate business support information. This we did with around fifty groups. However, our discussions with these intermediaries revealed a genuine desire for a closer engagement with business support issues and the broader objectives of the research. Consequently, we went 'beyond contract' by intensifying our involvement with such groups in a number of ways, including undertaking detailed interviews with twenty-one intermediaries, developing collaborative links with some groups, and brokering relationships with SUPPAG. In so doing, we transcended the potential limitations of a 'participatory action research' model by deliberately including participants beyond the project sponsors (Cassell and Johnson 2006). These exercises were more than simple data-gathering opportunities. They resembled 'developmental workshops' (Winter and Munn-Giddings 2001) in which participants outlined their views on wider issues of engagement with SUPPAG and the research team. SUPPAG and the researchers developed ongoing relationships with many of these intermediaries and business owners, thus broadening the potential 'users' of the research (Rappert 1999).

Designing the Survey: Contextualizing New Migrant Businesses

The differing perspectives of the researchers and SUPPAG officers toward ethnic minority enterprise were reflected in approaches to the design and implementation of the survey. We conducted 165 detailed semi-structured interviews with new migrant business owners. The objectives of the survey were threefold: to examine the experiences of business owners, elicit their business support needs, and promote awareness of SUPPAG. SUPPAG officers were primarily interested in ascertaining where new migrant businesses were located and alerting owners to sources of business support. The research brief required us 'to identify concentrations and baseline data on new migrant business owners' and 'engage with new migrant business owners on a one-to-one basis to develop awareness of business support'. This was part of an organizational discourse of responding to the business support 'needs' of 'ethnic minority' enterprises. Hence SUPPAG officials wanted the questionnaire to focus on the business support issues, for example, business problems, sources of business advice, and future business support needs.

However, our previous work on ethnic minority firms (Ram and Smallbone 2002) showed that the business support needs of minority business owners cannot be detached from the causal powers of the various contexts in which firms were embedded, notably personal resources, but also in the surrounding structural context of markets, competition, and the state regulatory regime. Consequently, in the present research, an adequate understanding of business support issues needed to be informed by an awareness of the influence of these contexts, together with the resources that owners brought to bear in their businesses. Accordingly, and in line with the process of retroduction, we devised a theoretically informed questionnaire to elicit data that would cast light on the causal mechanisms suggested by our previous work. Hence, it included questions on different kinds of capital (owners' social networks, experience and qualifications, sources of finance) and contexts (markets and competition, location and regulation). At the same time, we shared our thinking with SUPPAG practitioners and heeded their requests to elicit more 'fine-grained' information on the channels and types of business support used by new migrants.

Focus Groups

We conducted five focus groups with new migrant business owners in order to deepen our understanding of issues relating to the provision of business support to such firms. The dominant forms of focus group research have been criticized for being 'embedded in the epistemological and methodological assumptions of positivism, behaviourism, and empiricism, and in social relations which service power' (Johnson 1996: 516). However, we viewed the exercise as an opportunity to explore respondents' 'common-sense' perspectives on key elements of business support by linking their comments to the wider context in which such businesses operate. For example, the survey findings and comments by focus group respondents suggested that there were widespread perceptions of unfair treatment from financial institutions. One not untypical owner commented, 'there are better chances of me getting support from my community than from the banks', whilst another said that 'it's difficult to get a bank business loan here'. We pursued questions on the context of the firm, sector, and regulations (which are key elements of mixed embeddedness); this revealed a high level of 'irregular' businesses which would inevitably struggle to provide the paperwork required to access finance from banks.

Further, invoking Bhaskar's (1989) notion of a 'transformational act', the focus group has the potential to be used by social scientists to empower participants, thereby fusing 'social research and change' (Johnson 1996: 518). Although we do not claim that the focus groups in the present project merit the epithet of 'transformational', we nonetheless endeavoured to work with participants to explore the broader business support system. This was done in two ways. First, the focus groups were organized in collaboration with a social enterprise with community links and an ambition to work with 'mainstream' organizations like SUPPAG. The research team helped the respective organizations to collaborate, and also developed a working relationship that extended well beyond the duration of the project. Second, the focus group participants had an opportunity to interrogate SUPPAG officers on the nature of business support available to them. Many made contact with SUPPAG after the focus group activity.

The underlabouring role of CR in each of the methods deployed was important in drawing attention to three key features relating to the research object. First, it was clear that SUPPAG was captured by an essentialized theory in use which served to limit its effectiveness in respect of the provision of support to ethnic minority and new migrant businesses. Researchers' immersion in the organization highlighted how officers constructed minority businesses primarily in 'ethnic' terms. This was evident in the way in which such businesses were classified; reliance on 'ethnic' minority intermediaries for assessments of the needs of such businesses; and the appointment of 'champions' on the basis of their ethnic affiliation rather than business expertise. The compatibility of mixed embeddedness with CR is also evident. Officers' preoccupation with the empirical realm, without sufficient attention to the wider context of minority businesses, meant that undue attention was accorded to the 'ethnic' characteristics of such firms. Second, the capacity of SUPPAG to make a rational adjudication of the nature of new migrant businesses was hampered by its response to the pressure to categorize ethnic minorities in business, and by the organization's reliance on a narrow range of ethnic brokers for knowledge on such firms. Finally, the contextual account of new migrant businesses generated by the evidence from the survey and the focus groups painted a picture of marginal enterprises embedded in a range of social and economic relationships. The 'ethnic' dimension was of little significance when set against these sources of embeddedness. In the next section, we examine how the researchers worked with practitioners in each of these areas.

LEVER THREE: TAKING ENGAGEMENT SERIOUSLY

Taking agency seriously means 'finding ways to work with practitioners to help them understand their situation, identify barriers and opportunities for change, implement solutions, and evaluate the results while never losing sight of the ways in which generative mechanisms operate to constrain and/or enable change in particular settings' (Kontos and Poland 2009: 69). 'Critical reflection' is central to this approach to engagement within action research. It is a process of sharing and negotiation that enables participants to 'recognise the existence of alternative rationalities, the limitations of our immediate interpretations, and, consequently, possibilities for change' (Winter and Munn-Giddings 2001: 53). Critical reflection took a variety forms in the present study. Regular discussions were conducted in formal quarterly meetings with SUPPAG, where researchers had an opportunity to present detailed reports on findings as they arose. Informal bi-monthly meetings were also held to consider matters such as the most appropriate ways to refer business owners to SUPPAG. Its officers also sat in on some of our interviews with new migrant business owners, and researchers, in turn, participated in a number of SUPPAG advisor meetings with business owners in order to develop their understanding of the nature of such interactions. Such exchanges are central to action research (Whyte 1991); but they can equally serve as a resource for the realist ambition of furnishing participants with causal concepts to assess their perceptions and practices. Hence, there were regular discussions on mixed embeddedness and the nature of 'super-diversity', particularly in relation to how it was manifesting itself in the region. Researchers shared their conceptualization of new migrant business activity and the findings that were emerging from the survey as it was being carried out.

Reconstructing 'Ethnic Minority' Enterprise

Our project was instrumental in assisting SUPPAG to develop a more contextualized approach to supporting 'ethnic minority' businesses. The strength of the realist orientation lay in its role in revealing that minority business is not a single thing and that the causal powers of SUPPAG work only when connected in relevant ways with different kinds of firm. In effect, the researchers helped to expose and challenge the somewhat essentialist theories in use that governed SUPPAG approaches to ethnic minority and migrant business support needs, and posited an alternative theoretical understanding based on a more contextualized approach. This was achieved by sharing with officers the insights on their constructions of ethnic minority gained from the process of participant observation; discussing the findings of the contextually sensitive survey of new migrant business owners; and offering a conceptualization of minority businesses based on mixed embeddedness. This interactive process is similar to Rogers's (2004) CR-inspired depth investigation of organizational change. Rogers worked with participants to surface their theories-in-use; his goal was to 'develop an alternative account of the situation and events of interest that may better explain the predicament of the research participant' (2004: 259).

This shift in perspective was a gradual process, facilitated by researchers' 'immersion' in the practice setting. Practitioners valued these ongoing exchanges; as one SUPPAG officer remarked, 'I think that…the good thing was that all the information that was being held in the project wasn't being kept until the very end…I think that we did learn as we went along'. As an indication of the causal powers of the research with regard to SUPPAG's conceptualization of migrant businesses, one official commented:

> Before the project, most of our information on ethnic minority businesses came from specialist ethnic organizations. They tended to suggest that the key issues facing such businesses were ethnic issues… What the research was saying was that these businesses faced business issues, not necessarily ethnic ones. (SUPPAG officer)

Changes in SUPPAG's Practice

The reconceptualization of the ethnic minority and new migrant businesses that occurred during the project helped SUPPAG to develop a more nuanced view of its causal powers. One example is the re-assessment of some of its internal practices in relation to ethnic minority businesses. As noted earlier, SUPPAG appointed a number of 'champions' whose main role was to work with ethnic minority businesses. However, it became evident that these 'champions' were often diverted from this role by the other elements of their job; did not share their knowledge of ethnic minority firms systematically with other members of the organization; were insufficient in number to cover all parts of the region; and had little if any specialist knowledge of new migrant communities. Further, a community leader who had worked with SUPPAG commented, 'I have been in touch with SUPPAG several times, I have never heard about these ethnic minority champions.' Towards the end of the project, the decision to abolish the champions' role was taken. In effect, the causal powers of SUPPAG's approach of supporting ethnic minority businesses—that is, viewing such businesses in terms of ethnicity rather than the broader context in which they were embedded—were shown to be inadequate.

The project prompted SUPPAG to develop working relationships with a wide range of new migrant intermediary networks, many of which were unknown to it prior to the commencement of the research. SUPPAG began to hold regular meetings with these intermediaries. The meetings often served as precursors to a number of joint events and activities. The following extract from an email from one of the networks indicates their keenness to engage with SUPPAG:

> As part of one our projects, we will be displaying the products or services of at least twenty businesses... We would like [SUPPAG] to be present as we are trying to bring potential clients and funding bodies/business support together... I want to know that you will be available for interaction with the participants.

Our interactions also prompted SUPPAG to develop new ways of engaging with new migrant businesses. Rather than relying on a narrow group of 'ethnic' intermediaries (which usually represented established groups), the researchers and SUPPAG officers developed a close working relationships with several specialist media outlets that catered specifically for new migrant communities. This extract from the diary notes of a member of the research team describes the development initiative to promote their services to new migrant business owners through these new channels:

> Prior to the research SUPPAG had traditionally advertised through mainstream media. Our research showed that this was not an effective way to access the new migrant communities and we suggested to them [many alternative] networks, which SUPPAG were happy to adopt.

One possible indication of the success of this and other engagement efforts (for example, involvement of intermediaries and the focus groups) was the substantial increase in the recorded number of SUPPAG interactions with ethnic minority businesses. It rose from 2,999 in the year before the project to 4,214 after the end of the initiative. This increase was considerably more than expected. Although it is difficult to attribute it entirely to the project, a SUPPAG officer suggested that:

> We would like to think that some of that is down to the contact that we have made with intermediaries. I don't think that we should underestimate the efforts of just two people [the researchers]…I think certainly a lot of it was increased aware-ness of the [our] brand and engaging with businesses…With [researchers] out there on our behalf because of the research, and because they are talking about [SUPPAG]…The…referrals that are generated get back into the system.

Crucially, the process of critical reflection that permeated the project coin-cided with the gestation phase of a major SUPPAG investment in 'outreach' support. As the present project was drawing to close, SUPPAG initiated a 'community-based' advisor programme; it comprised the recruitment of six business support officers who would be based in particular geographic com-munities across the region. It was clear that the experience of the present pro-ject was an important influence upon the new initiative, as the responsible SUPPAG officer explained:

> The learning from the new migrant project was continually being fed into the community-based advisor programme. It was invaluable in helping us think through what we would want from the business advisors and how we would want them to operate.

This innovation went with the grain of some of the key tenets of super-diversity and mixed embeddedness. For example, rather than focusing solely on eth-nicity, the new initiative emphasized the importance of developing an under-standing of the *context* in which many new migrant business owners were located. Community-based business advisors were encouraged to develop long-term relationships with new and aspiring business owners in these areas; this proved helpful in developing tailored interventions rather than the pre-vailing 'one-size-fits-all' approaches. Finally, knowledge from these advisors was now being shared within SUPPAG, thus enhancing the organization's knowledge of diversity and enterprise in new migrant communities.

CONCLUSIONS AND IMPLICATIONS

This chapter has outlined the value of combining CR with AR as part of a pro-ject that aimed to promote greater engagement between the sponsor organiza-tion, SUPPAG, and new migrant businesses. The researchers and practitioners at SUPPAG had an active commitment to change which they were able to pursue without detracting from their own particular preferences. For the researchers, this involved the development of theory as well as practice, whilst for SUPPAG it concerned the utilization of evidence to promote engagement with new migrant businesses.

The theoretical pay-off for researchers was a deeper and fuller understanding of the agency-structure dialectic as it applies to entrepreneurial minorities, an enriched knowledge base yielding fresh insights and, equally valuable, confirmation of previous themes. As anticipated, the hands-on approach of action research, with its direct involvement of all relevant stakeholders—SUPPAG, focus groups, and intermediaries—enabled us to build a fuller picture than would have emerged had we confined ourselves exclusively to interviews with business owners At the same time, the proximity granted by action research is tempered by the distance afforded by realist philosophy, ensuring that there can be no confusion between the ideal and the actual, between what *ought* to be and what *is*. Moreover, by throwing all these parties into mutual engagement, we demonstrated a means of releasing the active potential of entrepreneurial agency, of providing even the most poorly resourced operators with some means of negotiating steep commercial obstacles. For SUPPAG, the practical outcomes included: enhancing the knowledge base of a key business support organization; establishing relationships with intermediaries; developing potentially important support networks; and facilitating the delivery of actual business support to new migrant communities.

A number of wider implications also follow from the project. First, AR provides CR with an opportunity to ground its ideals in practice. The detached and abstentionist stance of much CR theorizing tends to privilege analysis and explanation, with correspondingly little attention being accorded to the logic of practice (Clegg 2005; Rogers 2004). As Beirne (2008: 679) observes in his review of the critically oriented literature on workplace participation, 'the main preoccupations and achievements have been analytical and empirical, yet the momentum dissipates at that point'. Critical realist action research provides theorizing with an applied edge. At a minimum, it obliges researchers to think through the practical consequences of their theoretical conjectures.

Second, linking CR explicitly with AR also puts causal responsibility in participants' own hands (Friedman and Rogers 2009). Developing explanations of depth can help to generate more plausible explanations of participants' situations thereby enhancing the scope for actionable knowledge. The promoting of a critical consciousness amongst participants can reveal social constructions, structural conditions that constrain, and mechanisms that have the potential to operate in a more progressive manner. Schön and Rein's (1994: 204) concept of 'reflective transfer' is relevant here since it refers to 'the process by which patterns detected in one situation are carried over as projective models to other situations to generate new causal inferences'. This helps researchers and practitioners to consider the issue of generalizability in a manner that is consistent with the tenets of both CR and AR.

Third, combining CR with AR helps to overcome the 'the dual hurdles of relevance and rigor' (Van de Ven 2007:34). We addressed these objectives by changing organizational practice whilst also contributing to more theoretical debates on mixed embeddedness and super-diversity in the context of new migrant entrepreneurs. Exploiting the different knowledge base of scholars and practitioners is central to this process; such interaction is arguably more conducive to the generation of useful insights than either party working in isolation. Clearly critical realist action research is well placed to address practical as well as theoretical issues. But there is scope to pursue more 'engaged' research using other methods too. Van de Ven (2007) argues that 'engaged scholarship' is compatible with many other different types of social research, including basic social science with advice of key stakeholders, collaborative co-production of knowledge with stakeholders, and design science to evaluate an applied programme. Stakeholder views can inform each stage of the research process, including the grounding of the research problem, development of plausible theories, research design, and the application of findings to address the research problem. Active collaboration between researchers and practitioners is an important feature of engaged scholarship; it usually requires repeated interaction between the parties in order to explore meanings, generate new insights and develop better causal accounts. Importantly, the critical realist ontology of engaged scholarship and its commitment to 'deep explanation' militates against undue subjectivity and instrumentalism.

Finally, engagement with the complexities of practice that inevitably attends action research of this kind has implications for the skills of researchers. Although CR has a very clear analytical role for researchers, conflicting views on the purpose and impact of action research requires investigators to be political actors too. Institutional and political sophistication is required as well as intellectual effort (Rappert 1999); whether sufficient emphasis is accorded to these skills in the contemporary research environment is a moot point.

Yet there are also limits to what can be achieved. Engagement with SUPPAG far from enabled business owners to enact the context on their own terms. Re-interpret their roles they certainly can, but they cannot re-write the script. This point connects to CR's emancipatory agenda. In this particular case, emancipation was tightly constrained, and the subsequent abolition of the structures of regional government within which SUPPAG was embedded further underlined this fact. Yet in other circumstances the possibilities for emancipation may be greater; this case merely illustrates one situation.

But emancipation for whom? According to Sayer (2000: 158), CR 'gives a complacent account... in which *ought* follows straightforwardly from *is*'. If people do not want, or do not know that they want, to be emancipated, who are we as social scientists to tell them where their best interests lie? The underlying idea here is 'critical engagement' with practice. This may be contrasted with two other approaches. The first assumes that knowledge is produced and then applied. It has a mechanical view of what knowledge is, and also a naive view of how knowledge is applied in the context of power and inequality. The second approach speaks of the co-production of knowledge with practitioners. This helps in some ways but it leaves unresolved some key questions: if we co-produce with one set of practitioners, what of the interests of others; and will academics and practitioners even agree as to what the knowledge is that has been generated? Lessons to be drawn from research projects are often contested. The idea of critical engagement recognizes the need to relate with practitioners, but through a dialogue that may continue to be contested.

In the present case, SUPPAG's view of what it was doing, and of what a minority business really was (its essence, that is), was changed. We can also say that this marked an improvement. Such a claim is more than an assertion from a particular viewpoint, for in this case it was accepted by key actors in SUPPAG and was also embedded in relevant theory. There was a clear chain, and not a leap, from 'is' to 'ought'.

It is true that 'emancipation' for some is likely to affect other groups. In this case some interests may have been damaged. In particular, some groups representing minority firms had a definition of these firms' interests based in the ethnic origins of the firms' owners. The research helped to change this definition, potentially to the detriment of the groups concerned. But, we would argue, the definition was based on a view that could be demonstrated to be incorrect or at best partial. Such a demonstration may harm the groups' claim to expertise, but in so far as they also claim to know the nature of the ethnic business community they should also accept that some of their own interests are advanced. One could also point to balancing benefits, not least for the firms as opposed to these representative groups. Finally, these groups were not prevented from arguing their own case. Knowledge is always contested, but in this case we can say that there were genuinely emancipatory results.

Once we argue in terms of emancipation, it follows that some interests may be challenged and that interests are not taken as unquestionable. If there are grounds for challenging these interests, a CR project is defensible. In this case these grounds were reasonably clear, but in other situations this may not be the case. Claiming an emancipatory agenda requires that the analyst ask hard questions about each instance.

Action researchers need to consider whether a particular policy conclusion stems from the research in such a way that the effects of the policy on the various interest groups involved can reasonably be taken into account. In the central field of 'classic' AR, socio-technical design, an 'improvement' in some aspect of work organization can well have negative consequences for the workers affected. This is not necessarily to argue that the improvement not be made, but to point out the need to try to consider costs and benefits. In situations of this kind, realist action researchers would need to acknowledge that the decision was a political one. That is, the participants have to make a choice in light of available information, and CR can be helpful in explaining the nature of this information and also in insisting on the underlying causal processes and the actors involved in those processes: what may look like an improvement in a specific context of a work team may have negative consequences for other teams. But in our view CR would not have a privileged position in the making of one political choice rather than another.

Politics also shaped the intervention itself. As explained under 'lever one', Ram took a particular view of engagement with ethnic minorities that clashed with those of some groups. The design of the intervention reflected his own position and was not a piece of abstract science. But, we would claim, the intervention was designed in a transparent way without being predetermined, and the conclusions can be justified in evidence. Nonetheless, it is in the nature of any action intervention that it starts from a point of view, and this fact has to be acknowledged.

AR informed by CR can begin to engage with such large questions. Even if it does not, we can see how CR can begin to address action in practice, as opposed to the analytical importance of agency. CR researchers might give more attention to AR than they have done hitherto.

12

History and Documents in Critical Realism

Alistair Mutch

Many features of critical realism in practice suggest that we might pay more attention to the historical dimensions of analyses; it is the purpose of this chapter to consider what this might mean in more detail. I make the assumption that most readers are not intending to engage in historical analysis but to understand how they might draw upon such analyses to add to their primary focus. Accordingly, I seek to draw upon my own work, published in both historical and organizational theory journals, to consider what historical methods might mean in practice. Initially, I develop some of the reasons why those working in the critical realist tradition advocate the necessity of history (Fullbrook 2009: 21). While there tends to be an association between history and the archive, I recognize that for many it is secondary work that will be of importance and I review some considerations in using this. However, the question of archival sources remains important and I consider the ways in which some of the concerns of historians with the nature, provenance, and forms of archival sources can help to enrich contemporary research practices. I conclude with some thoughts on the construction of 'analytical narratives' and how these might consider the concatenation of mechanisms operating at different spatial and temporal levels.

A number of the examples to be explored below have been concerned with broad sweeps of time at a considerable level of abstraction, centred on entities such as societies and nations. However, for some working in the critical realist tradition such terms are rather too amorphous and they suggest a focus on more specific structures. Key amongst these is the organization. Elder-Vass (2010) has presented an account of organizations as key causal social structures. Organizations, he argues, are composed of roles and relationships: they, 'tend to be strongly structured by specialised roles; and secondly, they are marked by significant authority relations between at least some of these roles'

(Elder-Vass 2010: 152). On the basis of the coordinated interactions that these generate, he argues that an organization is 'a kind of hybrid entity: an entity that includes both people and other material things as its parts, and that depends on relations between both people and those other things to produce its emergent properties' (Elder-Vass 2010: 157). Such an entity endures over time and it is this property of endurance that makes history important. While the relationships that obtain between roles are constantly being negotiated, and whilst new roles can be specified and existing ones modified, the causal powers of the organization tend to be relatively enduring. In turn, as Elder-Vass notes, organizational members draw upon wider aspects of the social and cultural structures of which they are a part. Their actions will be an important part of change in those wider structures, but here in interaction with other organizations.

Here the notion of the organizational field, widely used in new institutional forms of organizational sociology, but drawn ultimately from Bourdieu, is of considerable value (Scott 2008). Drawn more broadly than terms such as 'sector', the field contains a variety of organizational actors and is an arena for establishing broader sets of understandings about how members operate. So, for example, Pollock and Williams (2009) point to the vital role of consulting firms in establishing classifications for software that shape the activities of both customers and suppliers. The organizational field is a space of positions and understandings that mediates between individual organizations and wider cultural and social structures. What we can see here is the potential for change at different levels and at different speeds. Such more enduring features are in turn likely to condition the actions that organizations can take, providing them with, in Archer's terms, 'situational logics' that point to appropriate courses of action. This distinction between levels is key to an appreciation of the historical dimension. This raises questions about how to unpick the evolution and interaction of levels through time. Such questions suggest that historical forms of analysis are vitally important, but probably often neglected. Before considering how historical methods might be used in practice, the next section considers some broader questions about the relationship between history and critical realism.

HISTORY AND CRITICAL REALISM

A number of the features of critical realism outlined in the introduction suggest the importance of a historical approach. Two key terms in the ontological armoury of CR are emergence and stratification. In the social world, structures which emerge from ongoing human interaction endure to shape future interactions. In so emerging they change at different paces. The great institutions of social life, such as the family and law, change at a different pace from, say, organizational routines. Indeed, change in these institutions can be so slow that it is only when we have temporal separation between two or more instances that we can register change. Thus, historical investigation can give us temporal, as opposed to spatial, contrasts to inform the contrastive explanation that, for example, Tony Lawson (2003) advocates in economics. It can also indicate to us just how emergence operates to create entities which, once emergent, cannot be reduced back to their constituent parts.

We have seen that CR employs a particular style of reasoning called retroduction. Here, the question that is asked is what must the world be like to enable the particular phenomenon that is of interest to us? Such a question then shapes the search for the range of generative mechanisms which might have combined to create the phenomenon. Such mechanisms might operate at a number of levels and, crucially, at a range of timescales. By its very nature, therefore, retroduction sends us back in time to look for antecedents. Just how far back is a matter of the particular phenomenon in question, but one might suggest that CR sensitizes one to go further back than a setting of the immediate 'context'.

In the study of the social world the most influential application of ideas drawn from CR is to be found in the work of Margaret Archer (1995). Over a series of books, she has stressed the need to examine the interplay of structure, culture, and agency over time. Her 'morphogenetic' approach can be summarized as follows:

> Every morphogenetic cycle distinguishes three broad analytical phases consisting of (a) a given structure (a complex set of relations between parts), which conditions but does not determine (b), social interaction. Here, (b) also arises in part from action orientations unconditioned by social organization but emanating from current agents, and in turn leads to (c), structural elaboration or modification—that is, to a change in the relations between parts where morphogenesis rather than morphostasis ensued. (Archer 1995: 91)

There is clearly a commitment here to a historical form of analysis, one which can be seen most clearly in her work on culture (Archer 1996). Here she argues for the existence of what Popper (1972) termed 'World 3' knowledge, what we might conceptualize as the world's library. This is the stock of knowledge that, separated from its conditions of production, endures and comes into logical relation with other forms of enduring knowledge. As such it forms both a resource for social action and a source of logical constraint, but those influences may sleep for generations until they are activated, perhaps by the emergence of new actors in the social domain. These are complex ideas developed at a high level of abstraction, but the implications for analyses closer to contemporary organizations is that they need to take account of the recursive relationship over time between agency and structure. Such inter-relationships

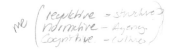

are unlikely to be convincingly examined by confining attention to one of the cycles outlined above. At the very least, attention will need to be paid, if we are to take conditioning seriously, to the formation of the structures within which social interaction takes place.

We can see a practical example of this attention to history in Archer's (1979) early work on the *Social Origins of Educational Systems.* Published in 1979 before her detailed engagement with CR, this work seeks to explore contrasts between the centralized nature of some systems and the decentralized nature of others. Over the space of 815 pages and 600 years, this account looked at four educational systems—those in England, Denmark, France, and Russia— in order to tease out the impact on education systems of long-term patterns of institutions and culture. She used this contrast to point to enduring mecha- nisms which lay behind the comparative success or failure of similar reforms when introduced into different systems. She also used it to critique the respec- tive positions of Pierre Bourdieu and Basil Bernstein, both significant theorists of educational transmission (Archer 1983). Both, she argued, failed to account in their analyses for the institutional specificity of their theories. Any analysis of the social world, therefore, has to pay serious attention to these long-run conditions.

Of course, such an enterprise is not just limited to those espousing CR. (Indeed, as we have noted, the inspiration for Archer's own work came in turn from works of sociology and it was the need for conceptual clarification that saw her engage with ideas from CR.) Others working in what we might term the domain of historical sociology have produced equally sweeping accounts seeking to elucidate underlying mechanisms. Robert Wuthnow (1989) for example, uses 583 pages to examine three key moments in the articulation of social structure and culture: the Reformation, the Enlightenment, and the origins of European Socialism. The parallels between his work and that of Archer have been noted, although not developed in detail, by Rambo and Chan (1990). Wuthnow concludes that:

> To understand how an ideology is shaped by its social environment, one must therefore examine the specific circumstances under which these expressions come into being, the audience to whom they are enunciated, the slogans and other materials that are available at the time for incorporation into discursive acts, the roles of speakers and audiences relative to one another and in relation to positions of power, and even the financial resources that make publishing activi- ties possible. Examining these contexts of ideological production enables one to establish with greater clarity why a particular constellation of ideas comes to be institutionalized successfully in a particular setting. (Wuthnow 1989: 540)

His work uses history to isolate these conditions and so to produce a gener- alized account of the articulation between ideas and social structures which might then be used in examining more contemporary situations. Another approach is to seek to uncover the longer-term mechanisms which, as with Archer's focus on degrees of centralization, shape current conditions for action. So, for example, Digby Baltzell examined three centuries of social life in Boston and Philadelphia with a view to demonstrating 'how class authority and leadership in the two cities was and still is related to the Puritan and Quaker ethics of their founders' (Baltzell 1979: 2). His source for this exploration was entirely secondary works of historical scholarship, as is common in works of historical sociology.

One can see much historical writing as involving explanations of the relative weights of agency and structure. On the one hand there are works in the tradition of Annales school in France, with a concentration on the *longue durée*, that is, the slowly changing and relatively enduring structures that frame and condition action (Veyne 1984). On the other hand there is a focus on more or less conscious agency, with a stress on the creative activities of actors in practice. This was most clearly seen in E. P. Thompson's discussion of class struggle as a process in his *The Making of the English Working Class* (Thompson 1968). Intruding into such debates has been the influence of the 'linguistic turn', which saw some arguing that history was nothing more than the construction of stories about the past (Evans 1997). The focus of historians should therefore be on the nature of such stories, rather than any search for a 'real' past. These arguments have led to historians being more sensitive to language and symbolism in their accounts, and to the ways in which traditions can be invented, but it is possible to assert that most history still adopts an approach broadly consistent with the relational approach espoused by critical realists such as Archer (Sewell 2005). It is not the purpose of this chapter to make a case for the claims of critical realist approaches in these debates, although their value and application seems clear. Rather it is to draw on historical work to see what lessons there might be for the study of organizations. This might start with the assertion that mainstream historians could be characterized as having a pragmatically realist approach. This is often not explicitly stated. As Chris Wickham, a noted Marxist historian, complains:

> Historians tend to avoid theorizing; it is one of the most characteristic cultural features of the discipline, in fact. But it is also one of its major weak points, for the attachment of historians to the empiricist-expository mode only too often hides their theoretical presuppositions, not only from others, but from the writers themselves. As a result, historians can fall into contradictory arguments, and risk overall incoherence; entire historical debates have, on occasion, depended on theoretical presuppositions which were indefensible, and which would have been immediately seen as such had they been articulated. (Wickham 2011: 221)

This is not to say that such theoretical commitments are not present (indeed, how could they not be) but that they are developed through the form of presentation rather than being explicitly laid out as is the expected style in organizational studies. For example, one historian who has attended to these matters in a work which examines the sense of local belonging in England and Wales between 1700 and 1950, and who does so as an explicitly declared 'social-science historian' provides a brief account of the 'real' which accords with broadly CR sensibilities (as opposed to broadly 'postmodern' approaches) but at the same time provides a rationale for not exploring 'theory' in detail. 'I have deliberately not engaged very openly with sociological and cultural theory in this book,' writes Keith Snell (2006: 23), 'even though there is some theoretical literature on the theme of belonging, and far more on communities identities, globalisation, and secularisation, from across the social sciences and humanities'. Part of his reasoning is that this would take up too much room, and so the concepts are integrated into the broader discussion of the evidence. But there is the further reason that 'some of the theoretical literature contains many historical mistakes, and it is probably best to use it as a jumping-off point, inspiring new questions, rather than regard it with too much respect' (Snell 2006: 23). However, he concludes that 'I have no problems in believing that the past was 'real', that much of that reality can be discerned and outlined, and that certain themes, emphases, patterns, experiences, and consistent personal accounts emerge repeatedly from the documentary and quantitative evidence' (Snell 2006: 26). This is not an uncommon approach and it means that those taking a CR perspective will need to read historical work against their general conceptual understanding; in other words, to return to the notion of CR as under-labourer in order to be able to distinguish those secondary works of most value in informing them of the historical context to their studies.

HISTORICAL METHODS IN ORGANIZATIONAL FIELDS

For many examining contemporary organizational practice, the value in historical work may simply be in supplying a richer and more extended context for their analyses. However, historical work also supplies a good deal of useful and rich guidance on how to extend the types of evidence that we bring to bear. Some of this guidance applies to often neglected sources such as documents and it can be useful to review how historians approach such sources. However, if we wish to delve into the historical evidence itself we are also faced by consideration of archival resources. Accordingly, in what follows I draw on some of my own work, conducted within the broad parameters of a morphogenetic approach, which engaged with historical sources at a number of levels. I do this to indicate the different types of evidence deployed in building historical accounts and how they might contribute to explanation. My work began with using largely secondary material to frame some aspects of contemporary

the brewery industry tended to have a strong focus on the tenancy model and to underplay the development of the direct management which was to prove so important later. What seemed important here was how companies interpreted the purpose of direct management. In companies with a long history of the employment of managers, notably Allied Breweries and Bass, the conception was one of control. By contrast, companies which came later to the practice had a looser conception, with more emphasis on the use of management to interpret customer needs. As we will see, Whitbread was more able to join this conception with the shift to retailing. Accordingly, this seemed a case to me where one could not rely on the existing accounts and where original historical investigation was needed. This leads us to a consideration of archival materials, and this is done in the next section.

THE HISTORY OF MANAGEMENT: PRINTED AND ARCHIVAL SOURCES

In tracing the history of the direct management of public houses it is useful to distinguish between two classes of evidence. One is those sources which were created at the time of the events we are studying, but which were created for the specific purpose of commenting on the phenomenon under investigation. Newspapers are the clearest example of such sources, but there are many more. The other is those documents which were created for other purposes but which might shed light on the phenomenon under consideration in more ARCHIVES indirect ways. Such might, for example, be the records which bear in their very existence the marks of a particular practice. Both were important in reconstructing the emergence of direct management.

My attention was drawn to the Liverpool firm of Peter Walker & Son by examination of the evidence given to a Royal Commission on the Licensing Laws in the 1890s (Mutch 2006b). These official investigations into particular social problems contain detailed testimony from the witnesses called and examined. Of course we have to be cautious about such evidence. The selection of witnesses and the questions asked reflected the predilections of the committee, which often had particular solutions in mind. The responses of witnesses might also be conditioned by their position as the representatives of particular bodies or their sensitivity to the issues. However, in this case there was an intriguing observation, one which had not been picked up in other historical work, by Ernest Ellis, secretary of Peter Walker & Son, that 'the founders of my company are generally credited with being the originators of the system [of direct management]' (UK Parliament 1898: 391). This observation in turn led to the discovery of a celebratory account of the company's operations which stoutly declared that 'the Managerial System, in fact, offers the prospect of order evolved from chaos' (Peter Walker & Son 1896: 56). Such claims suggested the potential origins of direct management and a site for further investigation.

It is worth observing that such printed sources of historical evidence are becoming more easy to find through electronic finding aids and to consult given the widespread digital imaging of printed sources. In the UK, for example, the Early English Online database contains digitized copies of virtually every work printed in England, Ireland, Scotland, Wales and British North America and works in English printed elsewhere from 1473–1700. The 19th Century British Library Newspapers collection contained, at the time of writing, full runs of forty-eight newspapers. Efforts continue to make a broader range of material accessible. Prior to these initiatives the need to consult these sources in specialist locations would often make their use impractical. Their existence now makes historical analysis using such sources more feasible, although it also raises some concerns with their status as evidence.

The primacy accorded to archival sources in traditional approaches to history was based in large measure on their insights into conduct based not on the interpretation of the actors but on the chance survival of documents which gave a window on their actions. Archives were therefore seen as a quarry for evidence. This was called into question by the linguistic turn, which raised new questions about the status of archives. These questions were about the genres embedded in their construction and the linguistic devices which not only mediated but shaped action. This broadened the class of evidence beyond documents to encompass other forms of material culture. It also gave a new status to the secondary documents, which were now seen not as a sort of evidence but as supplying an indication of the discourses which shaped the actions being recorded in the primary documents. This broader conceptualization was to be found in the influential works of Foucault, who used a selection of secondary literature, especially in the form of advice manuals, to shape his investigation of discourses. So, for example, *Discipline and Punish*, probably his most celebrated work, relies heavily on works such as a blueprint for Jesuit educational provision (Foucault 1991). In his later work, especially in the lectures on pastoral power, he recognizes the limitations of such work. So, for example, in his analysis of confessional techniques he notes of the advice books that he examines that they 'were effectively put to work in the formation of confessors themselves, rather than in the average faithful among the people' (Foucault 1999: 191) This points our attention to the networks in which such works were put into action, the type of considerations that Wuthnow outlines.

Citing Foucault may seem unusual in CR-influenced work, although there are those who point to the realism in his work (Pearce and Woodiwiss 2001). For our purpose the interest is in the way in which secondary works can illuminate that broader cultural framework, of outlining the possibilities and resources available to actors. The broader availability of such texts makes it more feasible now to consider the discourses that might have influenced action.

However, an examination of contemporary management practices would urge caution about a simple reading off of organization practices from handbooks of procedure or even declarations of adoption. We know from this work that what is adopted in practice often varies considerably in practice from the laid-down blueprint. And we also know that blueprints cannot contain all the answers; that routines have to be and are adapted to meet new circumstances. The implication of this is that, in some cases, we cannot escape the concrete investigation of practice, and such investigations force us to attend to primary sources.

The company records of Peter Walker & Son are held in Liverpool Record Office, but are quite fragmentary in nature. I was able to find managed house accounts dating from the late 1840s in this collection of papers, although they were not separately catalogued. What was frustrating were hints about the existence of others. I was aware that the main actor in the firm, Andrew Barclay Walker, had moved into the ranks of the landed gentry by a marriage and the purchase of a country estate at Osmaston in Derbyshire. Inquiries with the Derbyshire Records Office indicated that family papers relating to the Walker-Okeover family had been deposited there. However, they were only partially catalogued and, in the view of the archivist, contained only family material. However, examination of a box of material led to ledgers used for both family and business matters which contained a summary of managed house accounts. This in turn was supported by a large collection of managed house accounts, which enabled me to construct a detailed picture of the development and financial returns of this organizational practice (Mutch 2006b). So work in the archives is open to chance and serendipity. While directed by the questions that we ask initially, the nature of the sources might either constrain the answers we can give or suggest new directions. In forming explanations from the material, we need to use our theories to supply concepts which enable us to rise above the detail whilst acknowledging the particularity of specific events. This is where the guidance given by the broader tenets of critical realism is useful.

As with the printed sources, electronic finding aids have opened up archives and their holdings to a much broader audience. It has to be understood that such aids vary considerably in their usefulness. Some are a simple translation of paper finding aids, aids which were always intended to be used in conjunction with the implicit knowledge of the archivist and so often incomplete as a guide to collections (Cox 2007). Others, by contrast give a considerable amount of detail, detail that at times obviates the need for visits to archives. Indeed, some catalogues are so complete that much can be gained from an analysis of their contents. I have been, for example, able to draw some broad conclusions about the existence of separate accounts in the eighteenth-century Church of Scotland based on an analysis of catalogue entries which supplements the more detailed evidence gleaned from detailed local studies (Mutch 2013). Examples of catalogues

examples of
catalogues:

in the UK which give indications of records are those at the National Records of Scotland and Access2Archives, the latter covering many of the record offices in England. By this means the existence of records can easily be established. However, this does not necessarily remove the need for visits to the archives. This can be for two reasons. One is that such finding aids are often the only part of collections available electronically. While great strides are being made in making material available electronically, much remains difficult to digitize. The other is that archives often lack the resources to catalogue the material they do hold, so catalogues are often radically incomplete.

Another consideration is that it is useful to consider why an archive survives at all. The existence of an archive of papers, in the sense of a significant body of material, deliberately preserved, can shed some light on the nature of an organization and the broader context in which it exists. To draw upon my own work, there is a striking difference between the survival of the records of church administration at the local level in England and Scotland. In the Deanery of Bingham, Nottinghamshire (an administrative unit of the Church of England), for example, records for only twenty out of fifty parishes (the basic unit of church administration) for the eighteenth century survive in the local record office. By contrast, the comparable administrative unit of the Church of Scotland at the same time, the Presbytery of Garioch in Aberdeenshire, had sixteen parishes but extensive records, amounting to over 8,000 pages, for the thirteen that have survived in the National Records of Scotland (Mutch 2013). This difference points in turn to two very different systems, one national and systemic in character, the other local and fragmented. In England survival owes much to contingent local factors; in Scotland it was the product of a focus on record-keeping which extended back into the seventeenth century. In 1696, for example, one of the procedure manuals that I've referred to above laid down:

> That registers of all Judicatories may be better Preserved, it were fit, that every Session deliver their fair Register to the Presbytery every ten Year; and every Presbytery theirs, and the Sessions in to the synod, every fifteen Years; and that every Synod, every twenty Year, order all these, and their own fair Register, to be laid up in the publick Library of that University, which is next adjacent to them; where they may be safely keeped from Accidents, for the future benefit of the Church. (Anon 1696: 9)

This stipulation is significant in its right and it is reinforced by examination of the records, which suggest that it met with a considerable measure of success. That records survive at all, that is, raises questions about why certain records survive and not others, answers to which can in turn give us some hints about broader influences.

Another consideration is the form in which records survive. Often the use of archival material is associated with the archive as a quarry of *content*.

However, the examination of bodies of material can often indicate changes in *form* which can also be instructive. The idea of the genre can be useful here. Genres are taken for granted and accepted forms of communication whose patterns are often only seen in broad collections of material. Wuthnow, for example, explores the emergence of new genres such as the sermon, aided by technological developments such as printing, in his consideration of the Reformation. Jo-Anne Yates (1989) has used this category to particularly good effect to examine changes in management control in the development of American industry. She points to taken-for-granted and mundane innovations such as the development of vertical filing systems, accompanied by the refinement of the genre of the 'memo' and given material form in filing cabinets and typewriters, as being central to the control of large divisionalized corporations. In my own work on eighteenth-century Church of Scotland minutes it is noticeable how a legalistic language, initially promulgated in the procedure manuals I reviewed above, reaches down to the local level and shapes the recording of events. Here is one extract which indicates the tenor of such records:

> And then proceeding to revise the treasurers account & having diligently collated and compared them with the accounts kept by their clerk and finding them to agree in omnibus found that the hail money intromitted with by him from the Day of last clearance (vide page 61 & 62) amounts to the sum of Ninety six pounds ten shillings & Eight pennies Scots money [.] That he had at sundry times from the date foresaid with the knowledge of the session & by their orders & with their special approbation including the articles in his Discharge of this Date deburst all & whole the sum of sixty three pounds three shillings & four pennies Scots money, from whence it appeared that the sum remaining in his hands & now to be accounted for by him is thirty three pounds seven shillings & four pennies Scots.[2]

At a distance in time this can seem convoluted and slightly amusing, but such statements represent more than mindless clichés. They mark a serious tone which, it is conceivable, spreads into what Peter Hall (1984) calls for the United States the 'culture of organization', that is, the taken-for-granted ways of organizing. They also provide a link with not just the procedure manuals but also with the broader character of the law and its influence in this particular situation.

Genres also change over time, as Yates' work indicates. Indeed, such a concept can then be applied to contemporary organizations, with the emergence of genres such as the PowerPoint presentation (Kellogg, Orlikowski, and Yates 2006). However, the power of her account is the setting of such changes in a broader historical setting. It is interesting to note the impact of mechanization

---

[2] National Records of Scotland, CH2/310/5, kirk session minutes, Rayne, 25 July 1750.

on the genre of minutes in the case of UK brewing companies. The minutes of the board of directors of Whitbread start to be typewritten in 1934, replacing large handwritten folios. By contrast this does not happen at Bass, the largest company, until after the Second World War and this is perhaps an index of the conservatism of this company, something apparent in the examination of the annual reports discussed above. Attention to genre, that is, to the form as well as the content of documentary sources, can be extremely valuable, especially when then placed in the context of other evidence.

FORMING EXPLANATIONS

This discussion should give some indication of the value of not only archival research in some cases but also of paying attention to the nature of documentary evidence. I have suggested that historical work is not just a matter of the archives, but involves the use of a range of evidence. This might be a broader set of evidence than is normally considered in much organizational analysis. An intriguing example can be found in the work of Snell (2006) on the sense of place referred to above. He uses inscriptions from over 16,000 gravestones in eighty-seven burial grounds to examine the importance of place in the nineteenth century. Given the expense of carving memorial stones, he argues, what was recorded must have been considered to be of importance. He tracks how details of place vary over time, showing that it was considered important to record locations until the end of the nineteenth century, after which place becomes unremarked. As he concludes 'People were once described, given an identity, and their behaviour even accounted for, by their place and their occupation in it, however parochial that might be' (Snell 2006: 492). This is an example of an innovative use of evidence and shows historians will use a range of methods to answer the questions they pose.

These observations are drawn from sources which are not exclusively critical realist in their formation, but it is worth returning to the value of historical approaches in critical realism when we consider what we do with all this evidence. That is, we are examining these records for a reason, and that reason is a better explanation of a focal phenomenon. Margaret Archer suggests that the task is the writing of what she terms 'analytical narratives of emergence'. She explains this as follows:

> On the one hand, both proponents and opponents of the *grand narrative* rightly see that the possession of, or the misguided pretension to possess (depending upon which side they are on) some master-key to historical development immediately dispenses with any need to *analyse* history: the historical becomes illustrative of a prior explanatory principle and no amount of further analysis can add anything more than local colour to explanation. Yet the point here is that

analytical narratives of emergence can never ever be *grand* precisely because the imperative to narrate derives from recognizing the intervention of contingency and the need to examine its effects on the exercise or suspension of the generative powers in question—since outcomes will vary accordingly but unpredictably. On the other hand, *analytical narratives* are obviously distinct from any version of historical narration *tout court*, for although social realists in general have no difficulty in accepting the strong likelihood of uniqueness at the level of events, the endorsement of real but unobservable generative mechanisms directs analysis towards the interplay between the real, the actual and the empirical to explain precise outcomes. (Archer 1995: 343)

This passage well locates the centrality of historical explanation to any analysis informed by critical realism, but we also need to consider how we use concepts to make sense of the material we have collected.

If we return to the example of the shift from a production to a retailing logic in the large companies which dominated British brewing from 1950 to 1990, we can certainly see some of the traces of the shift in the practices which companies adopted, notably in the dramatic expansion in the numbers of managers employed to run public houses. As we have noted, while all the companies moved in similar directions in the adoption of such practices, the pace of change and the depth of commitment was very different from company to company. While one mechanism at operation was clearly adaptation to social and economic change, this was far from being the rational response predicted by economic theory. At one end of the spectrum Whitbread adopted retailing enthusiastically, to such an extent that soon after the end of the period it left brewing altogether. By contrast, Allied Breweries never made the transition and was to metamorphose into the drinks company Allied Domecq. In order to explain such differences we need to examine mechanisms at the level of both the individual organization and the field. At the field level one can see the consolidation of a retailing logic in changes in the remit of trade bodies. At the same time, the field became more open to influences from other business models, notably by the entry of new companies into a field which had traditionally been conceived of as the province of brewers. The trend for industrial conglomerates, a feature of the British economy more generally, was an important factor here (Mutch 2009). However, it is when we look at individual companies that history becomes important. Knowing what we do about the origins of the managed-house system in Liverpool, we can see how it became associated with a particular conception of management, one based on tight control and discipline, in Allied Breweries. Peter Walker & Son was a major component of this often uneasy merger of a number of companies, and it was their conception of management that was to win out (Mutch 2006c). By contrast, Whitbread had always positioned itself as a supplier to the free trade and was somewhat reluctant to become involved in running public houses directly. When it did so, however, its efforts were associated with the public house improvement of the 1920s and 1930s, which placed much greater stress on meeting perceived customer needs (Mutch 2010). That is, what 'management' means is conditioned by historical experience. The focus on management as control that was built up from early experience with the management of public houses in Liverpool in the mid nineteenth century meant that it was difficult for Allied Breweries to adapt to the broader conception that was needed to advance the cause of retailing in the 1970s. By contrast, Whitbread, having resisted direct management for so many years, was able to refashion it in the service of a more customer-focused approach. Historical investigations can, therefore, explain some of the mechanisms operating at the organizational level which then interact at the field level to produce particular outcomes.

I have drawn on the concept of the field from new institutionalism to enrich the morphogenetic approach and to indicate how we might employ historical methods to examine organizational change. I have shown how such methods might be used in the construction of analytical narratives. Such methods do not have to be about the use of archival materials. There is much that researchers can do with documentary sources. Perhaps the detail supplied here might encourage greater use of relatively neglected sources. However, in many cases if we are to probe the more enduring features of organizational life, we need to extend the temporal scale of our analyses. Here there is much value in attending to the nature of archival material. Here, I suggest that as well as viewing the archive as a quarry of material, it is valuable to consider the nature of the material that has survived. These can help in the development of analytical narratives in which we explore the interaction of agency and structure in contexts which have been shaped by longer-run factors. Simply focusing on the immediate context can mean that we neglect more significant mechanisms that provide situational logics for action. In the case of the adoption of the management of public houses in the UK in the second half of the twentieth century, these mechanisms included conceptions of what 'management' meant that were profoundly influenced by the historical experience of individual companies. While there might have been formal similarities at the level of the field, more detailed historical investigation suggested that how these field-level understandings played out in individual companies depended crucially on historically conditioned conceptions. This is not to deny the influence of other shorter-run mechanisms, such as demographics and geographical location, but it is to suggest the importance of history. The centrality of analytical narratives to critical realism suggests that researchers need to pay due attention to historical material. It has been the aim of this chapter to supply some concrete guidance about how this might be done.

13

Critical Realism and Mixed Methods Research

Combining the Extensive and Intensive at Multiple Levels

Scott A. Hurrell

INTRODUCTION

The aim of this chapter is to demonstrate how mixed methods research (MMR) can be utilized within critical realist (CR) ontology. The chapter uses the example of a study conducted at multiple levels of analysis (i.e. the economy (macro), organizations (meso), and individuals (micro)) and using multiple theoretical perspectives. The study to be discussed investigated the patterns of, and reasons for, soft (i.e. interpersonal and self-presentational) skills deficits (i.e. where an employer reports that a job applicant or worker lacks these skills) in Scotland. This chapter will show how a CR approach influenced the research process, choice of methods, and analysis of data with a particular focus on how research methods were combined. Weaknesses of the study are also discussed. The chapter begins with an overview of the methodological implications of other philosophies of science before addressing MMR and how this is commensurate with CR ontology.

MIXED METHODS AND CRITICAL REALISM

The traditional ontological dichotomy within social research is that of positivism vs. interpretivism with each having distinct epistemologies. Although a detailed rehearsal of these paradigms is not required here (see chs. 1 and 2), a brief interlocution into their methodological implications is necessary to then determine the distinct nature of MMR within CR.

In the case of positivists, quantitative methods typically give privileged access to social phenomena. Positivists believe in a single reality that exists independently of those experiencing it, which is amenable to observation and measurement (Tashakkori and Teddlie 1998). The focus on quantitative methods within positivism is inevitable, given that causality within this philosophy has traditionally been determined by the Humean notion of constant conjunctions of empirical events (Bhaskar 1978). Such an approach requires large samples of quantitative data in order to make time- and context-free generalization and predictions (Ragin 1994); further assuming closed systems (see chs. 1 and 2). CR views these closed systems as problematic as they do not represent the open, complex, and stratified systems of the social world (Bhaskar 1978, 1979). Quantitative analysis in the positivist sense may thus lead to reductionist theories that do not represent the complexity of reality.

Conversely, those who reject that an external social reality is knowable to researchers and who instead seek to uncover the *meanings* of social interactions (here referred to as interpretivists) favour qualitative methods. Indeed their attachment to this method is perhaps even stronger than the positivists' traditional attachment to quantitative methods. Following the rejection, by many, of positivism and the growing influence of anti-naturalism in social science following the 'paradigm wars' (Tashakkori and Teddlie 1998), some social scientists now reject *in totality* the usefulness of quantitative methods as a research methodology believing they *cannot* uncover social interactions (see, for example, Silverman 1993). Those who totally eschew quantitative approaches instead adhere to in-depth qualitative methods such as interviews, ethnography, or qualitative case studies. Therefore, there is a distinct 'epistemological chasm' between the use of qualitative and quantitative methods with particular antipathy evident from the qualitative side (Olsen 2004b: 103).

According to Olsen (2004b), however, this epistemological chasm is often driven by disciplinary differences rather than philosophical justifications, meaning that there is no reason why quantitative and qualitative methods may not be combined to utilize both of their strengths. A rejection of the quantitative/qualitative dichotomy has, in fact, been in existence for some time, with Bryman's (1988) oft-cited work *Quantity and Quality in Social Research* a prominent example. Even within positivist research there may be a role for qualitative methods, although the purpose is typically different from those taking an interpretive stance. Yin (1994), for example, describes how intensive qualitative research (specifically case-study research) is frequently used in the development of surveys and experiments. Traditionally, however, case studies were only deemed suitable for this exploratory stage, an assumption questioned by Yin. Downward and Mearman (2007) give the further example of Frankfort-Nachmias and Nachmias (2000). These authors opine that qualitative methods may be used within a positivist approach, where quantitative methods are not possible, although value-free hypotheses should still be tested. The pragmatic nature of Frankfort-Nachmias and Nachmias' argument is repeated by other methodological non-imperialists who advocate fitness for purpose and/or the use of multi-methods for data triangulation,[1] but without doing so from a particular ontological position (for example, Bryman 1988; Tashakkori and Teddlie 1998).

CR does not engage in the methodological imperialism of other approaches, but instead believes that methodological choices should 'depend on the nature of the object of study and what one wants to learn about it' (Sayer 2000: 19). Methods should thus display fitness for purpose. As Ackroyd (2004: 139) states when discussing the methodological choices facing CR researchers, 'only a child takes the hammer from the tool box every time'. Nevertheless, qualitative methods tend to predominate within CR research and especially case studies, given the emphasis on identifying causal mechanisms within particular contexts. Given CR's depiction of social reality as complex, differentiated, and where causal powers are contextually dependent (Bhaskar 1978, 1979), a preference for purely qualitative methods may seem intuitive. Such a preference for qualitative methods may appear stronger still as CR sees reality as mediated and influenced (if not determined) by agents' understanding and actions (Sayer 1992, 2000). Despite scepticism amongst some CR scholars regarding quantitative methods, however, (see chapter 16 for a detailed discussion) the choice of which methods to use remains, but goes beyond purely pragmatic concerns.

The choice of method within CR typically rests on Sayer's (1992, 2000) distinction between *extensive and intensive* research designs. Extensive research, as the name suggests, searches for large numbers of observations that can give significant relationships (i.e. quantitatively) and are, in Sayer's eyes, used purely for taxonomic purposes. Intensive methods, however, are concerned with, 'what makes things happen in specific circumstances', through examining the qualitative nature of phenomena and the intricacies of context, and are thus concerned with *causality* (Sayer 2000: 20). Essentially for Sayer, following Bhaskar, extensive relationships alone do not reveal causal mechanisms and he holds a commensurate cynicism for anything other than descriptive (rather than analytical) statistics.[2] The two research designs thus, 'have different purposes *but may be complementary in some research projects*' (Sayer

---

[1] Olsen (2004b) succinctly describes triangulation in social science as 'the mixing of data and methods so that diverse viewpoints or standpoints cast light upon a topic' (p. 103). MMR may be seen as a particular case of 'between-method' methodological triangulation (i.e. using different *types* of methods).

[2] For a defence of 'analytical' statistics within a CR perspective see Olsen and Wilson (2005).

2000: 20, emphasis added). Indeed it can be argued that combining extensive and intensive approaches provides the best of both worlds. Such combinations can highlight widespread phenomena of interest, drill down to explain *why* these may, or may not, have occurred in particular contexts, and provide depth not attainable through quantitative procedures alone (views echoed by Downward and Mearman 2007 and Olsen 2004b). MMR may thus overcome the weaknesses of using purely quantitative methods (i.e. a lack of intensity).

Developing the above themes further, Downward and Mearman specifically link the use of MMR within CR to the explanatory process of retroduction, the inferential process of establishing the causes of empirical phenomena through a posteriori explanation rather than deduction or induction (see also chs. 1 and 2). Building on Sayer's approach, they state that using different methods to explore different features of a phenomenon make MMR '*necessary* to reveal *different* features of the *same* layered reality' (Downward and Mearman 2007: 16, emphasis in original). Retroduction may for example help to describe phenomena through the 'quantitative analysis of data patterns and (then) qualitative investigations of the agencies and structures that produce the behaviour' (p. 18). Thus, for Downward and Mearman, MMR is not only *an* option it is *the* robust option for uncovering generative mechanisms whilst also constructing claims about which phenomena occur most frequently. Such an approach, however, does not conflate frequency with causality. Nor does CR MMR assume an artificial closed system; explanations are not deemed exhaustive (p.18) and there is no assumption of blanket monocausality either across or within contexts.

To summarize, unlike other philosophies of social science, CR does not engage in methodological imperialism recognizing the role of both quantity and quality within social research. MMR, however, still needs to be designed in a manner consistent with CR's ontological and epistemological assumptions. If these assumptions are adequately adhered to, CR MMR can allow different levels of reality to be established, and causality to be explained, whilst maintaining an open systems approach. The remainder of this chapter now illustrates how CR principles guided a particular piece of MMR in a study of soft skills deficits in Scotland.

THE CASE OF SOFT SKILLS DEFICITS

An Overview of the Project and Research Process

Surprising findings from the 2002 Scottish Employers' Skills Survey (SESS) motivated the empirical work described here (FSS 2003). This national survey revealed, contrary to popular understanding and media reports, that where Scottish employers reported skills deficits either with current staff ('skills gaps') or when recruiting new staff ('skills shortages') these were much more widely reported in 'soft'[3] rather than 'hard' skills. Soft skills included areas such as communication, customer-handling, and team-working,[4] whilst technical and practical skills, IT skills, and literacy were examples of 'hard' skills (FSS 2003). Following the 2002 SESS, the current study (published in full in Hurrell, 2009) was then established to further investigate the patterns of these skills deficits, why these occurred and how employers were responding to them. This chapter focuses on the patterns and causes, as space is limited. The study's inception is consistent with Lawson's (2003) explanation of retroductive social explanation as essentially 'backward looking': 'The essentially open nature of reality, both natural and social, necessitates that we very often start our explanatory endeavour from situations that have turned out to surprise, occasion a feeling of doubt, or otherwise interest us in some way' (p. 108). The task of explanation is therefore to explain such 'surprising' phenomena.

The study itself had two main stages with commensurate methods, following Sayer's (1992, 2000) extensive and intensive distinction. The details of each stage, the methods used therein, and the generative mechanisms considered, are discussed, in detail, in the sections that follow, whilst an overview is provided here. The first stage was an *extensive* secondary *quantitative* investigation of the 2002 SESS to gain a picture of the macro patterns of soft skills deficits (e.g. in which industries and occupations were they most widespread? Were differences apparent between soft skills shortages and gaps?). The second stage was an *intensive* case-study design with three case studies selected to represent particular organizations of interest, either reporting or not reporting soft skills deficits. The organizations thus provided, in Lawson's (2003) words, 'contrast spaces' where the existence or non-existence of a phenomena (in this case the reporting or not of soft skills deficits) can be contrastively examined to further elucidate upon the phenomena's nature and causes (i.e. why does it occur in some places and not others).

Within the case studies both extensive and intensive research methods were used. This MMR approach *within* the case studies was used to collect extensive contextual data (both qualitative and quantitative) and some quantitative data associations whilst using the qualitative data to obtain intensive depth. Essentially the qualitative data was used to elucidate upon the existence, or

---

[3] Hurrell, Scholarios and Thompson (2013: 162) define 'soft' skills as 'non-technical and not reliant on abstract reasoning, involving interpersonal and intrapersonal abilities to facilitate mastered performance in particular contexts'.

[4] 'Planning and organizing' and 'problem-solving' were considered to be soft skills during the secondary data analysis. Following the completion of the study, however, and the development of the definition reported above, these were considered not to fit the definition of 'true' soft skills but can instead be considered 'crossover skills' which may have characteristics of soft skills in certain contexts. The study thus allowed for the correction and development of a particular concept as discussed by Bhaskar (1998).

not, of certain theoretically informed, and retroductively established, generative mechanisms. The research was consistent with an open systems design allowing the role of various mechanisms within different contexts to be established and accepting that the same phenomena (i.e. whether or not soft skills deficits were reported) may have multiple contextual causes (Sayer 2000). The case-study method also allowed the emergence of mechanisms outwith those initially chosen to investigate the phenomena, further reinforcing an open systems perspective. A summary of the research design is contained in Figure 13.1.

Stage 1: Extensive Secondary Data Analysis of the Macro Patterns of Soft Skills Deficits in Scotland

The first stage of the research was secondary (macro) analysis of the 2002 SESS to further investigate the patterns of soft skills deficits in Scotland and inform the selection of case studies. This extensive stage was thus largely *descriptive* in the manner advocated by Sayer (1992, 2000). The focus here will be on the results and *how* these were used rather than on detail of statistical method, unless this is germane to the argument. The SESS was administered to 8,507 business establishments in Scotland and was taken by either the human resources (HR) manager or the primary manager responsible for HR issues. The survey (as in similar surveys conducted in other countries of the UK) was designed to gather intelligence on the functioning of the labour market and to

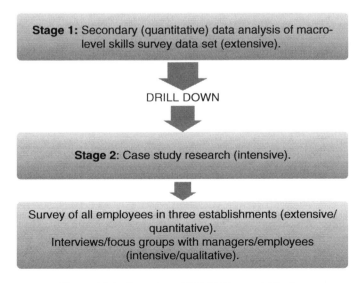

Figure 13.1 Overview of MMR Research Design

inform skills and employment policy. Areas covered in the SESS (amongst others) included: an establishment's skills and recruitment needs; the ease with which establishments could attract suitable staff; the perceived attractiveness of the establishment for job applicants; whether current staff were 'fully proficient' (i.e. whether any skills gaps existed); and whether the establishment had certain skills-related HR practices in place (i.e. a business plan, an HR plan, a training budget, training needs assessments, and staff appraisals). Where an organization identified a skills shortage in recruitment (i.e. reported that vacancies were hard to fill because applicants lacked the necessary skills) or a skills gap in any current staff they could indicate which skills were in deficit from a list of choices. Respondents also had an option where they could enter a 'free choice' although only approximately 0.5 per cent of respondents with a skills gap used this option. This may simply indicate that respondents found the SESS categories sufficiently covered their circumstances, although there were some notable omissions from the list. For example, the physical self-presentation of aesthetic labour, increasingly seen as important in interactive service sectors (Nickson and Warhurst 2007), was absent from the SESS survey (but was considered within the case studies reported below).

Simple frequencies revealed that organizations reported relatively few skills problems in the labour market with only 3 per cent reporting any kind of skills shortage, compared to 16 per cent reporting a skills gap. Soft skills were the predominant cause of both kinds of skills deficit accounting for approximately 70 per cent of both skills shortages and skills gaps.

The patterns of soft skills deficits were then examined with, in the first instance, simple cross-tabulations made between soft skills deficit rates and industry sector. The significance of any differences was tested using chi square ($\chi2$) analysis (see Table 13.1). It was found that the 'distribution hotels and restaurants' (hospitality) sector reported the highest rate of soft skills shortages (reported in approximately 3% of establishments); accounting for almost one-third of Scotland's soft skills shortages. Establishments in this sector also reported the highest proportion of soft skills gaps (approx. 14%); accounting for over one-fifth of Scotland's soft skills gaps. The 'retail and other consumer services' (retail) sector accounted for the highest proportion of all of Scotland's soft skills gaps (over a quarter) but had a lower within-sector rate of reported soft skills gaps (approx. 12%). The 'public administration and defence, education and health' sector (public sector) was also amongst the worst affected by both soft skills shortages and gaps. The public sector was, however, not as badly affected by either type of soft skills deficit as the hospitality sector, and also accounted for a lower proportion of Scotland's total soft skills gaps than the retail sector.

It was, however, not only service industries that reported high levels of soft skills gaps, with 11 per cent of manufacturing establishments also reporting these (although accounting for only approximately 7% of Scotland's soft skills gaps). A combined analysis of those sectors with the highest significant rates

Table 13.1 Sectoral Distribution of Soft Skills Deficits in Scotland 2002[a]

Soft skills shortages	% establishments reporting soft skills shortages within sector	% of Scotland's soft skills shortages attributable to sector
Distribution, Hotels, and Restaurants	3.3	31.4
Transport and Communications	2.5	5.9
Public Administration, Education, and Health	2.0	13.3

Soft skills gaps	% establishments reporting soft skills gaps within sector	% of Scotland's skills gaps attributable to sector
Distributions, Hotels, and Restaurants	13.8	22.3
Manufacturing	11.0	6.7
Public Administration and Defence, Education, and Health	12.9	15.0
Retail and Other consumer services	11.6	26.8

[a] *only those sectors with a greater frequency than would be expected under a chi square null model are reported*

of soft skills gaps and shortages, considering both the within-industry rate and the proportion of Scotland's soft skills deficits accounted for, confirmed that the hospitality sector was the 'worst' in Scotland for soft skills deficits followed by the retail and consumer services sector and then the public sector. Further analysis within these sectors revealed that the 'hotels and restaurants' industry was the worst affected overall.

Occupational analysis of soft skills deficits was then conducted, with respondents reporting skills deficits in the SESS, asked in which occupational groups these occurred.[5] Soft skills shortages were relatively evenly distributed, with administrative, personal service (for example beauty and security occupations), skilled trades, and elementary occupations (for example cleaners, shelf stackers, and waiting/bar staff) jointly the worst affected. When examining soft skills gaps only managers and senior officials, sales/customer service, and elementary occupations were reported as having soft skills gaps by 2 per cent or more of *all* establishments, with sales and customer service occupations the worst affected overall (having soft skills gaps in 2.9% of all establishments).

---

[5] As respondents were asked in which occupational groups skills deficits occurred directly, the analysis was univariate and thus no significance testing could be conducted.

Given the central importance of soft skills to front-line interactive service work (see for example Korczynski 2005; Nickson, Warhurst, and Dutton 2005), the kinds of industries and occupations worst affected appeared intuitively consistent (although, of course, still not revealing *why* some of these establishments reported soft skills gaps and others did not). Nevertheless, the descriptive statistics revealed complex patterns with non-service sector establishments also affected, albeit to a lesser degree. It was also not only lower-status occupational groups (such as front-line service workers) who were affected by soft skills deficits.

Given this complexity, the data was further described using logistic regression, in order to determine which factors contributed most to whether or not an establishment reported a soft skills gap.[6] Although a detailed appraisal of quantitative methods use within CR is given in chapter 15, some notes on this particular method are necessary. Whilst some influential CR authors explicitly or implicitly reject the use of analytical statistics (e.g. Sayer 1992, 2000; Ackroyd 2004; Fleetwood 2004; Fleetwood and Hesketh 2006b) the purpose of logistic regression here remained descriptive and was not used to make causal attributions. Olsen and Morgan (2005), in their sophisticated defence of analytical statistics from a realist perspective, use logistic regression as exemplar. Firstly, logistic regression can be used to analyse qualitative variables (such as whether or not an establishment reported a soft skills gap). Secondly, rather than seeking 'laws or universal patterns' as positivists do, the regression was used to find patterns within a population, using the subsequent intensive case studies to 'illuminate possible causal mechanisms' (Olsen and Morgan 2005: 271). The regression analysis was thus not used in isolation. Thirdly, multivariate analysis, such as logistic regression, can actually take into account the complexity of relationships within a data set by establishing the effects of certain factors, whilst also examining other data related to the phenomena which may 'counteract', 'mask', or 'blur' a particular pattern (Olsen and Morgan 2005: 271). For example, the fact that hospitality establishments appeared to report greater incidence of soft skills deficits than other establishments, may have been because they were concentrated in troublesome local labour markets, or because of high industry labour turnover rates. Bivariate statistics do not reveal such hidden patterns. Isolating the impact of certain factors whilst taking this complexity into account ('controlling' for the effects of other factors) does not, however, hold other factors 'constant or at bay' as in natural closed experiments (or social approximations of these) (Lawson 2003: 87). This is despite, for example, economists' use of the term '*ceteris paribus*' to explain the effects of factors in isolation from all others. The technique takes

---

[6] Only soft skills gaps were analysed due to the relatively low number of establishments reporting soft skills shortages, which, in any case, made logistic regression untenable (see Hair et al. 1998 for a full discussion of logistic regression).

into account the *actual* values of these other characteristics, or at least the data set's estimation of these, if we, in Olsen and Morgan's (2005) terms, assume these are 'ficts' which represent reality in a 'true enough' manner, rather than concrete social 'facts' (p. 277). These ficts are thus used to uncover whether significant relationships or patterns remain, whilst taking complexity into account. Finally, results were seen as 'demi-regularities' (demi-regs). These demi-regs are described by Lawson (2009: 150) as 'rough-and-ready patterns taking various forms' (reflecting the concept of 'ficts'), which can exist in open systems but do not necessarily endure over time.

The logistic regression analysis included the industry sector, occupation, and the location of the establishment and potential factors that may affect whether or not soft skills gaps were reported. The regression also included internal factors that may have contributed to an establishment's skills gaps; the size of the establishment, staff turnover rate, the number of formal skills-related HR practices in place (see above when discussing the content of the SESS survey), and the respondent's assessment of the attractiveness of the establishment for potential recruits. Even when adding these other factors the patterns in the descriptive statistics were largely supported, with the hospitality sector most likely to report a soft skills gap, followed by retail; and with sales and customer service occupations, followed by elementary occupations, most likely to be affected by soft skills gaps. When controlling for other factors managers were, however, amongst the occupations in which soft skills gaps were least likely. Other interesting factors also emerged. For example, (perhaps intuitively) establishments reported as more attractive for potential recruits were less likely to report a soft skills gap. More surprisingly, where an establishment had *more* formal skills-related HR practices in place they were *more* likely to report a soft skills gap. These findings not only informed the case-study selection but also contributed to the proposed generative mechanisms that were 'tested' within the case studies, as will be discussed below.

Stage 2: The Selection of Case Studies and Potential Causal Mechanisms

Having established the patterns of soft skills deficits at the macro level, case studies were then selected to 'drill down' below this data (see Figure 13.1) to try and establish what may have caused soft skills deficits and why they were reported in some contexts rather than others. Such an approach allows some of the 'complexity of social relations' to be uncovered in a way that quantitative data sets cannot (Olsen and Morgan 2005: 277). The case studies also allowed greater detail to be established on the nature of soft skills and the skills that caused soft skills deficits, going beyond the more closed questions on the SESS. The results from the secondary data analysis were used to guide the case study selection, with the following types of establishment included: an establishment from within the worst affected sector (hotels and restaurants) *reporting* soft skills deficits (both gaps and shortages), an establishment from the same sector *not* reporting any such deficits, and an establishment from a service sector relatively unaffected by soft skills deficits also not reporting such deficits. This approach allowed an inter- and intra-industry comparison of 'contrast spaces' of interest (Lawson 2003) to establish which mechanisms may have caused soft skills deficits to be reported or not.

The case studies were selected from the SESS 2004 data set (which asked the same questions regarding soft skills deficits and displayed similar data patterns) selecting establishments with over 100 employees, who were part of multi-site organizations. Such organizations were more likely to have formalized HR practices in place (Cully et al. 1999) and HR practices were investigated as one potential generative mechanism (see Table 13.2). Larger organizations were also selected to maximize the chance of achieving larger samples of respondents. The two establishments from the same sector were also drawn from the same labour market (Glasgow) in order to improve comparability. The establishment from a sector relatively unaffected by soft skills deficits (and not reporting any soft skills deficits itself) was drawn from the 'business services' sector, it being decided to limit the case studies to service establishments, given the higher importance of soft skills within such settings (see Grugulis 2006). Three (anonymized) establishments were thus selected, 'Fontainebleau' a four star hotel reporting soft skills deficits, 'Oxygen' a five-star hotel not reporting such deficits, and 'Silex' a scientific (geological) services establishment also not reporting soft skills deficits.

The use of comparative case studies within CR has been advocated elsewhere (e.g. Ackroyd 2010) and a brief comment on this method is needed. Ackroyd (2010) rightly rejects the use of comparative case studies in a method akin to experimental research. In such research cases would effectively 'be exactly the same as each other save in one precise, putatively causal "variable"' (p. 66).[7] Indeed, here, a multitude of possible generative mechanisms were examined, in depth, within each case study. In this research the *outcome* of interest differed between cases, to facilitate contrastive investigation that could retroductively explain the existence of soft skills deficits and why these occurred in certain contexts rather than others.

---

[7] Interestingly, although also rejecting the experimental method, Lawson (2003) appears at times to suggest that contrast spaces should be broadly similar in terms of causal factors besides the one causal factor being investigated. He does, however, believe that causality should still be ascertained retroductively, a posteriori, rather than deductively, once 'surprising and interesting' contrasts are discovered. Thus although Lawson's term 'contrast spaces' is used here, the manner of investigation was different to that postulated by Lawson, despite remaining consistent with CR.

A number of possible generative mechanisms were, therefore, investigated within these case studies to address the multilevel and complex nature of soft skills deficits. Such an approach was multi-disciplinary, consistent with how CR accepts complexity, multi-causality and shies away from 'disciplinary imperialism' (Sayer 2000) (see also Olsen 2004b; Olsen and Morgan 2005; Downward and Mearman 2007). The exploratory results of the descriptive statistics, described in stage one, also informed the selection of some of the potential mechanisms that were investigated within the case studies.

The potential reasons why soft skills deficits were reported or not were split roughly into three groups: those that related to the labour market and attractiveness of the establishments to potential recruits; those relating to organizations' 'skills-related' HR and organizational practices; and those relating to individual workers themselves. An overview of these possible causes is given in Table 13.2, alongside the manner in which these were investigated within the case studies (described in more detail in the next section).

In terms of the labour market and attractiveness of the establishment, this effectively looked outward at how the establishment engaged with its external context. Even despite the low level of skills shortages reported in the SESS survey some establishments still reported skills shortages on the external market and further depth was required on this issue. The role of the establishment in not being able to attract skilled applicants from the external market was also considered as a possible mechanism, rather than simply assuming that difficulties may occur because skilled applicants simply did not exist. This area of investigation appeared especially germane for further depth investigation given that the attractiveness of an establishment was associated with reduced likelihood of reporting a soft skills gap in the stage-one secondary data analysis. That the hospitality sector may have had difficulty in attracting suitably skilled applicants could potentially be associated with its reputation as having 'poor quality' employment (Siebern-Thomas 2005; Martin 2004) in the 'secondary' segment of the labour market (Doeringer and Piore 1971). Characteristics of this segment include low pay/low skill work, high employee turnover, poor promotion prospects, tight supervision, difficult working conditions, low unionization, and a high degree of contingent work patterns. Conversely business services may be associated with the 'primary' segment with conditions effectively the opposite of the secondary segment. The economic theory of dual labour markets (Doeringer and Piore 1971) was further reinforced by efficiency wage theory which posits that skilled workers are likely to price themselves out of low paying jobs (see e.g. Akerlof and Yellen 1986).

The investigation of organizations' HR practices was seen as a potential cause of soft skills deficits for a number of reasons. Firstly, the quantitative analysis in stage one revealed a surprising, counter-intuitive, finding (Lawson 2003) that the more formal HR practices in place, the more likely a firm was to report soft skills gaps. This, of course does not denote causality, but

Table 13.2 Generative Mechanisms and Methods Used to Investigate Them within Case Studies

Analytical level of generative mechanism	Specific elements investigated	Methods used to investigate
Labour market and attractiveness of establishment	Availability of suitable labour	Qualitative management interviews for both elements
	Perceived attractiveness of establishment for applicants	Qualitative employee interviews focusing on the attractiveness of the establishment
Skills-related HR policies and organizational practices	The main activities of each establishment	Descriptive statistics from employee surveys on incidence of training, induction, and appraisal
	Recruitment and selection	Qualitative management interviews on the details and effectiveness of HR policies
	Training and induction	Qualitative employee interviews regarding their experiences of HR practices and whether (and why) they could/could not carry out their job duties effectively
	Appraisal	
	Barriers-to-skills display	
Workers themselves	Skills withdrawal (via breaches in psychological contract)	Descriptive statistics regarding employees' psychological contract/work attitudes and social resource proxies
	Social resources and the development of soft skills	Analytical statistics (regression) on associations between employees' psychological contract/work attitudes/social resource proxies and their perceived competence in the soft skills requirements of their jobs
		Qualitative management interviews e.g. asking if (and why) employees' skills deteriorated over time and what characteristics were thought to develop soft skills
		Qualitative employee interviews e.g. asking the state of the psychological contract, whether (and why) they enjoyed their jobs and what they felt helped to develop their soft skills

stimulated interest within the intensive research as to how the *nature* of HR practices (rather than simply their existence) may have contributed to soft skills deficits. Given that organizations across Scotland also reported few soft skills shortages during recruitment but considerably greater rates of soft skills gaps (in current employees) recruitment and selection appeared a particularly fruitful area to investigate.[8] The incidence and details of training within the case studies was also considered as a generative mechanism due to the fact that training incidence had been found in the past to be lower in both the types of employee and sectors worst affected by soft skills gaps (Cully et al. 1999; Kersley et al. 2006). Employers may also have been less likely to engage in training if they considered soft skills to be 'general purpose human capital' transferable to other establishments (Becker 1993). Organizational barriers potentially hindering employees' use of soft skills were also considered.

Given that individuals may develop soft skills throughout their life and outside of the workplace (see, for example, Heckman 2000) it was also considered necessary to see *how* people believed soft skills were developed at the micro level. Of particular interest was the accumulation of Bourdieu's, social (e.g. accumulated networks), educational (e.g. qualifications and time spent at university), and economic capitals (see Bourdieu and Passeron 1977; Bourdieu 1986, 1991). Such capitals may have allowed people to practise social interactions in various contexts in order to develop a mastery of these (Bourdieu 1991). Given that some service employers had been seen to demand 'middle classness' in front-line employees (Witz, Warhurst, and Nickson 2003; Nickson and Warhurst, 2007), Bourdieu's work on cultural capital was also considered important as this is used by the middle classes to replicate and 'distinguish' themselves (Bourdieu 1986). The role of individuals was also considered in a second way; whether employer behaviour may have caused disaffection in workers, leading them to *withdraw* skills. This explanation was considered especially germane given the perceived location of hospitality establishments in the 'secondary' labour market. The findings in stage one of the study that soft skills gaps were more numerous than soft skills shortages *may* also have indicated that some employees who possessed skills upon entry to the firm withdrew them in this manner (see caveat in footnote 8). To this end the psychological contract was analysed to establish whether any breaches in this contract might have led to workers withdrawing or withholding skills. The psychological contract broadly consists of individual beliefs regarding the extent to which an organization has honoured their obligations to the employee and abided by the terms of the agreed exchange relationship, with its state (i.e. fulfilled or breached) changing over time (see for example Rousseau 1995; Morrison and Robinson 1997).

A note on the mode of explanation is required here to clarify the distinctiveness of the CR approach. Although potential causes were considered prior to the case study research, the approach remained essentially retroductive rather than deductive in trying to explain *why* soft skills deficits may occur

---

[8] Although the cross-sectional data did not examine whether it was the *same* employees who were deemed proficient at point of entry but later found to exhibit skills gaps, this potential causal mechanism remained salient.

in particular contexts. The study broadly follows Bhaskar's (1998: 637) RRREI mode of applied explanation. This first involves *re*solving a complex event (in this case why soft skills deficits were reported or not) into its components before *re*describing these theoretically and *re*trodicting back to possible causes, as shown above. The case studies then allowed *e*limination of non-salient causes[9] and *i*dentification of the causes that were most pertinent. This explanatory process also involves the practice of *abduction*. Here theoretical observations are generated from data, but in a manner that is non-inductive and also considers existing theories to 'test' which explanations best fit the data. Modell (2009: 213) described how abduction 'relies heavily on theories as mediators for deriving explanations... in the process of searching for empirical evidence that may shed light on the contingent conditions under which a particular event will occur... *By confronting alternative theories with additional empirical data, possibly derived from different data sources or methods, researchers may then assess their validity*' Morvell (2009: 213, emphasis added). It was not deduced that any one cause would be stronger than the others and the potential generative mechanisms were not deemed to be exhaustive, allowing through abduction, the emergence of explanation from the data itself. The approach thus differed markedly from the traditional closed-system, reductionist form of deduction as described, for example, by Fleetwood and Hesketh (2006b).

Combining the Extensive and Intensive within Case Studies

Although the focus within the case studies was on depth and the qualitative assessment of potential generative mechanisms, extensive and intensive methods were combined as in the study as a whole. The case studies included a survey of all employed in each establishment; semi-structured interviews with HR managers and the line managers responsible for the main employee groups within each establishment; and focus groups/interviews with employees. Table 13.3 shows respondents and response rates. The management interviews were more structured than employees' interviews as certain themes from the SESS needed to be (critically) compared, although managers were allowed to answer in depth and elucidate *why* certain phenomena occurred and *why* they held certain opinions. The interviews also allowed respondents to provide answers in a way that the more restrictive questions on the SESS and case-study surveys did not. HR respondents answered for the whole establishment whilst line managers answered for their own department. The methods were combined to investigate the potential generative mechanisms as

[9] Bhaskar (1998: 637) states that open systems '*always* constitute a plurality of possible causes', a mantra adopted within this research.

Table 13.3 Breakdown of Case-study Response Rates and Respondents

Case study	Survey response rate (%)	Management interview respondents	Employee interview respondents
Fontainebleau	22.3	5 (Including HR and functions such as F and B/ events, reception, and kitchen)	7 (Including front line workers in F and B/events and reception)
Oxygen	22.7	6 (As in Fontainebleau but also including housekeeping manager)	12 (8 as a focus group) (As in Fontainebleau)
Silex	47.2	7 (Including HR, head of establishment's administration and heads of scientific and technical departments)	3 (as a focus group) (Including scientific, technical, and support functions)

shown in Table 13.2, combining the strengths of each method and using them where most appropriate. As well as the areas covered in Table 13.2 contextual and descriptive data were also gathered such as demographics, the functions of various departments, the skills requirements of certain jobs, and the manner in which soft skills were enacted in the workplace.

When investigating the availability of suitably skilled labour and the attractiveness of the firm for potential recruits, qualitative management interviews were almost exclusively used, as managers were in the best position to comment on such issues. These questions were also used to establish skills shortages, *why* any hiring difficulties were evident and whether particular types of applicants were seen to lack certain skills. Employees were also asked what they liked/did not like about working for their establishments and employer. Although these questions were predominantly to gauge any disaffection with their employer for the skills withdrawal issue (see below), these were also used to gauge firm attractiveness.

The questions regarding the role of skills-related HR policies and organizational practices used all three methods, although the focus was very much on the qualitative experiences and opinions of managers and employees. The survey data was used descriptively to assess employees' experiences of the incidence of certain skills-related HR practices, where these were amenable to simple empirical measurement. Examples included whether they had received training (and if so, in what) and appraisal.[10] Managers were asked about the

---

[10] All employees in the establishment had clearly been successfully selected and piloting revealed confusion over survey questions asking *how* people had been recruited and selected. This HR practice was thus examined *purely* qualitatively, alongside depth investigation of the other HR practices.

details of HR practices and their views on their utility, whilst employees were asked about their experiences of the same. Employees were also asked whether there were any barriers in the workplace that inhibited their use of soft skills.

The final stage, assessing individuals and soft skills, used quantitative methods in a more analytical manner but alongside qualitative methods to elucidate whether any associations translated into generative mechanisms in any of the case studies. To ascertain the factors that may have contributed to individuals' soft skills development and in line with Bourdieu's cultural, economic, and educational capitals, regression models were used to ascertain whether associations were evident between various social resource 'proxies' and an individual's assessment of their ability to carry out soft skills' requirements of jobs. These proxies included social background, educational level, any time spent unemployed, and whether they were currently attending university (the experiences which may have added to social capital were seen as too complex to quantify). The soft skills competencies included communication skills, team-working, self-presentation, emotion work (e.g. dealing with emotional demands at work, managing emotions, and showing empathy and sensitivity) and an aggregated measure. Controls were included in the regressions including age, gender, contractual status (e.g. whether a part-time or temporary employee), and length of time in the organization and labour market (for a discussion of the use of control 'variables' see the discussion of logistic regression above, when discussing the secondary data analysis from stage one and Olsen and Morgan 2005). Clearly these proxies were rather blunt and could not show causality in isolation. It was certainly not assumed, for example, that people from less affluent backgrounds or without experience of university automatically did not possess soft skills. To complement the surveys both management and employees were asked qualitatively what they believed helped to develop soft skills, including consideration of areas not covered within Bourdieu's work, such as personality. The qualitative depth also allowed investigation of how the context of the case studies may have affected the factors seen as important for soft skills development (a key issue as will be seen below).

A similar process was engaged in when examining the possibility of skills withdrawal via breaches in the psychological contract. Regressions were performed on the state of employees' psychological contracts, outcomes of psychological contract breach (such as job satisfaction, commitment, the perceived state of employment relations, and motivation) and the soft skills competencies measures, whilst controlling for similar factors as in the social resource analyses above. The state of the psychological contract and its outcomes were also compared between establishments. As above, these regressions alone could not denote causality, but rather the *extent* of any associations within the case studies. Qualitative elucidation was thus essential in order to determine *whether* any causal effects were present and the nature of any disaffection within the case studies. Managers were thus asked, for example, whether employees' skills ever deteriorated over time, and if so why; whilst employee questions included whether the organization had upheld the obligations to them, how they reacted if not and, more generally, what they liked and did not like about working for their organizations.

Although a detailed discussion of quantitative methods within CR was given in chapter 15, it is necessary to briefly acknowledge and respond to critics of regression analysis. As has been stated throughout, many CR scholars are sceptical of analytical statistics. Fleetwood and Hesketh (2006b), for example, provide a robust rejection of 'scientistic' prediction within the social sciences achieved using quantitative techniques such as regression. They differentiate prediction into that which tries to predict the future and that which involves hypothesis testing. In terms of the former kind of prediction, the regression models here were used in a manner suggested by Ron (2002), 'retroactively, to identify (these) mechanisms and not to predict the future' (p. 137). If we assume that the Scottish labour market is essentially a complex, open system, such future prediction would, in fact, be impossible. Indeed the regression results were not used within the case studies to make mathematical predictions, for the same reason. Nevertheless, the regression results were used to 'bring forth evidence of otherwise hidden mechanisms' (p.121), although, to be considered as generative, such mechanisms needed to be related to theory *and supported by qualitative investigation*. This concurs with Fleetwood and Hesketh (2006b), that atheoretical quantitative investigations do not allow explanation; and that simply knowing certain quantitative variables are related to others does not explain *why* this is the case (p. 248, emphasis added).

The second type of prediction regards hypothesis testing, with Fleetwood and Hesketh (2006b) also rejecting the notion of using past occurrences to predict an outcome in the present. As described above, this study did seek to investigate, abductively, whether a number of proposed mechanisms could explain why soft skills deficits occurred in certain contexts. There was, however, no attempt to replicate previous studies (which did not exist in any case), or to predict the magnitudes of any effects within the case studies. 'Scientistic' deduction as described by Fleetwood and Hesketh (2006b) was, therefore, not practised. Systems were not considered closed, with any associations necessarily viewed as partial demi-regs, given the complexity of the other mechanisms considered within the case studies. Neither was there a reductionist attempt to isolate single cause or state a priori which cause would have the biggest effect.

The case studies thus combined the extensive and the intensive to investigate, in depth, the possible generative mechanisms that may have contributed to the existence of soft skills deficits. By combining both methods, their strengths were used to drill down below the SESS to take into account the meso (organizational) level; interactions between this level and the macro (labour market) and micro (employee) levels; and the micro level itself.

Outcomes of the Research: Explaining Complex Phenomena and Determining the Most Salient Mechanisms

Full results cannot be given here, but a synopsis of the generative mechanisms that appeared to contribute most to the existence of soft skills deficits within the case studies completes the picture. Firstly, the case studies broadly supported the results of the SESS, with soft skills deficits endemic in Fontainebleau (with 25%–30% of all staff affected by soft skills gaps, for example) and not reported by any manager in Silex. The picture was more complicated in Oxygen, as although the HR manager reported no soft skills deficits, two managers did report minor problems (in the management team and chefs/kitchen workers). These were, however, not considered a huge problem by management and no front-line service staff were affected by soft skills gaps, unlike Fontainebleau. Interestingly, the Oxygen front office manager initially reported that some of his staff had deficits in soft skills but then said they *could* all carry out their current job duties effectively (indicating no soft skills gaps). This finding shows the role of *hermeneutics* in the interpretation of whether or not soft skills deficits existed. This role was also apparent in Silex, with some managers reporting that despite no soft skills gaps existing, employees could still develop these skills further for the future.

Labour market factors (assessed qualitatively) constituted a weakly supported mechanism as managers reported that labour with the appropriate soft skills was generally available (despite the existence of some soft skills shortages). In the hotels, for example even though 'efficiency wages' (Akerlof and Yellen 1986) were not paid and some 'secondary' labour market conditions (Doeringer and Piore 1971) were apparent, there was a plentiful supply of students who were happy to take employment. Some minor problems did still exist for full-time positions in both hotels but there was little difference between the two establishments.

The group of causes that appeared to have the greatest explanatory power were certain HR practices—although what really mattered was their *form* as elucidated upon by the qualitative data. Firstly, and perhaps unsurprisingly the key activities of the establishment affected the importance of soft skills and, seemingly, whether managers reported deficits. Soft skills were essential throughout the hotels, especially in front-line staff. In Silex, however, although soft skills were deemed as important they were secondary to technical and scientific skills.

When examining training, through all data sources, there was no evidence that employers were reluctant to train in soft skills whether or not they reported soft skills gaps. Such a finding runs contrary to soft skills being classified as transferable 'general purpose' human capital (Becker 1993). What was apparent, however, was that the *form* of training differed between the hotels, with Oxygen allowing employees more agency in determining how they used their soft skills in enacting service requirements. A key emergent finding was that Oxygen employees also identified more with the organization, increasing the alignment of their skills with the brand and thus reducing the likelihood of soft skills gaps. A related emergent finding was that the allowance of discretion on the job itself appeared to further increase Oxygen employees' identification with the organization's style of service, further reducing the likelihood of soft skills gaps. Silex employees were also left almost complete discretion over how they performed their soft skills, although this appeared to be predominantly because of these skills' secondary nature in this establishment. Fontainebleau allowed employees the least discretion over their soft skills' use.

When qualitatively considering recruitment and selection, Fontainebleau managers appeared unselective and 'hyper deterministic' (Child 1997) in terms of the quality of labour they could attract. The other establishments, however, appeared highly selective. Both Oxygen and Silex, but not Fontainebleau, also had 'informal' stages to their selection process such as establishment tours, peer feedback on applicants, and (either in isolation or part of a wider process) interview 'chats'. Management believed these were highly effective in assessing soft skills and also allowed applicants a chance to decide for themselves whether they wanted to work for the establishment, in line with the 'social process' model of recruitment and selection (Herriot 1989). It was also apparent from the employee surveys that Fontainebleau had the worst incidence of employee appraisal of the three establishments. The qualitative research also revealed that Fontainebleau tended to rely exclusively on the formal appraisal system whilst the other establishments combined this with ongoing, more informal feedback. Management in these establishments rated the informal feedback as amongst the best methods to reduce soft skills gaps. Some Fontainebleau employees also reported barriers to their customer service skills, including understaffing and the behaviour of customers. No other establishment's employees reported barriers to *soft* skills use although Silex employees did report organizational barriers to the use of other, harder, skills.

There was mixed support for the micro-level mechanisms. When examining whether an individuals' social resources increased their proficiency in soft skills, the regression models were weak, with few significant coefficients or consistent patterns. Qualitative study, however, revealed that respondents believed social experiences (for example socializing, extra curricular activities, and travelling), work experiences, and time spent as a student, were particularly beneficial in soft skills development, as was an outgoing 'personality'. Of course as some experiences (such as travelling) tend to be available to the most affluent, economic capital may also have played an indirect role. Social background was not generally seen as important for developing soft skills, apart from in Oxygen where it was considered that 'polished' people typically from the middle classes were most consistent with the hotel's brand. This reflected Bourdieu's requirement for 'cultural capital' but only in certain qualitative contexts (see also Hurrell, Scholarios, and Thompson 2013; Hurrell and Scholarios 2011). This particular mechanism could thus, theoretically, have caused skills gaps in Oxygen, but remained latent.

The results for skills withdrawal via the psychological contract also yielded few significant regression results. The psychological contract was, quantitatively, generally upheld in each organization with generally good job satisfaction scores, although Silex had marginally worse scores regarding employee's perceptions of employment and social relations at work. The qualitative data generally supported these findings. Nevertheless, Silex, the establishment reporting no soft skills deficits, evidenced the most qualitative evidence of breach and dissatisfaction (typically with promotion and training). The qualitative data thus revealed something that the quantitative data did not. Nevertheless, there was some significant quantitative evidence that breaches in the psychological contract were associated with lower self-reported competency in soft skills involving emotion work in both Fontainebleau and Silex. Fontainebleau and Oxygen also revealed relationships between the same skills and job satisfaction and commitment respectively. All models were weak highlighting the importance of other qualitative factors not captured in the analysis. Some Fontainebleau managers stated that employees' skills sometimes deteriorated over time if they became disaffected, leading to skills gaps and appearing to place the blame on employees. Oxygen managers were, however, more aware of the demanding nature of certain jobs (such as housekeeping) and appeared more sympathetic to disaffected employees. In Silex, which had marginally the worst employee attitudes of the three, some managers believed an employees' *performance* may deteriorate due to (rare) disaffection with the establishment, but essentially employees' *skills* remained. Thus 'skills withdrawal' in Silex was not viewed as a skills gap, reinforcing the importance of management hermeneutics. Skills withdrawal thus appeared as a potential generative mechanism, but whether this was viewed as a skills gap depended very much upon the attitudes of managers in particular contexts.

Thus, the contexts in which generative mechanisms were exercised appeared to be where soft skills were an integral part of core employees' jobs. The manner in which organizations conducted recruitment and selection appeared to be a key generative mechanism as did the design of training, organization of work, and the manner in which appraisal was used. Essentially HR practices that 'institutionalized' informality (see Hurrell and Scholarios 2011), alongside allowing employee agency, appeared to be a large factor in determining whether employees could identify with, and align their soft skills to the organization and thus reduce the risk of soft skills gaps in the eyes of managers. There was also evidence that certain social experiences and 'personality' may have been beneficial in developing soft skills, although the role of 'cultural capital' was very much contextually mediated. Some partial evidence that psychological contract breach and negative work attitudes may have led to withdrawal of some soft skills also existed, although whether these were *defined* as skills gaps again depended upon the context. The role of management interpretation in defining what was a soft skills deficit was also important, reinforcing the hermeneutically mediated nature of social reality, although not of course denying that 'reality' exists. The importance of how managers interpreted skills gaps thus emerged as a key generative mechanism. Limitations to the study, which may guide future researchers, are now considered.

Limitations and What Could Have Been Improved

Although the case studies represented key contrast spaces of interest only a limited number of cases could be selected given time and resources. Future research may wish to look at the generative mechanisms present/absent in other contexts. The study also focused on larger multi-site organizations (as justified above) and investigation of smaller establishments may also be a fruitful area for further research.

Although the case-study stage retroductively followed the discovery of patterns at the macro level, the extensive and intensive case-study stages were conducted more or less simultaneously (with survey analysis not having been completed prior to the qualitative stage). Given time constraints this was necessary, but in an ideal world conducting survey analysis before beginning the qualitative stage may have allowed more 'surprising' issues from the surveys (using Lawson's [2003] terminology) to also be interrogated.

It was also relatively difficult to obtain qualitative participants in case studies, possibly because potential respondents had already been issued a survey and so may have been suffering from 'survey fatigue' (or perhaps more correctly here, 'research fatigue'). Although the main management contacts in each case study remained supportive they were reluctant to encourage participation too much, for the above reason and also to avoid annoying staff or other managers. Participation issues should thus be borne in mind when conducting MMR similar to that reported here.

Although originally deemed appropriate and analysed in a manner consistent with CR, the 'social resource proxies' used in the micro-level quantitative analysis were, perhaps, too far removed from the concepts they were trying to measure. This quantitative stage ultimately added little to the analysis (although its inclusion did not detract from the study).

In terms of presentation, the results around the psychological contract findings were originally discussed as hypotheses (Hurrell 2009). This was, in retrospect, inconsistent with the manner in which the study was conducted and these should have been expressed differently as the study was abductive rather than deductive. Indeed at some points when writing up the quantitative analysis, positivist language occasionally crept in. This was a mistake on the part of the researcher and the best advice is to remain consistent with your ontological approach when writing up, as well as designing, studies.

The psychological contract findings were originally aggregated across case studies to increase the sample size. Given the importance of organizational context in forming and delivering the contract, this aggregation was an error.[11] Although the case-specific qualitative investigation mitigated the risk of assuming a collective closed system, the decision was driven by data considerations rather than theory or philosophy, which should not have been the case. The advice again, is to remain consistent with the chosen ontology throughout.

CONCLUSION

This chapter has shown how an MMR design utilized within a CR perspective can in, Downward and Mearman's (2007: 92) terms, 'reveal different features of the same layered reality'. The research demonstrated here, combined methods and moved from quantitative patterns identified at the macro level to an in-depth retroductive and abductive explanation of generative mechanisms at the meso and, to a lesser extent, micro levels. Contextual factors within which certain mechanisms may or may not operate were also identified. Although results are heavily contextual and assume open systems, that is not to say that the generative mechanisms identified here cannot be considered within other similar contexts. This does not, however, mean that inductive generalizations of causality or deductive replications of these studies can be attempted. The chapter has shown how intensive depth and the appreciation of hermeneutics can elucidate upon social phenomena and help to uncover generative mechanisms and contextual mediators, but in a way that goes beyond interpretive research. The qualitative research here helped to elucidate *real* social processes, which can help us to interpret and most importantly *explain* empirical findings. Quantitative research also has a key role both descriptively and to look for 'hidden' data associations, but not in the sense of the positivist, empiricist, or naive realist. Instead these data were part of a more complete picture, used where they were appropriate but not relied upon to establish causality, both preceding and dovetailing with carefully designed qualitative investigation. CR MMR can help overcome the false qualitative/quantitative divide to achieve the 'best of both worlds' and, in doing so, can allow the complexity and mechanisms of the social world to come alive.

---

[11] The results discussed here are disaggregated by case study, but did not differ much from the original analysis.

14

Realist Synthesis

Joanne Greenhalgh

INTRODUCTION

Realist synthesis, developed by Ray Pawson (2006b) is a method of reviewing and synthesizing studies which evaluates complex social programmes. These are programmes which aim to change social processes at the individual, group, and organizational level and can be found in many different policy sectors from employment, health, education, welfare, and criminal justice. They range in reach and complexity from the Labour Government's New Deal for Communities or the Coalition government's plans to introduce Universal Credit for those in receipt of benefits through to the introduction of breakfast clubs or peer mentors in schools. Specific examples in organizational studies include performance management systems, 'lean thinking' production systems, employee skills training, or a programme to assist employees back to work after long-term sickness absence.

Realist synthesis rests on a central argument that such programmes represent *theories* about how best to remedy a particular problem and how participants are likely to respond to the solutions offered (Pawson 2006b). It thus operates through a process of developing, refining, and testing the theories that underlie complex social programmes (Pawson et al. 2005). The purpose of realist synthesis is explanation-building to create an understanding of which programmes work for whom, in what circumstances, and why (Pawson and Bellamy 2006).

While realist synthesis is underpinned by realist principles, Pawson is always at pains to stress that his version of realism is distinct from critical realism and does not take on board every proposition of critical realism. Important points of departure are Pawson's rejection (Pawson 2013) of Bhaskar's 'depth realism'. Points of convergence are that both are premised on an understanding of the generative nature of causality, the stratified nature of reality, and the centrality of the search for underlying mechanisms of action in understanding and building explanation. Undoubtedly, understanding these principles assists the reviewer in utilizing the method.

This chapter begins by taking a brief look at the complex nature of social programmes. It then offers a realist critique of positivist methods of evaluation and systematic review and sets out a realist framework for understanding and evaluating social programmes. Finally, the chapter considers how this has been operationalized in the process of realist synthesis and provides a step-by-step description of how to carry out a realist synthesis drawing on practical examples.

SOCIAL PROGRAMMES AND COMPLEXITY

Across many policy sectors, social programmes are inherently complex (Pawson 2013). They rely on human agency to make them work, depend on the actions of multiple stakeholders, and often require a multitude of different intervening processes to occur before they achieve their ultimate outcome. The link between human resource management (HRM) practices and the performance of a company provides a good illustration of this complexity (Guest 2011; Macfarlane et al. 2011). The implementation and impact of HRM practices relies on the cooperation of several stakeholders across different levels of the organization from chief executives, HR managers, line managers, team leaders, and workers themselves (Boxall and Macky 2007). HRM practices are not a single entity but involve many different interconnected policies and practices (Bowen and Ostroff 2004). These practices are dependent upon the intentions of the HR practice being translated into actual HR practice, which in turn is contingent upon how workers perceive such practices and their reactions to them before they influence organizational performance (Boxall and Purcell 2000).

However, the complexity of social programmes does not end in the programmes themselves. Such programmes are embedded into already complex systems, such as the existing network of relationships between workers and their managers and are often implemented alongside other organizational changes. Furthermore, programmes are implemented differently in different places, such that the programme is not standardized. They can even transform the conditions that make them work in the first place. Such complexity poses challenges for those seeking to learn transferable lessons from reviewing what previous evaluations can tell us about the fortunes of such programmes (Pawson 2003; Shepperd et al. 2009).

The dominant paradigm underpinning the evaluation of complex social programmes in many sectors is positivist and draws on quantitative methods. For example, within the health arena, the randomized controlled trial (RCT)

is held up as a gold standard method for evaluating programme effectiveness (Cochrane 1972; Sackett et al. 1996). In this study design, participants
are randomly allocated to 'control' and 'intervention' arms. Randomization is
assumed to produce a closed system in which the intervention can be 'switched
on' for the intervention group and 'switched off' for the control group. It is
then assumed that any difference in outcomes between the two groups can
be attributed to the intervention and not to differences in participants or settings. The RCT's sister methodology, the systematic review, is used to summate
the results of RCTs by simply adding their net effects together to determine
whether the programme works (Higgins and Green 2011). This method risks
ignoring crucial differences between the participants and settings in which
the RCTs occur in the search for a definitive answer to the question of 'what
works?' Similarly, the majority of the research examining the link between
HRM and company performance has been rooted in a positivist paradigm
(Fleetwood and Hesketh 2006a). As Fleetwood and Hesketh (2006a) argue,
the observation of a statistical association between packages of HRM practices
and company performance is taken as indicating a causal link between the
two, without any theorization of the underlying mechanisms through which
HRM practices might lead to changes in company performance. In the following section I draw on published examples of empirical work to provide a realist
critique of positivist methodologies such as the randomized controlled trial
and systematic review as methodologies for evaluating complex interventions.
Subsequently, I illustrate how a realist framework is better equipped to deal
with this complexity.

DEALING WITH COMPLEXITY: RCTS AND SYSTEMATIC REVIEWS

For experimental methods such as the randomized controlled trial and systematic review, dealing with complexity is a matter of control. These methodologies encapsulate a successionist view of causality, such that the programme
itself is deemed to have causal powers and is what gives rise to the change
in outcomes (Pawson and Bellamy 2006). In RCTs, human agency is viewed
as bias and contamination and the process of randomization seeks to erase
its effects. Existing complex social systems and the capacity for social programmes to adapt and change as they are implemented are tackled through
ceaseless attempts to standardize the programme through training, manuals,
and briefings. Thus, from a realist perspective, RCTs attempt to even out differences in the reasoning and reaction of participants to interventions that
may provide the very explanation for why the intervention does or does not

bring about change (Pawson 2006b, 2013). They endeavour to neutralize the circumstances which may influence the success or failure of the programme. However, such attempts are often not successful.

The evaluation of the Job Retention and Rehabilitation Pilots (JRRP) provides a good illustration of programme complexity and the shortcomings of the randomized controlled trial in addressing it. This programme was run jointly by the Department of Health and the Department of Work and Pensions and was designed to decrease sickness absence and increase job retention for people off work sick between six weeks and six months (Purdon et al. 2006). Evaluation ran alongside the programme in the form of a randomized controlled trial and represented the first attempt to use such a methodology in the evaluation of a large scale *voluntary* labour market programme in the UK. Participants were randomized to four arms (1) a 'health intervention' delivered away from the workplace to treat the mind or body and advise *only* about health; (2) a workplace intervention which focused on bringing about change in the workplace and could advise *only* about the workplace; (3) a combination of (1) and (2), and (4) no intervention. Of interest here are not simply the findings from the study—there were no statistically significant differences in rates of returning to work for thirteen weeks or more between the four arms (Purdon et al. 2006)—but also the reflections provided by the evaluators on the process of conducting an RCT of such a programme (Stratford et al. 2005).

As with all social programmes, entry to the programme was voluntary and thus required the active engagement of participants in the interventions offered to them in order to work. The programme had low recruitments rates; GPs in particular showed little interest in engaging with the programme but their involvement was necessary in order to identify potential candidates for enrolment. Participants who were enrolled in arms 1–3 underwent an assessment and an individualized action plan was devised. They were then offered access to a wide range of different services from physiotherapy, counselling, and complementary therapy for those in the health arm, ergonomic assessment, advice, and graduated return to work for the 'work' arm and any of these for the combined arm. Thus, each participant received a different combination of services and the policy architects were keen to ensure a clear distinction between 'health' services and advice and 'work' services and advice. However, in reality and despite numerous training workshops, this proved impossible to achieve (Stratford et al. 2005). In particular, providers found it extremely difficult not to give advice on health to those in the 'work' arm and vice versa as this conflicted with their professional code of ethics. Compounding this, the programme was implemented in six different locations and providers varied greatly in how they utilized the action plan with some constantly updating it whilst others used it simply as a formal contractual document (Stratford et al. 2005).

Here we see that programmes are embedded amidst complex social systems which govern professional practice, making it virtually impossible to create a closed system. Efforts to neutralize human agency through standardization lead to opposition from stakeholders. Instead, the programme was adapted to local circumstances and consequently there was a wide variation in how it was implemented. Furthermore, programmes with long implementation chains and multiple stakeholders can face an infinite number of stumbling blocks in achieving their end goals but the RCT rarely shines its torch into these murky depths. Finally, although some consideration was given to the different motivations that may drive participants to enrol on the programme and thus influence its success, these are assumed to be neutralized through the process of randomization. The programme worked for some but not others and it is therefore not surprising that no overall difference in return-to-work rates was found between the different arms of the trial.

Systematic reviews are the 'no overall effect' conclusion writ large and compound the failures of RCTs to deal with complexity. These are the dominant method of synthesizing research evidence in the healthcare arena, though their methods have also found their way into other policy sectors (for example, crime (Welsh and Farrington 2002), education (Torgerson and Elbourne 2002), and welfare (Bambra et al. 2005)). Their logic rests on pooling the results of RCTs within the same family of interventions in an additive fashion to provide an overall effect size or 'pass/fail' verdict on whether they work. This methodology ignores the differing circumstances in which programmes are implemented. Consequently it masks the factors that may explain why the intervention works in some circumstances and not others. For example, Hillage et al.'s (2008) review of programmes to reduce long-term sickness absence and improve job retention found a mixed pattern of outcomes across different types of interventions, settings, and populations. It concluded that, as the studies included in the review were heterogeneous, it was not possible to draw conclusions about the success or otherwise of specific interventions (Hillage et al. 2008). Such conclusions do not provide practical guidance to policymakers on which interventions to implement where or for whom.

DEALING WITH COMPLEXITY: REALIST SYNTHESIS

In this section I argue that a realist perspective is better able to deal with the complexity of social programmes and that a methodology such as realist synthesis (RS) can offer more useful advice to policymakers. Realist synthesis rests on a generative view of causality—it is not the programme or intervention that has causal powers; rather, programmes offer resources to people and it is people choosing or not to act on these resources that makes the programme work or not. In realist terms, these processes are 'mechanisms'. Programme resources may be interpreted in different ways by different participants, thus causal mechanisms may be multiple. For example, participants may have enrolled on the JRRP for various different reasons (Farrell et al. 2006) such as:

- to address a physical health problem that prevented their return to work;
- to tackle stress caused by a long-standing difficult relationship with their line manager;
- to receive support for a long-standing mental health problem;
- to help identify an exit route from a job they did not like.

However, choices people make are constrained by the circumstances in which they find themselves—therefore the context influences which causal mechanisms are fired. Furthermore, contextual influences are multiple and exist at many different levels (stratification)—for example, individual, group, organizational, and societal (Pawson, 2006b). As a result, programmes produce a whole pattern of outcomes, have a differential effect on different sorts of outcomes, produce different outcomes for different groups of people, and produce different outcomes in different settings. For example, the JRRP found that those who entered the trial with a mental health problem were much *less* likely to return to work after receiving an intervention while those with an injury were *more* likely to return to work after receiving an intervention (Purdon et al. 2006). RS aims to explain the whole pattern of outcomes, rather than deliver a pass/fail verdict on a particular intervention. Thus, we can hypothesize that very different mechanisms were at play for different subgroups of people depending on why they found themselves off work sick and how long they had been off sick in the first place. In essence, realism recognizes that the same intervention does not work in the same way in all circumstances and for all people and tries to understand for which people or groups and in which circumstances the intervention does or does not work.

RS thus offers a different approach to the task of systematic review. Here, the unit of analysis is the *theory*—the underlying assumptions or ideas about how the intervention is supposed to work, not the intervention. Indeed, the same intervention may 'work' through a range of different underlying mechanisms. For example, for people with mental health problems, participation in the JRRP may have led them to receive counselling or psychotherapy. This may have led to greater self-awareness of their problems which, in turn, may have either led to a realization that they needed more time off work to resolve them or indeed did not want to return. By contrast, for people with a physical health problem, participation in the JRRP may have led to the receipt of physiotherapy which in turn relieved their problem and thus the barrier to return to work. These represent theories that can each be tested through comparison with other studies exploring the trajectories of people returning to work following different reasons for sickness absence and then refined or refuted. Thus a central task of RS is to develop, test, and refine such theories in order to build explanation. The next section explains in more detail the practical steps involved in conducting RS.

A STEP-BY-STEP GUIDE TO REALIST SYNTHESIS

RS operates with an iterative, six-stage study design as outlined in Figure 14.1. Although what follows next is a somewhat linear description of the steps taken in realist synthesis, in reality there is much toing and froing between the steps and often different processes are intertwined rather than separate. What follows below is based on Pawson's (2006b) original exposition of the method.

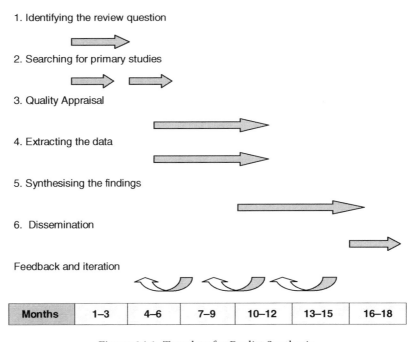

Figure 14.1 Template for Realist Synthesis

IDENTIFY THE REVIEW QUESTION

The basic unit of analysis in realist synthesis is not the intervention but the programme theories that underpin it (Pawson et al. 2005). The hypotheses that justify the programme and provide the reasons why it might work are also the hypotheses to be investigated in realist synthesis. Review thus begins by searching primary materials to identify the justifications, arguments, and programme logic of the interventions under review. Programme theories are to be found in policy guidance documentation, web- or paper-based descriptions of specific programmes produced by particular providers, promotional materials for the intervention or device, resource centre advice, management bulletins, position papers, thought pieces, advocacy pieces, and critical pieces. These forms of media and academic outputs are a useful source of programme theories because they describe, discuss, and dispute the underlying ideas and assumptions about how and why a programme is intended to work. For example, peer support has been suggested as a means of enabling people with a variety of physical and mental health problems or those excluded from society to regain meaningful employment. Figure 14.2 presents an edited description of a specific programme utilized by Cambridge and Peterborough Foundation NHS Trust (<http://www.cpft.nhs.uk/patients/peer-support.htm>) that aims to use peer support to help people recover from mental health or drugs and alcohol problems and ultimately, to gain meaningful employment.

This document is a source of programme theory. The description suggests that peer support 'works' through creating a trusting relationship between supporter and supportee based on mutual and shared experiences. This suggests that the relative status between supporter and supportee may be an important explanatory ingredient to the success of the peer support relationship. This relationship forms the foundation on which recovery can begin to occur through the provision of 'hope' ('someone else *like me* has done it—so can I') and as a safe place for trying new things. This theory is by no means the whole story or explanation about how and why peer support 'works'. Questions remain as to how the development of a trusting relationship could then ultimately lead to a person regaining employment. However, this initial theory may lead to the search for more formal academic theories of mentoring processes, for example, Kram and Isabella (Kram and Isabella 1985) make a distinction between 'career', 'psychosocial', and 'role model' mentoring. These theories can be added to the pool of candidate theories to be tested and can be assembled into an overall model to shape the focus of the review. The point here is that candidate theories can be drawn from a range of materials, not just academic journal papers.

It is likely that a large number of candidate theories on a particular programme can be assembled. It is not feasible for realist review to tackle them all. Thus, a crucial first stage in realist syntheses is careful deliberation and consultation on which programme theories to prioritize—which are the programme

---

What is peer support?

"Peer Support Specialists and Recovery Coaches are powerful recovery role models that engage each individual served in a personal recovery programme. Based on the person's goals the peer staff offer a wide range of support activities, skill building, and case management".

• Inspiring hope and optimism

• Empathy

• Mutuality (equals and co-learners)

• Friendship

What is a Peer Support Worker?

*"Someone with significant experience of mental distress, who works alongside others with similar difficulties in order to facilitate recovery through promoting hope and providing support based on common experiences"*Dr Julie Repper, Recovery lead Nottingham Healthcare Trust and Associate Professor in Mental Health and Social Care, University of Nottingham, 2009

• Someone with lived experience of mental health issues / mental illness

• Someone who is employed specifically as a result of their experience

• Someone who has the ability to share their recovery journey with others

• Someone who can motivate and encourage others

Why does it work?

*"When people identify with others who they feel are 'like them', they feel a connection. This is turn fosters an environment where individuals can share suggestions and tips for their recovery with each other, and try out different strategies, with the support of their fellow peers."*Sherry Mead, 2001

Figure 14.2 Web-based Description of a Programme as an Example of a Source of Programme Theories

theories whose further investigation is likely to foster the broadest improvement in the implementation and targeting of the social programme under study? One way of strengthening this process is to involve programme architects, programme implementers, and programme recipients in the process of identifying and prioritizing theories for review. This could involve presenting initial theories to key stakeholders at the start of the review to gain their views on which theories are actively at play in the implementation of the programme, asking them to modify the theory and suggest a whole range of 'ifs and buts' which may inform thinking about the contextual factors that might affect how and why the programme works.

The next step in realist synthesis involves developing a model to be tested through review. This sets out the configuration of contexts and mechanisms that lead to the programme outcomes. For example, the theory of peer support as 'befriending', described in embryonic form above, forms the first stage in a much longer model developed by Pawson (2004b) which provided the backbone of his realist synthesis of peer mentoring. This model hypothesized that peer mentoring works through a series of phases in which the peer support relationship first supports 'befriending', then through direction-setting, coaching, and finally sponsoring and advocating on behalf of the mentee to allow access to networks required for employment. It suggests that whether all of these stages are achieved depends heavily on the mentor's personal resources and it may be that only certain stages of the model are triggered by individual mentors. Thus, realist review takes the form of a set of linked sub-questions that can be tested through an exploration of the empirical literature.

SEARCHING FOR PRIMARY STUDIES

Literature searching in RS is ongoing and iterative throughout the review and search strategies and terms evolve as inquiry advances and understanding grows. For the purpose of description and explanation, I describe two main phases of searching here. The first, to support the stage described above, is the 'theory search' and its domain is the background policy documentation and unpublished literature described above. Searching and theory development are intertwined—searching for papers or policy documents on a particular theory inevitably leads to the discovery of another possible theory, which in turn, may initiate more searching and then more reading. Intermittently the reviewer also has to pause in order to consolidate reading and begin to draw diagrams, logic maps, or models of theories, before carrying out further searches and reading. This is somewhat similar to the process of qualitative data analysis, where the analyst constantly moves between immersion in the data (i.e. reading transcripts and applying codes) and reflecting on the analysis (developing categories, expanding and merging categories, writing reflective memos on how categories are related, drawing models to reflect this) (Charmaz 2006). The end result is a theory, expressed in terms of a set of interlinked questions and/or a framework to guide the review.

Once a preliminary model has been assembled and the subset of theories to be interrogated has been selected, RS commences an 'evidence search'. The aim of this search is to identify studies that will provide empirical tests of each component of the theory or subset of questions. Here the search domain covers more orthodox research reports and journal papers carrying empirical investigations of the programme under study. Unlike traditional systematic reviews, there is no limitation on study design; the search aims for a maximal sample of primary studies employing quantitative, qualitative, experimental, documentary, and historical analysis.

The evidence search in realist synthesis does not rest with comprehensive, pre-specified search strategies, as is usually the case in traditional systematic reviews. Such reviews generally rest on one, large, multi-component search strategy to identify all the studies that evaluate a predetermined and specific intervention in a predetermined population using particular outcome measures and a specific study design (usually the RCT). In RS, the search strategy takes the form of a series of linked searches to answer each specific sub-question.

Reference and citation tracking are often more useful than searches of electronic databases to identify high quality papers that are in hard-to-find locations (Greenhalgh and Peacock 2005). Reference tracking involves scanning the references lists of relevant papers to identify further papers that may contribute to building or testing theory. Citation tracking refers to using citation-tracking databases (for example, the Social Science Citation Index) to identify articles that have subsequently cited key papers. This technique of sampling papers for realist synthesis is akin to the process of the 'snowballing' strategy in qualitative research, where key informants introduce the researcher to other people that they know.

DATA EXTRACTION AND QUALITY APPRAISAL

In traditional systematic reviews, studies undergo a systematic series of vetting procedures to assess relevance and study quality before they can be included in the review. In a series of linear steps, the papers identified by the searches are filtered to assess their relevance to ensure that they first relate to the intervention, study population, and outcome being studied, and are of the appropriate study design. They are then checked to ascertain whether they meet predefined quality criteria with reference to quality checklists. Only then is data extracted from the paper using a standardized form, which then, in turn, provides the basis for this data to be synthesized. Only once all data has been extracted from the paper does synthesis begin.

These phases—an assessment of study relevance and quality, data extraction and synthesis are combined in RS (Pawson 2006a). The relevance of the study to the review can only be determined during the process of synthesis, not a priori according to a predetermined set of criteria relating to study population, outcome, or quality. Consequently, each fragment of evidence needs to be appraised, as it is extracted, for both its relevance for theory-testing and the rigour with which it has been produced. Different programme theories require substantiation in divergent bodies of evidence. Hypotheses about the optimal contexts for the intervention are tested in comparative outcome data; claims about the reactions of particular groups of subjects are tested using qualitative data; implementation ideas are tested in process research, and so on. Primary studies thus contribute specific bodies of evidence but each primary study plays a different role in the final synthesis. Quality appraisal is thus done on a case-by-case basis as appropriate to the method utilized in the original study.

Furthermore, empirical studies are rarely designed to directly test the whole theory under review. Rather, elements of the theory or specific sub-questions will be explored within a study. Each study is likely to provide only a partial test of the theory and/or only specific elements of a particular study may be used to test a particular element of the theory. As Pawson (2006a) argues, this then transforms the process of quality appraisal for RS; quality appraisal is not carried out against the study as a whole because it is usually only a fragment of data or an inferential claim that finds its way into the synthesis. Quality appraisal is thus an integral part of the synthesis itself and is set down as a caveat when the fragment of evidence and its contribution to theory-testing is discussed.

Pawson provides an example of this at play in his synthesis of mentoring relationships (Pawson 2004b). He begins by setting out a model of how mentoring relationships might work (described above) and then uses nine empirical studies with differing research designs (both qualitative and quantitative) to show how they have been used to test the theory. There is not sufficient space here to describe this process in detail but two important points can be noted. The first is that theory-testing is cumulative and is not an 'all-or-nothing' process—one study may provide some support for an aspect of the model but also suggest that a different element of it needs revising. Thus, Pawson shows how Colley's (2003) ethnographic study of a UK Government scheme of mentoring socially excluded young people provides support for the theory that mentoring itself is a long-term, stepped process in which it is not possible to 'jump' an individual step (Colley 2003). However, the same study also calls into question a different element of the theory—that there is a linear ladder of different types of mentor engagement and suggests that one mentor alone may not be able to encapsulate all steps. The second is that defensible claims can be obtained from flawed studies and used for the purpose of theory-testing. For example, Pawson (2006b) discusses the claims made by de Anda's (2001) qualitative evaluation of the RESCUE project ('Reaching Each Student's Capacity Utilizing Education') in which eighteen mentor-mentee dyads were interviewed about their experiences of the project. Pawson (2006b) argues that de Anda's claims, that engagement mentoring 'works', are not justified and probably represent biased reporting on the part of the researcher. Despite this, the study does provide a useful description of the mechanisms through which mentoring relationships might work. Furthermore, the caveats about study quality and precisely which evidential claims are being used to test theory are clearly set out in the synthesis (Pawson 2006a).

The theory and its linked sets of sub-questions provide a framework through which different fragments of evidence are sought and utilized from each study. There is no common 'data extraction form'. Both qualitative and quantitative data are compiled as well as the inferences and conclusions drawn from them. Data extraction thus requires active engagement with each document through note taking and text annotation. The reviewer considers how each fragment confirms, refutes, or revises the theory under consideration. Thus, judgements about relevance, data extraction, and quality appraisal form part of the process of synthesis itself, rather than being distinct, mechanistic processes of assembling data to be summated or analysed at a later stage.

SYNTHESIS

The role of synthesis in RS is not to offer a verdict, descriptive summary, or mean effect calculation on a family of programmes. Outcomes vary considerably according to how and where programmes are implemented. What is synthesized, therefore, are all the conditions and caveats that make for programme success. Many of these opportunities and stumbling blocks will have been anticipated in the original programme theories but after a total immersion in the data, more refined theories emerge as the key act of synthesis. Synthesis can take a number of different forms, summarized in Table 14.1.

A 'theory of change' synthesis is particularly useful for programmes that have long and complex implementation chains. They focus on mapping this

Table 14.1 Different Types of Realist Synthesis

Type	Key questions	Example
Theories of change	What are the main flows and blockages in the programme theory?	Pawson's synthesis of Megan's Law (Pawson 2002a)Greenhalgh et al.'s (2005) review of PROMs feedback in clinical practice (Greenhalgh et al. 2005)
Realist comparison	How does one theory fare in different contexts?	Pawson's synthesis of naming and shaming (Pawson 2002b)
Ajudication of rival theories	Which programme theory is most plausible?	Fung et al.'s (2008) review of the public release of performance data (Fung et al. 2008)

chain, challenging the assumptions underlying this chain and identifying the potential stumbling blocks that may prevent the programme from achieving its end points. An area where this form of review would be particularly insightful is the link between HRM practices and performance. Several narrative reviews exist in this area (see Boselie et al. 2005; Patterson et al. 2010) and most have focused on quantitative evidence examining the strength of the link between HRM practices and intermediate (employee motivation, job satisfaction, and turnover) and distal (company performance, profits, and market share) outcomes. Although some (Patterson et al. 2010) have attempted to look into the black box to specify the chain of events through which HRM practices lead to improved performance, these tend to be expressed in terms of event regularities under successionist logic. For example, Patterson et al. (2010) argue that superior HRM practices lead to a more skilled motivated, satisfied, and committed workforce who work harder, engage in more organizational citizenship behaviours, and thus improve organizational performance. However, this assumes that wherever superior HRM practices exist, all employees respond in the same way and takes no account of the different reactions that employees may have to these practices or the varying settings in which HRM practices are implemented. A realist synthesis in this area would seek to identify the different mechanisms through which HRM practices lead to organizational performance outcomes and explore the contextual influences on whether and how each different mechanism is fired. Thus, it would seek to explain the whole pattern of outcomes of the HRM-performance link, rather than examining what happens 'on average' or 'in most studies'.

A realist comparison synthesis is very powerful for interrogating programme theories that have found a home across a number of different policy arenas. The purpose of this form of synthesis is to shed light on how different contexts can influence the mechanisms through which such a programme works and thus explain its differential pattern of outcomes found in different settings. This form of review would be helpful in shedding light on the 'trade union-manager' relationship to explain how this produces different outcomes in different industries. For example, why do trade unions have more leverage to improve workforce conditions in some industries than in others? This form of review might begin by setting up a generic theory to explain the mechanisms through which trade unions influence managers and thus change working conditions and examine how these mechanisms operate in different contexts.

Pawson's synthesis of 'naming and shaming' also provides an example of this form of review (Pawson 2002b). As Pawson argues, naming and shaming has permeated almost every area of policy from the car crime index, school league tables, local press publication of the names of people who had not paid their poll tax bill in the UK, and sex offender registration in the US. Pawson sets up a generic theory to describe the process through which the identification of the behaviour and then its naming leads to public sanction and then to behavioural change on behalf of the recipient. He then provides evidence to show how recipients in different contexts have responded in different ways to the policy (discussed below). The revised theory accounts for these differential responses and presents a set of contingencies on which theory success is based.

Finally, in some areas of policy, rival theories are put forward to explain how a particular programme works. In these instances, a realist synthesis can be used to adjudicate between programme theories to determine which theory is best supported by the evidence. An example of this form of review is Fung et al.'s (2008) review of the public disclosure of hospital performance information as a means of improving the quality of care (Fung et al. 2008). Alert readers will recognize that this is a specific example of the generic 'naming and shaming' theory. Two rival theories are proposed. The 'change' theory argues that public disclosure leads to improved care through prompting hospital managers and clinicians to change their behaviour. 'Selection' theory argues that the public will choose better quality hospitals and that lower quality hospitals will lose their market share and eventually cease to operate. The review finds some evidence to support the change theory, but little evidence to support the selection theory; patients rarely consult performance data let alone use it to make decisions about hospital choice.

Thus, synthesis can take on different forms for a variety of purposes, but how is this operationalized in practice? The mechanics of the synthesis process have been described, in part, in previous sections. At its most basic, realist synthesis is a form of 'triangulation', bringing together information from different primary studies and different study types. It may, for instance, make use of: outcome data from studies 1, 2, and 3; implementation findings from studies 4, 5, and 6; subgroup findings from studies 7, 8, and 9; participant interpretations from studies 10, 11, and 12; temporal variation from studies 13, 14, and 15; contextual comparisons using studies 16, 17, and 18; and so on. To illustrate this, I will draw on a review I previously conducted with colleagues to understand the implementation pathway of the feedback of data from patient-reported outcome measures (PROMs) (Greenhalgh et al. 2005).

PROMs are questionnaires that measure patients' perceptions of the impact of a condition and its treatment on their health (Dawson et al. 2010). The theory is that if patients complete a PROM prior to their consultation and it is fed back to their doctor, this will enable the doctor to identify the patient's problems, discuss these with the patient, and intervene to address the problem, which will then improve the patient's health status. A starting point for the review was to describe and then explain the differential pattern of outcome data found in traditional systematic reviews of PROMs feedback (Greenhalgh et al. 2005). This indicated that PROMs feedback had found some success in changing communication within the consultation and increasing the recognition of problems for some subgroups of patients but had little impact on the ways in which patients were managed or their health status. A range of evidence was used to make sense of these outcome patterns. In particular, surveys revealed a considerable degree of scepticism from clinicians about the trustworthiness of PROMs data and qualitative studies showed that clinical and biological information plays a much greater role in treatment decision-making than PROMs data. Thus, the synthesis identified key stumbling blocks in the implementation chain that prevented the programme from working 'as planned'.

During the process of synthesis, each study is interrogated to determine the extent to which it supports, weakens, modifies, supplements, reinterprets, or refocuses the theory under question. After each successive encounter with a particular study, the original theory is thus revised. However, this process is not simply a 'one-study-at-a-time' process. Often, several studies will provide evidence concerning the same component of the theory; sometimes their evidence will be complementary but sometimes contradictory. At this point, the task for the reviewer is to juxtapose the evidence and 'adjudicate' or 'reconcile' the contending positions. This is not a matter of providing evidence to declare a certain standpoint correct and another one invalid. Rather, adjudication assists in understanding the respects in which a particular programme theory holds and those where it does not *and explaining why.* In other words, the theory is refined to account for the influence that context may have on the success or otherwise of the programme theory. Further evidence may be brought in to consolidate this revision. The end point of synthesis is a summary of how the model has been revised following such testing.

For example, in Pawson's (2002a) review of naming and shaming contrasts can be drawn between the reaction of different recipients of the policy in different settings according to the status of the shamed party. Poll tax protesters wore their naming as a badge of honour while sex offenders respond by going underground. Schools respond by game-playing to exclude 'hopeless' pupils from sitting exams and, focusing resources on ensuring those with middle grades achieve higher ones to inflate their performance. Car manufacturers, however, were embarrassed by the media response to their performance and responded by changing the security features of their car. Pawson concludes the review by setting out the circumstances under which the programme theory worked. In another paper he provides an explanation for how the status of the shamed party can explain their differential response by drawing on Merton's reference group theory (Pawson 2010). Through this lens, naming and shaming can be seen as attempts by an 'in-group' to remedy the behaviour of an 'out-group'. The theory argues that a group's reaction to policies is likely to depend on both their aspiration to belong to a salient 'in-group' and their eligibility for membership of that group. Thus, 'aspirational eligibles', such as Ford, will want to protect their position and respond to the policy of naming and shaming by complying positively under threats to their reputation.

DISSEMINATION

The purpose of RS is to improve the implementation and targeting of interventions. Accordingly, dissemination needs to focus on policymakers and decision-makers responsible for designing and implementing the programme under review. The outputs of RS are recommendations to assist decision-makers to target and implement the programme under review within the specific local conditions in their area and workplace. To maximize the chances that such recommendations are taken up by policymakers, Pawson recommends two strategies. First is to involve policymakers in the process of the review; particularly at the theory development and selection stage and at the synthesis stage, to ensure that the focus of the review addresses live policy issues and debates. The second is to frame the recommendations and outputs of realist synthesis in terms of viable policy options and in a language policymakers can understand. Thus policymakers require clear and concise conclusions to inform their decision-making. For example, Pawson's most recent synthesis to review the policy of banning smoking in cars carrying children exists in several different forms, ranging from an 18,000-word paper in the *American Journal of Evaluation* (Pawson et al. 2011) for hard core realist synthesis anoraks to an A4 summary of its key findings for policymakers.

CONCLUSIONS

Realist synthesis is a valuable addition to the evaluator's toolbox. It enables evaluators, policymakers and policy-implementers to move beyond an understanding of 'what works' to develop a more useful and practical understanding of 'what works for whom and in what circumstances'. Realist synthesis is particularly useful to review existing literature evaluating social programmes that:

- rely on human volition and on the action of multiple different stakeholders to make them work;
- have long implementation chains, such that a, b, c, d, and e need to happen before x and y can be achieved;
- vary in how they have been implemented in different settings;
- are inserted into complex existing social and organizational systems which are likely to influence how the programme works.

It can be particularly useful to:

- uncover the flows and blockages in the programme implementation;
- ajudicate between rival theories of how a particular programme works;
- explore how the same programme performs in different settings.

After compiling this list, it seems the reader might struggle to identify a social programme that does *not* fit these requirements, rather than one that does. Indeed, that is the point—the evaluation of existing research on all programmes aimed at changing the behaviour of individuals, groups, or organizations might be better serviced by conducting an RS. However, the focus of RS is to understand and refine the theory underlying the intervention, rather than the specificities of the intervention itself. So those wishing to understand how the provision of lifestyle advice to employees in small firms impacts their sickness absence might struggle to carry out an RS unless it is recognized that this is an example of a behaviour change theory. Thus, the ability of the intervention to support the process of behaviour change should be the focus of the synthesis, rather than the specifics of the intervention itself.

Further, while there may be few studies examining lifestyle advice to employees, there are countless studies examining interventions where the underlying theory is that of behaviour change. In this way, the lack of existing literature for an intervention need not be a reason for abandoning a realist synthesis; instead it is possible to draw on evidence from programmes that shared the same programme theory. Thus, it is more the focus of the evaluator's enquiry, rather than the programme itself or the level of existing evidence, which will determine the appropriateness of conducting a realist synthesis. It is more about a willingness to shift from wanting to simply answer the question of 'what works' to wishing to understand the contingencies that may affect the success of a programme. The answers to these questions are of much more practical use to policymakers.

15

Probability and Models

Malcolm Williams

INTRODUCTION—SOME PHILOSOPHICAL LIMITS AND POSSIBILITIES

Realism is a naturalistic doctrine; though defined in a number of ways, this is usually taken to mean in social science that human beings belong to an objective natural order. Whilst there is ontological difference between physical and social phenomena, there is no radical disjuncture between physical and mental (and therefore social) phenomena (Papineau 1993: 2–5). It follows that if there can be sciences of the physical world, then there can be sciences of the social world. If realism is a naturalistic doctrine, then realists must do scientific research and seek causal explanations and on the basis of these make generalizing statements about phenomena.

The objective of generalization is usually associated with quantitative methods. Much realist research has used qualitative methods (often with good effect), but there is a limit to the explanatory power of qualitative approaches for social structures or aggregate phenomena (Payne and Williams 2005; Williams 2000a). I will begin with a discussion of the limits of a realist methodology. The possibilities are then addressed through an explanatory strategy that begins with a case-based quantitative approach and then argues for and illustrates the use of models at three levels: theoretical, methodological, and statistical. The purpose is not to describe these models in detail but to argue that, if realism is to have relevance in quantitative research, it must embrace probability and models.

THE LIMITS OF A REALIST METHODOLOGY

One of the founders of what has become known as the 'causal analysis' tradition in social research, Hubert Blalock, wrote:

One admits that causal thinking belongs completely on the theoretical level and that causal laws can never be demonstrated empirically. But this does not mean that it is not helpful to think causally and to develop causal models that have implications that are indirectly testable. (Blalock 1961: 6)

In this sentence (and a number of times elsewhere) Blalock is proposing the existence of a reality and indeed one that is active, but he is also setting some limits to what a research programme can tell us about reality. This is not simply a Humean acknowledgement that there may be a reality but we cannot possibly know it, but rather an implicit admission that reality reveals itself to us partially and imperfectly. He goes on to say:

Reality, or at least our perception of reality, admittedly consists of ongoing processes. No two events are ever exactly repeated, nor does any object or organism remain precisely the same from one moment to the next. And yet, if we are ever to understand the nature of the real world, we must act and think as though events are repeated and as if objects do have properties that remain constant for some period of time, however short. (Blalock 1961: 7)

Blalock (perhaps unknowingly) was setting out a manifesto for a moderate realism that depended on some degree of invariance and some degree of visibility, but crucially the way through which we propose how the world is (our theories) will not and cannot be an equivalent of the way the world actually is. As Bhaskar put it, some decades later,

Things exist and act independently of our descriptions, but we can only know them under particular descriptions. Descriptions belong to the world of society and of men; objects belong to the world of nature…Science, then, is the systematic attempt to express in thought the structures and ways of acting of things that exist and act independently of thought. (Bhaskar 2008: 250)

Blalock was by training a mathematician who later turned sociologist, so for him a mathematical description of the world was entirely appropriate and indeed crucial for science. Mathematics can show both logical relations between concepts, but crucially quantity. We can reason through informal induction (and indeed we must) from one situation or set of characteristics to another. But more formal limits can only be expressed mathematically, or at least statistically in the form of probabilities.

This is where the first and most important limitation of realism arises. To what extent do our measures measure real things? Blalock was not greatly troubled by this (at a conceptual level), because the social scientist in common with other scientists must propose models that are testable empirically. His strategy was to make reasonable inferences about causal processes on the basis of a priori assumptions and statistical outcomes. Blalock's strategy can be described as one of heuristics: models of the world that incorporate a limited number of variables, because there must be a limit to the number of variables that can be articulated through a causal language, a mathematical language, and an operational language, but nevertheless provide an adequate description and explanation of some part of the social world. Blalock maintained that these languages are not reducible to each other and must forever remain the essential elements of the expression of the model (1961: 27).

At this point realists may be puzzled, or even annoyed, as to why I am spending time outlining the thinking of someone that many would see as much closer to empiricism than realism. The reason is simple and even implicit in the above: to what extent can methods uncover reality directly and to what extent must they rely on heuristics or approximations?

Realists have often been wary of models and heuristics in social science because of their alleged inability to capture the complexity of reality, or indeed to have practical adequacy. The result in critical realism has been an almost wholesale adoption of qualitative methods in what has been a fairly thin offering of empirical work since Roy Bhaskar's much lauded seminal work in the 1970s and 1980s. This is a pity, because the result has been that quantitative analysis has rarely benefited from the theoretical insights of realism and for many has remained synonymous with positivism. There are exceptions and I will mention some of these below.

An important and often critical discussion of the role of quantification in realism came early on from Andrew Sayer (1992). He specifically takes issue with the ability of mathematical language to capture reality, limited as it must be to being an ideal language (a fact not lost on Blalock). But equally he has a problem with (what Blalock termed) the 'operational language'. For example:

> Practically adequate forms of quantifying using interval scales can only be developed for objects and processes which are qualitatively invariant, at least in their fundamentals. As such, they can be split up and combined without changing their nature. We can measure them at different times or places in different conditions and know that we are not measuring different things. But there are far fewer occasions when we can be confident about this stability in social science than in natural science. (Sayer 1992: 177)

Sayer saw a role for descriptive data and statistics as a backdrop or framework for realist method, but these and quantitative methods more generally were less than enthusiastically embraced.

Neither Sayer, nor his critics who eschew theory and reify statistical models, have a monopoly of right and that is why I set out some of the epistemological and methodological limits to social science method. Sayer is wrong if he is claiming that interval measures of phenomena cannot be made practically adequate, though it is true that doing so can be hard.

For example, relatively simple measures, such as satisfaction scores, can achieve very good levels of validity across relatively wide cultural difference (e.g. Lucas and Diener 2009). It is true that cultural differences in responding to satisfaction measures exist, but can often be compensated through analytical strategies of aggregation or disaggregation, such as those used in cross-national surveys, for example the European Social Survey (ESS).[1] The depth of cultural differences can also be exaggerated. The ESS, for example, surveys sixteen European countries using around twenty-five different languages on topics such as civic activity, political affiliation, values, and the economy. Its base language is English, but it does not simply translate questions from English to other languages, but rather rigorously tests for meaning equivalence, at each level of measurement: nominal, ordinal, or interval. For example the concept of 'household' exists in some languages and cultures, but not others. If, however, one begins with a spatial definition of persons occupying a single defined dwelling space and then seeks equivalence in terms of dependencies of its occupants, then equivalence (which may not use the same question in each jurisdiction/language) may be achieved. Indeed equivalence of meaning (despite language) is remarkably consistent across much of Europe (see Jowell et al. 2007 for a detailed account of the methods of the ESS).

On one level the difficulties posed by cultural variance are technical, though not wholly so. For example, the transnational measurement of social class through occupation, income, lifestyle, and so on is a deeply theoretical activity that requires us to (for example) decide to what extent occupation can stand proxy for a way of life. However, once matters of principle are resolved calibrations of transnational equivalence can be achieved, though they and the starting theoretical assumptions will have their limits: we can translate between European, Australasian, and North American countries, but Rwanda or Egypt would be hard and maybe impossible. Thus, in criticizing the adequacy of models and seeing their limitations (which may actually be the limitations of social research anyway) we should be careful not to dismiss them out of hand. Indeed, in proposing modes of theoretical reasoning that posits causal powers or dispositions, realists are already constructing models. One of the best is the Context + Mechanism = Outcome (C+M=O) model of Ray Pawson (Pawson et al. 2005). I will return to the issue of models in some detail below.

PROBABILITY

Probability comes in two flavours: objective and subjective. The second, sometimes called Bayesian probability[2] like any other methodological or statistical method may have value for realism, but for the purposes of this discussion

[1] See <http://www.europeansocialsurvey.org/> (accessed 06/08/13).

[2] Bayesian probability is derived from Bayes Theorem, which is a method for calculating the conditional probability of an event from known prior events. It is subjective, because the initial prior estimate is not derived from any objectively known values, but instead is amended as a result of later confirmation/disconfirmation of the hypothesis.

I want to concentrate on objective probability, which itself divides into two main kinds: epistemological and ontological. In social research the epistemological has dominated in the form of the frequency theory of probability. This depends on the observation of the relative frequency of an event in a known sequence and usually takes the form of reasoning from a sample to a population. A sample is then a 'model' of reality and if one wishes to object to the use of models in realist research then the sample survey must be ruled out a priori, as must the statistical models that are then derived from this. Let me develop this line of argument further: each frequency in sample data, though derived from the observation of an actual person (or other unit of analysis), is for the purposes of statistical analysis an 'ideal' person who when aggregated with persons in the sample is considered statistically representative of some part of a wider population. The sample aims to model the population in its most salient features, and one reasons from the sample to the population. To reason from the sample to individuals or groups of individuals in the population is to commit an ecological fallacy. There are other statistical issues with the frequency theory of probability that I have discussed elsewhere (Williams 1999), but for our present purpose, suffice to say that this form of probabilistic reasoning can only ever *model* reality. However I will argue below that we should not reject models based on sample data that depend on the frequency theory.

There is another way! Sayer's critique of the survey in general, and interval data in particular, is grounded in the problem of variance. Here I use this term as an ontological characteristic of the social world, not to describe a statistical distribution. Variance implies flux and change between place and over time in the social world and this, even at a common sense level, is obviously true. We need think only of the issue of rationality which if held to be universal in form can only be demonstrated by example or examples which are trivial in their content, or at such a level of generality that they are not testable. Once rationality is specified in more detail it becomes culturally specific and imbued with particular and often 'local' meaning (see, for example, Taylor 1982). Yet there is also invariance, cultural stability, expressed through forms of rationality, which if not universal exist often quite widely across time and place. Indeed this must be the case for social life to be possible. This leads to the conclusion that if we observe the social world (even informally) we can observe two things: that some things are very much more likely than others, though never absolutely certain, and that things happen as a result of other things happening. We can say that the social world is ontologically probabilistic.[3]

---

[3] Statistically this is captured by variants of the 'normal curve'. The 'normal' curve is theoretical distribution under which measures of characteristics of most individuals or events fall under the central part of a bell-shaped curve. A perfect, or near perfect normal curve, in social life, is not that common and even when there is a distribution of characteristics that resemble a normal curve, there will usually be a long tail at one or other side of the curve that comprises 'outliers'.

Things will happen to an individual and as a result of these things happening, the probability of later other things happening to them will increase or decrease. The events themselves can be thought of as bifurcations, whereby a particular thing happens rather than any other thing. A truly realist method would measure the probability of an event's occurring in respect of an *actual* individual (or other unit of analysis). If this were possible, we would have derived the single case probability, the probability inherent in the thing itself and an ontological characteristic, rather than approximation of our knowledge. Single case probabilities were first mooted by Von Mises in the mid twentieth century (Von Mises 1951), but were taken up by Karl Popper. Single case probabilities are a form of the propensity theory of probability, which seeks to measure the propensity of an event's occurrence, rather than its relative frequency. One might say, as a metaphysical claim, that every single event in the world has a probability of occurrence, relative to every other event; however, to measure those individual case probabilities, as opposed to their relative position in a frequency distribution, is much harder.

Nevertheless this approach is possible in social research, but currently rarely used. It depends, first, on having a relational database of a given population, such as medical or criminal records that can record events over time. A sample will not do, because the analyses are based on actual cases.[4] The database is conceptualized as a number of tables (called relations or relational tables). This approach uses cluster analysis. Cluster analysis is an exploratory tool which classifies cases (not variables), for example, people, events, or objects, into groups, or clusters, so that the degree of similarity of characteristics is strong between members of the same cluster and weak between members of different clusters. Each cluster describes the class to which its members belong (see Everitt 1993). The more clusters are present, the greater the information about the cases, but the fewer the clusters the greater the generalizing power of the analysis. Cluster analysis can then be used to group cases according to their trajectories through time. For example, the social issue of homelessness is not dichotomous with not being homeless; rather it is a complex set of circumstances loosely characterized by housing need (Williams 2010). However, the types of housing need experienced by individuals can first be put into very specific clusters (e.g. street homeless, living in a squat, types of temporary accommodation, types of hostel) then re-clustered according to similarities and differences. Furthermore, this and other characteristics (loss of employment, release from prison, eviction, etc.) can be ordered through time to capture the dynamic process of an individual's 'homelessness' trajectory.

My point here is not to provide a technical overview of this method, which can be found in Williams and Dyer (2009), but rather to provide one example of

---

[4] The cases need not be individuals. They may be households, companies, families, countries, etc.

a quantitative method that does not depend either on samples, or reasoning from frequencies. Yet, this is not a realist magic bullet, because the method has a number of limitations. Firstly it can only be conducted on population data. Secondly it requires time series measures for each case and (though possibly not a disadvantage) the solutions tried in the clusters and the final interpretation are theory dependent. The homelessness example depends on beginning from a theorization of homelessness, however defined, as a social state worthy of investigation. One could have begun with a focus on, say, acute health crises, wherein types of homelessness are characteristics, along with diet, or other forms of poverty. Once clusters are established their probabilistic relationship to each other can be established using the technique of discriminant analysis (see Williams and Dyer 2009).

As a realist quantitative method, cluster analysis, that allows the derivation of single case probabilities, is about as realist as it gets. The cases themselves are 'real' and the bifurcations in the clusters represent life events (assuming the cases are actual people) that have causal consequences. Yet despite this the analyses are models for three reasons: first, as in variable analysis we cannot know whether the events recorded in the data file are all of those causally relevant to a final state (and in principle we could never know this). Second, it is a function of the cluster analysis that a decision must be made as to which clusters have the best explanatory power, which in turn is derived from a prior theoretical model. Third, because the decision to use (in my example) homelessness as the outcome state, equivalent to a 'dependent variable', is a theoretical choice and determines the key parameters of the analysis.

CAUSAL EXPLANATION

In practice single case probability analysis may not always be available so that social scientists must seek other methods. Simulations offer the complex modelling of artificial data (see Gilbert and Troitzsch 2005), but these are often somewhat removed from the quotidian concerns of the researcher called upon to find policy solutions or undertake evaluations (see for example Byrne 2011; Olsen 2004a; Pawson 2004a; Pawson and Tilly 1997). At this point realists have usually turned to qualitative methods and, whilst observations or interviews are very good at uncovering process and meaning, their ability to make causal generalizations is limited. Indeed in the work I have done with Geoff Payne (Payne and Williams 2005; Williams 2000a), we have acknowledged the possibility of *moderatum* generalizations, but have suggested that these should produce falsifiable propositions that would be (mostly) testable through quantitative methods. We need quantitative methods and we need some kind of variable-based analysis, but before I make the case for this there is a brief but necessary excursus into causality.

One cannot be a scientific realist without believing in causality. Nancy Cartwright (2002) has observed that causality is one word that can refer to many things. At a minimum we could say that it is a belief that B would not have happened if A had not occurred and that A should be prior in time to B. This statement has been more picked over by philosophers than any other and I do not want to labour these difficulties unduly. However, the key problems are that A may be multiple. Many things may have caused B, there may be intervening events between A and B, things other than A may sometimes cause B and in the social world at least what is B anyway? If B is a riot and A caused it, are we happy that our definition of riot captures B? We are faced with the problem of whether there are any necessary or sufficient conditions to bring about B, and B as an effect is often underdetermined.

But life and social research must go on. These exigencies were apparent to Blalock, just as they have been apparent to realists. In a recent paper, Ken Morrison (2012), provides an excellent critique of causal analysis. This covers the need to include relevant variables, the control of exogenous and endogenous variables, the problem of proving counterfactuals (the absence of a variable(s)), and the problem of transitivity (how far back to trace causal paths). One can add a further important one, that of asymmetry. The decision to treat B as the dependent variable is a theoretical one and not a mathematical function of a statistical mode. Morrison's assessment is correct but pessimistic. His solution? This begins from a premise it is hard to argue with (and I along with Dave Byrne [1998; 2011] have similarly argued) that the social world is ontologically complex and non-linear and our methods must begin from that point. So, his solution is to provide a methodological model that maps 'multi directionally interacting causes and effects that produce the phenomenon' (2012: 26). And who could argue with this? But it does not help us much with translating the search for causes into method.

Of the many things causality may be, here are three:

Single instance causality. It is enough to say (assuming we have an excellent observational account) that Denzil hitting Garfield caused him to fall over. Why he hit him may require us to look for reasons as causes and we cannot generalize beyond the situation about hitting and falling over. But beginning from these single instances and exploring reasons as causes is a frequently used qualitative strategy (see Hammersley 2008: chapter 4, for example).

Probabilistic causality. The probability of an event's coming about is not determined, but it is increased by earlier events happening. This is the basis of single case probability, which is essentially a causal theory of probability (Popper 1957, 1959, 1995). However, in frequency-based approaches, a causal model will show how the probability of an outcome variable is changed by addition of other variables to the model and is subject to the kind of criticisms advanced by Morrison and others. It can only ever be a heuristic model of reality.

Theoretical causality. In an ideal system outcome O is conditional upon mechanism M which will operate only in context C. This formulation is due to Ray Pawson and captures quite elegantly a realist model of causation. It is logically not different to saying (something like) heating water causes it to boil, but the temperature at which it boils depends on air pressure. If we know the air pressure, we can calculate the temperature at which water will boil and vice versa. In the social world the context and mechanisms are very much more variable than air pressure. The trick then (when we know O) is to also come to know C and M and to do this we need realist closure.

A realist methodological strategy can employ all three of these forms of causality, though quite often only the third of these is advocated, that is, causes are specified as theoretical properties of mechanisms. We may begin with the third of these and return to it, but empirically we must go via the first (in qualitative research) or the second. In the case of quantitative research on aggregate data, probabilistic causal claims seem unavoidable. As I have suggested, these may take the form of single case probabilities, though the opportunity to perform such analyses is limited. More likely we must use causal models derived from sample data.

MAKING MODELS

Whilst wanting to defend causality, no realist would deny the philosophical problems associated with it and many have been ready to identify the problems of operationalizing it in quantitative research. If realism wishes to pursue causal explanation a compromise is needed. That compromise requires a concession.

Models as Approximations

Models are not the world itself, but a realistic approximation of it. Implicit in much of what I have said so far has been the unavoidability of models, certainly at the theoretical level and most likely at the methodological level. Models imply translation processes and these require languages. Realists would assert that the world never presents itself to us in its raw or naked form. An observation is interpreted in context. Anything else is what C. W. Mills called 'abstracted empiricism' (1959: 50–75).

Realist quantitative research might be based on three interconnecting models (Skvoretz 1998): theoretical, methodological, and statistical. Whilst each uses a particular language and convention of expression, the specific content of each is derived from the other, and this is a dialectical relationship, in that testing of the statistical model will confirm, falsify, or change the theorized causal relationships in the theoretical model. There is an important caveat to enter here. Whilst each of these models is inevitably an approximation, the first two aim through their language to realistically represent the world. The statistical model is however an ideal representation of the relationships between the variables as measured and derived from the methodological model. Without implying conventionalism, in the philosophical sense, the statistical model relies on conventions. Ultimately the most important model is the theoretical model, for through this we aim to produce the best explanation of reality we can manage.

Theoretical Models

The aim of the theoretical model is to specify, as closely as possible, a hypothesized explanation for a given outcome. Realists will often use the term mechanism to describe a non-accidental ensemble of causal connections. The concept of a mechanism is familiar in such things as engines and clocks, but social mechanisms are not like these. Indeed Karl Popper (1979: chapter 6) used the analogy of clocks and clouds. A clock and its workings can be very closely specified and will be composed of a finite number of parts, which if assembled correctly and 'stimulated' by the energy of winding, or electricity, will work. Clouds, though they have shape, size, density, and chemical properties are all but infinite in the form they will take. Some mechanisms are closer to clocks, some closer to clouds. Social mechanisms are closer to clouds, though have more invariance than clouds (even though they may have many more properties). Particular social mechanisms can be identified, but they will be nested in other mechanisms and though more invariant than clouds, they will disappear or radically change in their properties, though some may persist relatively unchanged through time or place. Social mechanisms are as 'real' as clocks, but unlike a clock we cannot readily specify all of their components or properties.

On the shelf of my office I have a beautiful scale model replica of a Morris 1000 pick-up, very similar (right down to the rust patches) to the first vehicle I owned. The model captures the essence of a car I owned in the 1970s. It is indeed a very accurate model, but it is so because it is a replica of something that existed and had been built, whose precise characteristics were known. My toy Morris 1000 does not have an engine, a gearbox, or indeed a broken window-winding handle on the passenger side, but what is crucial is that we can specify exactly the properties of model, real car, and the difference between them. We cannot do this with social mechanisms. The issue is not just their complexity and their invariance; it is that we do not have in our possession a complete functioning social mechanism of which we can build a miniature. We have to build the miniature first and aim to make it as much like the real thing as we can, though we will never know whether we have got it absolutely right.

So we must build the best possible model and undertake tests which will tell us how closely it resembles reality. To do this we begin from an incomplete knowledge base, where some things are known with a good probability of their being correct and others we must infer from what we know.

Our theoretical models may be expressed in ordinary language terms as shorthand for concepts and their relations. Though less common these days, they may be formally expressed as logical axioms (Boudon 1974: 14–18). Whether expressed as axioms or in ordinary language, such models can be described as 'middle range' realism, a term coined by Ray Pawson (2000) to describe a realist specification of Merton's middle range theory. That is, they are 'models' (Pawson eschews this term) of mechanisms, hypothesized as a limited specification of social formations and interactions, that are capable of being empirically tested and if confirmed can be said to resemble that part of reality specified by the theory or model in its key features.

I do not believe we need worry too much about whether we refer to models of mechanisms, models, or mechanisms, the important thing is that they are representations of reality, and the more representative they are, the better. However a 'middle range' theory may be a much looser collection of inductive and deductive propositions than a theoretical model and one which will change in a relatively ad hoc way over time. A good example is counter-urbanization theory in population geography (Berry 1976), which arose from the serendipitous discovery that many rural areas in the United States had begun to experience a 'population turnaround': population movement from rural to urban areas of the kind that had dominated migration for more than a century was now supplanted by movement the opposite way, from urban to rural areas. The theory is very much of the middle range kind, but whilst retaining its central features, has undergone a number of modifications and iterations through research programmes over the years (see for example: Champion 1994; Fielding 1992; Mitchell 2004).

These research programmes have given rise to specific theoretical models, which could be defined (a little more formally) as a collection of basic sentences in a specified language, with deductive consequences that arise from those sentences. This, however, must then translate into variables, which themselves must be operationalizable into measurements. The model should also incorporate the nature of the relationships between the variables and what we might anticipate as the strength of that relationship, the job of the statistical model.

Methodological Models

As with theoretical models, the level of formality in a methodological model may vary. Indeed most researchers de facto move from theorizing to operationalization without too much consideration of variable-to-variable relationship. However, even informally, the way we think through the specification of variables, and their relationship to each other, constitutes a model. For example, if we wish to test a statistical hypothesis, stating the null hypothesis to be falsified, we must specify both the variables and the anticipated relationship. Indeed in the move from theory to measurement, the devil is in the detail. Much of this detail lies in the specification of the variable and its translation into measures that can adequately capture 'reality' and test the theoretical model. Some variables and especially those that relate to the physical world are relatively easily operationalized. Age, sex, postcode/zipcode come to mind, but also with some accuracy occupation, distance travelled to work, and housing characteristics can be measured and their specification in a methodological model can show likely relationships. Some kinds of models, particularly multilevel models (Goldstein 2010) transcend the methodological/statistical, because they require us to think at what 'level' relationships should be specified. Typically, these are used in education and may measure characteristics at an individual level and at a school level and propose the direction and strength of relationship between the levels.

But the operationalization of some kinds of characteristics and crucially attitudinal data is much more difficult, yet essential to the integrity of the theoretical model. Recently, I and colleagues, have given much thought to the operationalization of ethnicity (Williams and Husk 2012). Ethnicity is a nice example of where positivism and realism divide at the empirical level. In the UK (though mirrored in other jurisdictions) ethnicity is measured through a relatively simply specified variable that asks the respondent to select from around ten to twelve categories (sometimes subcategories are included) that reflect what are seen to be the main 'ethnic' groups in the country. These definitions have dubious historical origins rooted in the migratory concerns of the 1970s and although to some extent they can capture some key aggregate characteristics, they are a blunt instrument. For example, it can be fairly readily shown that African-Caribbean boys achieve less well educationally than members of other ethnic groups (as measured). There is an awareness of the bluntness of this kind of measurement and more fine-grained approaches have been adopted (Williams and Husk 2012). The problem is, however, seen as a technical one for many methodologists, but a realist approach begins from quite a different place. The theoretical model may propose a mechanism of ethnic stratification in say health, education, or employment, but (following Ray Pawson) such a mechanism will only fire in particular contexts. In order to differentiate these contexts we need to closely specify the ways in which the stratification can be measured, but also which ethnic groups will be measured.

Ethnicity is a slippery concept. There is plenty of evidence to show that people will say they are members of different ethnic groups at different times: not every one, not even most, but some (Platt et al. 2005). Some people with the same heritage background will assert their membership of different groups. The categories of ethnicity provided in a measurement instrument will best measure ethnicity if they reflect as accurately as possible the groups present according to the best consensus of what those groups are in any given location (Williams and Husk 2012). For example, in some locations Portugese or Polish might be provided and will be better measures of ethnic composition than they would be where there were significant numbers of Indian people. Again the latter may be too blunt a measurement and will require further refinement. Nevertheless, this is not a technical issue per se, but a theoretical one.

Nevertheless we need to remind ourselves that the methodological model needs to be of *sufficient* adequacy. There cannot be perfect measurement, but there can be good enough measurement. It is this I now address.

Statistical Models

A statistical model uses mathematical language to represent reality. A criticism of statistical models is that they are often elegant models of very little. Their specification is at such a level of abstraction that they do not capture reality, yet become reified as representing that reality. Often this is a fair criticism. For example, a model that proposes a statistical (indeed causal) relationship between an ethnic category called 'white' and some other variable(s) is indeed suspect, when 'white' is more a measure of the absence of ethnic identity, this is abstracted empiricism in its crudest form. But others and certainly Blalock, whilst acknowledging that statistical models are not reality, also argue that if operationalized carefully from our theories, they can be adequate for causal explanation and allow us to move from probabilistic causal explanation to mechanistic causal explanation.

Take, for example the logistic regression model, much loved amongst sociologists. It is based on assumptions of linearity, but allows the prediction of a discrete outcome, say migration (as a dependent variable), from a set of variables that may be dichotomous, discrete, or continuous (or a mix, though the dependent variable is usually dichotomous). The model allows us to seek the 'best fit' of the independent variables (the higher the G^2 the better the 'fit').

This first, or main, part of a logistic regression model shows the relative importance of the variables and a second part of the model shows how these variables are operating. A reference category of '1' is fixed and the other categories show the odds in relation to the reference category. Thus if another category is 2.0, then persons in that category have twice the likelihood of being in that category rather than the reference category; similarly if it is 0.5

then they have half the likelihood of being in this category than the reference category.

A historic example of migration. To illustrate how a statistical model may be used to develop a theoretical model I provide a further (simplified) migration example. Table 15.1 reports a logistic regression model that aims to provide a statistical explanation of migration from Cornwall, in the south-west of Great Britain, in a specific historic period of the 1980s. Table 15.2 shows the associated odds ratios.

Some background: firstly, that such an analysis was conducted at all depends on historic context motivating the research question: what were the characteristics of out-migrants from Cornwall in the 1980s? Cornwall, in the far south-west of Great Britain, had a history of migration going back to the mid nineteenth century. It was mostly associated with periods of economic difficulty in the traditional industries of mining and engineering and the demand for skilled labour elsewhere. This pattern of migration fitted the classical model of 'migratory elites' (Jackson 1986), that is those with particular social or economic capital are the ones most likely to migrate. In the mid 1980s Cornwall experienced a major and likely final collapse of its traditional industries. The theoretical model was derived from historic precedent, which had been an actualization of the migratory elite theory. Specifically it was hypothesized that those who had lost their jobs as a result of the economic collapse in mining, engineering, and associated industries would be those who would form the migratory pool, but mostly only those with skills in demand elsewhere would migrate.

The methodological model was predicated on some assumptions about the variables. Firstly that some variables directly operationalized an actual characteristic, for example age. Others, such as tenure, measured an actual state, but stood proxy for a set of circumstances associated with particular tenures. For example to live in owner occupation is associated with greater economic capacity than other tenures. However, the model was limited to what the Census measures (it does not measure income for example) and when applied in the statistical model, the necessity of statistical significance.

The model was crude, but powerful in ordering the important of the variables. A number of census variables were initially entered into the model, but only four were statistically significant: economic activity, tenure, age, and social class (Table 15.1). They were ordered by the reduction in scaled deviance achieved in the model (reduction in G^2), but although the variables were important, this does not tell us the way in which they were important. Table 15.2 provides the odds ratios for the categories in each variable, indicating that those who were unemployed in 1981 were two and a half times as likely to leave Cornwall as those who were employed. Students in 1981 were four times as likely to leave as those who were employed.

Those living in owner occupation were more than twice as likely to leave as those living in public housing. Those who were aged 17–25, in 1981, were three times as likely to migrate than those in older age groups. Those in manual

Table 15.1 Logistic Regression Main Effects Model of Variables Associated with Migration from Cornwall 1981–91 (1981 variables)

	G^2	df	change in G^2	Mean change in G^2
Null model	791.3	566		
Economic activity	700.3	562	−91.2	22.8
Tenure	644.9	560	−55.4	27.7
Age	615.5	557	−29.4	9.8
Social class	588.2	555	−27.3	13.7

Source: ONS Longitudinal Study, Williams 2000b.

Table 15.2 Odds Ratios of Variables Associated with Migration from Cornwall 1981–91 (1981 variables)

Economic activity	
Working	1
Unemployed	2.5
Student	4
Retired	Not significant
Other	Not significant
Tenure	
Owner occupied	1
Public housing	0.3
Private renting	Not significant
Age	
0–16	1
17–25	1.5
26–65	0.6
66+	0.6
Social class head of household	
Non-manual	1
Manual	0.6
Other	Not significant

Source: ONS Longitudinal Study, Williams 2000b.

classes were around half as likely to migrate as those in non-manual classes, but class was 'less important' than the other variables.

The statistical model mostly supported the theoretical model, but with some 'noise' in it. Firstly, that those living in owner occupation were more likely to migrate is probably explained by relatively low amounts of public housing in Cornwall and high owner occupation rates among those in skilled and semi-skilled manual classes. Moreover, students leaving Cornwall, though a different migratory stream, would have been much more likely to live in owner occupation (the tenure of their parents) prior to leaving. The social class odds were initially slightly puzzling, but further analysis indicated that they were much influenced by the out-migration of members of middle management, themselves earlier migrants to Cornwall ten years before.

I have deliberately used this rather crude model to illustrate its power to confirm simple macro-level tendencies. Statistical models do not accurately represent social reality, but they may nevertheless capture the key features of that reality, to allow us to modify and improve our theoretical models of social mechanisms. Does this represent a causal explanation? An *inference* of 'cause' is justified in a longitudinal model, because the data are representations of what actually happened to the same people over time. Each 'case' in the model was a person who migrated and the variables attached to them represent their characteristics prior to migration.

For a critical realist it would not constitute a causal explanation and indeed the association of variables, even in a longitudinal analysis do not really 'close in' on a cause, but they do provide evidence that supports the inference of a causal mechanism in the theoretical model, namely that those who migrated were the unemployed who had at least some resources, indicated by their tenure status and social class. A detective would not get a conviction on this quality of evidence, but it would be strong enough evidence to continue to support the line of inquiry. Simulations offer the complex modelling of artificial data (see Gilbert and Troitzsch 2005), but these are often somewhat removed from the quotidian concerns of the researcher called upon to find policy solutions or undertake evaluations (see for example Byrne 2011; Olsen 2004; Pawson 2004; Pawson and Tilly 1997). Indeed a further analysis (using a simple cross-tabulation) indicated that the destination jobs of the migrants were predominantly in managerial, skilled, or professional sectors (Williams and Harrison 1995).

Developing the Models

In the above example the initial theoretical models specified a middle range theory, that of migratory elites operating in a specific mechanism of late twentieth century post-industrial migration. Its context was that of Cornwall in the

1980s. The initial methodological model was specified through longitudinal Census data that hypothesized that individuals with certain characteristics would provide evidence for the operation of the proposed mechanism in the theoretical model. In turn the statistical model operationalized the variables in a logistic regression model. The results of this served to somewhat modify the theoretical model to incorporate managerial and student migration. Over the 1990s the mechanism proposed in the theoretical model was refined by further iterations into methodological and statistical models, but meanwhile the context changed. A theoretical model proposed in the late 2000s was very different (Husk 2011). Those with traditional skills had left and the new migratory elite are young people under twenty-six, whose parents moved to Cornwall between the 1970s and 1990s. The models are heuristics, partial representations of reality that help us to causally explain that reality—albeit imperfectly, because reality is dynamic and complex.

CONCLUSION

For many realists—at least critical realists, much of the foregoing is a heresy, indeed even a whole school of heresies. Whilst I have tried to remain faithful to the core principles of realism, that there is a social reality that operates independently of individuals' knowledge of it and can only ever be partially accessed through our methods, I have tried to suggest some broad pragmatic strategies for realist social research. I have concentrated on quantitative approaches, though I also believe such approaches remain as elements in a methodologically pluralist approach. Running throughout this chapter are two principles: the first is that the real character of the social world is that it is probabilistic. Here I am firmly among those, such as David Byrne, who suggest that at an abstract level there is an affinity between realism and complexity theory. My own foray (with Wendy Dyer) into developing a method that can truly bridge the demands of realism and the ontological probability inherent in the social world has been into the derivation of single case probabilities that would be compatible with the programme suggested by Byrne. But this approach, though immensely valuable in some contexts, is limited in many or most situations.

Thus, my second principle: that social researchers must use models. In practice I think realism implicitly does use models, at least at the theoretical and methodological level, if not the statistical one. Here, then, I am with Ray Pawson and his advocacy of 'middle range realism', though as I have noted, Pawson does not use the term models. I do, and the reason is to convey the important point that our theoretical or statistical representations of reality are not reality itself, nor could they ever be. Here I think I remain faithful to

Bhaskar's notion of the difference between the intransitive objects of nature and the transitive objects of science. The latter are our models.

As realists we should not conflate our epistemological position with either a methodological one or the methods of research. Certainly there is an argument (which I support) that the epistemological position should underpin our theorizing (and thus theoretical models) and it should also extend to developing the most 'realistic' methodological models possible—how we represent theories through measurement. But at this level and especially at the level of method, realism must use the available data and tools, both of which are often imperfect.

16

An Appraisal of the Contribution of Critical Realism to Qualitative and Quantitative Research Methodology

Is Dialectics the Way Forward?

Andrew Brown and John Michael Roberts

INTRODUCTION

The chapters of this book claim to demonstrate practical salience for critical realist philosophy. Qualitative, quantitative, and mixed method approaches are presented as being enhanced and developed through adoption of critical realism. As social scientists who are long standing, if sympathetic, critics of critical realism we have been asked in this chapter to offer a constructive critical eye over the claims made for critical realism in regard to practical application of critical realist philosophy. We will do this taking qualitative and quantitative methodology separately, as has become the norm (though, as will become clear we will go on to question this dichotomy) but by drawing on a core argument that is applicable to both.

Our argument will be that critical realism as presented in the chapters of this book and as it is most commonly found across the human and related sciences is most certainly of great value to local and specific social research but that it is also crucially lacking in respect of its treatment of the system as a whole, in particular the capitalist system and its historical development. The capitalist system is a dialectical whole and yet many critical realists lack dialectics. We believe this is rather strange, especially since the acknowledged founder of critical realism, Roy Bhaskar, goes to great lengths to incorporate dialectics in his later work (e.g. Bhaskar 1993). But by not following Bhaskar's direction many critical realists in our opinion tend to view social systems as straightforwardly 'open'. As a result they fail to help the social researcher uncover the systemic importance of local and specific events in the sense that 'open' local and specific events are not explored by them as being, in the words of Bhaskar (Bhaskar 1993: 167–70), 'diffractions' of relatively 'closed' systematic historical totalities. Our chapter will therefore take Bhaskar's later dialectical work seriously by analysing the power of dialectics in relation to critical realism. In particular, we argue that dialectics undermines the simple dichotomy between 'open' and 'closed' systems that critical realism espouses, as well as aiding the researcher in bridging the gap between the abstract and the concrete. In setting out our argument we thus draw on Bhaskar's dialectical critical realism but also make use of the wider literature on systematic and materialist dialectics.

The chapter will proceed as follows. In the next section we consider quantitative methods in relation to critical realism. The third section then considers qualitative methods in relation to critical realism. In the fourth section some problems of the critical realist method, in particular the open/closed-system dualism are introduced as a prelude to the fifth section, which tries to argue that dialectics can overcome such problems through proper methodological treatment of the social system as a totality. The sixth section concludes.

CRITICAL REALISM AND QUANTITATIVE METHODS

Within the literature and within several chapters of this book (most strongly in Williams's chapter) one can find arguments that there is a clear critical realist rationale for the application of quantitative methods within the social realm, alongside qualitative methods. Indeed, as a 'third way' between extreme positivism (associated with quantitative methods) and extreme interpretivism (associated with qualitative methods) critical realism might seem to be a clear candidate for underpinning mixed methods. However, the critical realist literature is in fact divided on the issue of quantitative methods. Critical realism is presented, by an important group of critical realists, via a critique of approaches that insist upon quantitative methods in social explanation. Below, we shall follow in particular the prominent arguments of Lawson (1997, 2003). We will see that Lawson draws on critical realist tenets to argue that the conditions required for quantitative methods to be applicable very rarely obtain in the social realm. In subsequent sections we will argue that attempts to justify quantitative methods on a critical realist rationale, such as that of Williams's chapter, characteristically do not explicitly meet the deep critical realist challenge to quantitative methods in social science made by Lawson. This gives rise, it will be argued, to an ongoing tension in the critical realist literature that is evident in this book.

Critical Realist Critique of Quantitative Methodology

Firstly, Lawson observes that, as used in social science, mathematics and statistics are centred on mathematical or statistical 'functions':

$$\text{A mathematical function ('deterministic'): } y = f(x) = bx^2$$

$$\text{A statistical function ('stochastic'): } y = f(x) = bx^2 + u$$

where
u is a 'random error term' that has a normal probability distribution, with mean zero;
x and y refer to social scientific variables, hence to 'events' or 'states of affairs'.

The next step of Lawson's argument is to translate the meaning of a function into English. Take the example of a function familiar in economics, the 'production function'. This function can be expressed as

$$y=f(x)$$

where
x is the quantity of labour employed by a particular firm (in hours);
y is the output produced by that firm in that time period.

In the case of the production function, to say that $x = 5$ is to stipulate the event that 5 hours of labour are undertaken. Likewise to say that $y = 2$ is to stipulate the event that 2 units of output have been produced. Given these variable values then the production function, translated into English, states, 'whenever 5 hours of labour are employed, 2 units of output are produced'. More generally, without any particular values being assigned, the production function states, 'whenever event x (employment of a definite quantity of labour), then event y (production of a unique corresponding amount of output)'. So, the production function is the statement of a strict event regularity, 'whenever event x then event y'.

The statistical version of the production function is exactly the same, except that a 'random error term' is added. This means that random deviations occur, which cancel out over repeated observations, so that the average deviation is zero. Translated into English we get an event regularity, 'whenever event x then event Y, on average', where Y is the average value of y. An event regularity is also assumed if the function is 'multivariate', that is, if there is more than one variable on the right-hand side of the function. For example, a 'long-run' production function includes both capital and labour and states, when translated into English, that 'whenever a certain amount, x, of labour is employed, and a certain amount, z, of capital is employed, then a certain amount, y, of output is produced'. Or simply, 'whenever event X [a given amount of capital and labour are employed] then event y [a given amount of output is produced]'. Whilst we have used the example of a production function, the same argument holds for all functions as used in social science, since these would simply involve changing the social events labelled by x and y. Hence Lawson concludes that the use of mathematics and statistics in social science implies the use of statements of social event regularities. This provides a very clear and strong link of quantitative methods to Humean empiricism and associated forms of positivism, (e.g. logical positivism) where causation is seen as nothing more than a constant conjunction of events.

The next step in Lawson's argument is to consider, given the critical realist social ontology, whether social event regularities are likely to occur. He finds the likelihood of the occurrence of social event regularities to be very low indeed. Firstly, consider the nature of social structures. In general, according to critical realism, a structure is comprised of internal relations by virtue of which an object possesses specific capabilities, powers, and tendencies to act in certain ways under particular conditions (Sayer 2000: 14; see also Danermark et al. 2002: 47; Porpora 1998: 344). These properties comprise the 'causal mechanism' of the object that enables it to act in certain ways under particular conditions. An example of a natural structure is H_2O by virtue of which water boils at 100 degrees, quenches a thirst, and so on. An example of a social structure would be the landlord-tenant relationship, by virtue of which landlord and tenant possess reciprocal enablements and constraints, for example, the tenant can use the accommodation but has to pay rent.

Natural structures such as water will display event regularities (describable by functions) only within the confines of an experiment, for example, water will regularly boil at exactly 100 degrees only in the purified conditions of the laboratory. In critical realist terms an experiment creates a 'closed system' where a closed system is defined as one that produces event regularities (conversely an 'open system' is one where event regularities do not occur). But one cannot in general perform experiments on social structures so social event regularities will not in general occur. Furthermore, social structures, unlike natural structures, are highly 'internally related', so that the occurrence of one structure, say of a capitalist firm, necessarily implies the occurrence of many others (commodities, money, labour, other firms, etc.). The isolation of one structure from all others is not even possible in principle, let alone in practice—they necessarily have to occur together, making the social world not merely open but 'quintessentially' open according to critical realism. Here, then, is a key reason why social event regularities will not occur. A second reason is the presence of human choice: humans could always have acted in a way other than they actually did, they are not automata so, again, social event regularities will not occur due to the very quintessence of the social world, comprised, according to critical realism, of social structures reproduced or transformed by the activities of individuals.

Lawson's conclusion regarding quantitative methodology is stark. The application within the social realm of standard quantitative techniques such as multiple regression and analysis of variance is without justification because they are closed-system techniques (they centrally involve functions and so statements of event regularities) and the social realm is, according to critical realism, quintessentially open not closed (event regularities do not occur). What do exist according to Lawson are what he terms 'demi-regularities' of events, these are 'rough-and-ready' patterns of events that can be captured with simple descriptive statistics. Therefore, for Lawson, the extent of the use of standard quantitative methods in social science is limited to the use of descriptive statistics to help get at 'demi-regularities' but that is it—there is no room for multiple regression or analysis of variance, or any other technique that centrally employs mathematical or statistical functions. We would observe that Lawson's argument seems impeccable in its grasp and use of critical realism, in particular the critical realist distinction between open and closed systems. Accordingly, in our view it lays strong claim to be considered *the* critical realist approach to quantitative methods (prior to the incorporation of dialectics). As we noted at the outset there are critical realists who argue otherwise. Before considering these arguments let us move on to consider a less contentious matter for critical realists: qualitative methods.

CRITICAL REALISM AND QUALITATIVE METHODS

There is no doubt that critical realism is in favour of qualitative methods. As a starting point in understanding the critical realist approach it is useful to consider the way qualitative methods are traditionally characterized and advocated. The distinctive approach of critical realism to qualitative methods, in terms of the focus on structures and mechanisms, and the corresponding shift in approach to data-gathering will then be outlined. We will go on to suggest that, though there is unanimity amongst critical realists on the importance of qualitative methods, the tension regarding quantitative methods discussed above also spills over into tensions regarding qualitative methods amongst critical realists, specifically regarding the issue of how to generalize from qualitative methods.

The Traditional Characterization and Advocacy of Qualitative Methods

Peter Winch (1958) famously argued that when we study any culture different to our own we must try to understand how the inhabitants evaluate their lives through their beliefs and meanings. Qualitative methods offer up a unique opportunity to conduct this sort of research because they seek to understand those human actions, meaningful beliefs, and symbolic practices that individuals and groups attach to their everyday lives, objects, and social relations. This is the so-called 'emic', or insider, view of society. As Guba and Lincoln (1994: 106) observe, this aspect of qualitative research enables the researcher to gain in-depth contextual information about a social setting that moves beyond the accumulation of set variable values associated with more quantitative approaches. Unlike quantitative methods, qualitative methods do not seek to strip down a context into subsets of discrete variables. A qualitative approach instead acknowledges that 'variables' rarely operate in subsets but instead congeal together in often contingent and unpredictable formations in real cultural and social contexts. In addition, qualitative methods allow research subjects to gain a 'voice' in the research process, especially those considered to be 'marginalized voices', and they also highlight the idea that historical events and historical processes are important elements for social investigation (Ragin 1994: 83–4).

Overall, then, qualitative methods can claim to be more attuned to the 'messiness' and 'openness' of real social life; the fact, for example, that everyday interaction is often fluid and escapes neat categorization, or that how we answer questions is often influenced by how the world is represented to us through (social) media, or that we all live and breathe through different social identities (gender, race, sexuality, class, and so on) which affect the way we experience and reflect about the world (Alvesson 2002: chapter 3). None of this is to say that qualitative researchers are all committed to some sort of anti-quantitative position. As Hughes and Sharrock (2007: 4) suggest, qualitative researchers not only often employ quantitative methods like questionnaires but also use quantitative expressions such as 'many' and 'several'. The point for qualitative researchers, however, is that quantitative methods are not the only research techniques available, and indeed they frequently push social scientists into making generalizations based on misleading and/or limited theoretical foundations.

Critical Realist Approach to Qualitative Methods

The critical realist approach emphasizing structures and mechanisms differs sharply from the anti-realism sometimes accompanying advocacy of qualitative methods. Like other qualitative approaches, critical realists pursue an *intensive* research strategy (Sayer 2000: 20; see also Collier 1994: 43) but this specifically means, for critical realism, exploring the internal structure of objects and their mechanisms before they analyse how one object (variable A) affects another object (variable B). Generative mechanisms are crucial to critical realists because they are the causal powers of an object that we cannot directly observe, yet give rise to observable events. These then involve rational models to be constructed about their intrinsic nature and how they might operate under enabling conditions (Harré and Secord 1972: 67–8).

The critical realist approach changes our orientation to the practice of qualitative empirical data-gathering. Flexibility in the process of gathering data is the preferred option for realists. As Pawson (1996) observes, when a researcher enters a research context s/he will at this point have a limited understanding of how particular mechanisms affect the context in question. There is then little point in entering a context with a one-policy-fits-all approach to research methods. Besides, to gain adequate information about mechanisms it is also critical that knowledge possessed by respondents is also taken seriously and not brushed aside as being 'inadequate' to the proscribed goals of a research project. Indeed, Pawson states that a researcher will have to ensure that respondents achieve some insight into the conceptual goals of a research project. The aim here is to enable the respondent to become more fully aware of potential mechanisms affecting the context being discussed (see also Pawson and Tilly 1997). Respondents are therefore encouraged to reflect on how they 'reason' about a particular context and what resources they feel enable or constrain them to act in particular ways in the context. 'The subject's task is to agree, disagree, and to categorize themselves in relation to the attitudinal patterns as constructed in such questions but also to refine their conceptual basis. It is at this point that mutual knowledge is really achieved' (Pawson 1996: 306). This approach to interviews is thus attuned to the *nature* of the interviewer and interviewee relationship. And so one further advantage of proceeding in this way is that one becomes aware of the *kind* of relationship being established, which enables the interviewer to minimize any type of exploitative bond with a respondent (Maxwell 2012: 101).

A standard criticism of qualitative research is that it offers no sound basis for generalization. It is in countering such a criticism that the critical realist approach really comes into its own. The key claim is that the critical realist notion of 'generative mechanisms' offers an approach to generalization from qualitative case studies. Edwards (2005) gives the example of the critical realist approach to case studies on teamwork, where teamwork can be understood in terms of the ontology of generative mechanisms. On such a critical realism-inspired understanding then each individual case study examines potentially the same mechanism (or mechanisms) in a different context and so the case studies can be brought together—synthesized—and hence generalized in terms of their findings regarding the nature of the generative mechanism and its operation in different contexts. In particular Edwards argues that the cumulative lesson of the numerous case studies on teamwork is to show how context really matters in determining whether teamwork mechanisms achieve their goals. Pawson's (e.g. 2002c) pioneering approach to realist synthesis and realist evaluation could be seen as having similar aspirations in looking to synthesize individual studies (quantitative as well as qualitative) through the notions of mechanism, context, and outcome.

Within this book we see various sophisticated developments of the basic insights of critical realism and of Pawson regarding generalizing from case studies (e.g. chapters by Bach and Kessler, Greenhalgh, and Saka-Helmhout). However, it must be said that the jury is still very much out on realist approaches to generalization. For example, Edwards (2005) feels there are too few examples of cumulative conclusions being drawn by critical realists from multiple case studies. Bach and Kessler's chapter noticeably draws from examples that do not profess affiliation to critical realism clearly unable to find sufficient material from avowedly critical realist sources. Greenhalgh can find no examples of actual realist syntheses regarding the link between human resource management practices and performance. Delving a little deeper we find Pawson and Manzano-Santaella (2012) arguing that, whilst over 120 articles *claim* to use Pawson's realist approach to evaluation or to synthesis, mistakes (from the point of view of realism) are typically made in many of these studies. Indeed the article is devoted to bringing out the various types of problem found across the literature. There remain very few examples that are properly illustrative of the approach to synthesis and to evaluation that Pawson recommends.

The chapters of this book also reveal what we would suggest are characteristic limits and limitations to critical realist approaches to generalization from qualitative case-study research via the notion of generative mechanisms. Pawson is quite clear that his approach is limited to 'middle range' theory, it simply does not penetrate to the theory of the system as a whole. Bach and Kessler and Saka-Helmhout focus on sound case-study design and limit themselves to generalizing about particular 'mechanisms' conceived of as spanning different levels. What is lacking is any sense of directing and integrating case-study research into an ongoing investigation of the system as a whole—it really does seem that mid-range theory is as far as case study goes for critical realism. Where system-wide concepts are concerned these tend to enter in the background as presumably informing the initial conceptions of the objects of study (e.g. the definition of the firm) and the tentative initial hypotheses that initiate case-study work. There is no sustained focus on the way in which the system as a whole brings together mechanisms. But surely the system as a whole cannot be outside the scope of case study because each study is examining a part of the system. We need help in comprehending the part in the whole system (and *vice versa*)—piecemeal mechanism by mechanisms theory is not enough. Marx, for example, relied on detailed description from Engels of the Manchester Mill that was part of the Engels family business, and Marx of course incorporates copious case detail into *Capital*. We would suggest, then, that a reason for the lack of good examples of critical realist generalization from case study might be that critical realism rather neglects the system as a whole. Let us consider problems with critical realist method more closely.

PROBLEMS WITH CRITICAL
REALIST METHOD

Reconsideration of Quantitative Methodology

The lack of successful examples of generalization from the above approaches might lead one to reconsider the use of quantitative methodology within critical realism. After all quantitative methodology is traditionally associated with the ability to generalize. One common response to anti-quantitative arguments within critical realism is to argue that multiple regression analysis (i.e. using statistical inference based upon 'multivariate' functions as discussed above) does not posit event regularities, *contra* Lawson and other critical realist critics of quantitative methodology. Or at least, multiple regression does not posit 'global' event regularities. All it posits is local and specific event regularities that are by no means held to be fixed for all time (e.g. Hoover 1997). An interesting drawback, from our point of view, is immediately apparent: this response takes away the ability of quantitative methods such as multiple regression to generalize! We will see below that Lawson also points out further drawbacks with this response. Another common response (e.g. see Downward 2003) is that the critical realist notion of social structure in fact implies some stability of social practices, norms, rules, or habits. Thus the reproduction of social structure (albeit there is always the possibility of transformation also) through agential activity would seem to imply a degree of regularity in social events, a regularity which would then legitimate the search for social event regularities undertaken by, say, multiple regression analysis. More generally, are not the 'demi-regs' that Lawson himself stresses, enough to legitimate multiple regression analysis?

Lawson (2003) notes these common responses and ripostes. Firstly, that the regularities the above arguments refer to are rarely if ever 'strict' so there is still no justification for using a language (of maths and statistics) which deals only in strict regularities. Secondly, that the regularities referred to above are rarely, if ever, *causal*. This is an important clarification of the overall critical realist argument (at least as interpreted by Lawson). By causal regularities Lawson means regularities of the form 'whenever event x then event y' where x causes y. For example in the case of the production function it is the labouring activity (x) that causes the output (y). Lawson does allow that 'concomitant' regularities which are 'quite' strict occur. These are regularities such as 'whenever the price goes up in this shop it goes up in that shop' or 'whenever people go to work this month they go to work next month'. Here the events are not causally related but rather are both caused by a third factor, for example, input cost rises in the first case and the common need to earn money in the second. For Lawson such regularities are trivial so they do not justify the use of multiple regression analysis. What is interesting to social science, according to Lawson, is when such a regularity unexpectedly breaks down, but this is a manifest breakdown not one that requires multiple regression to unearth.

There have been many other attempts to counter Lawson's arguments against standard quantitative methods in terms of the illicit closure assumption. For example, Olsen and Morgan (2005) suggest that 'mathematical' closure does not imply ontological closure so claim that the mathematical closure of, in their example, logistic regression is justified. But this common argument clearly fails to address Lawson's point. To see this it is first worth dwelling a little bit upon the closure conditions that logistic regression and all types of regression actually entail. One such condition, a crucial one, is the assumption of 'linearity'. This is the assumption that each independent variable has an effect on the dependent variable that is unaffected by the other independent variables. For example, in a logistic regression we use data to estimate 'coefficients' where each estimated coefficient is interpreted as the effect of one particular variable on the dependent variable, controlling for all other variables (logistic regression does this in terms of probabilities in a way which need not detain us here—see Williams's chapter in this book). Now, what are we to make of the claim that this is just a 'mathematical' closure condition but does not imply an 'ontological' closure condition? Well, if ontological non-linearity held this would mean that, in reality, the effect of each independent variable on the dependent variable *is* influenced by all other independent variables. It would no longer make any sense to 'control' for other independent variables so logistic regression would be a senseless exercise. The inescapable conclusion is that the applicability of techniques entailing mathematical closure does imply ontological closure *contra* Olsen and Morgan.

Similarly, Chick and Dow (2003) go to great lengths to define open and closed systems but ultimately fail to deal directly with Lawson's key argument that functions imply event regularities and that event regularities (closures) do not occur in the social world. Close examination of Williams's chapter in this book appears to us to reveal exactly the same problem. Williams initially stresses that the social world is a non-linear one and that logistic regression presupposes ontological linearity. So far so good. But Williams proceeds to endorse an example of the use of logistic regression (assuming linearity) in social analysis (where he agrees that linearity does not obtain)! The claim seems to be that it (logistic regression) 'works'—but why? Where has Lawson's reasoning (specifically in this case the argument that the closure condition of linearity does not obtain so logistic regression cannot be used) gone wrong? Williams does not say. In sum, there is an unresolved debate in which Lawson's key argument against quantitative methods such as multiple regression, resting on the point that the social world is quintessentially open, has not been clearly refuted despite many attempts to do just that.

Reconsideration of the Open/Closed System Distinction

We can begin to confront Lawson's argument head-on by reconsidering the critical realist open/closed system distinction. Critical realism stresses that the social word is highly internally related but still talks in terms of 'individuating' social structures and mechanisms without explaining how it is possible to individuate a particular social structure from an internally related totality (Brown 2012). The overall logic of the critical realist approach still rests on the open/closed system distinction, even as it argues that the social world is never closed but inherently open. There is, then, the belief that mechanisms can be isolated in the relatively closed and abstract confines of a distinct structure while its tendencies can be explored in the relatively open and concrete world of everyday life (Sayer 2000: 127). Bhaskar endorses this view to the extent that he poses a separation between structures (causal powers, and so on) and historical principles, 'i.e. those which only hold or apply for a certain period of the structure's duration' (Bhaskar 2009: 213). History, in this respect, refers to actual events, including the causal power of individuals, which affect structures in different overlapping ways. Archer also captures something of this dualism when she says that the ontological properties of structures pre-exist the ontological properties of human actions, the latter of which serve to reproduce the very same structures. Of course, social structures cannot be known without knowing something also about human actions, but these are *past* human actions of long gone generations which, when combined with one another, have helped to shape a particular structure in the present (Archer 1995: 148).

In these critical realist accounts a dualism is evident between the 'closed' world of abstract structures and mechanisms and the more open and concrete world of historical events where the empirical effects of structures interact with people, and where people interact with one another through their actions. Yet this implies that 'closed systems' and 'open systems' exist independently of one another—the former are associated with structures, the latter are associated with a host of concrete and contingent factors such as historical processes and human actions. 'On this basis', claims Carchedi (1983: 76), 'it is difficult to imagine how a satisfactory way…can be found of inquiring into what governs the functioning of a mechanism in an open world'. Closed and open systems are parallel and yet ultimately separate systems. As a result it is not at all clear how both can be satisfactorily brought together if an ontological chasm exists between both. Let's develop this point and see how dialectics can help.

A DIALECTICAL WAY FORWARD

One way forward to overcome some of these problems is suggested by Bhaskar himself. In his later dialectical work Bhaskar argues that structures are historical not because they enter the flow of linear, concrete history, but because their very essence reflects and refracts (or 'diffracts') historical systems, or 'totalities'. According to Bhaskar a totality refers to systems which are built on internally related elements. 'A may be said to be internally related to B if it is a necessary condition for the existence (weak form) or essence (strong form) of B, whether or not the converse is the case' (Bhaskar 1994: 75). Totalities thus comprise dialectical connections which are defined by Bhaskar as 'connections between entities or aspects of a totality such that they are in principle *distinct* but *inseparable*, in the sense that they are synchronically or conjuncturally internally related' (Bhaskar 1993: 58, original emphasis).

But Bhaskar also argues that many totalities are contradictory. At least one element of a dialectical contradiction is '*opposed*, in the sense that (at least) one of their aspects negates (at least) one of the other's, or their common ground or the whole, and perhaps vice versa, so that they are *tendentially mutually exclusive*, and potentially or actually tendentially transformative' (Bhaskar 1993: 58, original emphasis). Moreover, the form that dialectical contradictions assume in a specific totality is determined through 'an original *generative separatism*, split, or alienation of the immediate producers from the means and materials of their production' (Bhaskar 1993: 70). The most obvious generative separatism which determines the contradictory totality of capitalism is that between labour and the capital. But notice also that under this definition a totality is not located at a trans-historical level of abstraction. It is rather located firmly in a historical totality, with capitalism being an example here.

This might sound as if it is a rather trivial point. However, it is far from trivial and in fact fundamentally alters how we think about structures and their relationship to history in a number of ways. It suggests for example that history does not inhere in a different 'system' to that of structures but does in fact exist in the same system. That is to say, if we abstract an object in order to understand its internal structure we must do so in the confines of a historical system, or historical 'totality', in order to comprehend how the object in question internalizes or 'diffracts' in its own way the determinations of the system in question. Marx, in his theory of historical materialism, puts the point more plainly when he discusses how we might begin to understand consciousness and ideas, which in this instance he terms as 'spiritual production':

> In order to understand the connection between spiritual production and material production it is above all necessary to grasp the latter itself not as a general category but in *definite historical* form... If material production itself is not conceived in its *specific historical* form, it is impossible to understand what is specific in the spiritual production corresponding to it and the reciprocal influence of one on the another. (Marx 1969: 285, original emphasis)

For Marx, therefore, while there are trans-historical attributes of human behaviour (we need to eat, think, drink, find shelter, and so on), and while there are general human laws that exist across societies, to really understand their specificity these different objects have to be abstracted and examined as they develop in specific modes of production. It is for this reason that Marx announces in *Capital*, volume 1, that there are no general laws as such, but 'on the contrary... every historical period possesses its own laws' (Marx 1988: 100–1).

From this dialectical position social research should therefore aim to isolate the *determinant contradictory* relations—or 'generative separatism'—which gives a totality (or mode of production) its particular identity. Therefore, one will be isolating *historical structural relations* that are determinant in a mode of production. In this respect, one utilizes a historical approach insofar that one is interested in the *historical specificity* of structural relations. This is to isolate the inner and most abstract and determinant contradictory logic and connections of a particular totality. From here it is then possible to trace how these initial determinant contradictions contain within themselves further contradictions that can be unfolded through more concrete categories. The aim in doing this is to discover the social constitution of a self-expanding system.

These ideas are foreign to critical realism (prior to the addition of dialectics) and can be difficult to understand out of context so let us explain by way of examples. Taking the example of Marx, his theory in *Capital* attempts to abstract and isolate the most basic contradictions of the commodity-form in capitalism so that he can then trace how these inner and necessary contradictions develop into more complex systematic economic forms. At every stage in Marx's presentation, 'each category is the necessary condition for the category that follows and all the categories are necessary in order for the capitalistic commodity form to subsume economic life' (Albritton 2008: 237; see also Dean et al. 2006: chapter 3). Causality, or causal powers, at this historical level of abstraction therefore refers to the potential of contradictions to unfold and develop into more concrete contradictory forms. These are the essential and determinant structural contradictions of a systematic totality. Examples regarding qualitative and quantitative analysis can further help explain and develop these ideas and address the problems of critical realism identified above.

Qualitative Example of the Use of Dialectics
for Social Research

Dialectics offers us a way to respond to various criticisms of realist and materialist approaches to social research. For example, both realist and materialist approaches agree that qualitative research should aim to construct explanatory frameworks about the relationships evident in particular contexts, but which can also critically evaluate any misleading beliefs that people hold about the context at hand. For critics, however, this research strategy illicitly imposes values (in our case, our Marxist dialectical framework) on to the 'facts' obtained about a unique research context. According to critics, real concrete situations are far too complex to be reduced to single values, or a fixed ranking of values, in this way. As Hammersley (2009b) observes, there will nearly always be reasonable disagreement amongst social scientists about which values fit best in the context being investigated. Given this, critics suggest, a better way forward is to insist that social science should merely report about the factual knowledge it discovers through qualitative methods and then open it up to debate in the academic community as to its legitimacy (Hammersley 1995: 151). This 'liberal model' of research is thus indebted to the belief in 'the existence of conflicting views, and our inability to resolve many of these conflicts' (Hammersley 1995: 151).

From a dialectical perspective, however, this liberal model of research practice is far too idealistic. After all, Marxist dialectics teaches us that even at an abstract level research is never conducted in some sort of impartial and unbiased world. Research operates instead in the ideological confines of specific historical systems—what Bhaskar terms as totalities. Once this is accepted then the debate about 'factual knowledge' can be batted back to those who hold onto the 'liberal model'. If we do indeed conduct research in ideological historical systems, or totalities, then can the liberal model firstly define more precisely what portion of research knowledge is not tainted in some way or another by the ideological and political agendas associated with a specific totality, and, secondly, can they then tell us where the holy grail of 'factual knowledge' actually resides?

Of course, once we begin to explore the whereabouts of this elusive 'factual knowledge' it soon becomes apparent that it does not exist; at least not on planet earth. In reality qualitative research, or any type of research for that matter, is rarely, if ever, carried out in the sort of 'neutral' vacuum required by the liberal model. It is more accurate to say that qualitative research is always conducted in real cultural, historical, and social contexts that inevitably impact on our ideas about our research (Doyal and Harris 1986). Correspondingly, social scientists undertake research not in a political vacuum but in a world dominated by social and political agendas.

A simple example can illustrate this point. Since 1986 academic researchers and lecturers in the UK have had to endure countless research assessment exercises that endeavour to measure their output. Far from being a 'neutral' development these practices are in fact highly political. Successive research assessment exercises have established a form of market competition between academics and universities for a limited amount of research funds. This in turn has helped to legitimize the withdrawal of research funding from a number of departments who then instead have to rely on private funders. Viewing higher education as another market commodity thus helps to normalize a post-Thatcherite neo-liberal policy agenda at the level of academic practice (Elton 2000; Lynch 2006; Willmott 2003). Under these circumstances research becomes politicized irrespective of our actual research practice (Byrne 2011: 36).

Unless we adopt a dialectical reflexive attitude we may miss these political and social mediations of our own research practice and simply end up engaged in the sort of 'neutral' and 'rational' debate envisaged by Hammersley. While this observation is also made by other critical realists, we nevertheless feel that a dialectical perspective of the sort developed by Bhaskar in his later work, and one that is also evident in Marxism, provides a firmer foundation for a critical approach to issues of value neutrality in research. To give one brief illustration in terms of qualitative research: critical realist ethnographers are skilled at isolating the underlying causal properties of a particular context under investigation (see Porter 1993). However, they are often less adept at relating these causal mechanisms to wider dialectical totalities. Many empirical contexts, for instance, are governed in some way or another by distinctive rules and regulations which are also underpinned by legal mechanisms attached to the political apparatus of the state. But once this much is accepted then it makes sense to explore the ethnographic properties of an empirical context relative to the mediations of a historical system (or, historical totality) at different levels of abstraction. To what extent, for example, is an empirical context governed by a specific legal discourse? How does this legal discourse affect the ethnographic practices under investigation? How does it also affect our own ethnographic research practices when we enter the context in question? For instance, how do these abstract powers affect access to relevant funds to carry out research in the first place? And to what extent is this particular legal discourse an internally regulated moment of the more abstract causal structure of the capitalist legal form and/or the capitalist state? (Roberts 2001; Roberts and Sanders 2005). By asking these sorts of questions we can start to connect our own research practice to the complex mediations, ideologies, and power relations evident in historical totalities.

Quantitative Methods and the Self-reproduction of the Capitalist System

The dialectical approach to the capitalistic totality reveals a range of historically specific system-wide activities that necessarily coexist—commodity production, monetary purchase, working for a wage, making profit, charging interest, paying rent, and so on. Some of these are absolutely necessary to the persistence of the system, for example the system cannot exist without widespread commodity production, monetary exchange, wage-labouring and profit-making. Now it is true that from a local and specific perspective then these are not strict, causal regularities (as Lawson stresses). But from the system-wide perspective of dialectics they *are* strict regularities. Let us explain (see also Brown 2007).

Consider the following collective event regularity: 'whenever the events necessary to capitalism occur during one year in the UK, they occur during the next'. These are the collective events of widespread commodity and monetary exchange, widespread profit-making, widespread wage-labouring and so forth, all absolutely and strictly necessary to the capitalist system. To put this collective event regularity more formally, let the group of collective events, necessary to capitalism, that occur in the UK, at any given year, t, be denoted by C_t. Then the event regularity 'whenever the events necessary to capitalism occur during one year in the UK, they occur during the next' is simply 'whenever C_t then C_{t+1}'. This event regularity has been absolutely strict for the entire duration of developed capitalism in the UK. The regularity is a statement of actual fact, rather than a theory or prediction for the future. It is unlikely that capitalism will last for all eternity. More pertinently, it is a tenet of critical realism, as of other projects supportive of human emancipation, that choice is real and conscious change of social structures such as capitalism is therefore possible. This is a major reason why critical realism stresses that the social world is inherently 'open'. The fact, however, remains that the event regularity, 'whenever C_t then C_{t+1}', has been absolutely strict thus far.

Recall that, on Lawson's analysis, there is no causal connection between consecutive events of the form 'whatever happens today happens tomorrow'. Rather, a third causal factor is responsible for both. For the collective event regularity here under consideration, however, there is no third causal factor. In the absence of some outside factor, the system-wide activities necessary to capitalism have to be considered the cause of their own reproduction. In this light, collective event C_t is a 'trigger' and collective event C_{t+1} an 'actualization' of the *self*-reproductive power of the capitalist system. The triggering event (C_t) causes the 'actualization' of the power of self-reproduction, that is, it causes the persistence of the capitalist system through to the next time period and hence event C_{t+1}. In turn this actualization itself is a 'trigger' for the self-reproductive powers of capitalism, entailing persistence through to the subsequent time period (t+2), and so on. Thus, *contra* critical realism, the ongoing activities that are necessary to capitalism form a causal, as well as strictly regular, sequence through time because they are causal constituents of the self-reproduction of the capitalist system. From a collective system-wide point of view, then, as opposed to a local and specific point of view, strict and causal event regularities occur for the duration of capitalism and the system is, from this perspective, closed.

Here, then, we can see a new rationale for quantitative methods. The collective event regularities of capitalism, highlighted by a dialectical and systematic approach, imply, for example, an abstract aspect of commonality across capitalistic workplaces. There must be a predominance of commodity exchange, monetary transactions, hire or purchase of factors of production, profit-making, investment, and so on and, as labour process theory highlights, the employment relation must be predominantly characterized by a balance of conflict and consent. This persistence of abstract commonality across the system gives a role to econometrics on nationally representative data sets. Consider firstly the possibility of common co-variation through time, underpinned by common features of capitalist workplaces. An example here would be the impact of the economic cycle on general tightness of labour markets that may affect the general balance of conflict and consent across workplaces, in turn inducing common observable changes. Local contingencies of course will mean no strict regularity occurs at any given workplace—there will be myriad contingent local variations in labour market conditions, work relations, and so on, but the impact of local factors that are contingently related to the system will cancel out when considering all workplaces across the system (otherwise they would not be contingently related to the system). Thus the dialectical focus upon a single self-reproducing and self-developing system supports a socially specific version of the 'law of large numbers'.

One strand of our research has, for example, used large-scale data sets (e.g. WERS 1998–2004) to econometrically explore co-variation of tightness of labour market, perceptions of job security, the climate of employment relations, managerial responsiveness and job satisfaction over the period (Brown et al. 2008). The common aspects of workplaces also define enduring classes and groups which imply cross-sectional co-variation. For example, there are enduring differences between working and middle classes as regards work norms and expectations. These may lead to observable patterns which can be econometrically explored on large nationally representative data sets. Thus another strand of our research observes and explores a persistent U-shape of reported job satisfaction in earnings using ordered probit estimation (e.g. Brown et al. 2007). Dialectics provides the rationale for these quantitative approaches to system-wide theory that is missing from critical realism. To be precise, and to recapitulate the main point, dialectics reveals that, at the system-wide level of study of capitalism, there are strict, causal event regularities leading to interesting system-wide patterns that quantitative approaches can legitimately explore on nationally representative (system-wide) data. It thereby tackles head-on Lawson's argument against quantitative methods in social research because the crux of Lawson's argument is a denial of the existence of strict, causal event regularities in the social world.

CONCLUSION

This chapter has been concerned to show that critical realism represents important theoretical advances in qualitative and quantitative methods. At the same time the chapter has attempted to show that critical realism gains considerable explanatory power when its main methodological claims are wedded with a dialectical approach. Indeed, this is a move that Bhaskar also endorses in his later dialectical writings. Unfortunately, for whatever reasons, the majority of critical realists have not sought to develop this dialectical perspective to any great degree. However, there are signs in the critical realist community that this might be changing. Alan Norrie's recent book, *Dialectic and Difference* (2010), seeks to explain Bhaskar's dialectical work in relation to the critical realist project and then applies it to rethink some contemporary strands in social theory.

We welcome this move in critical realism and hope to see even more work in and around dialectics by critical realists in the future. In particular, and as our chapter touches upon, we would especially like to see critical realists use Bhaskar's insights as an opportunity to make stronger links with Marxism. Certainly, this project was one that was pursued with some enthusiasm by many critical realists in the 1970s. Yet by the 1980s and 1990s it had dropped out of favour, with many critical realists preferring instead to develop the more broad-based concepts of critical realism such as 'structure' and 'agency' in order to enhance the general and rather transcendental explanatory framework of critical realism. While this development has, of course, made critical realism attractive to many more social researchers, we feel nevertheless that critical realism lost some of its explanatory power along the way. Bhaskar seems to have recognized this too, which is probably why he went back to his Marxist roots in order to 'dialecticize' critical realism. But we would want to push this dialectical project even further towards Marxism simply because we feel that Marxism still retains the most important explanatory insights into how historical systems operate, and how internal and necessary contradictions serve to disrupt and halt the emancipatory potential inherent in such systems.

17

Concluding Comments

Paul K. Edwards, Steve Vincent, and
Joe O'Mahoney

This volume has endeavoured to demonstrate the value of critical realism in applied social research. The value of this approach is illustrated by the fact that many discussions of CR still tend to treat it as no more than a broad philosophy or perspective rather than also having a distinct empirical edge. An exchange in the *British Journal of Management* (Willmott 2012; Hodgkinson and Starkey 2012) is one example of this tendency. Given the rarity of detailed empirical applications, it cannot be expected that a single volume will have all the answers. We can, however, list aspects where, we claim, progress has been made, in the senses of at least illustrating that CR can drive empirical agendas and of helping to generate a better class of question to which answers can now be sought. We first indicate these aspects, before addressing some challenges to the CR project.

First, the volume has provided a series of specific examples of projects that have been informed by CR. As might be expected given the limited explicit guidance to date on using CR in practice, some of these projects were not explicitly designed using CR principles, but some were so designed, for example those on action research (chapter 11) and using mixed methods (chapter 13). And even those that were not explicitly CR-based clearly drew their principles from CR-like thinking. This is an advance on a previous collection, which included as examples of CR studies that might be seen as consistent with CR but which claimed no specific affinity with it (Ackroyd and Fleetwood 2000b). Indeed, chapter 2 concludes that 'there are valuable research procedures for the realist-inclined researcher to use'. It reaches this conclusion by identifying distinctive logics of discovery, classifying types of research design, and giving specific examples of research informed, albeit to different degrees and with differing levels of explicit commitment to CR, by realist principles.

Second, the chapters have grappled with the challenging question of how CR makes a difference. That is, a CR researcher might well deploy a technique such as interviewing, but just what about the practice is any different from that of a researcher from a different ontological or epistemological position? Part of the answer is obvious: a CR researcher will not take the view that all that an interview creates is the interview itself, in other words, that there are no facts or meanings outside the specific discourse. But, further, as chapters 3 and 6 showed, the CR researcher will, for example, use the interview to ask interviewees for their own causal accounts of the situation in which they find themselves. Interviewees may be challenged about their accounts so that their views of the structures in which they operate are brought to the surface. We would not draw hard boundaries here. That is, you do not have to sign up to CR to be willing to make a move of this kind. We recall the wise and profound approach of the very pragmatically oriented scholar, Keith Sisson. He often advised someone seeking the causes or effects of some process to begin by asking what participants themselves thought. This advice is useful in terms of specific technique. It also has implications for wider explanatory objectives. Suppose that we are interested in the causal powers of an equal opportunities policy. Asking relevant actors what it was designed to do and what unintended effects it might be having is one way to begin to address its causal powers.

As Rees and Gatenby point out in chapter 7, approaches informed by ideas of this kind have a long history. The ethnographies of the early anthropologists were sensitive to the material and the structural, and a later phenomenological turn weakened this emphasis. We would make a parallel point in relation to historical inquiry. As Mutch shows in chapter 12, a CR-informed approach is more likely to ask causal questions, and to seek the processes that produce causes, than are other approaches. In such fields, CR to some degree entails re-stating or re-discovering what researchers naturally did. But CR also offers some distinct ways to make analysis rigorous.

The discussions of identity, discourse analysis, and grounded theory (chapters 3–5) develop these points in particularly important ways, for these areas of study are often seen as stemming from a constructionist epistemology. Yet, as the chapters show, CR can deploy these methods. This is, moreover, not just a matter of, say, analysing discourse within a project whose main CR components lie elsewhere. It also means that the method itself can be opened up to CR principles. Sims-Schouten and Riley thus argue that non-discourse social structures provide the 'conditions of possibility' for social actors to generate different forms of discourse. These conditions can be addressed in three ways: background research on the relevant structural conditions and the broad kinds of discourse that they encourage; the production of discourse, together with attention to the ways in which conditions are rendered in talk; and analysis. In relation to identity, Marks and O'Mahoney argue that a CR researcher will focus more than others on structural factors that shape identity, will be more likely to use multiple levels of analysis, and will tend to 'triangulate' different sources of information (in the very specific sense discussed below). As for grounded theory, the approach is in some ways highly consistent with CR, for it aims to generate theory and explanation (as opposed to pure constructionism) in ways that are context-sensitive (as opposed to positivism). Yet it also, as Kempster and Parry explain, tends to eschew theory in the process of data collection, for fear of introducing bias. Yet how can bias ever be prevented? And is it not preferable to bring issues of structural conditions and causality directly into the research process, to generate what these authors call a retroductive approach?

Similar arguments arise around the case-study method (chapters 8–10). Some of the themes stressed in this volume are not peculiar to CR. Thus a stress on selecting cases to meet theoretical objectives, together with designing a comparative case study in light of the benefits of selecting on the basis of similarity or difference (chapter 10), is consistent with several analytical positions. But, we would argue, CR helps researchers in two key respects. First, it aids the making of the relevant choices in an explicit manner. Second, it alerts the researcher to the limits of any selection. The social world is necessarily open, and possible causal influences can never be wholly eliminated. Consider for example a design based on selecting to similarity, the purpose being to find two or more cases that are similar in key respects, so that differences can be attributed to other causal factors of theoretical interest. But two conditions will also be present. First, the factors that are controlled may not in fact be the 'same'. If we 'control' for gender by comparing two female-only organizations, it can still be true that gender exerts causal influences in one and not the other. This is because gender has a causal power that may be realized only when other factors are present. Second, other factors that are not controlled may also have an effect. CR does not resolve these challenges, but it helps to sensitize the researcher to them so that she will not conclude that, in this example, gender had no causal power in the contexts in question but, rather, consider how it might have effects in certain circumstances. This can be done by looking in detail within a specific situation or by devising further studies that capture variation in the influence of interest.

The discussion of 'realist synthesis' (chapter 14) makes a parallel point. Such an approach to policy evaluation is, as the chapter explains in detail, very different from the dominant method based on randomized control trials and meta-analyses of separate trials. It is also, the chapter argues, superior because the dominant method cannot deal with the fact that policy interventions often shift in their purpose and meaning. The chapter reaches the profound conclusion that 'the ability of [an] intervention to support the process of behaviour change should be the focus of the synthesis, rather than the specifics of the intervention itself'. In other words, for CR we do not take an intervention and ask about its effects in the abstract but, rather, consider the causal powers of an intervention in a specific context, which includes asking how the intervention came to be adopted and what sense participants themselves made of it.

There is a further simple but often neglected point here, identified by Ichniowski and Shaw (2009) in their assessment of field experiments in economics. Meta-analyses of 'average' effects take as their basis the median or modal organization. But organizations likely to utilize such experiments are not a random subset of all organizations, but are highly self-selected and almost by definition atypical. Effect sizes as measured from such experiments or from other kinds of organizational intervention may be both 'larger' and 'smaller' than conventional studies suggest: larger, because where they are adopted with vigour they are likely to be highly effective, but smaller because other organizations are so different that the effects do not carry over to them. We know only that an experiment has effects in a given context. This is not to argue against interventions of this kind, but to stress that the experiment and the context are closely connected and that assessments of interventions need to adopt a broader view than that of randomized trials and meta-analyses.

A feature of CR that cuts across individual methods is that a CR project is likely to embrace several techniques. The use of mixed methods is addressed directly by Hurrell, but other chapters also underline a range of methods. Kessler and Bach combined surveys with more intensive case-study methods. And the project discussed in the chapter on identity used interviews and observation to trace out the differing ways in which identities were constructed; using one method would have flattened this complex situation.

A second cross-cutting feature is 'triangulation' (see chapter 4). This metaphor is sometimes taken to mean that different methods can be used to produce an estimate of the true size of a phenomenon. There is, however, 'a difference between triangulation as a research method and triangulation as [a] claim that, given sufficient independent measurements, reality can be unambiguously discovered' (Edwards and Scullion 1982: 19). Chapters 4 and 9 give examples of both aspects: different tools are used to show that the nature of the thing being investigated has multiple aspects; people feel a strong sense of identity with their work, for example, in some respects but not others. The same idea informs such areas as realist synthesis (chapter 14). Such a synthesis will emphasize that the interventions being studied are not necessarily, or indeed normally, the same, and that teasing out their effects requires detailed causal reconstruction. CR-informed approaches will thus tend to stress the variability of both the dependent and independent variables. This approach is different from an ontological claim that reality can be retrieved if enough separate measurements are taken. CR certainly insists on the reality of the world, but it also stresses that we know that world through uncertain processes and also that different actors will define reality in different ways. A CR researcher will certainly want to explain, for example, why managers and workers might take a different view of the extent and meaning of 'teamwork', but will not suggest that there is a true single thing called teamwork.

Turning to the challenges facing CR, a major one relates to the 'critical' part of CR, which is generally taken to refer to an agenda that moves beyond analysis to action, with that action not merely being some form of engagement with the social world but also 'emancipation'. This idea is not separate from analysis but emerges clearly from it. CR aims to identify causal processes, knowledge of which then informs action. This book has identified some of the ways, ranging from the very specific to the broader, in which the links can be made. Ackroyd and Karlsson in chapter 2 outline several examples of projects where there was active engagement with the situations under study. In relation to the specific, Smith and Elger argue in chapter 6 that CR-informed interviewing, in contrast to other uses of the techniques, challenges participants' accounts and causal attributions. It does not just record what people say but uses these accounts to make links to causal explanations; and these explanations have implications for action, for example in exposing why participants take certain things for granted and by at least implying the kinds of action that they might take if these things are questioned. At a broader level, Ram et al. argue that a realist-informed action study was able to pose questions to actors' assumptions, in this case about the nature of 'ethnic' businesses, and they claim that such questioning changed these assumptions in ways that they deem to be beneficial—albeit recognizing that what is indeed beneficial is a contested issue. Similarly, Greenhalgh (chapter 14) shows that in the area of policy interventions a realist synthesis leads to results that have directly relevant conclusions at the level of policy and action. As Ackroyd and Karlsson put it, realist researchers do not offer specific advice about action; instead 'they provide practitioners with knowledge of structures, their mechanisms and tendencies that practitioners can apply to their specific contexts'.

That said, this book has not looked in detail at the links between research and practice. The justification is that the focus is research technique rather than the implications once the research has been done. But the dividing line here is not an easy one. Once we open up the idea of debating causal powers with participants and asking them to consider why they do what they do, we necessarily raise issues to do with changing such practice, with a view to changing the nature of the world in which it takes place. As Ram et al. point out, there are political choices to be made here, for views of the world are contested. CR may offer research designs that are 'better' than some alternatives, but it can claim no special wisdom in the making of these choices. It may be able to assist in the ways in which the choices are formulated, because it is interested in causal powers. It may, for example, be able to point out that choices may be wider than it seems at first sight. But these are matters that require a different kind of discussion from the aims of the present book.

The book has also addressed challenges to the explanatory power of the CR project. Many of the chapters recognize a fundamental problem of identifying causal mechanisms when these are not directly observable. This is perhaps the greatest issue facing CR as an explanatory project. Yet the chapters suggest several ways of grappling with it, for example using careful comparative research designs and addressing the conditions under which causal powers are put into effect. The challenge is not, moreover, peculiar to CR. It applies to any attempt to explain the social world, other than one that assumes that we can achieve conditions close to experimental closure. It is notable that fields that have taken the randomized controlled trial as the gold standard, for example studies of healthcare interventions, increasingly recognize the variability of interventions and the openness of the context in which they operate (Cox et al. 2007; Nielsen et al. 2010). They suggest that it is possible to make progress, for example by addressing how an intervention is defined and used in practice. Such an approach certainly makes it impossible to say whether 'an' intervention has necessary effects. But a search for such certainties is, CR tells us, inherently flawed. Once we start from this fact, we can begin to interrogate causal powers and how they are brought into existence.

Two chapters have also been included that take a more sceptical view of the CR project. For Brown and Roberts, there are issues in relation to both quantitative and qualitative methods. In relation to the former, they cite Lawson's view that CR is consistent only with the search for 'demi-regularities' and with statistics largely limited to overall descriptions of data, for example how many economists there are in Cambridge University. It is certainly the case, however, that many adherents to CR, including contributors to this book, use quantitative models of a much more formal kind. In our view, the use of the relevant techniques is consistent with CR, as long as their limitations are recognized and addressed. Suppose that we wish to explain patterns of job satisfaction across the working population, and also that theory tells us that workers with long length of service with an employer will have higher satisfaction than others. We can test for this statistically, controlling for other variables. We can also ask whether the relationship is linear, whether it is stronger in some settings than others, and so on. We can also examine the diagnostics in regression equations, looking for patterns of residuals that may suggest an error in the specification or looking for outliers that are poorly explained. A CR researcher, we suspect, would be more likely than a positivist to take the latter seriously: not eliminating them as exceptions but asking what causal factors lead to their presence and, possibly, instituting further inquiry to find out. We would claim that our own practice in quantitative analysis fits a realist programme. For example, if we are interested in whether a particular pay system causes strikes (and assuming that we have a theory as to why this might be the case), we can look at patterns in surveys and then investigate the specific conditions under which the association does or does not hold (Edwards 1987; see also Edwards et al. 1998, for a different example). Several of the chapters in this book, notably those by Bach and Kessler and by Hurrell, use quantitative methods along with others. Lawson cannot be taken as exemplary of the actual practice of CR researchers. It can of course then be argued that this practice is not consistent with CR, but we claim that that is not the case: as long as one is sensitive to context and mechanisms, and also to the assumptions of specific techniques, CR can use quantitative methods.

Quantitative methods are also the focus of Williams's chapter. His arguments for careful causal modelling are very cogently put, and he is surely right that quantitative methods call for more careful methodological consideration than is often the case. We would add that, in business and management studies, the use of techniques such as structural equation modelling may be running ahead of users' grasp of what the models are in fact doing. We see Williams's examples, notably that of migration from Cornwall, as consistent with what at least the realist part of CR is trying to do. Hurrell's use of mixed methods further illustrates a CR project; in many ways, the combination of methods could be seen as a fundamental CR approach, for it allows causal powers at different levels to be interrogated.

As for qualitative methods, Brown and Roberts conclude that the 'jury is still out' on the question of the ability of CR to generalize using such methods. We take a more sanguine view. In the field of workplace industrial relations, one project has been able to set out what it calls a strategy of 'holistic modelling' and argue for its superiority over a more inductively derived approach (Edwards and Bélanger 2008), and also use the approach to characterize (Edwards et al. 2006) and explain (Bélanger and Edwards 2007) specific patterns of workplace relations. The chapters on comparative cases and international comparison in this book also illustrate the possibilities of generalization. This is not of course to say that conclusions are fixed but it is to argue that realist-inspired analyses of causal powers permit generalization which has at least as much explanatory strength as other styles of inquiry.

Brown and Roberts then go on to discuss open and closed systems, and to suggest that a dialectical approach is the way forward. We make two comments. First, CR does not say that systems are either open or closed, or suggest that it is impossible to make links between one view of systems and the other. Any system is to a degree open, and any explanation—other than one saying that anything is possible, which is not really an explanation—is to a degree closed. In explaining something, we try to say what it is, what causes it, and how much variation in it we have captured. We have to draw boundaries. Take for example Burawoy's (1979) celebrated account of piecework bargaining in an engineering factory in Chicago in the 1970s. In our view, this is an exemplary study at the 'what-it-is' level: it characterizes and explains the internal dynamics of the regime. It is also powerful in explaining the causal conditions, notably the product-market context in which this workplace was located. It is less successful in explaining variation, in the sense of how far this workplace reflected the underlying principles of capitalism, for it is these principles that are Burawoy's central concern. The workplace was not 'typical' of Chicago, let alone America or advanced capitalism in general. It has also been argued that Burawoy's is a rather determinist account, in that worker 'subjectivity' is not addressed. On this latter point, the issue is to a considerable degree empirical: it is entirely consistent to argue that in this case structural conditions set such boundaries on workers' choices that subjectivity was of minor importance, while in other cases the actions and choices made by workers have real causal powers (see Bélanger and Edwards 2007, for examples). On the point about typicality, this one factory needs to be placed in a wider context to see what is peculiar to it, to manufacturing, to America, and so on. But points of this kind merely underline the openness of systems and the provisional nature of explanations. They do not say that there is a fundamental problem with thinking in terms of open systems while necessarily having to practise a degree of closure in making an explanation.

This brings us to dialectics. For ourselves, we do not dispute much of what Brown and Roberts say. But we are not convinced that the idea of dialectics is in any way inconsistent with CR, as indeed their use of Bhaskar's recent work suggests. It is not, moreover, clear how far these authors in fact pursue a dialectical analysis. Their prime example aims to show how dialectics can be used to unpick the necessary relations that inhere within the capitalist system. Yet the emphasis is on necessary features at a high level of abstraction that affect observable phenomena. This emphasis can be a reasonable one for certain purposes, notably the demonstration that capitalism is indeed a system. But a dialectical view also needs to avoid a determinist explanation of capitalism as a closed system. A dialectical view allows for variation by insisting that capitalism has several inherent processes that are in tension with each other, pressures for accumulation and legitimation being the classic example.

Whether other users of CR would agree is less clear, for CR is a meta-theory which fits a number of more empirical strategies. One can deploy CR without being committed to dialectics, and a dialectical approach is probably also consistent with several positions other than CR. The overall approach of Brown and Roberts implies a substantial empirical agenda. We take them as arguing that CR, as practised to date, is not so much wrong as incomplete. Given that, as an empirical project, CR is still relatively little developed, we see this as something of an endorsement of the project as a whole, and an effort to go further.

This book, however, represents an initial attempt to put CR into action at a relatively concrete level. There are certainly important ways in which it can be used to analyse the interconnections within a capitalist, or indeed any other, economic order. But there is a risk that such a project maintains CR at the level of a broad perspective. There is also the need to apply it in very specific research projects, and we hope that this book stimulates such projects. Our examples come mainly from business and management, though as pointed out in chapter 1, CR has been applied in a very wide range of other fields. Many of the illustrations here, for example as to how to use CR in interviewing, apply equally in other settings. But other themes may call for specific attention. For example, the meaning of emancipation, and hence the purchase of CR-oriented action research, is likely to differ between, say, such areas as education and social work. Moreover, though we have covered a range of methods, we have not addressed them all; the specifics of quantitative techniques, in particular, would merit more attention. And where we have addressed a technique, we give one example that may not be representative of the field. The empirical studies discussed illustrate the potential of CR, but other researchers using the relevant techniques would use it in different ways. The emphasis has also been on the doing of research in realist ways, with less attention to issues of action and emancipation. All these matters deserve further attention; we hope that the volume encourages such debate.

Bibliography

Ackroyd, S. (2004). 'Methodology for Management and Organisation Studies: Some Implications of Critical Realism', in S. Fleetwood and S. Ackroyd (eds), *Critical Realist Applications in Organisation and Management Studies.* London: Routledge, 137–63.

—— (2009). 'Research Designs for Realist Research', in D. Buchanan and A. Bryman (eds), *The SAGE Handbook of Organizational Research Methods.* London: Sage, 532–48.

—— (2010). 'Critical Realism, Organization Theory, Methodology and the Emerging Science of Reconfiguration', in P. Koslowski (ed.) *Elements of a Philosophy of Management and Organization.* London: Springer, 47–78.

—— and Fleetwood, S. (2000a). 'Realism in Contemporary Organisation and Management Studies', in S. Ackroyd and S. Fleetwood (eds), *Realist Perspectives on Management and Organisations.* London: Routledge, 3–25.

——eds (2000b). *Realist Perspectives on Management and Organisations.* London: Routledge.

—— and Muzio, D. (2007). 'The Reconstructed Professional Firm: Explaining Change in English Legal Practices', *Organization Studies,* 28: 729–47.

Aguilera, R. V. and Jackson, G. (2003). 'The Cross-National Diversity of Corporate Governance: Dimensions and Determinants', *Academy of Management Review,* 28: 447–65.

Akerlof, G. A. and Yellen, J. L. (1986). *Efficiency Wage Models of the Labor Market.* New York: Cambridge University Press.

Al-Amoudi, I. and Willmott, H. (2011). 'Where Constructionism and Critical Realism Converge: Interrogating the Domain of Epistemological Relativism', *Organization Studies,* 32(1): 27-46.

Al-Amoudi, I. (2007). 'Redrawing Foucault's Social Ontology', *Organization,* 14: 543–63.

Albritton, R. (2008). 'Marxian Crisis Theory and Causality', in R. Groff (ed.) *Revitalizing Causality.* London: Routledge, 220–41.

Alvesson, M. (2002). *Postmodernism and Social Research.* Buckingham: Open University Press.

—— (2011). *Interpreting Interviews.* London: Sage.

Anon. (1696). *Overtures Concerning the Discipline and Method of Proceeding in the Ecclesiastick Judicatories in the Church of Scotland.* Edinburgh: George Mossman.

Antonio, R. (1981). 'Immanent Critique as the Core of Critical Theory: Its Origins and Development in Hegel, Marx and Contemporary Thought', *British Journal of Sociology,* 32: 330–45.

Archer, M. S. (1979). *Social Origins of Educational Systems.* London: SAGE Publications.

—— (1983). 'Process without System', *Archives Européenes de Sociologie,* 24: 196–221.

—— (1995). *Realist Social Theory: The Morphogenetic Approach.* Cambridge: Cambridge University Press.

— (Ritical Realism: Essential Readings (1998) eds

—— (1996). *Culture and Agency: The Place of Culture in Social Theory*. Cambridge: Cambridge University Press.

—— (1998). 'Introduction: Realism in the Social Sciences', in M. Archer, R. Bhaskar, A. Collier et al. (eds), *Critical Realism: Essential Readings*. London: Routledge, 189–205.

—— (2000). *Being Human: The Problem of Agency*. Cambridge: Cambridge University Press.

—— (2003). *Structure, Agency and the Internal Conversation*. Cambridge: Cambridge University Press.

—— (2006). 'Structure, Culture and Agency', in M. D. Jacobs and N. W. Hanrahan (eds), *The Blackwell Companion to the Sociology of Culture*. Oxford: Blackwell, 17–34.

—— (2007). *Making our Way through the World: Human Reflexivity and Social Mobility*. Cambridge: Cambridge University Press.

—— (2012). *The Reflexive Imperative in Late Modernity*. Cambridge: Cambridge University Press.

Argyris, C. and Schön, D. (1996). *Organizational Learning II: Theory, Method and Practice*. Reading, MA: Addison Wesley.

Ashforth, B. E. and Mael, F. (1989). 'Social Identity Theory and the Organization', *Academy of Management Review* 14 (1): 20–39.

Au, Y. W. and Marks, A. (2012). 'Virtual Teams are Literally and Metaphorically Invisible": Forging Identity in Culturally Diverse Virtual Teams', *Work, Employee Relations* 34(3): 271–87.

Baltzell, E. (1979). *Puritan Boston and Quaker Philadelphia: Two Protestant Ethics and the Spirit of Class Authority and Leadership*. New York: Free Press.

Bambra, C., Whitehead, M., and Hamilton, V. (2005). 'Does "Welfare to Work" Work? A Systematic Review of the Effectiveness of the UK's Welfare to Work Programmes for People with a Disability or Chronic Illness', *Social Science and Medicine*, 60: 1905–18.

Bandura, A. (1977). *Social Learning Theory*. Englewood Cliffs, NJ: Prentice-Hall.

—— (1986). *Social Foundations of Thought and Action: A Social Cognitive Theory*. Englewood Cliffs, NJ: Prentice-Hall.

Banfield, G. (2004). 'What's Really Wrong with Ethnography?' *International Education Journal*, 4: 53–63.

Banta, B. (2013). 'Analysing Discourse as a Causal Mechanism', *European Journal of International Relations*, 19(2): 379–402.

Barker, J. (1993). 'Tightening the Iron Cage: Concertive Control in Self-Managed Teams', *Administrative Science Quarterly*, 38: 408–37.

Barley, S. R. (2008). 'Coalface Institutionalism', in R. Greenwood, C. Oliver, K. Sahlin-Andersson et al. (eds), *The SAGE Handbook of Organizational Institutionalism*. London: Sage, 491–518.

Barnes, C. and Mercer, G. (2010). *Exploring Disability*, 2nd edn. Cambridge: Palgrave.

Bartlett, C. A. (1979). 'Multinational Structural Evolution: The Changing Decision Environment in International Divisions', PhD dissertation (Harvard University).

—— and Ghoshal, S. (1989). *Managing Across Borders: The Transnational Solution*. Boston, MA: Harvard Business School Press.

Bateson, N. (1984). Data Construction in Social Surveys. London: Allen & Unwin.

Bawer, B. (2012). *The Victims' Revolution: The Rise of Identity Studies and the Closing of the Liberal Mind*. New York: HarperCollins.

Becker, G. S. (1993). *Human Capital: A Theoretical and Empirical Analysis with Special Reference to Education* (3rd edn). Chicago, IL: University of Chicago Press.

Becker, H. S., Geer, B., Hughes, E. C. et al. (1961). *Boys in White: Student Culture in Medical School*. Chicago, IL: University of Chicago Press.

Beirne, M. (2008). 'Idealism and the Applied Relevance of Research on Employee Participation', *Work, Employment and Society*, 4: 675–93.

Bélanger, J. and Edwards, P. (2007). 'The Conditions Promoting Compromise in the Workplace', *British Journal of Industrial Relations*, 45: 713–34.

Berg-Schlosser, D., De Meur, G., Rihoux, B. et al. (2009). 'Qualitative Comparative Analysis (QCA) as an Approach', in B. Rihoux and C. C. Ragin (eds), *Configurational Comparative Methods: Qualitative Comparative Analysis (QCA) and Related Techniques*. Thousand Oaks, CA: Sage, 1–18.

Berry, B. J. L. (1976). 'The Counterurbanization Process: Urban America since 1970', *Urban Affairs Annual Review*, 11: 17–30.

Beynon, H. (1973). *Working For Ford*. Harmondsworth: Penguin.

Bhaskar, R. (1978). *A Realist Theory of Science* (2nd edn). Brighton: Harvester Press.

—— (1979). *The Possibility of Naturalism*. London: Verso.

—— (1986). *Scientific Realism and Human Emancipation*. London: Verso.

—— (1989). *Reclaiming Reality: A Critical Introduction to Contemporary Philosophy*. London: Verso.

—— (1993). *Dialectic: The Pulse of Freedom*. London: Verso.

—— (1994). *Plato Etc.* London: Verso.

—— (1998a). 'General Introduction', in M. Archer, R. Bhaskar, A. Collier et al. (eds), *Critical Realism: Essential Readings*. London: Routledge, ix–xxiv.

—— (1998b). *The Possibility of Naturalism* (3rd edn). London: Routledge.

—— (2002). *Reflections on metaReality: Transcendence, Emancipation and Everyday Life*. London: Routledge.

—— (2008). *A Realist Theory of Social Science* (4th edn). London: Routledge.

—— (2009). *Scientific Realism and Human Emancipation* (2nd edn). London: Routledge.

—— (2011). 'Contexts of Interdisciplinarity', in R. Bhaskar (ed.), *Interdisciplinarity and Climate Change*. London: Routledge.

—— (2013). 'The Consequences of the Revindication of Philosophical Ontology for Philosophy and Social Theory', in M. Archer and A. Maccarini (eds), *Engaging with the World*. London: Routledge.

—— and Danermark, B. (2006). 'Metatheory, Interdisciplinarity, and Disability Research: A Critical Realist Perspective', *Scandinavian Journal of Disability Research*, 8: 278–97.

—— and Hartwig, H. (2010). *The Formation of Critical Realism: A Personal Perspective*. Abingdon: Routledge.

Billig, M. (1985). 'Prejudice, Categorisation and Particularisation: From a Perceptual Rhetorical Approach', *European Journal of Social Psychology*, 15: 70–103.

—— (2001). 'Discursive, Rhetorical and Ideological Messages', in M. Wetherell, S. Taylor, and S. J. Yates (eds), *Discourse Theory and Practice. A Reader*. London: Sage Publications, 210–22.

—— (2011). 'Writing Social Psychology: Fictional Things and Unpopulated Texts', *British Journal of Social Psychology*, 50: 4–20.

—— Condor, S., Edwards, D. et al. (1988). *Ideological Dilemmas: A Social Psychology of Everyday Thinking*. London: Sage Publications.

Birkhead, T. (2008). *The Wisdom of Birds: An Illustrated History of Ornithology*. London: Bloomsbury.

Birkinshaw, J., Brannen, M. Y., and Tung, R. L. (2011). 'From a Distance and Generalizable to Up Close and Grounded: Reclaiming a Place for Qualitative Methods in International Business Research', *Journal of International Business Studies*, 42: 573–81.

Blaikie, N. (2007 [1993]). *Approaches to Social Enquiry* (2nd edn). Cambridge: Polity.

Blalock, H. (1961). *Causal Inference in Nonexperimental Research*. Chapel Hill, NC: University of North Carolina Press.

Blau, P. (1955). *The Dynamics of Bureaucracy*. Chicago: University of Chicago Press.

Boselie, P., Dietz, G., and Boon, C. (2005). 'Commonalities and Contradictions in HRM and Performance Research', *Human Resource Management Journal*, 15: 67–94.

Boswell, T. and Brown, C. (1999). 'The Scope of General Theory: Methods for Linking Inductive and Deductive Comparative History', *Sociological Methods and Research*, 28: 154–85.

Boudon, R. (1974). *The Logic of Sociological Explanation*. Harmondsworth: Penguin.

Bourdieu, P. (1977). *Outline of a Theory of Practice*, translated by R. Nice. Cambridge.

—— (1986). *Distinction: A Social Critique of the Judgement of Taste*. London: Routledge.

—— (1991). 'Did You Say "Popular"?' in J. B. Thompson (ed.), *Language and Symbolic Power*. Cambridge: Polity Press, 90–102.

—— and Passeron, J.-C. (1977). *Reproduction in Education, Society and Culture*. London: Sage.

Bowen, D. E. and Ostroff, C. (2004). 'Understanding HRM-Firm Performance Linkages: The Role of the "Strength" of the HRM System', *Academy of Management Review*, 24: 203–21.

Bowlby, J. (1990). *Childcare and the Growth of Love*. Harmondsworth: Penguin.

Boxall, P. and Macky, K. (2007). 'High Performance Work Systems and Organisational Performance: Bridging Theory and Practice', *Asia Pacific Journal of Human Resources*, 45: 261–70.

—— and Purcell, J. (2000). 'Strategic Human Resource Management: Where Have We Come From and Where Should We Be Going?' *International Journal of Management Reviews*, 2: 183–203.

Brandist, C. (2002). *The Bakhtin Circle: Philosophy, Culture and Politics*. London: Pluto Press.

Brannan, M., Rowe, M., and Worthington, F. (2012). 'Editorial for the Journal of Organizational Ethnography: Time for a New Journal, a Journal for New Times', *Journal of Organizational Ethnography*, 1: 5–14.

Braverman, H. (1974). *Labor and Monopoly Capital: The Degradation of Work in the Twentieth Century*. London: Monthly Review Press.

Brown, A. (2007). 'Reorienting Critical Realism: A System-wide Perspective on the Capitalist Economy', *Journal of Economic Methodology*, 14: 499–519.

—— (2012). *Approach with Caution: Critical Realism in Social Research*, mimeo.

—— Charlwood, A., Forde, C. et al. (2007). 'Job Quality and the Economics of New Labour: A Critical Appraisal Using Subjective Survey Data', *Cambridge Journal of Economics*, 36: 941–71.

——, ——, (2008). 'Changes in Human Resource Management and Job Satisfaction 1998–2004: Evidence from the Workplace Employment Relations Survey', *Human Resource Management Journal*, 18: 237–56.

Brown, G. L. (2009). 'The Ontological Turn in Education', *Journal of Critical Realism*, 8: 5–34.

Brown, Steven D. and Peter Lunt. (1986). 'A Genealogy of the Social Identity Tradition: Deleuze and Guattari and Social Psychology', *British Journal of Social Psychology* 41.1 (2002): 1–23.

Bryman, A. (1988). *Quantity and Quality in Social Research*. London: Unwin Hyman.

—— (1989). *Research Methods and Organization Studies*. London: Unwin Hyman.

—— (2004a). 'Qualitative Research on Leadership: A Critical but Appreciative Review', *The Leadership Quarterly*, 15: 729–69.

—— (2004b). *Social Research Methods* (2nd edn). Oxford: Oxford University Press.

—— and Bell, E. (2003). *Business Research Methods*. Oxford: Oxford University Press.

Burawoy, M. (1979). *Manufacturing Consent*. Chicago, IL: Chicago University Press.

—— (1985). *The Politics of Production: Factory Regimes under Capitalism and Socialism*. London: Verso.

—— (1998). 'The Extended Case Method', *Sociological Theory*, 16: 4–33.

Burr, V. (1999). 'The Extra-Discursive in Social Constructionism', in D. J. Nightingale and J. Cromby (eds), *Social Constructionist Psychology: A Critical Analysis of Theory and Practice*. Buckingham: Open University Press, 113–27.

—— (2003). *Social Constructionism*. Hove: Routledge.

Byrne, D. (1998). *Complexity Theory and the Social Sciences: An Introduction*. London: Routledge.

—— (2002 [2004]). *Interpreting Quantitative Data*. London: Sage.

—— (2011). *Applying Social Science: The Role of Social Research in Politics, Policy and Practice*. London: Sage.

Carchedi, G. (1983). *Problems in Class Analysis*. London: Routledge and Kegan Paul.

Caroli, E., Gautié, J., Lloyd, C. et al. (2010). 'Delivering Flexibility: Contrasting Patterns in the French and the UK Food Processing Industry', *British Journal of Industrial Relations*, 48: 284–309.

Carter, B. (2000). *Realism and Racism*. Routledge: London.

Cartwright, N. (2002). *Causation: One Word, Many Things*. London: CPNS, London School of Economics.

Cassell, C. and Johnson, P. (2006). 'Action Research: Explaining the Diversity', *Human Relations*, 59: 783–814.

Champion, A. G. (1994). 'Population Change in Britain since 1981: Evidence for Continuing Deconcentration', *Environment and Planning A*, 26: 1501–20.

Charmaz, K. (2006). *Constructing Grounded Theory*. London: Sage.

Checkland, P. and Scholes, J. (1990). *Soft Systems Methodology: A 30-Year Retrospection*. Chichester: Wiley.

Chick, V. and Dow, S. C. (2005). 'The Meaning of Open Systems', *Journal of Economic Methodology*, 12: 363–81.

Child, J. (1997). 'Strategic Choice in the Analysis of Action, Structure, Organizations and Environment: Retrospect and Prospect', *Organization Studies*, 18: 43–76.

Child, J. and Smith, C. (1987). 'The Context and Process of Organizational Transformation-Cadbury Limited in its Sector'. *Journal of Management Studies*, 24(6), 565–93.

Chisholm, R. and Elden, M. (1993). 'Features of Emerging Action Research', *Human Relations*, 46: 275–99.

Clark, P. (2000). *Organizations in Action: Competition between Contexts.* London: Routledge.

Clarke, I. and Mackaness, W. (2001). 'Management Intuition: An Interpretive Account of Structure and Content of Decision Schemas using Cognitive Maps', *Journal of Management Studies*, 38: 147–72.

Clawson, A. (1944). *Shipyard Diary of a Woman Welder*. New York: Penguin.

Clegg, S. (2005). 'Evidence-based Practice in Educational Research: A Critical Realist Critique of Systematic Review', *British Journal of Sociology of Education*, 26: 415–28.

Cochrane, A. L. (1972). *Effectiveness and Efficiency: Random Reflections on Health Services.* London: Nuffield Provincial Hospitals Trust.

Cockburn, C. (1983). *Brothers: Male Dominance and Technological Change.* London: Pluto Press.

Colley, H. (2003). 'Engagement Mentoring for Socially Excluded Youth: Problematising an "Holistic" Approach to Creating Employability through Transformation of the Habitus', *British Journal of Guidance and Counselling*, 31: 77–98.

Collier, A. (1989). *Scientific Realism and Socialist Thought*. London: Pluto.

—— (1994). *Critical Realism: An Introduction to Roy Bhaskar's Philosophy.* London: Verso.

—— (1998). 'Explanation and Emancipation', in M. Archer, R. Bhaskar, A. Collier et al. (eds), *Critical Realism: Essential Readings*, London: Routledge, 444–72.

Collins, H. (1992). *Changing Order: Replication and Induction in Scientific Practice.* Chicago, IL: University of Chicago Press.

Collinson, D. (1992). *Managing the Shopfloor: Subjectivity, Masculinity and Workplace Culture.* New York: De Gruyter.

—— (2003). 'Identities and Insecurities: Selves at Work', *Organization*, 10 (3): 527–47.

Condor, S. (1996). 'Social Identity and Time', in W. P. Robinson (ed.) *Social Groups and Identities: Developing the Legacy of Henri Tajfel.* Oxford: Butterworth Heinemann, 285–315.

Conger, J. A. (2004). 'Developing Leadership Capability: What's Inside the Black Box?' *Academy of Management Executive*, 18: 136–9.

Cooke, B. (2006). 'The Cold War Origin of Action Research as Managerialist Co-optation', *Human Relations*, 59: 665–93.

Costas, J. and Fleming, P. (2009). 'Beyond Dis-identification: A Discursive Approach to Self-alienation in Contemporary Organizations', *Human Relations*, 62: 353–78.

Cox, R. (2007). 'Revisiting the Archival Finding Aid', *Journal of Archive Organization*, 5: 5–31.

Cox, T., Karanika, M., Griffiths , A. et al. (2007). 'Evaluating Organizational-level Work Stress Interventions: Beyond Traditional Methods', *Work and Stress*, 21: 348–62.

Crinson, I. (2001). 'A Realist Approach to the Analysis of Focus Group Data', *5th Annual IACR Conference*, Denmark, 17–19 August.

—— (2007). 'Nursing Practice and Organisational Change within the NHS: A Critical Realist Methodological Approach to the Analysis of Discursive Data', *Methodological Innovations Online*, 2: 32–43.

Cromby, J. (2012). 'Feeling the Way: Qualitative Clinical Research and the Affective Turn', *Qualitative Research in Psychology*, 9: 88–98.

—— and Harper, D. J. (2009). 'Paranoia: A Social Account', *Theory & Psychology*, 19: 335–61.

—— and Nightingale, D.J. (1999). 'What Is Wrong with Social Constructionism?' in D. J. Nightingale and J. Cromby (eds), *Social Constructionist Psychology: A Critical Analysis of Theory and Practice*. Buckingham: Open University Press, 1–21.

Crouch, C. (2005). *Capitalist Diversity and Change: Recombinant Governance and Institutional Entrepreneurs*. Oxford: Oxford University Press.

Cruickshank, J., ed. (2003). *Critical Realism: The Difference It Makes*. London: Routledge.

Cully, M., Woodland, S., O'Reilly, A. et al. (1999). *Britain at Work: As Depicted by the 1998 Workplace Employee Relations Survey*. London: Routledge.

Dalton, M. (1959). *Men Who Manage*. New York: Wiley.

Danermark, B., Ekström, M., Jakobsen, L. et al. (2002). *Explaining Society: Critical Realism in the Social Sciences*. London: Routledge.

Daniel, P. and Ivatts, J. (1998). *Children and Social Policy*. London: Macmillan.

Davies, C. A. (2008). *Reflexive Ethnography: A Guide to Researching Selves and Others* (2nd edn). London: Routledge.

Dawson, J., Doll, H., Fitzpatrick, R. et al. (2010). 'The Routine Use of Patient-Reported Outcome Measures in Healthcare Settings', *British Medical Journal*, 340, c186.

Daycare Trust (2001). 'Quality Matters: Ensuring Childcare Benefits Children', *Childcare for All: Thinking Big, 2*. London: Daycare Trust, National Childcare Charity.

de Anda, D. (2001). 'A Qualitative Evaluation of a Mentor Program for at risk Youth: the Participants' Perspective', *Child and Adolescent Social Work Journal*, 18(2): 97–117.

Deakins, D., Ram, M., and Smallbone, D. (2003). 'Addressing the Business Support Needs of Ethnic Minority Firms in the United Kingdom', *Environment and Planning C*, 21: 843–59.

Dean, K., Joseph, J., Roberts, J. M. et al. (2006). *Realism, Philosophy and Social Science*. London: Palgrave Macmillan.

Delbridge, R. (1998). *Life on the Line in Contemporary Manufacturing*. Oxford: Oxford University Press.

Denzin, N. K. (1989). *The Research Act*, 3rd edn. New York: McGraw-Hill.

Diener, E. and Diener, M. (2009). 'Cross-Cultural Correlates of Life Satisfaction and Self-Esteem', *Culture and Well-Being Social Indicators Research Series*, 38: 71–91.

DiMaggio, P. J. and Powell, W. W. (1983). 'The Iron Cage Revisited: Institutional Isomorphism and Collective Rationality in Organizational Fields', *American Sociological Review*, 48: 147–60.

Dixon, M., Roscigno, V. J., and Hodson, R. (2004). 'Unions, Solidarity, and Striking', *Social Forces*, 83: 3–33.

Dobson, P. J. (2002). 'Critical Realism and Information Systems Research: Why Bother with Philosophy?' *Information Research*, 7, (2). [online] Available at: <http://InformationR.net/ir/7-2/paper124.html> accessed 7 August 2013.

Doeringer, P. and Piore, M. J. (1971). *Internal Labor Markets and Manpower Analysis*. Lexington, MA: Heath Lexington Books.

Doherty, C. (2007). 'The Effectiveness of Jurisdictional Change on Professionalisation in Nursing', DPhil thesis (King's College, London).

Down, S. (2006). *Narratives of Enterprise: Creating Entrepreneurial Self-Identity in a Small Firm*. Cheltenham: Edward Elgar.

—— (2012). 'A Historiographical Account of Workplace and Organizational Ethnography', *Journal of Organizational Ethnography*, 1: 72–82.

Downward, P., ed. (2003). *Applied Economics and the Critical Realist Critique*. London: Routledge.

—— and Mearman, A. (2007). 'Retroduction as Mixed-Methods Triangulation in Economic Research: Reorienting Economics into Social Science', *Cambridge Journal of Economics*, 31: 77–99.

Doyal, L. and Harris, R. (1986). *Empiricism, Explanation and Rationality*. London: Routledge and Kegan Paul.

Drummond, J. and Themessl-Huber, M. (2007). 'The Cyclical Process of Action Research: The Contribution of Giles Deleuze', *Action Research*, 5: 430–48.

Dubois, A. and Gadde, L.-E. (2002). 'Systematic Combining: An Abductive Approach to Case Research', *Journal of Business Research*, 55: 553–60.

du Gay, P. (2007). *Organizing Identity: Persons and Organizations 'After Theory'*. London: Sage.

Easton, G. (2010). 'Critical Realism in Case Study Research', *Industrial Marketing Management*, 39: 118–28.

Eden, C. (1992). 'On the Nature of Cognitive Maps', *Journal of Management Studies*, 29: 261–5.

Edley, N. and Wetherell, M. (1999). 'Imagined Futures: Young Men's Talk about Fatherhood and Domestic Life', *British Journal of Social Psychology*, 38: 181–94.

Edwards, D. (1995). 'Two to Tango: Script Formulations, Dispositions, and Rhetorical Symmetry in Relationship Troubles Talk', *Research on Language and Social Interaction*, 28: 319–50.

—— (1997). *Discourse and Cognition*. London: Sage.

Edwards, P. K. (1986). *Conflict at Work: A Materialist Analysis of Workplace Relations*. Oxford: Blackwell.

—— (1987). 'Does PBR Cause Strikes?' *Industrial Relations Journal*, 18: 210–17.

—— (1990). 'Understanding Conflict in the Labour Process: The Logic and Autonomy of Struggle', in D. Knights and H. Willmott (eds), *Labour Process Theory*. London: Macmillan, 125–52.

—— (2005). 'The Challenging but Promising Future of Industrial Relations: Developing Theory and Method in Context-Sensitive Research', *Industrial Relations Journal*, 36: 264–82.

—— and Bélanger, J. (2008). 'Generalizing from Workplace Ethnographies: From Induction to Theory', *Journal of Contemporary Ethnography*, 37: 291–313.

——, ——, and Wright, M. (2006). 'The Bases of Compromise in the Workplace: A Theoretical Framework', *British Journal of Industrial Relations*, 44: 125–46.

—— Collinson, M., and Rees, C. (1998). 'The Determinants of Employee Responses to Total Quality Management: Six Case Studies', *Organization Studies*, 19: 449–75.

——and Scullion, H. (1982). *The Social Organization of Industrial Conflict: Control and Resistance in the Workplace*. Oxford: Blackwell.

Edwards, T. (2004). 'Corporate Governance, Industrial Relations and Trends in Company-Level Restructuring in Europe: Convergence towards the Anglo-Saxon Model?' *Industrial Relations Journal*, 35: 518–35.

Eisenhardt, K. (1989). 'Building Theories from Case Study Research', *Academy of Management Review*, 14: 532–50.

*Elder-Vass, D. (2010). *The Causal Power of Social Structures: Emergence, Structure and Agency*. Cambridge: Cambridge University Press.

Elger, T. (2010). 'Critical Realism', in A. J. Mills, G. Durepos, and E. Wiebe (eds), *Encyclopaedia of Case Study Research, i*. Los Angeles: Sage, 253–57.

——and Smith, C., eds (1994). *Global Japanization? The Transnational Transformation of the Labour Process*. London: Routledge.

—— — (2005). *Assembling Work: Remaking Factory Regimes in Japanese Multinationals in Britain*. Oxford: Oxford University Press.

Elton, L. (2000). 'The UK Research Assessment Exercise: Unintended Consequences', *Higher Education Quarterly*, 54: 274–83.

Erzberger, C. and Kelle, U. (2003). 'Making Inferences in Mixed Methods: The Rules of Integration', in A. Tashakkori and C. Teddlie (eds.) *Handbook of Mixed Methods in Social and Behavioral Research*. Thousand Oaks, CA: Sage.

Evans, R. (1997). *In Defence of History*. London: Granta.

—— and Lewis, P. (2012). 'Mark Kennedy Hired as Consultant by US Security Firm', *The Guardian*, 21 June.

Everitt, B. (1993). *Cluster Analysis*. London: Heinemann.

Ezzy, D. (1998). 'Theorizing Narrative Identity: Symbolic Interactionism and Hermeneutics', *The Sociological Quarterly*, 39: 239–52.

Fairclough, N. (2002) 'Language in New Capitalism', *Discourse and Society* 13 (2): 163–6.

——(2003). *Analysing Discourse: Textual Analysis for Social Research*. London: Routledge.

—— (2005). 'Peripheral Vision: Discourse Analysis in Organization Studies, the Case for Critical Realism', *Organization Studies*, 26: 915–939.

—— Jessop, B., and Sayer A. (2002). 'Critical Realism and Semiosis', in I. Parker (ed.), *Social Constructivism, Discourse and Realism*. London: Sage.

Farrell, C., Nice, K., Lewis, J. et al. (2006). 'Experiences of the Job Retention and Rehabilitation Pilot', Research Report. Leeds: Department for Work and Pensions.

Fassinger, R. E. (2005). 'Paradigms, Praxis Problems and Promise: Grounded Theory in Counseling Psychology Research', *Journal of Counseling Psychology*, 52: 156–66.

Ferner, A., Almond, P., and Colling, T. (2005). 'Institutional Theory and the Cross-National Transfer of Employment Policy: The Case of "Workforce Diversity" in US Multinationals', *Journal of International Business Studies*, 36: 304–21.

Fielding, A. (1992). 'Migration and Social Mobility: South East England as an Escalator Region', *Regional Studies*, 26: 1–15.

Fielding, Nigel. (2008) 'Analytic density, postmodernism, and applied multiple method research'. Advances in mixed methods research: 37–52.

Fiss, P. C. (2011). 'Building Better Causal Theories: A Fuzzy-Set Approach to Typologies in Organization Research', *Academy of Management Journal*, 54: 393–420.

Fleetwood, S. (2004). 'An Ontology for Organisation and Management Studies', in S. Fleetwood and S. Ackroyd (eds), *Critical Realist Applications in Organisation and Management Studies*. London: Routledge, 25–50.

—— (2005). 'Ontology in Organization and Management Studies: A Critical Realist Perspective', *Organization*, 12: 197–222.

—— and Ackroyd, S., eds (2004). *Critical Realist Applications in Organisation and Management Studies*. London: Routledge.

—— and Hesketh, A. (2006a). 'HRM-Performance Research: Under-Theorized and Lacking Explanatory Power', *International Journal of Human Resource Management*, 17: 1977–93.

—— ——(2006b). 'Prediction in Social Science: The Case of Research on the Human Resource Management-Organisational Performance Link', *Journal of Critical Realism*, 8: 228–50.

—— ——(2010). *Explaining the Performance of Human Resource Management*. Cambridge: Cambridge University Press.

Fleming, P. and Sturdy, A. (2010). 'Being Yourself in the Electronic Sweatshop: New Forms of Normative Control', *Human Relations*, 64: 2177–200.

Foucault, M. (1991). *Discipline and Punish: The Birth of the Prison*. Harmondsworth: Penguin.

—— (1999). *Abnormal: Lectures at the Collège de France 1974–1975*. New York: Picador.

Frank, T. (2007). *What's the Matter with Kansas?: How Conservatives won the Heart of America*. Macmillan.

Frankfort-Nachmias, C. and Nachmias, D. (2000). *Research Methods in the Social Sciences* (6th edn). New York: Wadsworth.

Friedman, V. and Rogers, T. (2009). 'There Is Nothing so Theoretical as Good Action Research', *Action Research*, 7: 31–47.

Fullbrook, E. (2009). *Ontology and Economics: Tony Lawson and his Critics*. London: Routledge.

Fung, H. C., Lim, Y. W., Mattke, S. et al. (2008). 'Systematic Review: The Evidence that Publishing Patient Care Performance Data Improves Quality of Care', *Annals of Internal Medicine*, 148: 111–23.

Gaskin, I. M. (2002). *Spiritual Midwifery*. Summertown, TN: Book Publishing Company.

Gatenby, M. (2008). 'Teamworking: History, Development and Function', PhD thesis (Cardiff University).

—— and Rees, C. (2011). 'The Restructuring of Public Sector Work: A Critical Realist Analysis', *29th International Labour Process Theory Conference*, Leeds, 5–7 April.

Geering, J. (2007). *Case Study Research: Principles and Practices*. Cambridge: Cambridge University Press.

Geertz, C. (1973). 'Thick Description: Toward an Interpretive Theory of Culture', in C. Geertz (ed.) *The Interpretation of Cultures: Selected Essays*. New York: Basic Books, 3–30.

George, A. L. and Bennett, A. (2005). *Case Studies and Theory Development in the Social Sciences*. Cambridge, MA: MIT Press.

Gergen, K. J. (1971). *The Concept of Self*. London: Holt, Rinehart and Winston.

—— (1985). 'The Social Constructionist Movement in Modern Psychology', *American Psychologist*, 40: 266–75.

Gherardi, S., Nicolini, D., and Odella, F. (1998). 'Toward a Social Understanding of How People Learn in Organisations: The Notion of Saturated Curriculum', *Management Learning*, 29: 273–97.

Giddens, A. (1984). *The Constitution of Society: Outline of the Theory of Structuration.* Cambridge: Polity.

—— (1991). *Modernity and Self-Identity: Self and Society in the Late Modern Age.* Cambridge: Polity.

Gilbert, N. and Troitzsch, K. G. (2005). *Simulation for the Social Scientist* (2nd edn). Maidenhead: Open University Press.

Gillon, A. (2011). 'Does OD Practice within the HR Profession in the UK Reflect the Academic Rhetoric?' *Leadership & Organization Development Journal*, 32: 150–69.

Glaser, B. G. and Strauss, A. L. (1967). *The Discovery of Grounded Theory: Strategies for Qualitative Research.* Chicago, IL: Aldine.

—— (1972). Relations in Public. Transaction Books.

Goffman, E. (1983). 'The Interaction Order', *American Sociological Review*, 48: 1–17.

Goldstein, H. (2010). *Multilevel Models* (4th edn). Chichester: Wiley.

Goldthorpe, J. (2000). *On Sociology: Numbers, Narratives and the Integration of Research and Theory.* Oxford: Oxford University Press.

Gómez-Estern, B. M., Amián, J. G., Sánchez Medina, J. A. et al. (2010). 'Literacy and the Formation of Cultural Identity', *Theory & Psychology*, 20: 231–50.

Gomm, R., Hammersley, M., and Foster, P. (2000). *Case Study Method.* London: Sage.

Gouldner, A. W. (1954). *Wildcat Strike: A Study of an Unofficial Strike.* London: Routledge.

Greckhamer, T., Misangyi, V. F., Elms, H. et al. (2008). 'Using Qualitative Comparative Analysis in Strategic Management Research: An Examination of Combinations of Industry, Corporate, and Business-Unit Effects', *Organizational Research Methods*, 11: 695–726.

Greenhalgh, J., Long, A. F., and Flynn, R. (2005). 'The Use of Patient-Reported Outcome Measures in Clinical Practice: Lacking an Impact or Lacking a Theory?' *Social Science and Medicine*, 60: 833–43.

—— and Peacock, R. (2005). 'Effectiveness and Efficiency of Search Methods in Systematic Reviews of Complex Evidence', *British Medical Journal*, 331: 1064–5.

Greer, I. and Hauptmeier, M. (2008). 'Political Entrepreneurs and Co-Managers: Labour Transnationalism at Four Multinational Auto Companies', *British Journal of Industrial Relations*, 46: 76–97.

Griffin, C. (2007). 'Being Dead and Being There: Research Interviews, Sharing Hand Cream and the Preference for Analysing "Naturally Occurring Data"', *Discourse Studies*, 9: 246–69.

Grugulis, I. (2006). *Skills, Training and Human Resource Development: A Critical Text.* Basingstoke: Palgrave Macmillan.

Guba, E. G. and Lincoln, Y. S. (1994). 'Competing Paradigms in Qualitative Research', in N. K. Denzin and Y. S. Lincoln (eds), *Handbook of Qualitative Research.* Thousand Oaks, CA: Sage, 105–17.

Guest, D. E. (2011). 'Human Resource Management and Performance: Still Searching for Some Answers', *Human Resource Management Journal*, 21: 3–13.

Gunaratnam, Y. (2003). *Researching 'Race' and Ethnicity: Methods, Knowledge and Power.* London: Sage.

Gustavsen, B. (2004). 'Making Knowledge Actionable: From Theoretical Centralism to Distributive Constructivism', *Concepts and Transformation*, 9: 147–80.

Hair, J. F., Anderson, R. E., Tatham, R. L. and Black, W. C. (1998). *Multivariate Data Analysis*, Upper Saddle River, NJ: Prentice-Hall, 5th edn.

Hall, P. (1984). *The Organization of American Culture, 1700–1900: Private Institutions, Elites and the Origins of American Nationality*. New York: New York University Press.

Hall, P. A. and Thelen, K. (2009). 'Institutional Change in Varieties of Capitalism', *Socio-Economic Review*, 7: 7–34.

Hall, S. (2011). 'The Neoliberal Revolution', *Soundings*, 48: 9–28.

Hammersley, M. (1992). *What's Wrong with Ethnography? Methodological Explorations*. London: Routledge.

—— (1995). *The Politics of Social Research*. London: Sage.

—— (2008). *Questioning Qualitative Inquiry: Critical Essays*. London: Sage.

—— (2009a). 'Challenging Relativism: The Problem of Assessment Criteria', *Qualitative Inquiry*, 15: 3–29.

—— (2009b). 'Why Critical Realism Fails to Justify Critical Social Research', *Methodological Innovations Online*, 4: 1–11.

—— and Atkinson, P. (2007 [1995]). *Ethnography: Principles in Practice* (3rd edn [2nd edn]). London: Routledge.

Haraszti, M. (1977). *A Worker in a Workers' State: Piece Rates in Hungary* (trans. M. Wright). Harmondsworth: Penguin.

Harré, R. (1975). *The Principles of Scientific Thinking*. Chicago, IL: University of Chicago Press.

—— (1984). *The Philosophies of Science* (new edition). Oxford: Oxford University Press.

—— (1990). 'Exploring the Human Umwelt', in R. Bhaskar (ed.) *Harré and His Critics: Essays in Honour of Rom Harré with His Commentary on Them*. Oxford: Blackwell, 297–362.

—— and Bhaskar, R. (2005). 'How to Change Reality: Story vs. Structure—A Debate between Rom Harré and Roy Bhaskar', in J. Lopez and G. Potter (eds), *After Postmodernism: An Introduction to Critical Realism*. London: Continuum International Publishing, 22–39.

—— and Madden, E. H. (1975). *Causal Powers*. Oxford: Basil Blackwell.

—— and Secord, P. F. (1972). *The Explanation of Social Behaviour*. Oxford: Basil Blackwell.

Harrison, D. and Easton, G. (2004). 'Temporally Embedded Case Comparison in Industrial Marketing Research', in S. Fleetwood and S. Ackroyd (eds), *Critical Realist Applications in Organisation and Management Studies*. London: Routledge, 194–210.

Harrison, R. and Leitch, C. (2000). 'Learning and Organization in the Knowledge-Based Information Economy: Initial Findings from a Participatory Action Research Case Study', *British Journal of Management*, 11: 103–19.

Heckman, J. J. (2000). 'Policies to Foster Human Capital', *Research in Economics*, 54: 3–56.

Hepburn, A. and Wiggins, S. (2007). 'Discursive Research: Themes and Debates', in A. Hepburn and S. Wiggins (eds), *Discursive Research in Practice: New Approaches to Psychology and Interaction*. Cambridge: Cambridge University Press, 1–28.

Herrigel, G. (2008). 'Roles and Rules: Ambiguity, Experimentation and New Forms of Stakeholderism in Germany', *Industrielle Beziehungen*, 15: 111–32.

Herriot, P. (1989). 'Selection as a Social Process', in M. Smith and I. Robertson (eds), *Advances in Selection and Assessment*. New York: John Wiley and Sons.

Hesketh, A. and Fleetwood, S. (2006). 'Beyond Measuring the Human Resource Management-Organizational Performance Link: Applying Critical Realist Meta-Theory', *Organization*, 13: 677–99.

Higgins, J. P. T. and Green, S., eds (2011). *Cochrane Handbook for Systematic Reviews of Interventions*. London: The Cochrane Collaboration.

Hill, L. A. (2003). *Becoming a Manager: How New Managers Master the Challenges of Leadership*. Cambridge, MA: Harvard Business School Press.

Hillage, J., Rick, J., Pilgrim, H. et al. (2008). *A Review of the Effectiveness and Cost Effectiveness of Interventions, Strategies, Programmes and Policies to Reduce the Number of Employees Who Move from Short-Term to Long-Term Sickness Absence and to Help Employees on Long-Term Sickness Absence Return to Work*. London: National Institute of Clinical Excellence.

Ho, K. (2009). *Liquidated: An Ethnography of Wall Street*. Durham: Duke University Press.

Hockey, J. (1986). *Squaddies: Portrait of a Subculture*. Exeter: University of Exeter Press.

Hodgkinson, G. and Starkey, K. (2012). 'Extending the Foundations and Reach of Design Science', *British Journal of Management*, 23: 605–10.

Hodson, R. (2004). 'A Meta-Analysis of Workplace Ethnographies: Race, Gender, and Employee Attitudes and Behaviors', *Journal of Contemporary Ethnography*, 33: 4–38.

Hogg, M. A. and Terry, D. J. (2000). 'Social Identity and Self-Categorization Processes in Organizational Contexts', *Academy of Management Review*, 25: 121–40.

Holmer-Nadesan, M. (1996). 'Organizational identity and space of action', *Organization Studies*, 17(1), 49–81.

Holstein, J. A. and Gubrium, J. F. (1995). *The Active Interview*. Thousand Oaks, CA: Sage.

—— (1997). 'Active Interviewing', in D. Silverman (ed.) *Qualitative Research: Theory, Method and Practice*. London: Sage, 113–29.

Hoover, K. D. (1997). 'Econometrics and Reality', UC Davis Working Paper no. 97–28. Available at SSRN: <http://papers.ssrn.com/sol3/papers.cfm?abstract_id=54984> accessed 10 October 2013.

—— (2002). 'Econometrics and Reality', in U. Mäki (ed.) *Fact and Fiction in Economics: Models, Realism, and Social Construction*. Cambridge: Cambridge University Press, 152–77.

Houston, S. (2001). 'Beyond Social Constructionism: Critical Realism and Social Work', *British Journal of Social Work*, 31: 845–61.

Huff, A. S. (1990). *Mapping Strategic Thought*. Chichester: John Wiley.

Hughes, J. and Sharrock, W. W. (2007). *Theory and Methods in Sociology*. London: Palgrave.

Hurrell, S. A. (2009). 'Soft Skills Deficits in Scotland: Their Patterns, Determinants and Employer Responses', PhD thesis (University of Strathclyde).

—— and Scholarios, D. (2011). 'Recruitment and Selection Practices, Person-Brand Fit and Soft Skills Gaps in Service Organizations: The Benefits of Institutionalized Informality', in M. J. Brannan, E. Parsons, and V. Priola (eds), *Branded Lives: The Production and Consumption of Identity at Work*, Cheltenham: Edward Elgar, 108–27.

—— ——and Thompson, P. (2013). 'More than a "Humpty Dumpty" Term: Strengthening the Conceptualization of Soft Skills', *Economic and Industrial Democracy*, 34: 161–82.

Husk, K. (2011). 'Ethnicity and Social Exclusion: Research and Policy Implications in a Cornish Case Study', *Social and Public Policy Review*, 5: 7–25.

Hutchby, J. and Wooffitt, R. (1998). *Conversation Analysis*. Cambridge: Polity.

Hycner, R. H. (1985). 'Some Guidelines for the Phenomenological Analysis of Interview Data', *Human Studies*, 8: 279–303.

Ibarra, H. (1999). 'Provisional Selves: Experimenting with Image and Identity in Professional Adaptation', *Administrative Science Quarterly*, 44: 764–92.

Ichniowski, C. and Shaw, K. (2009). 'Insider Econometrics: Empirical Studies of How Management Matters', *NBER Working Paper 15618*. Cambridge, MA: National Bureau of Economic Research.

Jackson, B. and Parry, K. (2001). *The Hero Manager: Learning from New Zealand's Top Chief Executives*. Auckland: Penguin Books.

Jackson, J. (1986). *Migration*. London: Longman.

Jacobi, O., Keller, B., and Müller-Jentsch, W. (1998). 'Germany: Facing New Challenges', in A. Ferner and R. Hyman (eds), *Changing Industrial Relations in Europe*. Oxford: Blackwell, 190–238.

Janesick, V. J. (1998). 'The Dance of Qualitative Research Design: Metaphor, Methodolatry, and Meaning', in N. K. Denzin and Y. S. Lincoln (eds), *Strategies of Qualitative Inquiry*. Thousand Oaks, CA: Sage, 33–55.

Janson, A. (2008). 'Extracting Leadership Knowledge from Formative Experiences', *Leadership*, 4: 73–94.

Jaros, S. (2010). 'The Core Theory: Critiques, Defences and Advances', in P. Thompson and C. Smith (eds), *Working Life: Renewing Labour Process Analysis*. Basingstoke: Palgrave Macmillan, 70–88.

Jefferson, G. (1985). 'An Exercise in the Transcription and Analysis of Language', in T. A. Van Dijk (ed.) *Handbook of Discourse Analysis: Discourse and Dialogue, iii*. London: Academic Press, 25–34.

Jenkins, M. and Johnson G. (2001). 'Entrepreneurial Intentions and Outcomes: A Comparative Causal Mapping Study', *Journal of Management Studies*, 34: 895–920.

Jenkins, R. (2004). *Social Identity*, 2nd edn. London: Routledge.

Jenkins, S., Delbridge, R., and Roberts, R. (2010). 'Emotional Management in a Mass Customised Call Centre: Examining Skill and Knowledgeability in Interactive Services Work', *Work, Employment and Society*, 24: 546–64.

Johnson, A. (1996). ' "It's Good to Talk": The Focus Group and the Sociological Imagination', *Sociological Review*, 44: 517–38.

Joseph, J. (1998). 'In defence of critical realism'. *Capital & Class*, 22(2), 73–106.

Jowell, R., Roberts, C., Fitzgerald, R. et al., eds (2007). *Measuring Attitudes Cross-Nationally: Lessons from the European Social Survey*. London: Sage.

Kaposi, D. (2011). 'The Crooked Timber of Identity: Integrating Discursive, Critical, and Psychosocial Analysis', *British Journal of Social Psychology*, doi: 10.1111/j.2044-8309.2011.02074.x.

Karlsson, J. C. (2011). 'People Can not only Open Closed Systems, They Can also Close Open Systems', *Journal of Critical Realism*, 10: 145–62.

Kazi, M. A. F. (2003). *Realist Evaluation in Practice: Health and Social Work*. London: Sage.

—— Blom, B., Morén, S., et al. (2002). 'Realist Evaluation for Practice in Sweden, Finland, and Britain', *Journal of Social Work Research and Evaluation*, 3: 171–86.

Kellogg, K., Orlikowski, W. J., and Yates, J.-A. (2006). 'Life in the Trading Zone: Structuring Coordination across Boundaries in Post-Bureaucratic Organizations', *Organization Science*, 17: 22–44.

Kelly, G. A. (1955). *The Psychology of Personal Constructs*. New York: Norton.

Kempster, S. J. (2006). 'Leadership Learning through Lived Experience', *Journal of Management and Organization*, 12: 4–22.

—— (2009). *How Managers Have Learnt to Lead: Exploring the Development of Leadership Practice*. Basingstoke: Palgrave Macmillan.

——and Cope, J. (2010). 'Learning to Lead in the Entrepreneurial Context', *International Journal of Entrepreneurial Behaviour and Research*, 16: 6–35.

—— and Parry, K. W. (2011). 'Grounded Theory and Leadership Research: A Critical Realist Perspective', *The Leadership Quarterly*, 22: 106–20.

Kersley, B., Alpin, C., Forth, J. et al. (2006). *Inside the Workplace: Findings from the 2004 Workplace Employment Relations Survey*. London: Routledge.

Kessler, I., Bach, S., and Heron, P. (2006). 'Understanding Assistant Roles in Social Care', *Work, Employment and Society*, 20: 667–85.

—— Heron, P. and Dopson, S. (2012). *The Modernization of the Nursing Workforce: Valuing the Healthcare Assistant*. Oxford: Oxford University Press.

Ketokivi, M. and Mantere, S. (2010). 'Two Strategies for Inductive Reasoning in Organizational Research', *Academy of Management Review*, 35: 315–33.

Kilduff, M., Mehra, A., and Dunn, M. B. (2011). 'From Blue Sky Research to Problem Solving: a Philosophy of Science Theory of New Knowledge Production', *Academy of Management Review*, 36: 297–317.

Kincaid, H. (1996). *Philosophical Foundations of the Social Sciences: Analyzing Controversies in Social Research*. Cambridge: Cambridge University Press.

Kirkpatrick, I., Ackroyd, S., and Walker, R. (2004). *The New Managerialism and Public Service Professions: Developments in Health, Social Services and Housing*. Basingstoke: Palgrave Macmillan.

Kloosterman, R. (2010). 'Matching Opportunities with Resources: A Framework for Analysing (Migrant) Entrepreneurship from a Mixed Embeddedness Perspective', *Entrepreneurship and Regional Development*, 22: 25–45.

Knijn, T. (1998). 'Participation Through Care? The Case of the Dutch Housewife', in J. Bussemaker and R. Voet (eds), *Gender, Participation and Citizenship in the Netherlands*. Aldershot: Ashgate, 65–79.

Kogut, B. and Ragin, C. C. (2006). 'Exploring Complexity when Diversity is Limited: Institutional Complementarity in Theories of Rule of Law and National Systems Revisited', *European Management Review*, 3: 44–59.

Kontos, P. and Poland, B. (2009). 'Mapping New Theoretical and Methodological Terrain for Knowledge Translation: Contributions from Critical Realism and the Arts', *Implementation Science*, 4: 1–10.

Korczynski, M. (2005). 'Skills in Service Work: An Overview', *Human Resource Management Journal*, 15(2): 3–14.

Kral, M. J., Ramírez García, J. I., Aber, M. S. et al. (2011). 'Culture and Community Psychology: Toward a Renewed and Reimagined Vision', *American Journal of Community Psychology*, 47: 46–57.

Kram, K. E. and Isabella, L. A. (1985). 'Mentoring Alternatives: The Role of Peer Relations in Career Development', *Academy of Management Journal*, 28: 110–32.

Kuhnert, K. W. and Russell, C. J. (1990). 'Using Constructive Developmental Theory and Biodata to Bridge the Gap between Personnel Selection and Leadership', *Journal of Management*, 16: 595–607.

Kunda, G. (1992). *Engineering Culture: Control and Commitment in a High-Tech Corporation*. Philadelphia, PA: Temple University Press.

Kundnani, A. (2000). 'Stumbling On: Race and Class in England', *Race and Class*, 41: 1–18.

Lafrance, M. N. (2009). *Women and Depression: Recovery and Resistance*. London: Routledge.

Lane, C. (1996). 'The Social Constitution of Supplier Relations in Britain and Germany: An Institutionalist Analysis', in R. Whitley and P. H. Kristensen (eds), *The Changing European Firm: Limits to Convergence*. London: Routledge, 271–304.

Lather, P. (2007). *Getting Lost: Feminist Efforts toward a Double(d) Science*. New York: State University of New York Press.

Lauber, V. and Schenner, E. (2011). 'The Struggle over Support Schemes for Renewable Electricity in the European Union: A Discursive-Institutionalist Analysis', *Environmental Politics*, 20: 508–27.

Lave, J. and Wenger, E. (1991). *Situated Learning: Legitimate Peripheral Participation*. Cambridge: Cambridge University Press.

Lawson, T. (1997). *Economics and Reality*. London: Routledge.

——(2003). *Reorienting Economics*. London: Routledge.

——(2009a). 'Applied Economics, Contrast Explanation and Asymmetric Information', *Cambridge Journal of Economics*, 33: 405–19.

——(2009b). 'Triangulation and Social Research: Reply to Downward and Mearman', in E. Fullbrook (ed.), *Ontology and Economics: Tony Lawson and his Critics*. London: Routledge, ch. 8.

Layder, D. (1998). *Sociological Practice: Linking Theory and Social Research*. London: Sage Publications.

Layman, L. (2009). 'Reticence in Oral History Interviews', *Oral History Review*, 36: 207–30.

Leary, M. R. and Kowalski, R. M. (1990). 'Impression Management: A Literature Review and Two-component Model'. *Psychological bulletin*, 107(1): 34.

Leca, B. and Naccache, P. (2006). 'A Critical Realist Approach to Institutional Entrepreneurship', *Organization*, 13: 627–51.

Levin-Rozalis, M. (2004). 'Searching for the Unknowable: A Process of Detection—Abductive Research Generated by Projective Techniques', *International Journal of Qualitative Methods*, 3: 1–18.

Lindqvist, S. (1978). *Gräv där du står. Hur man utforskar ett jobb (Dig Where You Stand: How to do Research on a Job)*. Stockholm: Bonniers.

——(1979). 'Dig Where You Stand', *Oral History*, 7 (2): 24–30.

Littler, C. (1990). 'The Labour Process Debate: A Theoretical Review' in D. Knights and H. Willmott (eds) *Labor Process Theory*, London: MacMillan.

Locke, R. M. and Thelen, K. (1995). 'Apples and Oranges Revisited: Contextualized Comparisons and the Study of Comparative Labor Politics', *Politics and Society*, 23: 337–67.

Lounsbury, M. (2001). 'Institutional Sources of Practice Variation: Staffing College and University Recycling Programs', *Administrative Science Quarterly*, 46: 29–56.

Lucas, R. E. and Diener, E. (2009). 'Personality and Subjective Well-Being', in E. Diener (ed.), *The Science of Well-Being*. Dordrecht: Springer.

Luong, P. J. (2002). *Institutional Change and Political Continuity in Post-Soviet Central Asia: Power, Perceptions, and Pacts*. New York: Cambridge University Press.

Lupton, T. (1963). *On the Shopfloor: Two Studies of Workshop Organization and Output*. Oxford: Pergamon.

Lynch, K. (2006). 'Neo-liberalism and Marketisation: The Implications for Higher Education', *European Educational Research Journal*, 5: 1–17.

Macdonald, S. and Hellgren, B. (2004). 'The Interview in International Business Research: Problems We Would Rather Not Talk About', in R. Marschan-Piekkari and C. Welch (eds), *Handbook of Qualitative Research Methods for International Business*. Cheltenham: Edward Elgar, 264–82.

Macfarlane, F., Greenhalgh, T., Humphrey, C. et al. (2011). 'A New Workforce in the Making? A Case Study of Strategic Human Resource Management in a Whole-System Change Effort in Healthcare', *Journal of Health Organization and Management*, 25: 55–72.

Mahoney, J. and Rueschemeyer, D. (2003). *Comparative Historical Analysis in the Social Sciences*. Cambridge: Cambridge University Press.

Malinowski, B. (1922). *Argonauts of the Western Pacific*. New York: Dutton.

Marchal, B., van Belle, S., van Olmen, J. et al. (2012). 'Is Realist Evaluation Keeping its Promise? A Review of Published Empirical Studies in the Field of Health Systems Research', *Evaluation*, 18: 192–212.

Marginson, P., Armstrong, P., Edwards, P. K. et al. (1995). 'Extending Beyond Borders: Multinational Companies and the International Management of Labour', *International Journal of Human Resource Management*, 6: 702–19.

—— Arrowsmith, J., and Gray, M. (2008). 'Undermining or Reframing Collective Bargaining? Variable Pay in Two Sectors', *Human Resource Management Journal*, 18: 327–46.

Marginson, P., Hall, M., Hoffman, A. et al. (2004). 'The Impact of European Works Councils on Management Decision-Making in UK and US-Based Multinationals: A Case Study Comparison', *British Journal of Industrial Relations*, 42: 209–33.

Marks, A. and Thompson, P. (2010). 'Beyond the Blank Slate: Identities and Interests at Work', in P. Thompson and C. Smith (eds) *Working Life: Renewing Labour Process Analysis*. London: Palgrave Press.

Markus, H. and Nurius, P. S. (1986). 'Possible Selves', *American Psychologist*, 41: 954–69.

Marsh, C. (1982). *The Survey Method*. London: Allen and Unwin.

—— (1988). *Exploring Data: An Introduction to Data Analysis for Social Scientists*. Cambridge: Polity Press.

Martin, E. (2004). 'Who's Kicking Whom? Employees' Orientation to Work', *International Journal of Contemporary Hospitality Management*, 16: 182–8.

Marx, K. (1852). 'The Eighteenth Brumaire of Louis Bonaparte', in D. McLellan (ed.) (1977), *Karl Marx: Selected Writings*. Oxford: Oxford University Press, 300–5.

—— (1969). *Theories of Surplus Value, Part 1*. Moscow: Progress Publishers.

—— (1988). *Capital, i*. London: Penguin.

Mauss, M. (1925). 'Essai sur le Don: Forme et Raison de l'Échange dans les Sociétés Archaïques', *l'Année Sociologique*, nouvelle série, I: 30–186.

Maxwell, J. A. (2012). *A Realist Approach for Qualitative Research*. London: Sage.

McCall, M. W., Lombardo, M. M., and Morrison, A. (1988). *The Lessons of Experience*. Lexington, MA: Lexington Books.

Michael, M. (1990). 'Intergroup Theory and Deconstruction', in I. Parker and J. Shotter (eds), *Deconstructing Social Psychology*. London: Routledge.

Miles, M. B. (1979). 'Qualitative Data as an Attractive Nuisance: The Problem of Analysis', *Administrative Science Quarterly*, 24: 590–601.

—— and Huberman, A. M. (1994). *Qualitative Data Analysis: An Expanded Source Book* (2nd edn). London: Sage.

Miles, R. E. and Snow, C. C. (1978). *Organizational Strategy, Structure, and Process*. New York: McGraw Hill.

Mill, J. S. (1967 [1843]). *A System of Logic Ratiocinative and Inductive: Being a Connected View of the Principles of Evidence and the Methods of Scientific Investigation*. Toronto: University of Toronto Press.

Miller, D. (1986). 'Configurations of Strategy and Structure: Towards a Synthesis', *Strategic Management Journal*, 7: 233–49.

Mills, C. W. (1959). *The Sociological Imagination*. New York: Oxford University Press.

Mingers, J. (2003). 'The Place of Statistical Modelling in Management Science: Critical Realism and Multimethodology', *Working Paper Series No. 45* (Canterbury Business School, Canterbury).

—— (2006). *Realising Systems Thinking: Knowledge and Action in Management Science*. New York: Springer.

Mitchell, C. (2004). 'Making Sense of Counterurbanisation', *Journal of Rural Studies*, 20: 15–34.

Modell, S. (2009). 'In Defence of Triangulation: A Critical Realist Approach to Mixed Methods Research in Management Accounting', *Management Accounting Research*, 20: 208–22.

Mole, K., Hart, M., Roper, S. et al. (2011). 'Broader or Deeper? Exploring the Most Effective Intervention Profile for Public Small Business Support', *Environment and Planning A*, 43: 87–105.

Montano, S. and Szmigin, I. (2005). 'Case Study Research: A Critical Realist Approach', in A. Brown and D. Remenyi (eds), *Proceedings of the 4th European Conference on Research Methods*. Reading: Academic Conferences.

Morais, R. (2011). 'Critical Realism and Case Studies in International Business Research', in R. Piekkari and C. Welch (eds), *Rethinking the Case Study in International Business and Management Research*. Cheltenham: Edward Elgar, 63–84.

Morgan, J. and Olsen, W. K. (2007). 'Defining Objectivity in Realist Terms: Objectivity as a Second-Order "Bridging" Concept', *Journal of Critical Realism*, 6: 250–66.

—— (2008). 'Defining Objectivity in Realist Terms: Bridging to Praxis', *Journal of Critical Realism*, 7: 107–32.

Morrison, E. W. and Robinson, S. L. (1997). 'When Employees Feel Betrayed: A Model of How Psychological Contract Violation Develops', *Academy of Management Review*, 22: 226–56.

Morrison, K. (2012). 'Searching for Causality in the Wrong Places', *International Journal of Social Research Methodology*, 15: 15–30.

Moth, R. (forthcoming). 'How Do Practitioners in Community Health Teams Conceptualise Mental Distress? The Pentimento Model as a Laminated System', ICCR working paper.

Moustakas, C. (1994). *Phenomenological Research Methods*. Thousand Oaks, CA: Sage.

Muller, M. (1999). 'Human Resource Management under Institutional Constraints: The Case of Germany', *British Journal of Management*, 10 (S1): 31–44.

Musson, G. and Duberley, J. (2007). 'Change Change or Be Exchanged: The Discourse of Participation and the Management of Identity', *Journal of Management Studies*, 44 (1): 164–85.

Mutch, A. (1980). 'The Mechanisation of the Harvest in South-West Lancashire 1850–1914', *Agricultural History Review*, 29: 125–132.

—— (2000). 'Managers, Information and Teams: A Tale of Two Companies', *The New Review of Information Behaviour Research*, 1: 151–66.

—— (2006a). *Strategic and Organizational Change: From Production to Retailing in UK Brewing 1950–1990*. London: Routledge.

—— (2006b). 'Public Houses as Multiple Retailing: Peter Walker & Son 1846–1914', *Business History*, 48: 1–19.

—— (2006c). 'Allied Breweries and the Development of the Area Manager, 1950–1984', *Enterprise and Society*, 7: 353–79.

—— (2007). 'Reflexivity and the Institutional Entrepreneur: A Historical Exploration', *Organization Studies*, 28: 1123–40.

—— (2009). 'Dominant Logic, Culture and Ideology', *Research in the Sociology of Organizations*, 27: 145–70.

Mutch, Alistair. (2010). 'Improving the public house in Britain 1920-1940: Sir Sydney Nevile and "social work"', *Business History*, 52(4): 517–35.

—— (2013). 'Data Mining the Archives: The Emergence of Separate Books of Account in the Church of Scotland 1608–1800', *Scottish Archives*.

Naess, P. (2004). 'Predictions, Regressions and Critical Realism', *Journal of Critical Realism*, 3: 133–64.

Neimark, M. (1992). *The Hidden Dimensions of Annual Reports: Sixty Years of Social Conflict at General Motors*. New York: Markus Wiener Publishers.

Nichols, T. and Beynon, H. (1977). *Living with Capitalism: Class Relations and the Modern Factory*. London: Routledge.

Nickson, D. and Warhurst, C. (2007). 'Opening Pandora's Box: Aesthetic Labour and Hospitality', in C. Lashley, P. Lynch, and A. Morrison (eds), *Hospitality: A Social Lens*. Amsterdam: Elsevier, 155–72.

——, —— Dutton, E. (2005). 'The Importance of Attitude and Appearance in the Service Encounter in Retail and Hospitality', *Managing Service Quality*, 15 (2): 195–208.

Nielsen, K., Taris, T. W., and Cox, T. (2010). 'The Future of Organizational Interventions: Addressing the Challenges of Today's Organizations', *Work and Stress*, 24: 219–33.

Nightingale, D. J. and Cromby, J. (2002). 'Social Constructionism as Ontology: Exposition and Example', *Theory & Psychology*, 12: 701–13.

Norrie, A. (2010). *Dialectic and Difference*. London: Routledge.

Norris, A. (1987). *Derrida*. Cambridge, MA: Harvard University Press.

Nussbaum, M. C. (2006). *Frontiers of Justice: Disability, Nationality, Species Membership.* Cambridge, MA: Harvard University Press.

O'Connell Davidson, J. and Layder, D. (1994). *Methods: Sex and Madness*. London: Routledge.

O'Dougherty, D. and Willmott, H. (2009). 'Avoiding Debate and the Immobilisation of Labour Process Theory: Strawmanning or Friedmanning?' in A. Pullen and C. Rhodes (eds), *Bits of Organisation*. Copenhagen: Copenhagen Business School Press, 38–55.

O'Mahoney, J. (2011). 'Embracing Essentialism: A Realist Critique of Resistance to Discursive Power', *Organization*, 19 (6): 723–41.

—— Heusinkveld, S. and Wright, S. (2013). 'Commodifying the Commodifiers: The Impact of Procurement on Management Knowledge', *Journal of Management Studies*, 50 (2): 204–35.

Olsen, W. (2004a). 'Methodological Triangulation and Realist Research: An Indian Exemplar', in B. Carter and C. New (eds), *Making Realism Work: Realist Social Theory and Empirical Research*. London: Routledge, 135–50.

—— (2004b). 'Triangulation in Social Research: Qualitative and Quantitative Methods can really Be Mixed', in M. Holborn and M. Haralambos (eds), *Developments in Sociology*. Ormskirk: Causeway Press, 103–21.

—— ed. (2010). *Realist Methodology* (4 vols.). London: Sage.

—— and Morgan, J. (2005). 'A Critical Epistemology of Analytical Statistics: Addressing the Sceptical Realist', *Journal for the Theory of Social Behaviour*, 35: 255–84.

—— and Wilson, J. (2005). 'A Critical Epistemology of Analytical Statistics: Addressing the Sceptical Realist', *Journal for the Theory of Social Behaviour*, 35: 255–84.

Outhwaite, W. (1987). *New Philosophies of Social Science: Realism, Hermeneutics, and Critical Theory*. New York: St. Martin's Press.

Pajunen, K. (2008). 'Institutions and Inflows of Foreign Direct Investment: A Fuzzy-Set Analysis', *Journal of International Business Studies*, 39: 652–69.

Papineau, D. (1993). *Philosophical Naturalism*. Oxford: Blackwell.

Park, R. and Burgess, E. (1921). *Introduction to the Science of Sociology*. Chicago, IL: University of Chicago Press.

Parker, I. (1992). *Discourse Dynamics: Critical Analysis for Social and Individual Psychology*. London: Routledge.

—— (2002). *Critical Discursive Psychology*. London: Palgrave.

Parry, K. W. (1998). 'Grounded Theory and Social Process: A New Direction for Leadership Research', *The Leadership Quarterly*, 9: 85–105.

Patterson, M., Rick, J., Wood, S. et al. (2010). 'Systematic Review of the Links between Human Resource Management Practices and Performance', *Health Technology Assessment*, 14 (51): 1–334.

Pawson, R. (1989). *A Measure for Measures: A Manifesto for Empirical Sociology*. London: Routledge.

—— (1996). 'Theorizing the Interview', *The British Journal of Sociology*, 47: 295–314.

—— (2000). 'Middle Range Realism', *European Journal of Sociology*, 41: 283–325.

—— (2002a). 'Does Megan's Law Work? A Theory-Driven Systematic Review', Working Paper 8. Queen Mary University of London: ESRC UK Centre for Evidence Based Policy and Practice.

—— (2002b). 'Evidence and Policy and Naming and Shaming', *Policy Studies*, 23: 211–30.

—— (2002c). 'Evidence-Based Policy: The Promise of a "Realist Synthesis"', *Evaluation*, 8: 340–58.

—— (2003). 'Nothing as Practical as a Good Theory', *Evaluation*, 9: 471–90.

—— (2004a). 'Evidence Based Policy: A Realist Perspective', in B. Carter and C. New (eds), *Making Realism Work: Realist Social Theory and Empirical Research*. London: Routledge, 26–49.

—— (2004b). 'Mentoring Relationships: An Explanatory Review', ESRC UK Centre for Evidence Based Policy and Practice Working Papers. Leeds: ESRC UK Centre for Evidence Based Policy and Practice.

—— (2006a). 'Digging for Nuggets: How Bad Research Can Yield Good Evidence', *International Journal of Social Research Methodology*, 9: 127–42.

—— (2006b). *Evidence-based Policy: A Realist Perspective*. London: Sage.

—— (2010). 'Middle Range Theory and Program Theory Evaluation: From Provenance to Practice', in J. Vaessen and L. Leeuw (eds), *Mind the Gap: Perspectives on Policy Evaluation and the Social Sciences*. New Brunswick: Transaction Publishers.

—— (2013). *The Science of Evaluation*. London: Sage.

—— and Bellamy, R. (2006). 'Realist Synthesis: An Explanatory Focus for Systematic Review', in J. Popay (ed.), *Moving Beyond Effectiveness in Evidence Synthesis: Methodological Issues in the Synthesis of Diverse Sources of Evidence*. London: National Institute for Clinical Excellence.

—— Greenhalgh, T., Harvey, G. et al. (2005). 'Realist Review—A New Method of Systematic Review Designed for Complex Policy Interventions', *Journal of Health Services Research and Policy*, 10 (Suppl.1) :21–34.

—— and Manzano-Santaella, A. (2012). 'A Realist Diagnostic Workshop', *Evaluation*, 18: 176–91.

—— and Tilley, N. (1997). *Realistic Evaluation*. London: Sage.

—— Wong, G. and Owen, L. (2011). 'Known Knowns, Known Unknowns, Unknown Unknowns: The Predicament of Evidence-Based Policy', *American Journal of Evaluation*, 32: 518–46.

Payne, G. and Williams, M. (2005). 'Generalisation in Qualitative Research', *Sociology*, 39: 295–314.

Pearce, F. and Woodiwiss, T. (2001). 'Reading Foucault as a Realist', in J. López and G. Potter (eds), *After Postmodernism: An Introduction to Critical Realism*. London: Athlone Press, 51–62.

Peirce, C. S. (1955). 'Abduction and Induction', in J. Buchler (ed.) *Philosophical Writings of Peirce*. New York: Dover Publications, 150–56.

Pettigrew, A. (1997). 'What is Processual Analysis?' *Scandinavian Journal of Management*, 13: 337–48.

Piekkari, R., Welch, C., and Paavilainen, E. (2009). 'The Case Study as Disciplinary Convention: Evidence from International Business Journals', *Organizational Research Methods*, 12: 567–89.

Platt, L., Simpson, L., and Akinwale, B. (2005). 'Stability and Change in Ethnic Groups in England and Wales', *Population Trends*, 125: 31–46.

Polanyi, M. (1958). *Personal Knowledge: Towards a Post-Critical Philosophy*. London: Routledge and Kegan Paul.

Pollert, A. (1981). *Girls, Wives and Factory Lives*. London: Macmillan.

Pollock, N. and Williams, R. (2009). *Software and Organisations: The Biography of the Enterprise-Wide System or How SAP Conquered the World*. London: Routledge.

Popper, K. R. (1957). 'The Propensity Interpretation of the Calculus of Probability, and the Quantum Theory', in S. Körner (ed.) *Observation and Interpretation*. London: Butterworth Scientific.

—— (1959). 'The Propensity Interpretation of Probability', *British Journal for the Philosophy of Science*, 10: 25–42.

—— (1979 [1972]). *Objective Knowledge: An Evolutionary Approach* (2nd edn). Oxford: Oxford University Press.

—— (1995). *A World of Propensities*. Bristol: Thoemmes Continuum.

Porpora, D. V. (1998). 'Four Concepts of Social Structure', in M. Archer, R. Bhaskar, A. Collier, et al. (eds), *Critical Realism: Essential Readings*. London: Routledge, 339–55.

Porter, S. (1993). 'Critical Realist Ethnography: The Case of Racism and Professionalism in a Medical Setting', *Sociology*, 27: 591–609.

—— (2000). 'Critical Realist Ethnography', in S. Ackroyd and S. Fleetwood (eds), *Realist Perspectives on Management and Organisations*. London: Routledge.

—— (2002). 'Critical Realist Ethnography', in T. May (ed.), *Qualitative Research in Action*. London: Sage, 53–72.

—— and Shortall, S. (2009). 'Stakeholders and Perspectivism in Qualitative Policy Evaluation: A Realist Reflection', *Public Administration*, 87: 259–73.

Potter, J. and Edwards, D. (2001). 'Discursive Social Psychology', in W. P. Robinson and H. Giles (eds), *The New Handbook of Language and Social Psychology*. Chichester: Wiley, 103–18.

—— and Hepburn, A. (2005). 'Qualitative Interviews in Psychology: Problems and Possibilities', *Qualitative Research in Psychology*, 2: 38–55.

—— and Wetherell, M. (1987). *Discourse and Social Psychology: Beyond Attitudes and Behaviour*. London: Sage.

Prahalad, C. K. (1975). 'The Strategic Process in a Multinational Corporation', PhD dissertation (Harvard University).

Price, L. (forthcoming). 'Reflections on Interdisciplinarity and Violence against Women', ICCR working paper.

Pujol, J. and Montenegro, M. (1999). 'Discourse or Materiality? Impure Alternatives for Recurrent Debate', in D. J. Nightingale and J. Cromby (eds), *Social Constructionist Psychology: A Critical Analysis of Theory and Practice*. Buckingham: Open University Press, 83–96.

Purdon, S., Stratford, N., Taylor, R. et al. (2006). *Impacts of the Job Retention and Rehabilitation Pilot*. Leeds: Department of Work and Pensions.

Radley, A. (1995). 'The Elusory Body and Social Constructionist Theory', *Body & Society*, 1(2): 3–23.

Ragin, C. C. (1987). *The Comparative Method: Moving Beyond Qualitative and Quantitative Strategies*. Berkeley, CA: University of California Press.

—— (1994). *Constructing Social Research: The Unity and Diversity of Method*. Thousand Oaks, CA: Pine Forge Press.

Ram, M. and Smallbone, D. (2002). 'Ethnic Minority Business Support in the Era of the Small Business Service', *Environment and Planning C*, 20: 235–49.

Ram, M., Theodorakopoulos, N., and Jones, T. (2008). 'Forms of Capital, Mixed Embeddedness and Somali Enterprise', *Work, Employment and Society*, 22: 427–46.

Rambo, E. and Chan, E. (1990). 'Review: Text, Structure and Action in Cultural Sociology: A Commentary on "Positive Objectivity" in Wuthnow and Archer', *Theory and Society*, 19: 635–48.

Randall, V. (2000). *The Politics of Child Daycare in Britain*. Oxford: Oxford University Press.

Rao, H. (1998). 'Caveat Emptor: The Construction of Nonprofit Consumer Watchdog Organizations', *American Journal of Sociology*, 103: 912–61.

Rappert, B. (1999). 'The Uses of Relevance: Thoughts of a Reflexive Sociology', *Sociology*, 33: 705–23.

Ratcliffe, P. (2001). 'Sociology, the State and Social Change: Theoretical Considerations', in P. Ratcliffe (ed.) *The Politics of Social Science Research*. Basingstoke: Palgrave Macmillan, 3–17.

Reed, M. (1985). *Redirections in Organizational Analysis*. London: Tavistock.

——(2000). 'The Limits of Discourse Analysis in Organization Analysis', *Organization*, 7: 524–30.

—— (2005). 'Reflections on the "Realist Turn" in Organization and Management Studies', *Journal of Management Studies*, 42: 1621–44.

——(2008). 'Critical Realism: Philosophy, Method, or Philosophy in Search of a Method', in D. Buchanan and A. Bryman (eds), *The SAGE Handbook of Organizational Research Methods*. London: Sage, 430–48.

Rees, C. (2009). 'Theorising National Institutions and MNE Actors: What Scope for Critical Realism?' *International Industrial Relations Association (IIRA) 15th World Congress*, Sydney, 24–27 August.

—— (2012). 'Agency and Institutions in MNC Research: The Contribution of Critical Realism', *28th European Group for Organizational Studies (EGOS) Colloquium*, Helsinki, 5–7 July.

Richards, J. and Marks, A. (2007). 'Biting the Hand that Feeds: Social Identity and Resistance in Restaurant Teams', *International Journal of Business Science and Applied Management*, 2 (2).

Rihoux, B. (2003). 'Bridging the Gap between the Qualitative and Quantitative Worlds? A Retrospective and Prospective View on Qualitative Comparative Analysis', *Field Methods*, 15: 351–65.

—— and Lobe, B. (2009). 'The Case for Qualitative Comparative Analysis (QCA): Adding Leverage for Thick Cross-Case Comparison', in D. Byrne and C. C. Ragin (eds), *The SAGE Handbook of Case-Based Methods*. London: Sage, 222–42.

—— Ragin, C. C., Yamasaki, S. et al. (2009). 'Conclusions: The Way(s) Ahead', in B. Rihoux and C. C. Ragin (eds), *Configurational Comparative Methods: Qualitative Comparative Analysis (QCA) and Related Techniques*. Thousand Oaks, CA: Sage, 167–77.

Riley, S. C. E. (2002). 'Constructions of Equality and Discrimination in Professional Men's Talk', *British Journal of Social Psychology*, 41: 443–61.

——Thompson, J., and Griffin, C. (2010). 'Turn On, Tune In, But Don't Drop Out: The Impact of Neo-Liberalism on Magic Mushroom Users' (In)ability to Imagine Collectivist Social Worlds', *International Journal of Drug Policy*, 21: 445–51.

Roberts, J. (2001). 'Dialogue, Positionality and the Legal Framing of Ethnographic Research', *Sociological Research Online*, 5. Available at: <http://www.socresonline.org.uk/5/4/roberts.html> accessed 8 August 2013.

—— (2005). 'The Power of the "Imaginary" in Disciplinary Processes', *Organization*, 12: 619–42.

Roberts, J. M. and Sanders, T. (2005). 'Before, During and After: Realism, Reflexivity and Ethnography', *The Sociological Review*, 53: 294–313.

Rogers, T. (2004). 'The Doing of a Depth-Investigation: Implications for the Emancipatory Aims of Critical Naturalism', *Journal of Critical Realism*, 3: 238–69.

Rolfsen, M. and Knutstad, G. (2007). 'Transforming Management Fashions into Praxis: Action Research Project in AutoParts', *Action Research*, 5: 341–57.

Ron, A. (2002). 'Regression Analysis and the Philosophy of Social Science: A Critical Realist View', *Journal of Critical Realism*, 1: 119–42.

Rousseau, D. M. (1995). *Psychological Contracts in Organizations: Understanding Written and Unwritten Agreements*. Thousand Oaks, CA: Sage.

Roy, D. (1959). ' "Banana Time": Job Satisfaction and Informal Interaction', *Human Organization*, 18: 158–68.

Ryant, C. (1988). 'Oral History and Business History', *Journal of American History*, 75: 560–66.

Sackett, D. L., Rosenberg, W. M. C., Gray, J. A. M. et al. (1996). 'Evidence-Based Practice: What It Is and What It Isn't', *British Medical Journal*, 312: 71–2.

Saka-Helmhout, A. (2011). 'Comparative Historical Analysis in International Management Research', in R. Piekkari and C. Welch (eds), *Rethinking the Case Study in International Business and Management Research*. Cheltenham: Edward Elgar, 383–407.

Sandelowski, M., Voils, C. I., Barroso, J. et al. (2008). "Distorted into Clarity": A Methodological Case Study Illustrating the Paradox of Systematic Review', *Research in Nursing and Health*, 31: 454–65.

Sayer, A. (1992). *Method in Social Science: A Realist Approach*, 2nd edn. London:Routledge.

——(2000). *Realism and Social Science*. London: Sage.

——(2005). 'Class, Moral Worth and Recognition'. *Sociology*, 39(5): 947–63.

——(2011). *Why Things Matter to People*. Cambridge: Cambridge University Press.

Schneider, M. R., Schulze-Bentrop, C., and Paunescu, M. (2010). 'Mapping the Institutional Capital of High-Tech Firms: A Fuzzy-Set Analysis of Capitalist Variety and Export Performance', *Journal of International Business Studies*, 41: 246–66.

Schön, D. A., and Rein, M. (1994). *Frame Reflection: Toward the Resolution of Intractable Policy Controversies*. New York: Basic Books.

Schutz, A. (1973). *Structures of the Life-World*. Evanston: Northwestern University Press.

Scott, W. (2008). *Institutions and Organizations: Ideas and Interests*. London: Sage.

Searle, J. (1995). *The Construction of Social Reality*. New York: Free Press.

Selznick, P. (1949). *TVA and the Grass Roots: A Study in the Sociology of Formal Organization*. Berkeley: University of California Press.

Sepulveda, L., Syrett, S., and Lyon, F. (2011). 'Population Superdiversity and New Migrant Enterprise: the Case of London', *Entrepreneurship and Regional Development*, 23: 469–97.

Sewell, W. (2005). *Logics of History: Social Theory and Social Transformation*. Chicago, IL: University of Chicago Press.

Sharpe, D. (2004). 'The Relevance of Ethnography to International Business Research', in R. Marschan-Piekkari and C. Welch (eds), *Handbook of Qualitative Research Methods for International Business*. Cheltenham: Edward Elgar, 306–23.

—— (2005). 'Contributions of Critical Realist Ethnography in Researching the Multinational Organisation', *4th International Critical Management Studies (CMS) Conference*, Cambridge, 4–6 July.

Shepperd, S., Lewin, S., Strauss, S. et al. (2009). 'Can We Systematically Review Studies that Evaluate Complex Interventions?', *PLoS Medicine*, 6 (8): e1000086.

Siebern-Thomas, F. (2005). 'Job Quality in European Labour Markets', in S. Bazen, C. Lucifora, and W. Salverda (eds), *Job Quality and Employer Behaviour*. Basingstoke: Palgrave MacMillan.

Siegel, J. I. and Larson, B. Z. (2009). 'Labor Market Institutions and Global Strategic Adaptation: Evidence from Lincoln Electric', *Management Science*, 55: 1527–46.

Siggelkow, N. (2007). 'Persuasion with Case Studies', *Academy of Management Journal*, 50: 20–4.

Silverman, D. (2001 [1993]). *Interpreting Qualitative Data: Methods for Analyzing Talk, Text and Interaction*. London: Sage.

Sims-Schouten, W. (2000). 'Child Care Services and Parents' Attitudes in England, Finland and Greece', in A. Pfenning and T. Bahle (eds), *Families and Family Policies in Europe: Comparative Perspectives*. Frankfurt/New York: Peter Lang, 270–86.

——Riley, S. and Willig, C. (2007). 'Critical Realism in Discourse Analysis: A Presentation of a Systematic Method of Analysis Using Women's Talk of Motherhood, Childcare and Female Employment as an Example', *Theory & Psychology*, 17: 101–24.

Skocpol, T. and Somers, M. (1980). 'The Uses of Comparative History in Macrosocial Inquiry', *Comparative Studies in Society and History*, 22: 174–97.

Skvoretz, J. (1998). 'Theoretical Models: Sociology's Missing Links', in A. Sica (ed.) *What Is Social Theory: The Philosophical Debates*. Malden, MA: Blackwell, 253–70.

Smets, M., Morris, T., and Greenwood, R. (2012). 'From Practice to Field: A Multilevel Model of Practice-Driven Institutional Change', *Academy of Management Journal*, 55: 877–904.

Smith, Chris (2005). 'Beyond Convergence and Divergence: Explaining Variations in Organizational Practices and Forms', in S. Ackroyd, R. Batt, P. Tolbert et al. (eds), *The Oxford Handbook of Work and Organization*. Oxford: Oxford University Press, 620–35.

——Child, J. and Rowlinson, M. (1990). *Reshaping Work: The Cadbury Experience*. Cambridge: Cambridge University Press.

—— and Meiksins, P. (1995). 'System, Society and Dominance Effects in Cross-National Organisational Analysis', *Work, Employment and Society*, 9: 241–67.

Smith, Christian.(2010). *What is a Person?* Chicago, IL: University of Chicago Press.

Snell, K. D. M. (2006). *Parish and Belonging: Community, Identity, and Welfare in England and Wales, 1700–1950*. Cambridge: Cambridge University Press.

Speer, S. A. and Potter, J. (2000). 'The Management of Heterosexist Talk: Conversational Resources and Prejudiced Claims', *Discourse & Society*, 11: 543–72.

Spradley, J. P. (1979). *The Ethnographic Interview*. New York: Holt, Rinehart and Winston.

—— (1980). *Participant Observation*. New York: Holt, Rinehart and Winston.

Stake, R. (2005). 'Qualitative Case Studies', in N. Denzin and Y. Lincoln (eds), *Sage Handbook of Qualitative Research* (3rd edn). London: Sage, 443–66.

—— (1992). *Method in Social Science: A Realist Approach* (2nd edn). London: Routledge.

—— (2000). *Realism and Social Science*. London: Sage.

—— (2011). *Why Things Matter to People*. Cambridge: Cambridge University Press.

Steinmetz, G. (1998). 'Critical Realism and Historical Sociology', *Comparative Studies in Society and History*, 40: 170–86.

Stratford, N., Taylor, R., Legard, R. et al. (2005). *The Job Retention and Rehabilitation Pilot: Reflections on Running a Randomised Controlled Trial*. Leeds: Department of Work and Pensions.

Strauss, A. and Corbin, J. (1998). *Basics of Qualitative Research: Techniques and Procedures for Developing Grounded Theory* (2nd edn). Thousand Oaks, CA: Sage.

Streeck, W. and Thelen, K., eds (2005). *Beyond Continuity: Explorations in the Dynamics of Advanced Political Economies*. Oxford: Oxford University Press.

Swanborn, P. (2010). *Case Study Research: What, Why and How?* London: Sage.

Syed, J., Mingers, J., and Murray, P. A. (2010). 'Beyond Rigour and Relevance: A Critical Realist Approach to Business Education', *Management Learning*, 41: 71–85.

Sylva, K., Melhuish, E., Sammons, P. et al. (2010). *Early Childhood Matters: Evidence from the Effective Pre-School and Primary Education Project*. London and New York: Routledge.

Tajfel, H. (1972). 'La catégorization sociale', in S. Moscovici (ed.), *Introduction à la psychologie sociale*, i. Paris: Larousse.

—— and Turner, J. C. (1986). 'The Social Identity Theory of Intergroup Behaviour', in S. Worchel and W. G. Austin (eds.), *Psychology of Intergroup Relations*, 2nd edn. Chicago: Nelson-Hall, 7–24.

Tajfel, H., Billig, M. G., Bundy, R. P., and Flament, C. (1971). 'Social categorization and intergroup behaviour', *European Journal of Social Psychology*, 1(2): 149–78.

Tashakkori, A. and Teddlie, C. (1998). *Mixed Methodology: Combining Qualitative and Quantitative Approaches*. Thousand Oaks, CA: Sage.

Tavecchio, L. W. C. (2002). *Van Opvang naar Opvoeding (From Child Care to Child-Rearing)*. Amsterdam: Vrije Universiteit, Faculteit der Maatschappij en Gedragswetenschappen.

Taylor, C. (1982). 'Rationality', in M. Hollis and S. Lukes (eds), *Rationality and Relativism*. Oxford: Blackwell, 87–105.

Taylor, P. and Bain, P. (2003). ' "Subterranean Worksick Blues": Humour as Subversion in Two Call Centres', *Organization Studies*, 24: 1487–509.

—— —— (2004). 'Humour and Subversion in Two Call Centres', in S. Fleetwood and S. Ackroyd (eds), *Critical Realist Applications in Organisation and Management Studies*. London: Routledge, 250–71.

—— —— (2005). ' "India Calling to the Far Away Towns": The Call Centre Labour Process and Globalization', *Work, Employment and Society*, 19: 261–82.

Teddlie, C. B. and Tashakkori, A. (2009). *Foundations of Mixed Methods Research: Integrating Quantitative and Qualitative Approaches in the Social and Behavioral Sciences*. London: Sage.

Ten Have, P. (1999). *Doing Conversation Analysis: A Practical Guide*. London: Sage.

Thompson, E. P. (1968). *The Making of the English Working Class*. Harmondsworth: Penguin.

Thompson, J. D. (2003 [1967]). *Organizations in Action: Social Science Bases of Administrative Theory*. New Jersey: Transaction Publishers [New York: McGraw-Hill].

Thompson, Paul [b. 1951]. (1990). 'Crawling from the Wreckage: The Labour Process and the Politics of Production', in D. Knights and H. Willmott (eds), *Labour Process Theory*. London: Macmillan, 95–124.

—— (2003a). 'Disconnected Capitalism: Or Why Employers Can't Keep their Side of the Bargain', *Work, Employment and Society*, 17: 359–78.

—— and Smith, C. (2010a). 'Debating Labour Process Theory and the Sociology of Work', in P. Thompson and C. Smith (eds), *Working Life: Renewing Labour Process Analysis*. Basingstoke: Palgrave Macmillan.

—— and Smith, C. (2010b). *Working Life: Renewing Labour Process Analysis*. Basingstoke: Palgrave Macmillan.

—— and Vincent, S. (2010). 'Beyond the Boundary: Labour Process Theory and Critical Realism', in P. Thompson and C. Smith (eds), *Working Life: Renewing Labour Process Analysis*. London: Palgrave.

Thompson, Paul [b. 1935]. (2003b). *Voice of the Past: Oral History*. Oxford: Oxford University Press.

Torgerson, C. J. and Elbourne, D. (2002). 'A Systematic Review and Meta-Analysis of the Effectiveness of Information and Communication Technology (ICT) on the Teaching of Spelling', *Journal of Research in Reading*, 25: 129–43.

Turner, John C. and Penelope J. Oakes. (1986). 'The Significance of the Social Identity Concept for Social Psychology with Reference to Individualism, Interactionism and Social Influence', *British Journal of Social Psychology*, 25.3 (1986): 237–52.

UK Parliament (1898). *Royal Commission on the Licensing Laws: Third Volume of Evidence*. London: UK Parliament.

Van de Ven, A. (2007). *Engaged Scholarship*. Oxford: Oxford University Press.

Van Maanen, J. (2011). 'Ethnography as Work: Some Rules of Engagement', *Journal of Management Studies*, 48: 218–34.

Vertovec, S. (2007). 'Super-Diversity and its Implications', *Ethnic and Racial Studies*, 30: 1024–54.

Veyne, P. (1984). *Writing History: Essay on Epistemology*. Manchester: Manchester University Press.

Vincent, S. (2005). 'Really Dealing: A Critical Perspective on Inter-Organisational Exchange Networks', *Work, Employment and Society*, 19: 47–65.

—— (2008). 'A Transmutation Theory of Inter-Organizational Exchange Relations and Networks: Applying Critical Realism to Analysis of Collective Agency', *Human Relations*, 61: 875–99.

Von Mises, R. (1951). *Probability, Statistics and Truth* (2nd edn). London: George Allen and Unwin.

Walker, Peter & Son (1896). *Walker's Warrington Ales*. Warrington: Peter Walker & Son.

Walkerdine, V., Lucey, H., and Melody, J. (2001). *Growing Up Girl: Psychosocial Explorations of Gender and Class*. London: Palgrave.

Walton, J. R. (1973). 'A Study in the Diffusion of Agricultural Machinery in the Nineteenth Century', *University of Oxford School of Geography Research Paper*, 5.

Watson, T. J. (2001). *In Search of Management: Culture, Chaos and Control in Managerial Work*. London: Thomson.

—— (2011). 'Ethnography, Reality, and Truth: The Vital Need for Studies of "How Things Work" in Organizations and Management', *Journal of Management Studies*, 48: 202–17.

—— (2012). 'Making Organisational Ethnography', *Journal of Organizational Ethnography*, 1: 15–22.

Webb, J. (2004). 'Organizations, Self-Identities and the New Economy', *Sociology* 38: 719–38.

Welsh, B. and Farrington, D. P. (2002). 'Crime Prevention Effects of Closed Circuit Television: A Systematic Review', *Home Office Research Studies*. London: Home Office.

Wenger, E. (1998). *Communities of Practice: Learning, Meaning, and Identity*. Cambridge: Cambridge University Press.

Wengraf, T. (2001). *Qualitative Research Interviewing*. London: Sage.

Wetherell, M. (1998). 'Positioning and Interpretative Repertoires: Conversation Analysis and Poststructuralism in Dialogue', *Discourse & Society*, 10: 387–412.

—— (1999). 'Negotiating Hegemonic Masculinity: Imaginary Positions and Psycho-Discursive Practices', *Feminism & Psychology*, 8: 335–56.

—— and Potter, J. (1992). *Mapping the Language of Racism: Discourse and the Legitimation of Exploitation*. Columbia: Columbia University Press.

Whitbread. (1955). *Annual Report and Accounts*, London: Whitbread Ltd.

Whitley, R. (1999). *Divergent Capitalisms: The Social Structuring and Change of Business Systems*. Oxford: Oxford University Press.

—— (2007). *Business Systems and Organizational Capabilities. The Institutional Structuring of Competitive Competences*. Oxford: Oxford University Press.

Whyte, W. F. (1948). *Human Relations in the Restaurant Industry*. New York: McGraw Hill.

—— ed. (1991). *Participatory Action Research*. Newbury Park, CA: Sage.

Wickham, C. (2011). 'The Problems of Comparison', *Historical Materialism*, 19: 221–31.

Wiggins, S. and Riley, S. (2010). 'QM1: Discourse Analysis', in M. Forrester (ed.), *Doing Qualitative Research in Psychology: A Practical Guide*. London: Sage, 135–53.

Wilkins, M. (1974). 'The Role of Private Business in the International Diffusion of Technology', *The Journal of Economic History*, 34: 166–88.

Wilkinson, I. and Young, L. (2004). 'Improvisation and Adaptation in International Business Research Interviews', in R. Marschan-Piekkari and C. Welch (eds), *Handbook of Qualitative Research Methods for International Business*. Cheltenham: Edward Elgar, 207–23.

Williams, G. (2001). 'Theorising Disability', in G. L. Albrecht, K. D. Seelman, and M. Bury (eds), *Handbook of Disability Studies*. London: Sage, 123–44.

Williams, M. (1999). 'Single Case Probabilities and the Social World: The Application of Popper's Propensity Interpretation', *Journal for the Theory of Social Behaviour*, 29: 187–201.

—— (2000a). 'Interpretivism and Generalisation', *Sociology*, 34: 209–44.

—— (2000b). 'Migration and Social Change in Cornwall 1971–1991', in R. Creeser and S. Gleave (eds), *Migration within England and Wales using the ONS Longitudinal Study*. London: The Stationery Office.

—— (2010). Can We Measure Homelessness? A Critical Evaluation of Capture-Recapture', *Methodological Innovations Online*, 5 (2): 49–59.

—— and Dyer, W. (2009). 'Single Case Probabilities', in D Byrne and C. Ragin (eds), *The SAGE Handbook of Case-Based Methods*. London: Sage, 84–100.

—— —— Harrison, E. (1995). 'Movers and Stayers: A comparison of migratory and non migratory groups in Cornwall 1971-91', *Cornish Studies*, 2nd Series, Vol. 3: 176–94.

—— and Husk, K. (2012). 'Can We, Should We, Measure Ethnicity?' *International Journal of Social Research Methodology*, doi:10.1080/13645579.2012.682794.

Willig, C. (1998). 'Constructions of Sexual Activity and Their Implications for Sexual Practice: Lessons for Sex Education', *Journal of Health Psychology*, 3: 383–92.

—— (1999). 'Beyond Appearances: A Critical Realist Approach to Social Constructionist Work', in D. J. Nightingale and J. Cromby (eds), *Social Constructionist Psychology: A Critical Analysis of Theory and Practice*. Buckingham: Open University Press, 37–52.

Willis, P. (1977). *Learning to Labour*. Westmead: Saxon House.

—— and Trondman, M. (2000). 'Manifesto for Ethnography', *Ethnography*, 1: 5–16.

Willmott, H. (1993). 'Strength is Ignorance, Slavery is Freedom: Managing Culture in Modern Organizations', *Journal of Management Studies*, 30: 515–52.

—— (2003). 'Commercialising Higher Education in the UK: The State, Industry and Peer Review', *Studies in Higher Education*, 28: 129–41.

—— (2012). 'Reframing Relevance as "Social Usefulness"', *British Journal of Management*, 23: 598–604.

Willott, S. and Griffin, C. (1997). '"Wham Bam, Am I a Man?" Unemployed Men Talk About Masculinities', *Feminism & Psychology*, 7: 107–28.

Winch, P. (1958). *The Idea of a Social Science*. London: Routledge and Kegan Paul.

Windschuttle, Keith. (2000). *The Killing of History: How Literary Critics and Social Theorists are Murdering our Past*. Encounter Books.

Winter, R. and Munn-Giddings, C. (2001). *A Handbook for Action Research in Health and Social Care*. London: Routledge.

Witz, A., Warhurst, C., and Nickson, D. (2003). 'The Labour of Aesthetics and the Aesthetics of Organization', *Organization*, 10: 33–54.

Wong, G., Greenhalgh, T., and Pawson, R. (2010). 'Internet-Based Medical Education: A Realist Review of What Works, for Whom and in What Circumstances', *BMC Medical Education*, 10 (12): 1–10.

Wuthnow, R. (1989). *Communities of Discourse: Ideology and Social Structure in the Reformation, the Enlightenment, and European Socialism*. Cambridge, MA: Harvard University Press.

Yates, J.-A. (1989) *Control through Communication: The Rise of System in American Management*. Baltimore: Johns Hopkins University Press.

Yin, R. K. (1981). 'The Case Study Crisis: Some Answers', *Administrative Science Quarterly*, 26: 58–65.

—— (2009 [1994]). *Case Study Research: Design and Methods* (4th edn). London: Sage.

Index

abduction 17, 18, 19, 24, 27, 30, 32, 34, 36, 39, 41, 43, 55, 57, 81, 149, 150, 155, 157, 159, 160, 255, 258, 262, 263
abductive logic 23, 25, 26
abductive redescription vii, viii, ix
abductive retrodiction vii
Aberdeenshire 236
absence xii, 31–2, 73, 102, 153, 154, 182, 187, 188, 189, 200, 201, 289, 294, 315
   sickness 264, 267, 268, 269, 281
accumulation 156, 325
Ackroyd, Stephen vi, vii, 1, 11, 31, 35, 36, 131, 144, 146, 149, 170–1, 205, 243, 249, 251, 318, 322
action research 36, 37–9, 41, 43, 318, 326
   implementing 205–22
AfC (Agenda for Change) pay
   agreement 177–8, 180
African-Caribbean boys 293
agency x, 8, 70, 75, 97, 197, 265
   apparent in morphostasis 170
   collective 125
   constraint on 178, 191, 195
   efforts to neutralize through
     standardization 268
   employee 260, 261
   enabling 191, 195
   entrepreneurial 219
   explaining underlying generative
     mechanisms that shape 137
   greater scope for 174
   individual 125, 137
   influence of structural factors on 138
   iterative 191, 192, 193, 195, 200, 201, 202
   macro-institutional dynamics could play a
     role in 194
   management 124, 125, 127, 138, 145
   national policies and practices the
     product of 178
   projective 192, 193, 196, 200–1, 202
   pulling the levers of 205–22
   realist promotion of 76
   reflexivity and 69, 79, 110, 123
   residual importance of 183
   revised sense of 128
   transaction-cost economics based on
     economist's view of 166
   unleashing in institutionally diverse
     settings 189–92

viewed as bias and contamination in
   RCTs 266
   see also structure-agency relationship
Aguilera, R. V. 195
Akerlof, G. A. 252, 259
Al-Amoudi, I. 70 n., 75
alienation 72, 118, 311
Allied Breweries 230, 231, 233, 239
Allied Domecq 239
Allied Machine Shop 31
Alvesson, M. 119, 122, 305
analysis of variance 303–4
analytical narratives 223, 238–9, 240
anomie 72
anthropology 100, 134, 135, 319
   cultural 102
   social 102
anti-reductionism x–xii, xiv
Antonio, R. 14
apprenticeship 101, 102, 192
approximations 31, 32, 133, 284, 287
   models as 290–1
   social 249
Archer, Margaret 14, 27, 33, 69, 71, 74, 81, 89, 103, 122–4, 131, 149, 170, 224, 225, 226–7, 238–9, 310
Argyris, C. 206
Ashforth, B. E. 68, 102
asymmetry 289
Atkinson, P. 109, 110, 112, 114, 115–16, 119, 123, 131, 140
attachment theory 56, 59, 64
   see also maternal attachment
Au, Y. W. 82
authenticity 76, 113, 211
   cultural 71

Bach, Stephen 127, 150, 307, 321, 323
Bain, P. 31, 144, 151, 153, 154, 157, 163
Baltzell, Digby 227
Bambra, C. 268
Bandura, A. 101, 102
Banfield, G. 137, 147
Banta, B. 70
barefoot research 27, 36, 41–3
Barker, J. 151, 153, 154, 156–7, 163
Barnes, C. 74
Bartlett, C. A. 185, 191, 195
Bass 231, 233, 238

Bateson, N. 34
Bawer, B. 66
Bayesian probability 285–6
Becker, G. S. 254, 259
Becker, H. S. 145
behavioural norms 160
behaviourism 136, 214
Beirne, M. 219
Bélanger, J. 324, 325
beliefs 1, 71, 85, 130, 186, 254, 289, 310
    ability to justify 19
    clarity of 101
    endorsed 123
    false vi, 12, 19
    knowledge compared to 5–6
    lives evaluated through 304
    meaningful 304
    misguided 205
    misleading 313
    philosophical 133
    prior 205
    sanctioned 30
    self 19, 125–6, 127, 129
    true 12
    understanding of 136
Bell, E. 95
Bellamy, R. 264, 266
Bennett, A. 185, 189
Bennett, Alex 230
Berg-Schlosser, D. 187
Bernstein, Basil 226
Berry, B. J. L. 292
Beynon, H. 23, 28, 122, 128–9
Bhaskar, Roy v, vii, viii, ix, x, xi, xii, xiii, xiv,
    2, 7, 10, 11, 14, 27, 47, 48, 52, 67, 73 n.,
    87, 90, 97, 102, 103, 116, 122, 137, 139,
    147, 186, 203, 214, 242, 243, 245 n., 255,
    264, 283, 284, 299, 300–1, 310, 311, 313,
    314, 317, 325
Billig, M. 50, 57, 68
biological structures 79
Birkhead, T. 110
Birkinshaw, J. 138, 145, 185, 186, 203
bivariate statistics 249–50
    see also analysis of variance; correlations;
        dependent variables; independent
        variables
Blaikie, N. 3
Blalock, Hubert 282–4, 289, 294
Blau, P. 29
Boolean algebra 188
Boselie, P. 277
Boston 227
Boswell, T. 188
Boudon, R. 292
Bourdieu, Pierre 69, 81, 224, 226, 254,
    257, 261

Bourneville 125, 127
    see also Cadbury-Schweppes
Bowen, D. E. 265
Bowlby, John 53, 56
Boxall, P. 265
Brannan, M. 145
Braverman, H. 5, 158
brewery industry, see Allied Breweries; Bass;
    Scottish & Newcastle; Whitbread
Britain, see UK
British Chem 189, 190, 191, 193, 196, 198,
    200, 201
British Journal of Management 318
British Library Newspapers 234
British North America 234
Brown, A. 310, 315, 316, 323, 324, 325
Brown, C. 188
Brown, Gordon x
Brown, S. 69
Bryman, A. 95, 172, 173, 205, 242, 243
Burawoy, M. 23, 28, 29–30, 31–2, 149, 324–5
Burgess, Ernest 133
Burr, V. 47, 49, 74 n.
Business Links 207
Byrne, David 28, 34–5, 288, 289, 298, 314

Cadbury-Schweppes 124, 125, 126, 127
California 42
call centres 157, 161
    workplace humour and collective
        identity 153
Cambridge and Peterborough Foundation
    NHS Trust 271
Canadian law firms 35
capital and labour 42, 43, 144
    structured antagonism between 156
capital markets 154
capitalist system 6, 7, 18, 43, 300, 303, 311
    advanced 325
    basic contradictions of the
        commodity-form 312
    competition 156, 158
    empirical instances of commodification 19
    managerial 144
    neo-liberal 8–9
    organization of 30
    possession of causal imperatives within
        institutional mechanisms 155
    quantitative methods and self-reproduction
        of 314–17
    underlying principles 324
car manufacturers, see Daimler-Chrysler;
    Ford; GM; VW
Carchedi, G. 310
career pathways 102, 182
Caroli, E. 175
Carter, B. 211

Cartwright, Nancy 289
case studies x, 27, 37–8, 124, 128, 131, 243,
    247, 259
  aggregated 263
  case for 23–5
  critical realism and 170–2
  exceptional 157
  explanatory power of 185, 186
  exploratory 156–7
  extensive 255–8, 262
  generalization from 144, 307
  intensive 249, 255–8, 321
  multiple 172, 307
  prevailing positivistic stereotype about 185
  qualitative 242, 306, 307
  selection of 246, 250–5, 320
  smaller sub-contractor 130
  synthesized 306
  using ethnography 35
  see also case-study design; comparative
    case studies; OCSs
case-study design 28–30, 43, 172
  intensive 245
  sound 307
Cassell, C. 205, 206, 213
causal dynamics 102, 162
causal explanation 11, 91, 97, 104, 138, 282,
    288–90, 297, 322
  better 158, 165
  configurational 163
  converging and diverging 81
  deeper 141
  mechanistic 294
  normative 162–3
  probabilistic 294
  recognizing 105
  rival, powerful techniques for
    eliminating 188
  statistical models can be adequate for 294
causal inferences 196, 219
  unwanted 186
causal mechanisms 10, 13, 22, 81, 158,
    213, 303
  characteristic vii
  classifying 151–5
  context can often trigger or retard
    actualization of 16
  cross-cutting 169
  discourse represented as 70
  empirical tendencies generated by 78
  evidence that supports inference of 297
  explanation and generalization
    through 203
  hidden 17
  identifying 24, 168, 243, 322
  interacting with major ontological
    entities 142

multiple 269
  possibilities at deeper levels 11
  possible 249
  potential 250–5
  relating to wider dialectical totalities 314
  underlying 116, 169
  unobservable 186
  ways of gaining insight into 146
causal powers xiii, 8, 51, 104, 134, 216, 217,
    266, 269, 285, 305, 310, 312, 319
  abduction and retroduction of 150
  activated 138
  assumption of 91
  connectivity of themes with 103
  context and 87–90, 93, 106, 107, 243
  creation of 106
  debating with participants 322
  distinct 123
  explanation of 97, 98, 150
  external 106
  framework for dissecting 148
  generative 93, 105, 106, 107, 108
  genesis of 159
  identifying 86, 102, 103, 105, 106, 108
  impact of 100
  indeterminacy of 137
  interaction of 151, 152
  interrogated 323, 324
  local 108
  needs of minority business owners cannot
    be detached from 213
  objective but unobservable structures
    with 203
  ongoing obviation of 11
  possible 97
  private 106
  real 98, 325
  realist-inspired analyses of 324
  realized 320
  relatively enduring 224
  self-employed 106
  shaping leadership learning 86, 87, 95,
    98, 100
  significant for revealing causes of
    institutional mechanisms 162
  stratification and 9
  understanding 139
  wiping out 207–8
causality 168, 186, 242, 243, 257, 264,
    288–89, 312
  ascertained retroductively 251 n.
  attaining 203
  context and 16, 24, 202, 203
  generative view of 268
  holistic xiii, xiv
  inductive generalizations of 263
  inferring 202

causality (*Cont.*)
    intentional, of reasons ix
    probabilistic 289–90
    reconciling tension between
        meaning-making and 206
    single-instance 289
    successionist view of 266
    theoretical 290
    'thick' 208
    without correlation vii
    see also mono-causality; multi-causality
causation 16, 171, 180–3, 185, 203, 303
    context and 168–9, 183
    covert nature of 170
    critical realism has strong interest in 168
    downwards 151, 152
    failing to indicate 202
    in-depth analysis allows for focus on 170
    realist model of 290
    search for 170
    sequences of 17, 24
    social xi
    underlying 173, 176
    upwards 151, 152
CBA (category-bound activity) 60
cement industry 41, 42
centralization 143, 189, 195, 196, 226
    focus on degrees of 227
    high 188
CHA (comparative historical analysis)
        185–92, 196, 202, 203–4
Challenger, Carol 126
Champion, A. G. 292
Chan, E. 226
Charmaz, K. 273
Checkland, P. 103
Chemco 128
Chicago 29, 31, 324–5
Chicago School (sociology) 133–4
Chick , V. 309
Child, J. 124, 260
childcare 46, 59–60, 64, 123
    benefits of 61, 62, 63
    decisions regarding 52, 53, 54, 55,
        57, 61, 63
    high-quality 56
    institutional 51, 56, 58
    local provision 55, 56
    national provision 55
    older women are more likely to use 52
    private provision 56
Chisholm, R. 205
Church of England 236
Church of Scotland 235, 236, 237
citation-tracking 274
Clark, Peter 33

Clarke, I. 103
class differences 71
    see also social class
Clawson, A. 145
Clegg, S. 219
closed systems x, 242, 255, 266, 301, 303–4,
        310–11, 324
    artificial 244
    capitalism as 325
    collective 263
    defined 300, 309
    virtually impossible to create 267–8
cluster analysis 179, 287, 288
CM (context + mechanism) viii, 10, 14, 25–7,
        29, 31–3, 35, 36, 39–40, 78, 144, 269,
        272–3, 277, 293, 306
    relations between 37
CMO (context-mechanism-outcome)
        configuration viii, 37, 39, 40, 44, 120,
CMO 285, 290, 306
Cochrane, A. L. 266
Cockburn, C. 158–9
Codes of Practice 10
Colley, H. 275
Collier, Andrew x, 1, 2, 12, 73 n., 137, 305
Collier, John 206
Collinson, D. 76, 145
comparative case studies 30–2, 168–204,
        251, 320
    theory-driven approach 127
    value of 144
complexity xii, 39, 81, 113, 119, 172, 188,
        189, 242, 249–50, 258, 263, 264, 292
    activity systems to summarize and
        simplify 103
    affinity between realism and 298
    alleged inability of models and heuristics to
        capture 284
    approach consistent with how CR
        accepts 252
    dealing with 266–70
    generality given precedence over 186
    open systems characterized by viii
    range of methods considered useful for
        exploring 54
    social programmes and 265–6
concrete utopianism xiv
Condor, S. 68
configurational analysis 159–60, 162,
        163–4, 165
Conger, J. A. 103
Conservative Government (UK) 207
conservative values 71
constellationality xiii–xiv, 52, 164–5, 203, 226
constructivism vii, 16, 19, 38, 69, 102
    critical realism takes stance against 136

see also social constructionism
social vi, 67
context ix, 7, 8, 11, 15, 43, 46, 91, 109, 113,
    130–3, 142, 151, 160, 161, 176–9, 186,
    211, 220, 221, 226, 238, 244–6, 279,
    321, 323
    attitudes inherently variable and highly
        reflective of 34
    broader 4, 17, 18, 150, 152, 159, 162,
        217, 236
    causality and 16, 24, 202, 203
    causation and 168–9, 183
    changing 37, 156, 298
    comparisons of 278
    cultural 18, 313
    differentiating between meaning in 99
    discursive 54, 56, 64
    economic 31, 146, 210
    embodied 54, 58, 61, 64
    empirical 16, 71, 80, 81, 314
    enterprise 208
    environmental 188
    examining the intricacies of 243
    explaining theory-building within 104–7
    external 152, 252
    extra-discursive 56
    genealogical 50
    historical 146, 228, 295, 313
    host 191, 192, 193, 194–5, 200, 201, 202
    immediate 225, 240
    impact of whole entity in isolation
        from 164
    inability to address 86
    institutional 32, 51, 54, 58, 61, 64, 143,
        146, 162, 189, 195, 197, 200, 210
    local 146
    material 54, 58, 61, 64, 147
    meaning seen as closely tied to 170, 172
    naturally occurring x
    negative labour process 158
    optimal 275
    organizational 18, 29, 171, 263
    placing common themes back into 99
    political 31, 210
    practical 207, 208
    product-market 324
    properties of gravity in 9–10
    qualitative 261
    quantitative data can be revelatory
        about 35
    recipes applied independent of 41
    relative ignorance of 42
    research 306, 313
    self-employed 95
    sensitivity to 169, 172, 183, 320, 324
    social-structural 51

societal 54
socio-historic 50
soft skills deficits in 250, 251, 254–5, 257,
    258, 262
structural 140, 183–4, 213
structured 145
understanding 115, 167, 218
validity of 93
variety of 97, 103
varying 116
wider 49, 115–16, 117, 124, 127, 214,
    215, 325
work experience and relative
    ignorance of 42
see also CM; CMO; contextualization;
    CSMO; social contexts; specific contexts
contextualization 118, 120, 124, 137, 140–1,
    149, 191, 203, 262
    critical realist emphasis on 146
    desire for 108
    ethnic minority business 216
    new migrant businesses 213–14, 215
    see also recontextualization
Cooke, B. 206
Cope, Jason 105
Corbin, J. 98, 103, 191, 197
Cornwall 295–8, 324
correlations 3, 5, 16, 25, 44, 186
    causality and vii
    direct 212
    reification of 4
Costas, J. 76
counterfactuals 289
Courage 230
Cox, R. 323
creativity ix, 17, 136, 227
    eclecticism and 22–3
    intellectual 22
Crinson, I. 140, 141, 146
critical reflection 215, 218
criticality 75–6, 80
Cromby, J. 48, 49, 51, 50, 54
cross-case comparisons/analysis 187,
    192–6, 197
Crouch, C. 195
Cruickshank, J. 1, 14, 15, 72
crystallization 80
CSMO (context, structure, mechanism,
    outcome) viii
Cully, M. 251, 254
cultural norms 4, 153

Daimler-Chrysler 176
Dalton, M. 145
Danermark, Berth ix, x, 2, 17, 18, 26, 27, 30,
    32, 34, 70 n., 104, 137, 303

Daniel, P. 56
data analysis 86, 87, 88, 139, 148, 159–63
  avoiding bias in 97
  case-oriented approach to 186
  central tenet shaping 91
  consequences for 81
  constructing critical realist-informed
    grounded theory 97–8
  metaphors to enrich and liberate 102
  phenomenological 98
  secondary 245 n., 246–50, 252, 257
  use of extant theory during 100
data collection 14, 16, 82, 86, 87, 88, 190
  avoiding bias in 97, 320
  central tenet shaping 91
  cycles of 203
  critical realist approach to specifics of 15
  detailed procedures for 23
  explicitly CR approach to 112
  focus of 77
  leadership learning/lived experience 93–7
  measures and methods of 56–7, 59, 63, 78,
    80, 132, 146
  outcomes become apparent during 196–7
  particular techniques of 139
  qualitative, context-rich 92
  quantitative 35
  realist theory of 116, 131
  realists often see problems with 34
  rigorous exploration of 149
data extraction 274–6
Davies, C. A. 133, 134, 136, 137
Daycare Trust (UK) 60
  see also childcare
Deakins, D. 210
Dean, K. 105, 107, 312
Deanery of Bingham 236
decentralization 198, 226
deduction vii, 18, 24, 104, 244
  closed-system, reductionist form of 255
  scientistic 258
deductive logic 32
Delbridge, R. 23, 31, 144, 145
demi-regularities 169, 170, 171, 172, 250, 304
  search for 323
Denmark 226
Denzin, N. K. 80
Department of Health (UK) 267
Department of Work and Pensions (UK) 267
dependent variables 3, 288, 289, 294,
    309, 321
Derbyshire Records Office 235
Derrida, Jacques 67
detachment 123, 205
  involvement and 26, 27–8
  relative 26

developmental psychology 52
diachronic analyses 43
dialectics v, xi, xiv, 72, 78, 84–5, 291, 300–17,
    324, 325
  agency-structure 219
  epistemological xii–xiii
Dig-where-you-stand-movement 42
DiMaggio, P. J. 157
discourse analysis 70, 76, 232, 319
  critical 46–65, 129–30
dissemination 212, 270, 280
division of labour 36, 120, 121
Dixon, M. 186
Doeringer, P. 252, 259
Doherty, C. 172
domain-specific theory 14, 15, 69, 85, 139
Dow, S. C. 309
Down, S. 145, 147
Downward, P. 171, 242–3, 244, 252, 263, 308
Doyal, L. 313
DREIC model vi, vii, ix
Drummond, J. 205
Du Gay, P. 69, 75
Duberley, J. 70
Dubois, A. 30
Durkheim, Emile 72
Dutch Chem 189, 190, 191, 193, 196, 198,
    200, 201
Dutch childcare, 55, 56, 57, 60–3
Dyer, Wendy 287–8, 298

Early English Online database 234
Easton, G. 30, 88–9, 170, 172, 186
Eden, C. 103
Edley, N. 50
educational systems 50, 226
Edwards, D. 57
Edwards, P. K. 1, 31, 32, 33, 62, 143, 144, 156,
    169, 306, 307, 321, 323, 324, 325
Edwards, T. 174
Eisenhardt, K. 172, 173
Elbourne, D. 268
Elden, M. 205
Elder-Vass, D. 2, 7, 10, 27, 74, 139, 141, 150,
    151, 152, 164, 168, 223–4
Elger, Tony 121, 124, 127, 128–9, 130, 134,
    140, 144, 322
Ellis, Ernest 233
Elton, L. 314
email 81, 82, 83, 84, 141, 217
embeddedness 23, 67–8, 70, 76, 89, 120,
    130, 170, 174, 213, 214, 217, 221, 234,
    265, 267–8
  mixed 210, 215, 216, 218, 220
emergence xii, 27, 28, 34, 70, 93, 100, 168,
    225, 237, 246, 255

acceptance of 107
analysis of 124
analytical narratives of 238–9
CR commitment to 15–16
ontological 147
open systems characterized by viii
reconstructing 233
relational 150, 151
shaping 86–7, 105
stratification and 6–9, 69–70, 74, 75, 83, 147, 224
testing the presence of generative casual powers contributing to 107
understanding 7, 86–7, 150
empiricism 8, 75, 149, 227, 263, 284
abstracted 290, 294
anti-philosophical thinking in ethnographic literature 133
classical vi
epistemological and methodological assumptions 214
Humean 303
realist commitment to an objective world 3
realist OCSs are substantively different from 148
see-sawing between discourse and 86
'thin' accounts of research phenomena 4
employee skills training 264
endogenous variables 289
engagement 44, 169, 175, 191, 206, 209, 210, 213, 222, 226, 229
active 205, 267, 276, 322
concrete 207
critical 220, 221
management 200
mentor 275
mutual 219
promoting 212, 219
taking it seriously 215–18
worker 192, 200
Engels, Friedrich 307
England 226
Access2Archives 235
church administration records 236
digitized copies of virtually every work printed in 234
England and Wales 228
English regions 177
entities 19, 52, 54
and parts 141, 142
and powers 8, 9, 11, 78, 81
epistemology vi, viii, xii–xiii, 5,, 21, 43, 47, 48, 91, 92, 135, 136, 172, 214, 284, 299
clashing 49
constructionist 319

distinct 241, 242
ontology and xiv, 1, 16, 69, 170, 244, 286, 319
relativist 70 n., 71, 206
EPPE (Effective Provision of Pre-school Education) study 56 n.
Erzberger, C. 80
ESRC (UK Economic and Social Research Council) 210–11
ESS (European Social Survey) 295
essences 8, 49, 87, 99, 291, 311
ethnic minority communities 207, 222
businesses 208–10, 212–17
ethnicity 106, 111, 294
operationalization of 293
ethnography x, 16, 22, 30, 35, 66, 107–8, 109, 131, 157, 242, 275, 319
critical realism and 132–47, 314
realist interviewing 112, 114–16, 119–20
thick description' in 148
Evans, R. 75 n., 227
event regularities 277, 304
causal 316–17
collective 315, 316
functions imply 309
global 308
novel explanations of 165
social 303, 308
statements about 3
strict 302, 315, 317
Everitt, B. 287
EWCs (European Works Councils) 176, 193, 194, 195, 196, 199, 200, 201
exogenous variables 289
explanation vii, viii, xi n., 4, 7, 27, 40, 48, 106, 110, 115, 123, 147, 206, 208, 227, 228, 254, 258, 266, 271, 273, 279, 284, 320, 324
a posteriori 244
a priori 173
abductive 263
accurate 9, 13
alternative 167
applied 255
attempting to construct 117
better 6, 18, 149, 161, 205, 216, 238
building 163, 167, 264, 265, 270
closed 203
competing 188, 202
complete 10
contingent 97, 107
contrastive 86, 88, 90, 105, 108, 225
convergence of 82, 93
correct 9
critical realist 13, 138, 165, 166, 185, 203
deep(er) 186, 220

explanation (*Cont.*)
  determinist 325
  developing 148, 150, 165, 176,
    196–202, 219
  emerging 87, 91, 92, 108, 255
  enabling 78
  fine-grained 55
  focus of 128
  forming 235, 238–40
  full and proper 144
  generalized 17
  historical 239
  hypothesized 291
  institutional 159, 162–3
  literal 83
  necessary historicity introduced into 136
  non-reductionistic xii
  novel 165
  nuanced 169
  plausible 17, 107, 183, 219
  potential 17, 188
  realistic 140
  reliable 9
  retroductive 88, 98–104, 107, 244, 245, 263
  richer 16, 72
  satisfactory 26
  scientific 29
  searching out 168
  single-factor 188
  social 245, 301
  statistical 295
  strengthening of 176
  sufficient 79
  tentative 179, 183
  theoretical 13, 16, 81
  thick 19
  thin 6, 16
  transferable 167
  wider 72
  see also causal explanation
extant theory 14, 87, 97, 98, 100, 102,
    106, 108
Ezzy, D. 102

Fairclough, N. 11, 51, 57, 69, 129–30
false positives 189
farm mechanization 230–2
Farrell, C. 269
Farrington, D. P. 268
Fassinger, R. E. 106
female employment 55, 57
Ferner, A. 192
field analysis 159, 160, 161–2, 165–7
Fielding, A. 292
Fielding, N. G. & J. L. 81
Fiss, P. C. 187, 189

Fleetwood, S. 1, 4, 6–7, 11, 88, 89, 90, 91,
    105, 143, 144, 146, 147, 208, 249, 255,
    258, 266, 318
Fleming, P. 76
focus groups 81, 109, 140, 171, 211, 214–15,
    217, 219, 246, 255, 256
Fontainebleau 251, 256, 259, 260, 261
Ford 176, 279
formalization 185, 188, 189
  emphasis on 193, 194
Foucault, Michel 67, 75, 234
four planar social being x–xi, xiv
France 174, 175
  Annales school 227
  educational system 226
  functional flexibility by food processing
    companies 183
Frank, Thomas 70–1
Frankfort-Nachmias, C. 243
frequency-based approaches 289
Friedman, V. 206, 207, 219
Fullbrook, E. 223
Fung, H. C. 276, 278

Gadde, L.-E. 30
Garioch Presbytery 236
Gaskin, I. M. 47
Gatenby, Mark 30, 141, 319
Geering, J. 168
Geertz, C. 148
gender 4, 106, 111, 158, 257, 305, 320
gender-based violence xi n.
gender equality 48
gender identity 17
generalizations 3, 5, 62, 68, 78, 81, 93,
    140, 144, 185, 187, 203, 219, 287, 289,
    304, 308
  based on misleading and/or limited
    theoretical foundations 305
  causal 288
  context-free 242
  desire for 108
  empirical 37
  explanatory 30
  inductive 263
  justifiable 31
  law-like 111
  leverage for 202, 204
  moderatum 288
  modified 19
  need for 104
  no basis for 23, 306
  objective of 282
  positivist 16, 18
  possibilities of 324
  potential 17

producing 186, 226
realist approaches to 307
theoretical vii, 18, 36–7, 40, 91, 106, 133, 148, 167
generative institutional analysis 27, 254
generative institutional investigations 32–4
generative mechanisms 28, 29, 32, 33, 35, 38, 55, 140–1, 144, 158, 171, 181, 215, 245, 246, 254, 257, 305, 307
  causally efficacious, identification of vii
  clues about the character of 30
  clues to 183
  deep structures and 137
  distinguished from actual empirical occurrences 70
  entities that combine/interact to form/create 52, 54
  exploring the complexity of 54
  given, emergence of a 27, 34
  insight into 206
  intensive research is focused on the discovery of 25
  interactive 147
  key 261, 262
  known 36, 37
  labour process as part of 31
  methods used to investigate them within case studies 253
  nature and operation in different contexts 306
  novel 157
  ontology of 306
  plausible 138
  possibility of reconstructing 39
  possible 251, 258
  potency across the NHS 181
  potential 251, 255–6, 261
  proposed 250
  real but unobservable 239
  recognition of precise nature of 30
  restructuring direct attention towards 174
  search for 170, 225
  social contexts and 129
  soft skills deficits and 259
  teamwork understood in terms of ontology of 306
  theoretical model of 167
  uncovering 178, 244, 263
  underlying 137, 168, 183
  understanding of 36
  wider patterns and 169
geo-history xi, xiii
George, A. L. 185, 189
Gergen, K. J. 47, 102
Germany 153, 162, 174, 189, 191–6, 200, 201
gestalt 99

Gherardi, S. 102
Ghoshal, S. 191, 195
Giddens, A. 72
Gilbert, N. 288, 297
Gillon, A. 232
Giorgi, A. 99
Glaser, B. G. 92, 96, 98, 103, 160, 161
Glasgow 251
GM (General Motors) 176, 229
Goffman, E. 69, 72, 76
Goldstein, H. 293
Goldthorpe, J. 111
Gómez-Estern, B. M. 48, 49
Gomm, R. 170
Gouldner, A. W. 23, 28, 29
Greckhamer, T. 186–7
Green, S. 266
Greenhalgh, J. 4, 13, 21, 40, 274, 276, 278, 307, 322
Greer, I. 176
Griffin, C. 50
grounded theory 13, 86–108, 319, 320
Grugulis, I. 251
Guba, E. G. 305
Gubrium, J. F. 111, 112–14
Guest, D. E. 265
Gunaratnam, Y. 211
Gustavsen, B. 38

Hacking, I. 68
Hair, J. 249 n.
Hall, P. 237
Hall, P. A. 195
Hall, S. 56
Hammersley, M. 109, 110, 112, 114, 115–16, 119, 123, 131, 133, 140, 289, 313, 314
Haraszti, M. 31
Harper, D. J. 48, 49, 51
Harré, R. 47, 48, 138, 305
Harris, R. 313
Harrison, D. 88–9, 170, 172
Harrison, E. 297
Harrison, R. 206
Hartwig, H. 14
Hauptmeier, M. 176
HCAs (healthcare assistants) 169, 171–2, 177–83
health, *see* HCAs; hospitals; JRRP; NHS; PROMs
Heckman, J. J. 254
Hegelian dialectic xiii
Hellgren, B. 120, 131
Hepburn, A. 57
hermeneutics ix, x, 259, 262
  appreciation of 263
  orthodox 140

Herriot, P. 260
Hesketh, A. 4, 208, 249, 255, 258, 266
heuristics xii, 96, 283, 284, 290, 298
Higgins, J. P. T. 266
Hillage, J. 268
historical systems 311, 313, 314
  explanatory insights into how they
    operate 317
history 6, 7, 11, 14, 15, 33, 34, 44, 70, 74–5,
    89, 135, 136, 139, 144, 146, 150, 223–40,
    273, 295, 300, 301, 305, 310, 319
  causal 208
  materialist view of 147, 311–12
  oral 45, 131
  personal 48, 57
  social 48
  structures and their relationship
    to 311, 312
  see also barefoot research; CHA;
    geo-history; historical systems; natural
    history; socio-historic context
Ho, K. 145
Hockey, J. 135
Hodgkinson, G. 318
Hodson, R. 145
Hogg, M. A. 102
holistic orientation xiii, xiv, 94, 95, 103,
    170–1, 172, 183, 324
Holmer-Nadesan, M. 72–3
Holstein, J. A. 111, 112–14
homelessness 12, 287–8
Hoover, K. D. 308
hospitality sector 247–8, 249, 250, 252, 254
hospitals xii, 171, 178–83, 184
  acute 177
  public disclosure of performance 278
Houston, S. 51
HRM (human resource management) 265,
    266, 277
  superior practices 277
Huberman, A. M. 30, 99, 103
Huff, A. S. 103
Hughes, J. 305
Hume, David 283, 303
Hungary 31
Hurrell, S. A. 4, 43, 245, 261, 262, 321,
    323, 324
Husk, K. 293, 294, 298
Hutchby, J. 62
Hycner, R. H. 98, 99

Ibarra, H. 102
ICT (information and communications
    technology) 79, 85, 230
IDB (SUPPAG Information, Diagnostic and
    Brokerage) service 208

idealism 5, 131, 313
identity x, 5, 228, 238, 312
  aspirational 102
  collective 153
  development of (becoming) 102, 106
  differing ways in which constructed 321
  dominant positions on 67–9
  ethnic 294
  gender 17
  structural factors that shape 319
  virtual teams 82–5
  see also self-identity; SIT
identity research 46–85
immanent critique 14
independent variables 3–4, 294, 309, 321
induction vii, 18, 24, 104, 203, 244, 253
  informal 283
inductive logic 34
interdependence 142, 146, 186, 198
  subject-specific theory of 143
international business 185–204
Internet 8, 161
  medical education 40–1
interpretivism 186
  extreme 301
  positivism vs. 241–2
interviews 15, 17, 51, 53, 54, 58–63, 66, 70,
    75, 77–85, 160, 161, 171, 179, 182, 206,
    215, 219, 242, 246, 260, 275, 288, 306,
    319, 321
  active 111, 112–14
  analysed 57, 109, 114
  case 98, 104
  construction of knowledge through 97
  critical realism and 109–31, 322, 326
  depth 22
  detailed 212, 213
  ethnographic 112, 114–16, 119–20
  exploring lived experience through 88
  face-to-face 142
  formal 82, 84, 191
  necessarily taken at face value 67
  non-directive 94
  orientations described in 192
  pilot 93–6
  problems with data collection and
    recording in 34
  qualitative 109, 111, 140, 253, 256
  semi-structured 57, 118, 127, 191, 213,
    255
  structured 255
  theory-driven 116–18
  transcripts of 98–9, 100, 101, 197
Ireland 135, 234
Isabella, L. A. 271
Ivatts, J. 56

Jackson, B. 103
Jackson, G. 195
Jackson, J. 295
Jacobi, O. 195
Janesick, V. J. 95, 100
Japanese companies 128, 129, 130
  British subsidiaries 121, 127
Jaros, S. 156
Jay's (engineering firm) 31
Jenkins, M. 103
Jenkins, R. 72
Jenkins, S. 157, 161
Jesuit educational provision 234
Johnson, A. 214
Johnson, G. 103
Johnson, P. 205, 206, 213
Jones, Will 125–6
Joseph, J. 73 n.
Jowell, R. 285
JRRP (Job Retention and Rehabilitation
  Pilots) 267, 269

Kaizen 194
Kansas 70–1
Kantianism vi
Kaposi, D. 49
Karlsson, Jan C. vi, vii, 34, 149, 322
Kazi, M. A. F. 39, 43, 44
Kelle, U. 80
Kellogg, K. 237
Kelly, G. A. 94
Kempster, S. J. 13, 86, 87, 89, 90, 92, 93, 94–5,
  96, 97, 98–9, 100, 102, 103, 104, 105,
  106, 107–8, 320
Kenny, Martin 125
Kessler, Ian 127, 146, 150, 171, 177, 178, 307,
  321, 323
Ketokivi, M. 19
Kilduff, M. 205
Kirkpatrick, I. 31
Kloosterman, R. 210
Knijn, T. 61
knowledge vi, 30, 37, 114, 116–17, 136, 143,
  155, 165, 167, 215, 237, 298, 322
  accrued 166
  actionable 219
  adoption of 195
  applied 221
  approximation of 287
  attempts to activate 113
  beliefs compared to 5–6
  complex 40
  conceptual 40
  construction of 97, 110
  contested 221
  contextual 140

co-production of 140, 220, 221
creation of 195, 206
developing 31, 149, 195
diffusion of 195
discourse has the potential to structure 49
discursive 3, 5
distinction between object and xiii–xiv
enduring 225
enhancing 218
existence of 67
experience and 84, 104, 212
expert 120
exploiting 220
factual 313
gaps in 127
implicit 235
in-depth 200
inadequate 306
interpreted subjectively 3
intimate 162
lack of 58, 208
limited 13
links between areas of 36
local 119, 121, 209
mutual 306
objective 5, 45
possibility of 67, 70
production of 36, 115, 186, 211, 220
scientific 24
shared 38, 197, 217
situated character of 119
socially-constructed 97
sociological 135
specialist 217
stocks of 113, 205, 225
subject to reinterpretation 5
tacit 92, 95, 96
tainted 313
taken-for-granted 47, 115
theoretical viii, 14, 38
theory-laden 97
transitive 74
see also knowledge base; knowledge
  transfer; KSF
knowledge base 220
  enhancing 219
  enriched 219
  incomplete 292
knowledge transfer 195
  cross-national 185
  MNE structures for 200
Knutstad, G. 38
Kogut, B. 186
Kontos, P. 215
Kowalski, R. M. 76, 84
Kral, M. J. 48

Kram, K. E. 271
KSF (Knowledge and Skills Framework) 178, 180
Kuhnert, K. W. 96
Kunda, G. 145
Kundnani, A. 208

Labour Government (UK) 264
labour process theory, *see* LPT
labour transnationalism 176, 184
Lacan, Jacques 67
laminated systems 7, 139
  anti-reductionism and x-xii, xiv
  distinct but related 140
  restructuring of 142
Lancashire 232
Lane, C. 195
Larson, B. Z. 188
Lather, P. 49
Lauber, V. 48, 51, 64
Lave, J. 100, 102
Lawson, Tony 86, 90, 108, 142, 169, 225, 245, 249, 250, 251, 252, 262, 301–4, 308–10, 315, 316–17, 323–4
Layder, D. 34
Layman, L. 131
leadership learning:
  biographical data on 96
  causal configurations of 105
  causal powers of 106
  causes influencing 102, 103
  grounded theory of 105
  lived experience of 88, 93–7, 98, 100, 101, 104
  manager's perspective of 97
  shaping 86, 87, 88, 95, 96, 97, 98, 101, 103
  suggestions to explain 100
lean manufacturing/production systems 194, 264
learning ix, 17, 39, 74, 122, 205
  informal 103
  naturalistic 103
  teaching and 117
  virtual 41
  see also leadership learning; observational learning; organizational learning; situated learning; social learning theory
learning difficulties 52, 63
Leary, M. R. 76, 84
Leca, B. 137
Leitch, C. 206
Levin-Rozalis, M. 55
Lewin, Kurt 205, 207
Lewis, P. 75 n.
Lincoln , Y. S. 305
Lindqvist, S. 41–3

linguistic turn 227
Littler, C. R. 156
Liverpool 33, 230, 233, 239, 240
  Record Office 235
Lobe, B. 186, 187, 202
Locke, R. M. 168–9, 174
logistic regression 249, 250, 257, 294–5, 296, 298
  justified 309
London 82, 177
London School of Economics 133
Lounsbury, M. 197
LPT (labour process theory) 31, 127, 155–6, 158, 316
Lucey, H. 48
Lunt, P. 69
Luong, P. J. 186
Lupton, T. 31, 145
Lynch, K. 314

Macdonald, S. 120, 131
Macfarlane, F. 265
Mackaness, W. 103
Macky, K. 265
Mael, F. 68, 102
Malinowski, Bronislaw 133
Manchester Mill 307
Mantere, S. 19
Manzano-Santaella, A. 307
Marchal, B. 39
Marginson, P. 35, 175, 176
Marks, Abigail 70–1, 76, 82, 166, 319
Markus, H. 102
Marsh, C. 34
Martin, E. 252
Marx, Karl xiii, 29, 71 n., 72, 144, 146–7, 227, 307, 311–12, 313, 314, 317
materiality 46, 48, 49, 50, 51, 52, 55, 57, 59, 79
  historical 74–5
maternal attachment 51, 53, 57
mathematical functions 302, 304
Maxwell, J. A. 212, 306
MBA (Master of Business Administration) programmes 94, 95
McCall, M. W. 103
Mead, Sherry 272
meaning(s) 3, 11, 50, 72, 106, 122, 134, 319, 321, 326
  associated 67
  attributed 22
  categories of 71
  causality and 206
  closely tied to context 170, 172
  clusters of 99, 100, 101, 102, 104
  construction of 5, 110, 111, 112

context-specific 85
converging or diverging 81
core 99
differentiating in context 99
used to convey 144
empirical phenomena 81
enriching and validating 99
equivalence of 285
holistic 95
lives evaluated through 304
local 286
observations or interviews very good at
uncovering 288
policy interventions shift in purpose
and 320
production of 112, 113, 115
range and complexity of 113
repeated interaction in order to
explore 220
researchers seek to uncover 242
situated 82
social 5
subjective 5, 135, 148, 149
substantive 112, 113
translating 302
unconstrained and free 74
understanding 99, 135, 136
units of 99, 100, 101, 102
variations in 80, 85
means of production 311
Mearman, A. 171, 242–3, 244, 252, 263
mechanisms:
actualization 15, 19
countervailing 9
entities and 19
institutional 51, 148–67
operative 31
problem 44
social 13, 21, 51, 146, 149, 291–2, 297
see also causal mechanisms; CM; CMO;
CSMO; generative mechanisms
Meiskins, P. 33
Melody, J. 48
Mercer, G. 74
Merton, R. K. 279, 292
meta-explanation 98
metaphor 102, 108, 321
alternative 80
theory and 96–7, 98, 100
meta-theory xiv, xv, 12, 26, 97, 137, 165,
206, 325
domain-specific 15
general realist 15
methodological models 289, 291, 293–4, 295,
298, 299
Michael, M. 68

middle-range theory 187, 292, 297–8, 307
Miles, M. B. 30, 99, 103, 171
Miles, R. E. 188
Mill, John Stuart 187, 202
Miller, D. 188
Mills, C. W. 290
Mingers, J. 19, 186
Mises, R. von 287
Mitchell, C. 292
MMR (mixed methods research) 80, 241–63
MNEs (multinational enterprises) 144, 145,
189, 193
strategic responses to overcome
institutional contradictions 192
structures 191, 194, 195, 196, 197, 198,
200, 201–2
see also subsidiaries
Modell, S. 80, 81, 82, 83
mono-causality x, 244
Montano, S. 18
Montenegro, M. 77
Morgan, J. 206, 207, 208, 249, 250, 252,
257, 309
morphogenesis 14, 103, 139, 142, 143,
170, 228
field concept and 240
summarized 225
morphostasis 11, 103, 139, 142, 143,
170, 225
Morrison, E. W. 254
Morrison, Ken 289, 290
Moth, R. xi n.
motherhood 55, 57, 64
biological and social theories of 59
full-time 61
see also maternal attachment
Moustakas, C. 98
MPB (managed professional business)
model 35
Muller, M. 151, 153, 154, 162
multi-causality 252
multinational enterprises, *see* MNEs
multiple regression analysis 303–4, 308, 309
Munn-Giddings, C. 206, 208, 211, 213, 215
Musson, G. 70
Mutch, Alistair 33–4, 150, 152, 229, 232, 233,
235, 236, 239, 240
Muzio, D. 33, 35, 36

Naccache, P. 137
Nachmias, D. 243
Naess, P. vii
naming-and-shaming policy 276, 277–8, 279
National Childcare Trust (UK) 56
National Records of Scotland 236, 237 n.
natural history 110

necessary and sufficient conditions 187, 197,
    201, 202
Neimark, Marilyn 229
Netherlands 174, 189
    see also Dutch childcare
New Guinea 133
new migrant businesses 208, 209, 211,
    212, 218
    conceptualization of 216
    contextualization of 213–14, 215
    engaging with 207, 217, 219
    identification of 210
NHS (UK National Health
    Service) 169, 177–84
    see also Trusts
Nichols, T. 128–9
Nickson, D. 247, 249, 254
Nightingale, D. J. 48, 50
non-participant observation 82
normative analysis 159, 160–1, 162, 164, 165
Norrie, Alan 317
Norway xi
Nottingham Healthcare Trust 272
Nottinghamshire 236
Nurius, P. S. 102

objective reality 5, 178, 185, 186
objectivism 3
objectivity 46, 67, 108, 207
    claims to 5, 47
    context-free 92
    critical realist approach to 206
observational learning 101
O'Connell Davidson, J. 111
OCSs (organizational case studies) 148–67
O'Dougherty, D. 76
Olsen, W. 1, 55, 206, 207, 208, 242, 243 n.,
    244, 249, 250, 252, 257, 288, 297, 309
O'Mahoney, Joe x, 5, 8, 47, 49, 52, 54, 64, 67,
    69, 70, 77, 149–50, 166, 187, 188, 319
ontology v, viii, ix, 19, 21, 66, 81, 85, 93, 135,
    136, 137, 142, 150, 243, 263, 282, 287,
    289, 298, 309, 310, 321
    constructionist 76, 77
    constructivist 38
    depth 6, 9–11, 70–1, 78, 116
    domain-specific 139, 140
    emergent 69, 147, 224
    empirical 3
    epistemology and xiv, 1, 16, 69, 170, 244,
        286, 319
    generative mechanisms 306
    irreducible levels x
    layered 122
    major entities and parts 142
    meta-theoretical 15

positivist 9, 38
primacy in the research process vi
realist 1, 67, 69, 75, 77, 87–8, 98, 132, 220,
    241, 303
    scientific 139
    social 303
    stratified 11, 51, 69, 75, 147, 224
    viable, organizations and management 146
open systems vii, ix, x, xiii, 8, 203, 250, 255
    n., 263, 301, 303, 304, 310–11, 324, 325
    characterized viii
    complex 4, 34, 258
    defined 309
    emergent properties in 15
    maintaining 244
    reinforcing 246
    social phenomena only ever occur in viii
    stratified 6
organizational learning 206
organizational performance 188, 264, 277
    correlation between firms that implement
        teamwork and 16
    high 189
Orlikowski, W. J. 237
Osmaston 235
Ostroff, C. 265
Outhwaite, W. 138
Oxbridge intellectualism 126, 127
Oxygen 251, 256, 259, 260–1

Pajunen, K. 187
Papineau, D. 282
Park, Robert 133
Parker, I. 46, 48, 75
Parkinson (TV programme) 94–5
Parry, Ken 13, 86, 90, 92, 93, 98, 100, 103,
    106, 107, 320
participant observation 146, 191, 211,
    212–13, 216
    detailed 142
Passeron, J.-C. 254
patterns of regularities 54
    capturing 196–202
    expected, single deviation from 188
    identifying 191
Patterson, M. 277
Pawson, Ray 28, 34, 37, 39–40, 87–8, 110,
    112, 116–23, 131, 264, 265–6, 269, 270–
    1, 273, 274–7, 279–80, 285, 288, 290,
    292, 293, 297, 298, 306–7
Payne, G. 282, 288
Peacock, R. 274
Pearce, F. 75, 234
peer support 271–3
Peirce, C. S
pentimented social being xi

performance management 178, 264
Pettigrew, A. 172
phenomenology 98, 99, 132, 134, 135–6, 140,
   147, 319
   qualitative 116
Philadelphia 227
philosophy of metaReality v
   dialectical critical realism and xii–xiv
Piekkari, R. 185
Piore, M. J. 252, 259
Platt, L. 294
Poland, B. 215
Polanyi, M. 69
political analysis/actions 208–11
Pollert, A. 23, 28
Pollock, N. 224
Popper, Karl vi, 225, 287, 289, 291
Porpora, D. V. 303
Porter, S. 30, 34, 134, 135–6, 206, 211, 314
positivism vi, vii, 9, 15, 16, 19, 23, 24, 37, 38,
   44, 45, 67, 91, 97, 107, 109, 110, 111, 122,
   172–3, 186, 203, 243, 249, 263, 266, 293,
   320, 323
   accounts of scientific procedures 116
   active interviewing in opposition to 112
   assumptions underpinning quantitative
      research 34
   belief in single reality that exists
      independ-ently of those
      experiencing it 242
   critical realism takes stance against 136
   deductive research and design
      characteristic of 138
   epistemological and methodological
      assumptions 214
   extreme 301
   favour of large and quantitative
      data-sets 3, 22
   interpretivism vs. 241–2
   leadership studies and leadership
      learning 86, 101
   logical 303
   meta-analysis 40, 41, 43
   method-driven experimental and
      quasi-experimental evaluations 39
   prevailing stereotype about the case
      study 185
   qualitative ethnographic research
      formulated in opposition to 114
   quantitative 116, 242
   quantitative analysis synonymous with 284
   realist commitment to an objective
      world 3
   realist critique of methods 265, 266
   research heavily influenced by 38
   'straw man' critique 113

'thin' accounts of research phenomena 4
   unsocial and unreflective basis of research
      practice 34
postmodernism 67, 109, 110, 114, 132, 134,
   135–6, 137, 138, 144, 228
Potter, J. 46, 57, 58, 68
Powell, W. W. 157
Prahalad, C. K. 185
Price, L. xi n.
probability 282–299, 302, 309
production functions 302, 308
project and research process 244–6
PROMs (patient-reported outcome
   measures) 278
PRP (performance-related pay) 4, 153
psychological contract 254, 263
   breaches in 253, 257, 261, 262
psychological structures 79
psychology x, 56, 73, 75
   depth xi
   discursive 46–9, 51–4, 57–9, 63
   popular 60
   social constructionist 48
   use of ethnography 136
   see also developmental psychology; gestalt;
      social psychology
Pujol, J. 77
Purcell, J. 265
Purdon, S. 267, 269

qualitative methods 43, 54, 243, 257, 282,
   288, 301, 313, 323, 324
   approaches typically aligned with 3
   critical realism and 304–7, 317
   in-depth 242
   wholesale adoption of 284
qualitative research x, 22, 54, 114, 185, 260,
   263, 290, 305, 313, 314
   common experience in 46
   explanatory claims based on 204
   intensive 242
   snowballing' strategy in 274
   standard criticism of 306
quantitative data-sets 3, 34–6
quantitative methods 43, 44, 54, 185, 242,
   243, 244, 257, 265, 284, 323
   approaches typically aligned with 3
   CR and 249, 258, 288, 300, 301–4, 317, 324
   objective of generalization usually
      associated with 282
   qualitative researchers often employ 305
   reconsideration of 308–10
   self-reproduction of the capitalist system
      and 314–17
quantitative research x, 22
   common feature of 35

quantitative research (*Cont.*)
  key role of 263
  positivist assumptions underpinning 34
  problems of operationalizing
      causality in 290
  realism and relevance in 282
  realist 291

Ragin, C. C. 186, 188, 189, 202, 203, 242, 305
Ram, Monder 38, 208–11, 212, 213, 222, 322
Rambo, E. 226
randomization, *see* RCTs
Rao, H. 197
Rappert, B. 213, 220
Ratcliffe, P. 212
rationality 286
  axial xiv
Rayne 237 n.
RCTs (randomized controlled
      trials) 265–6, 274
  and systematic reviews 266–8
realist evaluation 306
  extensive 27, 43–4
  intensive 27, 39–41
realist synthesis 264–82, 307, 320, 321, 322
  pioneering approach to 306
recontextualization vii, viii
redescription iii
  abductive vii, viii, ix
Reed, M. 29, 30, 76, 137, 139, 143
Rees, Chris 30, 141, 319
reference-group theory 279
reflexivity 5, 72, 74, 75, 118
  agency and 69, 79, 110, 123
  importance of 114
  interview as tool for
      investigating 110, 122–4
  respondent 97
regression analysis 44, 249, 253, 260, 261, 323
  critics of 258
  see also logistic regression; multiple
      regression
regularities vii, 29, 52, 137, 160
  causal 107, 308, 315
  concomitant 308
  empirical 10, 161
  generative mechanisms that affect 54
  observed 3, 4, 10, 17
  statistical 3
  strict 308, 315, 316
  trivial 308–9
  see also demi-regularities; event
      regularities; patterns of regularities
Rein, M. 219
relational tables 287
relativism 5, 49, 71, 76, 135, 136–7

epistemological 70 n., 77, 206
Repper, Julie 272
Republicans (US) 71
RESCUE project 275
research 4
  engaged 36–44, 220
  ethnographic 114, 134
  IB 185
  identity 46–85
  intensive and extensive 25, 26–7
  mixed methods 80, 241–63
  positivist 43
  primacy of ontology in vi
  retroductive strategy 138
  social science 1, 3, 108
  see also action research; barefoot research;
      qualitative research; quantitative
      research; social research
retrodiction viii, ix
  abductive vii
retroduction vii, ix, 17, 18, 19, 27, 34, 36, 42,
      43, 70, 71, 77, 79, 81, 86–7, 132, 138, 139,
      140, 149, 150, 155, 159, 161, 162, 165,
      170, 179, 181, 183, 184, 186, 205, 213,
      225, 246, 251, 254–5, 262, 320
  manifestation of 171
  see also DREIC
retroductive argumentation 98, 104, 108
  development of 93
  empirical foundation for 105
  four stages of 90–1
  identifying socially real phenomena
      through 97
retroductive explanation 88, 98–104, 107,
      244, 245
  in-depth 263
retroductive grounded theory 88, 90, 91–3,
      98, 102
  creation of causal powers through 106
retroductive logic 23, 24, 26
rhythmics xi-xii, xiii
Richards, J. 76
Rihoux, B. 186, 187, 202, 203
Riley, S. C. E. 48, 50, 53, 57, 319
Roberts, J. M. 76, 314, 323, 324, 325
Robinson, S. L. 254
Rogers, T. 206, 207, 216, 219
Rolfsen, M. 38
Ross, Ronald 25
Rousseau, D. M. 254
Rowlinson, M. 124
Roy, D. 145
Royal Commission (Licensing
      Laws 1890s) 233
RRREI mode 255
RRREIC model vvii-viii, ix

Rueschemeyer, D. 187, 188
Russell, C. J. 96
Russia 226
Ryant, Carl 41

Sackett, D. L. 266
Saka-Helmhout, Ayse 174, 186, 307
salience 102, 106, 120
    practical 300
    uneven 130
Sanders, T. 314
Sayer, A. 9, 11, 12, 26, 27, 34, 70, 88–9,
    97, 102, 138, 168, 186, 203, 230, 243–4,
    245, 246, 249, 252, 284, 286, 303, 305,
    310
Schenner, E. 48, 51, 64
Schneider, M. R. 187
Scholarios, D. 245 n., 261
Schön, D. 206, 219
Schutz, Alfred 134
Scotland 33, 241, 253
    church administration records 236
    digitized copies of virtually every work
        printed in 234
    see also Church of Scotland; National
        Records of Scotland; SESS
Scott, W. 224
Scottish & Newcastle 231
Scullion, H. 31, 32, 321
Searle, J. 137
Secord, P. F. 305
selecting-to-difference 174, 175, 177
selecting-to-similarity 176
self-identity 103
    autonomous-reflective 33
semiotics 11, 78
sense-making 50, 51, 55–6, 58–9, 61, 63, 64
    conditions of possibility for 52
Sepulveda, L. 208
SESS (Scottish Employers' Skills
    Survey) 244–8, 250, 251, 252,
    255, 258–9
seven scalar social being xi
Sewell, W. 227
Sharpe, D. 145
Sharrock , W. W. 305
Shepperd, S. 265
Shield Project 44
Shortall, S. 206, 211
Siebern-Thomas, F. 252
Siegel, J. I. 188
Siggelkow, N. 32
Silex 251, 256, 259, 260, 261
Silverman, D. 60 n., 242
Sims-Schouten, W. 48, 49, 50, 51, 56, 58,
    64, 319

simulations 288
Singapore 82, 83, 84
Sisson, Keith 319
SIT (social identity theory) 73, 75, 101,
    103, 305
    discredited 69
    emergent properties have
        consequences for 74
    personal identity and 68, 71, 72, 76, 78, 79,
        80, 83, 84–5
    significant limitations based upon
        ontological weaknesses 66–7
situated learning 102
    influential argument for 100
Six Sigma 194
Skocpol, T. 188
Skvoretz, J. 291
Smallbone, D. 210, 213
Smith, Chris 33, 121, 124, 125, 126, 127,
    128–9, 130, 134, 140, 144, 169, 322
Snell, Keith 228, 238
Snow, C. C. 188
social activity 117
    see also TMSA
social class 295, 296, 297
    transnational measurement of 285
social constructionism 3, 14, 70, 76, 160
    critical debates between critical
        realists and 47
    denial of better truths 6
    derision of any personal properties as
        'essentialism' 73
    discourse analysis and 47, 54
    realist OCSs are substantively different
        from 148
    significant limitations based upon
        ontological weaknesses 66–7
    social structures are entirely
        determined by 149
    strong emphasis on language 48
    strong/weak 5
    typical approach 46
social contexts xii, 40, 52, 64, 68, 146,
    305, 313
    child's 44
    generative mechanisms and 129
    leadership perspectives and 101
    materially, embodied, and institutionally
        and discursively structured 65
    relationships to 123
    subjective understanding of 111
social learning theory 101
social norms 14, 17, 73
social programmes 267, 272, 280
    complex 264, 265–6, 268
social psychology 101

social reality xiv, 7, 113–14, 135, 149, 298
  character of 116, 119, 129
  complex 119, 129, 243
  external 111, 242
  objective 111
  reinforcing the hermeneutically mediated
    nature of 262
  sophisticated and nuanced
    representation of 8
  statistical models do not accurately
    represent 297
social research ix, x, 110, 111, 112, 113, 119,
    123, 131, 139, 286, 287, 289, 298, 300
  applied 318
  argument against quantitative methods
    in 316–17
  causal analysis tradition in 282
  commonest method of 109
  effective method of 135
  engaged scholarship is compatible with
    many other different types of 220
  fusing change and 214
  implications of critical realism for 124
  knowledge produced in the detached
    mode of 36
  limitations of 285
  nature of 66
  objects of 137
  quantity and quality within 244; *see
    also* Bryman
  traditional ontological dichotomy
    within 241
  use of dialectics for 312, 313–14
Social Science Citation Index 274
social world viii, ix, 4, 7, 9, 10, 37, 122, 136,
    137, 242, 284, 303, 322
  ACR in v
  agency central to critical realist
    conception of 72
  analysis of 226
  attempt to explain 323
  causal effects upon subjectivities of
    individuals 134
  complexity of 263, 289
  describing 14–16
  event regularities do not occur in 309, 317
  ideas in 50, 225
  inherently/necessarily open 310, 315, 320
  interpretation of 135
  layered 110, 124–30
  mechanisms of 263, 290
  ontological characteristic of 286
  powers in 8
  produced 27, 47
  real character of 298
  reconstructed by actions of participants 27

  role of social processes in constituting 47
  sciences of 282
  sophisticated representation of 19
  structures in 139, 224
  theoretical explanation for 13
  widespread condition in xiii
socialization 17, 60, 61, 157, 260
  organizational 195
socio-historic context 47, 50, 64
sociology 1, 6, 132, 135, 146, 228, 283, 294
  Chicago School 133–4
  ethnographic research 134
  historical 186, 226, 227
  organizational 224
  social-constructionist 14
soft skills deficits 241, 244–63
solidarity 29, 73, 192
  universal xiv
Somers, M. 188
South Africa xi n.
spatio-temporalities xi
specific contexts viii, 85, 105, 107, 118, 207
  causal powers in 93, 106, 320
  creation of knowledge in 206
  experience embedded in 120
  explanatory accounts found in 29
  how organizational members actually
    behave in 160
  structures, mechanisms and tendencies
    that practitioners can apply to 37, 32
  work team 222
Spradley, J. P. 96, 140, 141
Stake, R. 148–9, 157, 160, 161, 167
Star Trek 194
Starkey, K. 318
statistical functions 302, 304
statistical models 284, 286, 291, 292,
    294–7, 298
  see also theoretical models
Steinmetz, G. ix
Strategic Partnership 163–7
Stratford, N. 267
stratification 11, 18, 51, 129, 242, 269
  embodied personality xi
  emergence and 6–9, 69–70, 74, 75, 83,
    147, 224
  ethnic 293
  hierarchical 147
  interaction between structure and
    agency in 168
  internal 170, 179
  multi-relational 140
  temporal 151
stratified reality 74, 88, 93, 95, 203, 264
  assumption of causal powers within 91
  awareness of 92

critical realist potential for analysis of 83
  deep 105
  explicit expectation of 100
  exploration of 98
  insight into 94
  seeking to illuminate 96
Strauss, A. L. 92, 96, 98, 103, 160, 161,
    191, 197
Streeck, W. 195
structured antagonism 156
structure-agency relationship 72–4, 79, 85,
    86, 89, 91, 103, 168, 169, 173, 174, 177,
    183, 240, 317
  calls to to re-examine the value of 143
  culture and 225
  deeper and fuller understanding of 219
  distinctive configuration of 176
  events and experiences that address 129
  explanation of the way in which social
    discourses arise out of 147
  opportunity to explore and clarify 179, 184
  patterns emerged from 180
  qualitative investigations of 244
  recursive, need to take account of 225
  relative weights 227
  relatively autonomous 176, 181
  serious and separate attention to 210
Sturdy, A. 76
subjective probability 285–6
subjective reality 149
subjectivism 2–3, 5, 135
subjectivity x, 48, 50, 116, 123, 134, 207
  neo-liberal 53
  undue 220
  worker 325
subsidiaries 121, 189, 191–2, 194–200
  conventional accounts of character of 127
  headquarters relations with 144, 145
  key characteristics 190
SUPPAG (business support
    intermediary) 206–21
Swanborn, P. 171
Sweden 35, 41, 42
Sylva, K. 56 n.
synchronic analyses 43
Szmigin, I. 18

Tajfel, Henri 67, 68
Tashakkori, A. 171, 242, 243
Tavecchio, L. W. C. 56
Taylor, C. 286
Taylor, P. 31, 144, 151, 153, 154, 157, 163
Taylorism 24
teamwork 142–3, 306, 321
  importance of 101
  organizational performance and 16

self-managed 153
  subject-specific entities for 141
Teddlie, C. 171, 242, 243
temporal specialization 69
temporality 80
Terry, D. J. 102
testing theory 88, 107, 108, 274
Thatcher, Margaret 127
Thelen, K. 168–9, 174, 195
Themessl-Huber, M. 205
theoretical models 166, 167, 288, 291–2, 293,
    295, 297–8, 299
theory-building 93, 102
  explaining within a particular
    context 104–7
  retroductive 98
Thompson, E. P. 6, 227
Thompson, J. 50
Thompson, J. D. 143, 144, 151, 154, 163, 169
Thompson, P. 70–1, 76, 144, 155, 169, 245
    n., 261
Tidbury, Sir Charles 230
Tilley, N. 28, 39–40, 87–8, 110, 112, 116–23,
    131, 288, 297, 306
Tina compromise form xiv, xv
TMSA (transformational model of social
    activity) x, 73 n.
Torgerson, C. J. 268
transcendental properties vi–xii
transcription conventions 65
transfer of knowledge, *see* knowledge
    transfer
transitivity problem 289
treacherous bind 211–15
triangulation 81, 82, 83, 96, 131, 278,
    319, 321
  mixed methods 80, 171
  multi-methods for 243
  respondent 95, 97, 100
Troitzsch, K. G. 288, 297
Trondman, M. 133
Trusts (NHS) 181–2, 184, 271, 272
Turner, J. C. 68

UK (United Kingdom) xi, 42, 82–4, 121, 127,
    174, 189
  call centres 153, 157
  childcare 54, 55, 56, 60, 61
  developed capitalism 315
  employment practices of transnational
    companies 35
  functional flexibility by food processing
    companies 183
  government mentoring scheme 275
  labour process in factories 31
  main social science funding body 210–11

UK (United Kingdom) (*Cont.*)
  managerial work in
    telecommunications 145
  public house managers 229
  solicitor firms 35, 36
UK Parliament 233
uncertainty 72, 114, 115, 166, 170, 321
  absolute 135
  environmental 188
  exposed 127
Universal Credit 264
universals 3, 18, 104, 105, 106, 249, 286
  concrete xiii
USA (United States of America)
  law firms 35

value chains 151, 154
Van de Ven, A. 220
Van Maanen, J. 134
Vertovec, S. 209, 210
Veyne, P. 227
Vincent, Steve x, 18, 47, 52, 54, 64, 67, 69,
    149–50, 155, 163, 165, 166
VPS (variable pay schemes) 175
VW (Volkswagen) 176

Wales 234
Walker, A. B. 33, 235
Walker, R. 31
Walker (Peter) & Son 230, 233–4, 235, 239
Walker-Okeover family 235
Walkerdine, V. 48
Walton, J. R. 230–2
Warhurst, C. 247, 249, 254
Watneys 230
Watson, T. J. 132, 136, 137, 145, 147
Webb, J. 5, 72

Welsh, B. 268
Wenger, E. 100, 102
Wengraf, T. 94
Wetherell, M. 46, 50, 57, 58, 68
Whitbread 230, 231, 232, 233, 238,
    239–40
Whitley, R. 190, 195, 197
WHO (World Health Organization) x
Whyte, W. F. 215
Wickham, Chris 227
Wiggins, S. 57
Wilkins, M. 185
Wilkinson, I. 131
Williams, G. 74
Williams, M. 4, 282, 286, 287–8, 293, 294,
    297, 301, 309, 324
Williams, R. 224
Willig, C. 48, 51, 54
Willis, P. 133
Willmott, H. 5, 50, 70 n., 76, 314, 318
Wilson, J. 243 n.
Winch, Peter 304
Windschuttle, K. 66
Winter, R. 206, 208, 211, 213, 215
Witz, A. 254
Wong, G. 40
Woodiwiss, T. 75, 234
Wooffitt, R. 62
Works Councils, see EWCs
'World 3' knowledge 225
Wuthnow, Robert 226, 234, 237

Yates, J.-A. 237
Yellen, J. L. 252, 259
Yin, R. K. 23, 149, 161, 168, 170, 171, 172–3,
    183, 185, 189, 242
Young, L. 131

Stratified Ontology:

Empirical
Actual
Real.

Emergent entities

Power
Possess
Exercise
Actualised

Relational Emergence = causal powers of
entities (= parts + relations)
‿
emergence

Abduction

Retroduction

Relational Approach (p. 227)

Content Analysis for documents (p. 229) : language
construction of documents; how are they shaped?
formats = genre, preservation, etc
└ illuminate the broader cultural framework (possibilities + resources available to authors) p. 234

Context

Entities

Mechanisms

CMO = Context
(p.43)   Mechanisms
(p.88)   Outcome

Conditions
    Mechanisms

Structure
Agency
Culture

(Archer p.225)
_____
RELATIONAL APP

- Generative mechanisms = real (p.231)
- Underlying mechanisms
- long-term mechanisms → historical analysis
                              ↓
              situational logics for action (p.240)

long-term
mechanisms
that shape
conditions
(P. 227)
H&Doc

→ Conditions (p.203) CHA

↓

Same mechanisms ⟹ different events

Same events ⟹ different causes

↑

Conditions

Situational
Logics for action
(p 240)

Types of
Causal
Powers
(p 152)

< Normative powers & potentials < 1 upward causation
2 downward ''

Configurational '' '' < 3 upward causation
4 downward ''

Case Studies

Explactory + Exceptional CS
(p. 156)

Analysis of Data

Configurational analysis ⎤
Normative analysis   ⎬ Institutional Explanation.
Field analysis   ⎦

Objective

theoretical replication

18274607R00238

Printed in Great Britain
by Amazon